TEACHER PREP

**MERRILL
PRENTICE HALL**

Teacher Preparation Classroom

Your Class. Their Careers. Our Future. Will your students be prepared?

We invite you to explore our new, innovative and engaging web site and all that it has to offer you, your course, and tomorrow's educators! Preview this site today at www.prenhall.com/teacherprep/demo. Just click on "go" on the login page to begin your exploration.

Organized around the major courses pre-service teachers take, the Teacher Preparation site provides media, student/teacher artifacts, strategies, research articles, and other resources to equip your students with the quality tools needed to excel in their courses and prepare them for their first classroom.

This ultimate online education resource will provide you and your students access to:

Online Video Library. More than 250 video clips—each tied to a course topic and framed by learning goals and Praxis-type questions—capture real teachers and students working in real classrooms.

Student and Teacher Artifacts. More than 200 student and teacher classroom artifacts—each tied to a course topic and framed by learning goals and application questions—provide a wealth of materials and experiences to help your students observe children's developmental learning.

Lesson Plan Builder. Step-by-step guidelines and lesson plan examples support students as they learn to build high-quality lesson plans.

Articles and Readings. Over 500 articles from ASCD's renowned journal *Educational Leadership* are available. The site also includes Research Navigator, a searchable database of additional educational journals.

Strategies and Lessons. Over 500 research-supported instructional strategies appropriate for a wide range of grade levels and content areas.

Licensure and Career Tools. Resources devoted to helping your students pass their licensure exam; learn standards, law, and public policies; plan a teaching portfolio; and succeed in their first year of teaching.

How to ORDER *Teacher Prep* for you and your students:

- For students to receive a *Teacher Prep* Access Code with this text, please provide your bookstore with ISBN 0–13–241942–4 when you **place** your textbook order. The bookstore **must** order the text with this ISBN to be eligible for this offer.

Upon ordering *Teacher Prep* for their students, instructors will be given a lifetime *Teacher Prep* Access Code. To receive your access code, please email **Merrill marketing@pearsoned.com** and provide the following information:
- Name and Affiliation
- Author/Title/Edition of Merrill text

Assessment and Grading in Classrooms

Susan M. Brookhart
Duquesne University

Anthony J. Nitko
University of Arizona

PEARSON

Merrill
Prentice Hall

Upper Saddle River, New Jersey
Columbus, Ohio

Library of Congress Cataloging-in-Publication Data

Brookhart, Susan M.
  Assessment and grading in classrooms/Susan M. Brookhart, Anthony J. Nitko.
    p. cm.
  ISBN 0-13-221741-4
1. Educational tests and measurements—United States. 2. Grading and marking
(Students)—United States. 3. Educational evaluation—United States. I. Nitko, Anthony J.
II. Title.
  LB3051.B727 2008
  371.27—dc22

                                                                2007017668

Vice President and Executive Publisher: Jeffery W. Johnston
Publisher: Kevin M. Davis
Development Editors: Autumn Crisp Benson, Christina Robb
Editorial Assistant: Sarah N. Kenoyer
Production Editor: Mary Harlan
Production Coordination: GGS Book Services
Design Coordinator: Diane C. Lorenzo
Text Design and Illustrations: GGS Book Services
Cover Design: Ali Mohrman
Cover Image: SuperStock
Production Manager: Laura Messerly
Director of Marketing: David Gesell
Marketing Manager: Autumn Purdy
Marketing Coordinator: Brian Mounts

This book was set in New Baskerville by GGS Book Services. It was printed and bound by Edwards Brothers. The cover was printed by Phoenix Color Corp.

All chapters are based largely on content in *Educational Assessment of Students*, Fifth Edition, by Anthony J. Nitko and Susan M. Brookhart, copyright © 2007 by Pearson Education.

Pearson Education Ltd.   Pearson Education Australia Pty. Limited
Pearson Education Singapore Pte. Ltd.   Pearson Education North Asia Ltd.
Pearson Education Canada, Ltd.   Pearson Educación de Mexico, S.A. de C.V.
Pearson Education–Japan   Pearson Education Malaysia Pte. Ltd.

10 9 8 7 6 5 4 3 2
ISBN-13: 978-0-13-221741-5
ISBN-10:   0-13-221741-4

To our loving spouses
Veronica V. Nitko
and
Frank Brookhart

Preface

The goal of *Assessment and Grading in Classrooms* is to help preservice teachers and classroom teachers assess their students well and to use the assessment results to further student learning. *Assessment and Grading in Classrooms* focuses on the professional practices of elementary and secondary schoolteachers and is intended as a core textbook for an undergraduate course in educational assessment. This book is particularly geared to the needs of classroom teachers, focusing on the core concepts teachers need to know to assess and grade students, emphasizing sound approaches to gathering both formative and summative information about student achievement of classroom learning targets, interpreting standardized tests for classroom purposes, and using information from multiple sources to help students learn. Concepts are treated conceptually, not mathematically. For example, the sections on validity, reliability, item analysis, and interpreting standardized test scores define and describe the respective scores, values, or indices without presenting formulas for calculating them. The emphasis is on interpretation and use.

Organization of the Text

The text is organized to develop and support sound teacher assessment practices. Chapter 1 begins with the big questions of purpose. This chapter frames assessment information as the basis for decisions teachers make about teaching and students make about learning. It introduces teacher and student rights and responsibilities with regard to assessment. It introduces current accountability requirements (including the No Child Left Behind legislation). Finally, it discusses the nature and purpose of various assessment accommodations for students with special needs.

Chapter 2 continues the "big issues" with treatments of validity and reliability, which are fundamental principles of assessment information quality. Validity and reliability for large-scale and classroom assessments are discussed separately, and special emphasis is given to practical strategies for assuring validity and reliability in classroom practice.

Chapters 3 through 11 change the focus of the lens, from big picture assessment issues to classroom applications. Chapter 3 discusses learning goals, especially their role in driving assessment. Taxonomies of thinking skills are also introduced here. Chapter 4 discusses higher-order thinking skills like problem solving and critical thinking: what they are, why they are important learning goals, and how to assess them. Chapter 5 discusses planning for assessment and instruction. This chapter emphasizes the need to plan assessment and instruction simultaneously, basing both on appropriate learning targets. Chapter 6 discusses formative assessment: As students and their teachers focus on the quality of student work in relation to learning goals, students are enabled to use strategies for further learning and self-regulation of learning. Practical suggestions for formative assessment are given.

Chapters 7 and 8 move to summative assessment and discuss test items: short-answer and completion (Chapter 7) and essay questions (Chapter 8). Chapter 9 discusses how to design performance assessment tasks. Chapter 10 takes a comprehensive approach to scoring all these assessments, emphasizing that no matter what the type of item or task, the scoring design is what "translates" student performance into a metric. That metric needs to be not only valid and reliable but also informative and useful. Various types of scoring schemes are discussed, including four types of rubrics. Chapter 11 discusses how to combine sets of indicators of achievement into grades for official reporting. Grading methods based on communicating achievement of classroom learning targets (criterion-referenced methods) are recommended and illustrated.

Chapter 12 discusses standardized tests. The emphasis is on the needs of classroom teachers to interpret student performance and use sound information to communicate with parents and to plan instruction. The section on interpreting standardized test scores takes a practical approach—what does each type of score mean and how is it used?—and does not require the use of mathematical formulas.

Special Features

The following special features highlight the practicality of this text:

- Each chapter begins with a vignette that illustrates the main chapter concepts. These help set the purpose for reading the chapter.

- Each chapter begins with a list of key concepts, which serve as an advance organizer for readers and can also be used as a chapter summary. These concepts become the section headings for the text, encouraging chapter study that is truly focused on the main concepts to be learned. The conclusion to each chapter then reminds readers of the "bigger picture"; a brief restatement of chapter purpose reminds readers "where they are" in the logical progression of assessment content and foreshadows what comes next.

- Key terms appear in bold type the first time they are used in the text. These terms are defined in a glossary at the end of the text.

- Chapter features include both visual organizers for concepts (Tables and Figures) and organizers for assessment practices (Examples and Guidelines). Brief examples are included within the text; the Example features include more extended examples. Guidelines are included for all major assessment practices that classroom teachers use as they are planning, writing, and interpreting assessments. Each Guidelines chart can be used prior to work, as true guidelines for proceeding, or after work, as a checklist for assuring quality.

■ Each chapter ends with open-ended exercises, mostly at the Application level, so students can apply chapter content. Appendix H presents key elements of good answers for these exercises.

Supplementary Materials

Companion Website

The Companion Website provides a wealth of resources for students. For each chapter of the book the Companion Website includes two student self-tests: multiple-choice and essays. The multiple-choice questions are a self-scoring quiz. The essays section contains open-ended exercises (with feedback) designed to help students check their own understanding of chapter content. The multiple-choice questions are different from those in the *Instructor's Manual*. The open-ended exercises are different from those in the textbook and require more extended responses. Both of these assessments can be submitted to the instructor online. Suggestions for using the Companion Website quizzes and exercises as formative assessment during instruction are included in the *Instructor's Manual*.

The textbook Key Concepts and the Glossary are also available online, for students' reference as they work. Finally, the Companion Website includes Web links to a wide range of websites related to the course.

To access the Companion Website, go to www.prenhall.com/brookhart.

Online PowerPoint® Slides

Each chapter has a file of PowerPoint slides containing an outline of the chapter content. These slides could be used in several ways: to accompany an instructor's lecture, to outline chapter content for students who want or need organizers for notes or reading, and/or to structure individual study or class review for exams.

The Online PowerPoint Slides are available on the Instructor's Resource Center. To access the Online PowerPoint Slides, go to www.prenhall.com and click on the Instructor Resource Center. Here you will be able to login or complete a one-time registration for a user name and password to access the online supplements for this text.

Instructor's Manual/Test Bank

The *Online Instructor's Manual/Test Bank* provides resources for course instructors, in three sections. (1) For each chapter, the manual includes a summary of the full range of instructional and assessment resources available in the set of supplements for the text, suggestions for pre-instructional assessment, and questions for class discussion. (2) The manual includes complex performance assessments that combine key concepts across chapters. (3) The manual also includes a test bank. The test bank is organized by chapter, and items are indexed to key concepts to help instructors construct their own test blueprints.

The *Online Instructor's Manual/Test Bank* is available on the Instructor's Resource Center. To access the *Online Instructor's Manual/Test Bank*, go to www.prenhall.com and click on the Instructor Resource Center. Here you will be able to login or complete a one-time registration for a user name and password to access the online supplements for this text.

Acknowledgments

A project of this magnitude requires the help of many persons. We are very much indebted to the reviewers whose critical readings contributed greatly to the technical accuracy, readability, and pedagogy: Stacey Neuharth-Pritchett, University of Georgia; Joseph M. Ryan, Arizona State University; and John T. Willse, University of North Carolina at Greensboro.

We also thank Kevin Davis, Autumn Benson, Christie Robb, Sarah Kenoyer, and Mary Harlan at Merrill. To all of these people, and others we have failed to mention, we offer our most sincere thanks and appreciation.

Special thanks to Veronica Nitko and Frank Brookhart, whose support and encouragement have been, as always, invaluable.

About the Authors

Susan M. Brookhart is a Senior Research Associate at the Center for Advancing the Study of Teaching and Learning in the School of Education at Duquesne University. She is also an independent consultant in the field of educational assessment and serves on state assessment Technical Advisory Committees in two states. She is a former Professor and Chair of the Department of Educational Foundations and Leadership at Duquesne. Previous to her higher education experience, she taught both elementary and middle school. Her research interests include the role of both formative and summative classroom assessment in student motivation and achievement, the connection between classroom assessment and large-scale assessment, and grading.

Professor Brookhart is the 2007–2009 editor of the journal *Educational Measurement: Issues and Practice.* She has served as the Education columnist for *National Forum,* the journal of Phi Kappa Phi, and as newsletter editor for the National Council on Measurement in Education. Some of the journals in which her research has appeared are *Applied Measurement in Education, Assessment in Education, Educational Measurement: Issues and Practice, Journal of Educational Measurement, Journal of Educational Research, Review of Educational Research,* and *Teachers College Record.* She serves on the editorial boards of *Teachers College Record* and *Applied Measurement in Education.*

Professor Brookhart is a past president of the American Educational Research Association's Special Interest Group on Classroom Assessment, and was program co-chair for the 2004 NCME Annual Meeting. She is the author of two books: *The Art and Science of Classroom Assessment* and *Grading.* She is the author of a notebook of materials for teachers: *Formative Assessment Strategies for Every Classroom.* With Anthony J. Nitko, she is the co-author of the textbook *Educational Assessment of Students* (5ᵗʰ edition).

Anthony J. Nitko is an adjunct professor of the Department of Educational Psychology, University of Arizona, and professor emeritus and former chairperson of the Department of Psychology in Education at the University of Pittsburgh. His research interests include curriculum-based criterion- referenced testing, integration of testing and instruction, classroom assessment, and the assessment of knowledge and higher-order thinking skills. His publications include the chapter "Designing Tests That Are Integrated with Instruction" in the third edition of *Educational Measurement.* He co-authored (with C. M. Lindvall) *Measuring Pupil Achievement and Aptitude,* (with T. C. Hsu) *Pitt Educational Testing Aids* (PETA, a package of computer programs for classroom teachers), and (with R. Glaser) the chapter "Measurement in Learning and Instruction" in the second edition of *Educational Measurement.*

Professor Nitko has been editor of the journal *Educational Measurement: Issues and Practice* and also *d'News,* the AERA Division D newsletter. Some of the journals in which his research has appeared are *American Educational Research Journal, Applied Measurement in Education, Educational Evaluation and Policy Analysis, Educational Measurement: Issues and Practice, Educational Technology, Journal of Educational Measurement,* and *Research in Developmental Disabilities.*

Professor Nitko has been a member of several committees of the American Educational Research Association, was elected secretary of AERA Division D, served on committees of the National Council on Measurement in Education, and was elected to the board of directors and as president of the latter. He received Fulbright awards to Malawi and Barbados and has served as a consultant to various government and private agencies in Bangladesh, Barbados, Botswana, Egypt, Ethiopia, Indonesia, Jamaica, Malawi, Namibia, Oman, the United States, Vietnam, and Singapore.

Brief Contents

APPENDIXES

Contents

Note: Every effort has been made to provide accurate and current Internet information in this book. However, the Internet and information posted on it are constantly changing, and it is inevitable that some of the Internet addresses listed in this textbook will change.

Classroom Decision Making

KEY CONCEPTS

1. Teaching involves making decisions.
2. Assessment provides teachers information for decisions about teaching.
3. Assessment provides students information for decisions about learning.
4. High-stakes assessments provide those in authority with the information they use to classify and sanction schools.
5. Teachers have professional responsibilities in assessment.
6. Students have rights and responsibilities as test takers.

Maria, newly certified and happy to be finished with a semester of day-to-day substituting, was settling in to her first full-time teaching position. In January, she took over the third-grade classroom of a teacher who had left in December. She had learned so much about students and classrooms during her semester of substituting and increased her repertoire of instructional strategies, and she was feeling good about that. The same was not true about assessment. Her experience with assessment had been limited to administering paper-and-pencil tests, mostly from textbooks. As a new full-time teacher, she continued her unquestioned use of textbook tests and some tests "left" to her in the former teacher's files. It never occurred to her to review or question their contents, or to use the results for anything besides assigning grades. Her approach to assessment was simply "to do" it, not to think about or use the results.

A moment of panic came when she needed to put something in the column under "oral reading" in the gradebook she had inherited. She had not been taught principles for performance assessment and had no idea what to do. For a while, she used 100 to mean "good," 90 to mean "pretty good," and 80 to mean "needs work," simply to have something to write down. She did not use criteria in any systematic way, and it felt like she was making things up. It also felt like shortchanging her kids.

Everything about Maria's story except her name is true. Her situation is pretty common. And it doesn't have to be that way!

Teaching involves making decisions

Like Maria, you may view assessment strictly as a way to assign grades. However, information obtained by assessments can and should be used, not simply to assign grades, but to make informed decisions to improve your teaching and your students' learning. In fact, teachers make a decision every 2 to 3 minutes (Shavelson & Stern, 1981) and spend from one third to one half of their time in assessment-related activities (Stiggins, Conklin et al., 1992). You will have to do this, and you will want to be better equipped than Maria.

Table 1.1 lists types of educational decisions teachers make and gives some examples. All are important, but because this book is about classrooms, we highlight classroom instruction and management decisions in more detail.

Instruction and management decisions include planning your instruction, sequencing learning, monitoring progress, diagnosing learning difficulties, providing students and parents with feedback, evaluating teaching effectiveness, and assigning grades. Maria's incomplete understanding limited her to simply planning instruction and assigning grades. No wonder she felt something was

Table 1.1 Types of Educational Decisions

Type of decision	Definition	Example
Classroom Instruction and Management Decisions	Decisions made for daily classroom teaching	
Modeling Learning Targets	Designing assessments that embody learning goals	The learning goal is about persuasive writing, and the assessment asks students to write persuasively.
Motivating Students	Designing and using assessments to encourage and support student engagement in learning	In your class, assessments are at an appropriate level of challenge, and mistakes are treated as opportunities to learn.
Providing Feedback to Students	Providing information to students comparing their work with the learning target and suggesting how to improve	A teacher gives feedback on all major assignments that is clear, specific, and frequent.
Providing Feedback to the Teacher	Using information to evaluate classroom teaching and learning and plan future teaching	I won't take as much time on the photosynthesis unit next year because it seemed easy for everyone.
Grading	Using information to assign marks for reporting	Sharonda gets an A in Reading this quarter.
Classification Decisions	Categorizing students	
Selection Decisions	Categorizing students as "in" or "out" of a program	A certain private school will not accept Peter.
Placement Decisions	Categorizing students into different levels	Latisha is in the "Bluebirds" reading group.
Counseling and Guidance Decisions	Helping students explore career options, plan future education, and the like	Brad will take as much math and science in high school as he can because he wants to be a doctor and has the potential.
Credentialing and Certification Decisions	Deciding whether students have met certain standards	Aisha cannot graduate from high school because she did not pass the state graduation exam.

missing! Below we connect assessment to these key instruction and management decisions.

Modeling learning targets

Assessments serve as examples for students by showing them what you want them to learn. Ask a student, "What did you learn in school today?" and most will respond by describing the activities and assignments they did. Thus, assessment tasks and their scoring criteria *must* embody learning targets and show students what is important. For example, if you grade students' original paragraphs mostly on the basis of neatness and grammar, they will conclude that's what you want them to know about writing a paragraph. On the other hand, if you grade students' original paragraphs based on content, they will conclude that content is what they should focus on when writing a paragraph.

Motivating students

Assessments may motivate students to study. For example, if you tell students there will be a test on the periodic table of elements, most will study it.

Assessments can also motivate students to learn. Assessments that help students get a clear picture of the goals for learning, or provide feedback that helps them improve, contribute to motivation as well as learning. These types of assessments support student self-regulation of learning—when students take control of their own learning—and thus self-efficacy and feeling "in control." Classrooms where the assessment environment is conducive to learning from mistakes, instead of being punished for them, encourage students to view learning as possible for all students (not just "smart" ones) and to persevere.

Providing feedback to students

Assessments provide feedback to students about their learning. In order to improve learning, feedback must give students specific guidance about what they must do, at the time they need it, in language they can understand. Therefore, teachers who simply give students a grade on a paper or test are not providing enough feedback to help students improve. Feedback must be integrated into your instructional process in order to improve learning. An atmosphere of trust must exist, where it is "safe" for students to receive suggestions and constructive criticism without feeling "put down."

Providing feedback to the teacher

Assessments provide feedback to you about how well students have learned and how well you have taught. If students have failed to grasp important points, re-teach the material before proceeding to new material. If students have accomplished their short-term learning goals, you can enrich or extend learning in that area or move on to another area.

Grading

Although you continually assess students' progress in informal ways, you also must officially record your evaluations of students' progress through grades. The grades or symbols (A, B, C, etc.) that you report represent your *summative* (final) evaluations or judgments about how well your students have achieved important learning targets. Use a mixture of assessment formats to provide the information you need to make these evaluations. Good teaching practice and common sense indicate that grades should be based on more than test scores. For example, you may have a combination of tests, short essays, and performance assessments for a unit in Social Studies.

Assessment provides teachers information for decisions about teaching

Assessment is a process for obtaining feedback for making a particular educational decision. The general public often uses the terms *assessment, test measurement,* and *evaluation* interchangeably, but it is important for you to distinguish among them. For example, in one Eskimo language, Central Alaskan Yupik, there are at least 15 different words for "snow." Fine distinctions (tiny flakes, drifting flakes, clinging flakes, and so on) are important in central Alaska. The distinctions in assessment information are just as important to educators as the distinctions in snow are to central Alaskans. Table 1.2 lists some terms that describe different aspects of assessment information. As you read what at first may seem like fine distinctions, imagine the differences these distinctions make in education practice.

Assessment terms

Assessment is a broad term meaning a process for obtaining information that is used for making decisions about students; curricula, programs, and schools; and educational policy (see AFT, NCME, & NEA, 1990). A large number of assessment techniques may be used to collect this information. These techniques include formal and informal observations, oral questions and discussion, paper-and-pencil tests, homework, lab work, research papers, projects, and analyses of student records. We will discuss these techniques in greater detail throughout this book.

A common way to assess students is by using a test. A **test** is an instrument or systematic procedure for observing and describing one or more characteristics of a student, using either a numerical scale or a classification scheme. Test is a narrower concept than assessment. In schools, we usually think of a test as a paper-and-pencil instrument with a series of questions that students must answer, scored as percent correct.

Measurement is a procedure for assigning numbers (usually called scores) to a specified trait or characteristic of a person in such a way that the numbers describe the degree to which the person possesses the trait. An important feature of the

Table 1.2 Assessment Terms and Purposes

Term	Definition	Examples
Basic terms		
Assessment	Obtaining information for making decisions about students, curricula, programs, schools, and educational policy	• Student admissions interviews for college • First-grade teacher's observation of holding a pencil • Class projects • Exams
Test	An instrument or systematic procedure for observing and describing one or more characteristics of a student using either a numerical scale or a classification scheme	• Test after a unit of classroom instruction • SAT • TerraNova • Wechsler Intelligence Scale for Children • State accountability test
Measurement	Assigning numbers (usually called scores) to a specified attribute or characteristic of a person such that the numbers describe the degree to which the person possesses the attribute	• Scores on tests • Ratings based on observations • Rubric levels based on student projects
Evaluation	The process of making a value judgment about the worth of a student's product or performance	• Sam needs to rewrite his paragraph. • School A is not making adequate yearly progress.
Assessment purposes		
Formative	Providing information for improvement	• Observation and feedback on student work in class • Conferencing with students
Diagnostic	Providing information about strengths and weaknesses	• Pretest analyzed for error types • Student writing analyzed for specific needs
Summative	Providing information for a final judgment of worth or accomplishment	• Grades • Final exams

number-assigning procedure in measurement is that the resulting scores maintain the order that exists in the real world among the people being measured. For example, if you are a better speller than Billy, a test that measures your spelling abilities should result in your score (your measurement) being higher than Billy's score.

Thus, assessment may or may not provide measurements. If a procedure identifies a student by descriptive labels or categories, the student is assessed, but not measured in the sense used here. Assessment is a broader term than measurement, because not all types of assessments yield measurements.

Evaluation is the process of making a value judgment about the worth of a student's product or performance. For example, you may judge a student's writing as exceptionally good for his grade placement. To make this evaluation, you would first have to assess his writing ability. You may gather information by reviewing the student's journal, comparing his writing to other students and to known quality standards of writing, and so on. Evaluations are the bases for decisions about what course of action to follow.

Evaluation may or may not be based on measurements or test results. Evaluations may be based on counting things, using checklists, or using rating scales. However, you can—and probably often do—evaluate students on the basis of assessments such as systematic observation, without measuring them. For example, you may observe students using lab equipment and decide from those observations which students to put in charge of clean-up.

Evaluations may be based on a combination of measurements (test results, for example) and observations leading to *category judgments*. Diagnoses of certain kinds of learning disabilities are done this way, using combinations of test results and teacher, parent, or psychologist observations. Kindergarten screening is typically done this way, too, using a combination of test results and child observations leading to the designations "ready" or "not ready" for kindergarten.

Assessment purposes

You may assess students for formative, diagnostic, or summative purposes. **Formative assessment** of students' achievement means judging the quality of a student's achievement while the student is still in the process of learning. Formative assessments of students help you and the students take the next learning steps. For example, you ask questions in class to see whether students understand the lesson. You can then adjust your lesson if students do not understand, and help them see what they don't understand. Good formative assessment boost student achievement (Black & Wiliam, 1998).

Sometimes the instruction an individual student receives is not effective. The student may need special remedial help or special instruction with alternative methods or materials. Assessments that provide some of the information needed to make this type of decision are called diagnostic assessments. **Diagnostic assessment** centers on the question, "What learning activities should I use to best adapt to this student's individual requirements and thereby maximize the student's opportunities to attain the learning target?" Diagnosis implies identifying both the appropriate content and the types of learning activities that will help a student attain the learning target (Nitko, 1989).

Summative assessment of students' achievement means judging the quality or worth of a student's achievement after the instructional process is completed. Giving letter grades on report cards is one example of reporting your summative evaluation of a student's achievement.

In this book, we will use the convention of calling assessment of students done for formative purposes *formative assessment*. Similarly, we will use the term *summative assessment* for assessment of students done for summative purposes. This terminology will differentiate classroom processes from program- or school-level evaluations. You can look at information about schools, programs, or materials for formative and summative purposes, as well.

For example, you might evaluate a particular district's K–12 science curriculum. Or you might evaluate the effectiveness of an after-school tutoring program. We will term these kinds of things *formative evaluation* and *summative evaluation*, respectively.

Getting good information from classroom assessments.

Classroom assessment activities should focus on the information you need to make particular instructional and management decisions. Guideline 1.1 gives a set of guiding principles that you should follow to select and use classroom assessments meaningfully.

1. *Be clear about the learning targets you want to assess.* The knowledge, skills, and performances you want students to learn are sometimes called **achievement targets** or **learning targets**. The more clearly you specify the learning targets, the better you will be able to select the appropriate assessment techniques.

2. *Match your assessment techniques to each learning target.* Assessments must match the learning targets with respect to both content *and* cognitive process. To find out how well students solve real-world problems, for example, you need to give them some real-world problems to solve. Two other things must also be in place for the match to really work. First, the directions and assessment tasks or items must make this match—and clearly identify what the students need to do. For example, if an essay question asks students to analyze a poem, they must clearly understand that. Otherwise, they might just repeat what the poem said and not realize they were supposed to add their own analysis.

In addition, the *criteria* for good work must match the learning target(s) and be clear to students. Even if everything else is coordinated, if the criteria do not match the learning target, then the information won't, either. We once worked with some eighth-grade science teachers who used a wonderful group simulation task. Students were given a simulated community map and had to decide on 12 locations (from among 30 potential spots) to "dig" and test water (samples were supplied in a lab), record and interpret their findings, and then recommend where a well should be placed. After all that, their work was graded like a 12-point quiz, one point for each water test they did. Using the information to zero in on the best location to dig a well did not figure in to the scoring or feedback. Arguably this was the whole point of the exercise, and it certainly was the place where higher-order thinking came into play. Students' scores on the 0 to 12 scale had nothing to say about that.

3. *Your assessment techniques should serve the needs of the learners.* Proper assessment tools give students concrete examples of what they are expected to do with their learning. Assessment techniques should provide learners with opportunities for determining specifically what they have achieved and specifically what they must do to improve their performance. Therefore, you should select assessment methods

Guideline 1.1 Guidelines for selecting and using classroom assessments

1. Be clear about the learning targets you want to assess.
2. Match your assessment techniques to each learning target.
3. Your assessment techniques should serve the needs of the learners.
4. Whenever possible, use multiple indicators of performance for each learning target.
5. When you interpret the results of assessments, take their limitations into account.

that allow you to provide meaningful feedback to the learners. You should be able to tell students how closely they have approximated the learning targets. Chapter 6 gives more details about how to give good feedback.

4. *Whenever possible, use multiple indicators of performance for each learning target.* Only using one format of assessment (such as short-answer questions or matching exercises) provides an incomplete picture of what a student has learned. Getting information about a student's achievement from several assessment modalities usually enhances the validity of your assessments. Matching exercises, for example, emphasize recall and recognition of factual information; essay questions emphasize organizing ideas and writing skill under the pressure of time limits; and a month-long project emphasizes freely using resources, research, and more thorough analyses of the topic. All three of these assessment techniques may be needed to ascertain the extent to which a student has achieved a given learning target.

5. *When you interpret the results of assessments, take their limitations into account.* Assessments in schools cannot completely reproduce those things we want students to learn in "real life." The information you obtain, even when you use several different types of assessments, is only a sample of a student's attainment of a learning target. Because of this, information from assessment contains sampling error. Factors such as a student's physical and emotional conditions further limit the extent to which we can obtain truly accurate information. Make decisions with these limitations in mind. In addition to helping you make decisions about teaching, assessment also helps guide student learning.

Assessment provides students information for decisions about learning

Some students will use any information they can get to help them with their learning. You may have been one of those students who always checked your graded tests to see what you got wrong, and tried to understand why. You can increase the impact of your assessments on learning by handling assessments in such a way that *most* students can use information from your classroom assessments for their own learning. This occurs during formative assessment while the students is still in the process of learning.

Chapter 6 will give you more detail about the formative assessment process. We introduce this important function briefly in this first chapter because we think it deserves a spot in your basic, foundational thinking about assessment. People commonly think of *teachers* using assessment information. It is less common, but really more important, to help *students* use assessment information. Classroom assessments can help students (Sadler, 1989):

- focus on the learning target,
- compare their work with the target, and
- take action to improve.

We have already described how good classroom assessments help students focus on the learning target. Students experience your assessments (and other assignments) as "what you want them to do." No matter what your learning goals or objectives say on paper, students will conclude that what you ask them to do is what you want them to learn. Therefore, assignments that embody the learning targets in both content and cognitive process, that are clear to students, and that have clear and appropriate criteria help students focus on the learning target.

You can help students understand how their work compares with the target in three ways: by sharing the criteria for good work (by telling or by using examples), by giving good feedback, and by giving students opportunities to evaluate their own work. Good feedback is specific, descriptive, and clear, and includes suggestions for improvement. However, good feedback should also let the students take action to improve. If you "pass back" papers with feedback, but then move right on to a different topic, students can't use the feedback very well. Build opportunities for practice and growth into your lessons.

Most of your classroom learning targets will be based on state standards. Giving students opportunities to practice and grow, using formative assessment information, will no only help students in the short term, but will also prepare students well for assessments created externally to your classroom, including state assessments.

High-stakes assessments provide those in authority with the information they use to classify and sanction schools

Legally mandated assessment programs place constraints on your teaching. You need to be aware of these as you plan your instruction. Tests are called **high-stakes tests** when their results will have serious consequences for school administrators, teachers, or students. Example 1.1 gives three examples.

In Example 1, the consequences of assessment are quite serious for individual students. If they do not pass all subjects, they may not get a job because the employers require a secondary school certificate. If they do not do well on the examinations, they have no opportunity for attending a university. The stakes are high in Example 2, but not quite as high as in Example 1. Students can stay in school for several years, prepare for the tests, and retake the tests each year. In Example 3, there are high stakes for school administrators and teachers, but not for individual students. In fact, the tests may be low stakes for the students, since there appear to be no consequences to them for doing poorly on the tests.

Although the use of high-stakes testing in the United States can be traced back to Horace Mann in the 1850s, modern high-stakes testing in the United States grew out of school reform movements that developed during the 1980s. Assessment that is used to hold individual students or school officials responsible for assuring that students meet state standards is called **accountability testing**. Usually accountability testing is accompanied by high-stakes consequences. Check your state's education department web site for its current regulations regarding individual and school accountability.

■ EXAMPLE 1.1 Examples of high-stakes testing

Example 1

In a certain country, at the end of their secondary schooling, students must pass an examination for each subject they studied. The examinations cover the concepts and skills that are in the curriculum. Students are marked as A, B, C, D, and F for each examination. Students must get no Fs in order to be awarded the secondary school certificate. People without a secondary school certificate find it difficult to get a job in the country since employers see the certificate as indicating that candidates for a job have minimum competencies needed. Students who fail may study on their own time and take the examination again, but they cannot repeat the schooling because there is only a limited number of places in secondary schools. Students must have As and Bs but no Ds or Fs to be considered for a place in one of the few universities.

Example 2

In a certain state, students must pass tests in English, writing, and mathematics before grade 12; otherwise they cannot receive a high school diploma. They begin taking the test in grade 10, and once each year up to grade 12, they may repeat the tests they failed. Students who do not pass all of the tests by the end of grade 12 receive only an attendance certificate.

Example 3

In another state, students take the state-mandated tests annually in reading and mathematics from grades 3 through 11. Students do not have to pass the tests, but each school is evaluated by how well its students do. If a school's students do not show a pattern of continued improvement on the test, the state places a sanction on the school by dismissing the administrative staff and perhaps some of the teachers. It turns over the running of the school to a state-appointed team until such time the test scores show regular improvement.

Federal laws now cover matters of assessment participation and accommodation that apply to school districts and states receiving federal funds. These include the Fifth and Fourteenth Amendments to the U.S. Constitution, Section 504 of the Rehabilitation Act of 1973 (Public Law 93–112), the Family Education Rights and Privacy Act of 1974 (Public Law 93–380), the Education of All Handicapped Children Act of 1975 (Public Law 94–142), the Education of the Handicapped Act Amendments of 1986 (Public Law 99–457), the Individuals with Disabilities Education Amendments Act of 1990 (IDEA, Public Law 101–476), the Rehabilitation Act of 1973 (Public Law 93–112), the Americans with Disabilities Act of 1992 (Public Law 101–336), 1997 Amendments to the Individuals with Disabilities Education Act (Public Law 105–17), the No Child Left Behind Act of 2001 (Public Law 107–110), and the Individuals with Disabilities Education Improvement Act of 2004 (Public Law 108–446).

The *No Child Left Behind* Act is important to our discussion of high-stakes assessment because it requires states to establish challenging content standards and performance standards (referred to as *achievement standards* in the NCLB Act literature), and to demonstrate by way of tests and other assessments how well students have attained high levels of achievement on these standards. A state's failure to provide this demonstration will result in loss of federal education funds. Assessment under the NCLB Act is a school-level accountability tool.

Content standards describe the subject-matter facts, concepts, principles, and so on that students are expected to learn. **Performance standards** describe the things students can perform or do once the content standards are learned.

When students in a school are assessed on a state's standards, they are classified into at least three groups for purposes of reporting to the federal government: basic, proficient, and advanced. A state may have more than three categories, but they must be aligned to these three. Nebraska, for example, has four categories: beginning, progressing, proficient, and advanced. Under the NCLB Act, the goal is for 100% of the students in each school to reach the proficient level or higher on the state's content and performance standards by 2014. In addition, schools must show *adequate yearly progress* (AYP) towards this goal; otherwise, sanctions will be imposed.

An important provision of the NCLB Act is that a state must report test summaries at the school level and must disaggregate the data. To **disaggregate** test results means to report separately for subgroups of students such as the poor, minorities, students with limited English proficiency, and students with disabilities in addition to reporting on the total population. The federal government wants to assure that states are accountable for all students learning the challenging state standards, including those in these subgroups. In some instances in the past, states reported only on the whole groups of students, thus masking the fact that some subgroups of students were not receiving quality education.

The sanctions and corrective actions that follow a school's failure to make adequate yearly progress after two years include the following:

- parents may choose to have their children attend another school in the district that is making AYP,
- the school staff may be replaced,
- a new curriculum may be implemented,
- the authority of the administrative staff of the school may be changed,
- the school year may be extended,
- the school may be reorganized,
- the school may be reopened as a charter school,
- the state may contract with a private company to run the school, and
- the school may be taken over by the state.

To illustrate the effects of NCLB on public schools, let's look at the following report.

The Center for Education Policy (CEP) is an independent, nonprofit research and advocacy organization. Jennings and Rentner (2006, pp. 110–112) summarized the findings of four years of CEP studies of the effects of NCLB on the public schools into 10 generalizations. Some of the effects are positive and some are negative. Of course, these are statements about average effects, and the experience of some schools may be different.

- Student achievement on state tests is rising; it's not clear, however, that gains are as large as percentages of proficient scores make it seem.
- Schools are spending more time on reading and math, sometimes by spending less time on nontested subjects.
- Curriculum, instruction, and assessment are more closely aligned than previously, and state test results are more carefully analyzed than previously.
- Schools that were restructured because of low performance for the most part have not been radically changed (for example, by being disbanded or being taken over by the state).
- Good progress has been made at meeting required teacher qualifications, but many educators are not sure that this will improve teaching in the classroom.
- Students are taking more tests.
- Attention is being directed to the achievement of subgroups, and to achievement gaps between groups.
- The number of schools labeled as "needing improvement" because of not making adequate yearly progress two years in a row has leveled off (to about 10%), although they are not the same schools each year.
- The role of the federal government in education has expanded.
- The role of state governments and school districts in schools has also expanded, by federal mandate but often without federal funding.

Assessment of students with disabilities

Under the NCLB Act all students must be assessed. Two main assessment issues for students with disabilities are *participation* and *accommodation* (Salvia & Ysseldyke, 2004). **Participation** means that students with disabilities have the right, and sometimes the obligation, to be assessed, including taking part in accountability assessment programs. In the past, students with disabilities were sometimes excluded from taking accountability tests. If existing school programs did not serve students with disabilities well, there was no information to use to hold schools accountable for that.

For NCLB assessment, 95% of students with disabilities must participate in grade-level assessments. Students' disabilities may be used as a basis for accommodations to the assessment process for those students unable to participate in the assessment under the standardized conditions set for the general school population. Further, alternative assessment methods must be found to assess those students who cannot participate even with accommodations.

States are now granted some limited flexibility in adjusting content and performance standards for students with severe cognitive impairments (U.S. Department of Education, May 10, 2005). A state may exempt Limited English Proficient students (LEP students who have attended schools in the U.S. for less then twelve months) from one administration of the state's reading/language arts assessment; however, these students must take their state's mathematics assessment (U.S. Department of Education, September 11, 2006).

Assessment accommodations or modifications[1] are changes in either the conditions or materials of assessment that allow the achievement of students with disabilities to be evaluated in the same areas as students who are evaluated with unmodified assessments.

Accommodations may be grouped into four types (National Center on Educational Outcomes, 2005):

- *Presentation of the test* (e.g., repeat directions, read aloud, use of larger bubbles, etc.)
- *Response of students* (e.g., mark answers in book, use reference aids, point, etc.)
- *Setting where test is administered* (e.g., study carrel, special lighting, separate room, etc.)
- *Timing/scheduling of the test administration* (e.g., extended time, frequent breaks, etc.)

The NCLB Act requirement that 95% of the students with disabilities be tested on grade-level standards in a state's accountability assessment program is in conflict with the IDEA legislation that permits the development of an **individual education plan** (IEP). Each student's IEP is developed by a child study team from the school and is approved by a student's parents. It specifies for the student learning targets, appropriate teaching methods, and classroom accommodations. Often assessment conditions and accommodations are specified, too. That IEP may result in students with disabilities being taught a curriculum that is below their grade level. Thus, one law, the NCLB Act, requires students to be tested at levels for which they have not been taught, but their curriculum has been authorized by another law, IDEA (Phillips, 2005).

As we have outlined in this section, you must recognize that high-stakes assessment will have an impact on what and how you teach. High-stakes testing will require you to carefully determine how the content and learning targets of your teaching and your student assessment are aligned with your state's standards. This is just one of your assessment responsibilities.

Teachers have professional responsibilities in assessment

Formal and informal assessment tools help you gather information for making hundreds of decisions about your students. Each decision you make will have positive or negative consequences for your students. You must base all decisions, especially those with serious consequences, on high-quality information. This is critical!

---

[1]Some distinguish between *accommodations*, meaning changes that do not affect score meaning, and *modifications*, changes that may affect score meaning.

Appendix A (*Standards for Teacher Competence in Educational Assessment of Students*) and Appendix C (*Code of Professional Responsibility in Educational Measurement*) describe in detail teachers' **professional responsibilities** for gathering and using assessment information appropriately.

Guideline 1.2 applies these principles to the assessment activities of a classroom teacher. We discuss each in turn.

Guideline 1.2 Teachers' responsibilities in assessment

Responsibility	Explanation	Strategies
Creating assessment procedures	When you develop your own assessment procedures, ensure they are of high quality.	• Use sound principles of assessment planning, assessment design, task development, item writing, rubric development, and assessment marking.
Choosing assessment procedures	When you choose or select assessment procedures that others have created, make sure that they are appropriate for your intended use.	• Keep assessment procedures free from characteristics irrelevant to assessing the learning target and free of bias and stereotypes. • Accommodate in appropriate ways students in your class with disabilities or special needs. • Obtain permission necessary to use copyrighted material. • Present the assessment results in a way that encourages students and others to interpret them properly. • Ensure accuracy in assessment content, instructions, and scoring key or rubrics. Correct errors if you find any, and re-score or re-administer the assessment.
Administering assessment procedures	When you administer assessment procedures, ensure that your administration process is fair to all students and will not result in uninterpretable results.	• Give students sufficient information. • Establish a healthy classroom assessment environment. • Accommodate students with disabilities. • Follow established procedures for administering standardized and mandated tests.
Scoring assessment results	When you score students' responses to an assessment, evaluate the responses accurately and report the results to students in a timely manner.	• Classroom assessment scoring should be accurate, fair, and timely. Explain your scoring and give feedback that will help students improve. • Follow established procedures for scoring standardized and mandated tests.
Interpreting and using assessment results	When you interpret and use assessment results, ensure that your interpretations are as valid as possible, are used to promote positive student outcomes, and are used to minimize negative student outcomes.	• Interpret assessment information in light of students' learning targets. • Interpret multiple sources of evidence (more than one source of assessment information should inform decisions about each learning target).
Communicating assessment results	When you communicate assessment results, provide complete, useful, and correct information about students' performance that will promote positive student outcomes and minimize negative student outcomes.	• Communicate clearly and frequently. • Explain assessment terminology to parents, students, or community members as needed.

Choosing or creating assessment procedures

Your main professional obligations in using assessments are the same whether you select assessments, adapt them, or create your own. Assessment results must (a) be valid for your intended interpretation and use and (b) have an appropriate degree of reliability for importance of the decision(s) you will make. *Validity* refers to how you interpret and use information. *Reliability* refers to how dependable the assessment results are. The strategies in Guideline 1.2 will help you do this. Here are two brief examples. We will expand on validity and reliability in Chapter 2.

Regarding validity, suppose your state's standards require schools to teach a student to solve real-life problems using mathematics principles and generalizations. If your assessment procedure required students only to recall facts and generalizations, to solve problems that are unlike real life, and to demonstrate general comprehension of mathematics concepts, you couldn't make valid decisions about whether students met the standard.

Regarding reliability, suppose you are deciding what grade to give a student for the term. If you based the term grade decision on only a few questions or a short performance assessment, you would be in effect expecting a few pieces of information to be a dependable indicator of term-long learning, and they're not.

Administering assessment procedures

Usually, classroom assessments are meant to be opportunities for students to demonstrate their best performance. For students to perform at their maximum, they need basic information about the assessment, including:

- when it will be given,
- the conditions under which they are expected to perform,
- the content and abilities that will be assessed,
- what the assessment will emphasize,
- the standard or level of performance expected,
- how the assessment performance will be scored, and
- the effect the results of this assessment will have on any decisions (e.g., grades) you will make from the results.

Provide this information to students routinely.

The way you handle assessments sends messages to students. Giving students assessments they find meaningful and worthwhile will help motivate them to do their best. Establish an atmosphere where students don't feel threatened if they need to ask for help. For example, some teachers have a policy or class rule that there are "no stupid questions," and sometimes its corollary, "what's stupid is to wonder something and not ask about it."

Establish a climate of respect, as well. For example, rushing students unnecessarily or distracting them as they work creates unfair conditions if the goal is to have students do their best.

If you have students with disabilities in your class, you have a professional and possibly legal responsibility to make reasonable accommodations to assess them properly. As a general rule, the accommodations an IEP prescribes for students in your classroom learning environment would be appropriate accommodations for administering a classroom assessment. Do not introduce accommodations for the first time during the assessment (National Center on Educational Outcomes, 2005).

For standardized tests or other district or state tests, follow established procedures for administration.

- Fully inform students and parents about the testing and how the results will be used.
- Carefully follow the administration instructions in the test manual.
- Maintain security.
- Maintain testing conditions appropriate for maximum performance.

The same modifications you make in your classroom assessments might not be appropriate for standardized and state-mandated tests. This is especially true if a student's score is to be interpreted using national norms. Follow the test administration instructions from your school's test director and the state's guidelines. Since the passage of the NCLB Act, a state's accountability assessment program specifies what accommodations are permitted and the criteria students must meet in order for those accommodations to be permitted. Visit the National Center on Educational Outcomes web site (www.education.umn.edu/nceo/TopicAreas/Accommodations/StatesAccomm. htm) to see the latest requirements of each state.

Scoring assessment results

Teachers' assessment responsibilities extend to scoring, too.

- Score student responses accurately. Use the appropriate tools such as scoring keys, scoring rubrics, checklists, or rating scales.
- Score students fairly. Remove from the scoring process anything that would cause unfair results.
- Provide students with feedback that helps them to improve their learning. Show students what they did incorrectly and what their expected performance level is.
- Explain to students the rationale for the correct answers and for the scoring rubrics you use. This clarifies the learning target and teaches students the standards they are expected to meet.
- Give students the opportunity to review their evaluations individually. Go over your evaluation of a student's response if the student requests it.
- Score and return results in a timely manner. For feedback to be effective, it must be timely. The amount of time will vary with the assessment, but even a big test should normally be scored within a week.
- Correct errors in scoring and make necessary adjustments as quickly as possible.

Occasionally you may be asked to score standardized tests or other tests mandated by your school district or state. In such cases, follow the scoring procedures given in the test manual or in other materials or training. Be sure you understand how to apply the scoring guidelines before you score. Be honest! You have probably heard stories about some districts putting pressure on teachers to report high scores. Even if you are pressured in this way, it is your responsibility to score students' responses honestly and report the actual results.

Interpreting and using assessment results

Interpreting and using classroom assessment results are probably the most important teacher responsibilities.

- Interpret students' performance on one assessment in light of the learning targets you taught and emphasized. Students should be held accountable for the learning targets you taught. So if you taught a unit on the solar system, an "extra credit" report on rockets might be nice, but if it does not provide evidence about your solar system learning targets, then it doesn't belong in a grade or in any other feedback about how the student learned what you taught.

- Give students multiple opportunities and different ways to show their abilities with respect to the curriculum learning targets. No single assessment procedure is comprehensive enough to cover every important learning target. Realize the limitations of each assessment procedure you use. For example, you may combine a test to see if students know facts and concepts about plants and a seedling project to see if they can apply that knowledge, if your learning targets intended both.

- Help students and parents properly interpret assessment results. Some parents make too much of a test score or the result of a single assessment. Others do not see the pattern of success or failure that develops over time.

- Use assessment results to evaluate attainment of learning targets, not as a weapon for punishing or controlling students' behavior.

- Keep classroom assessment results confidential and protect students' rights of privacy. For example, do not post students' names and assessment results on the classroom wall or reveal your students' results to other teachers who have no right to know them. Sometimes a parent will ask how a neighbor's child performed in relation to the parent's own child. Don't honor this request.

Communicating assessment results

Communicate the proper interpretations of assessment results to students, parents, and school authorities. Describe classroom assessment results in terms of classroom learning targets. External tests do not exactly match the curriculum learning targets and your teaching emphasis. Help students and parents avoid misinterpreting external test results and understand the effects of school factors. Further, external test results are often reported as norm-referenced scores (e.g., percentile ranks, grade equivalents). You may need to teach a parent the meaning of certain types of scores or assessment concepts.

Make sure you communicate frequently. Establish and follow a regular communication schedule to report student progress to parents. Your school may have a policy to communicate progress to parents when grades are sent home. These policies usually specify minimum communication patterns. However, you may need more frequent communication depending on the community and the students you teach.

Students have rights and responsibilities as test takers

Student rights

Check with the superintendent of your school district for information on your state's requirements regarding student and family rights. Your school should also have its own written policy on (a) maintenance and release of assessment results, (b) release of nonconfidential information, (c) nondiscrimination, and (d) representational consent information.

In addition to legal requirements, test takers have the right to:

- be informed of their rights and responsibilities as a test taker;
- be treated with respect and courtesy;
- be given tests that are appropriate for the purpose for which they plan to be used and that have been developed to meet professional standards;
- receive an explanation prior to being tested about the purpose for testing, who will receive the test results, and what the plans are for using the results;
- be told what accommodations are available and be tested with appropriate accommodations;
- be informed in advance about when the test will be administered, when you will receive the results, and the cost of testing;
- have the test administered and interpreted by appropriately trained persons who follow professional codes of responsibility;
- be told the consequences of not taking a test, not completing a test, or canceling the scores on a test already taken;
- receive an explanation of the results of testing in easily understood language and in a timely manner;
- have test results kept confidential within the limits of law; and
- present any concerns about the testing process or results.

Among the major issues for a classroom teacher are fairness to each student, respecting students, opening up student evaluation processes, and correcting errors in student evaluations as soon as possible.

Student responsibilities

Students also have responsibilities in an assessment situation. Students have the responsibility of studying and preparing for tests and examinations in their classes. The same Test-Takers' Rights Working Group (1999) that prepared test-taker's rights has prepared a list of test-taker's responsibilities. These include students' responsibilities to:

- pay attention to explanations of their rights and responsibilities as a test taker;
- be respectful and courteous toward others during testing;
- ask questions and clarify before the testing when uncertain about the purpose of testing, the manner in which it will be administered, what they will be expected to do, and how the results will be reported and used;
- attend to written or oral instructions;
- inform the examiner in advance of what accommodations or modifications are needed;
- inform the examiner in advance of any current illness that may affect their performance;
- inform the examiner if they had difficultly understanding the language of the test;
- learn the date, time, and place of the test;
- pay for the test if necessary;
- arrive for the testing on time, with the requisite materials, and be prepared to begin the test;
- follow the examiner's instructions;
- respond and behave honestly during the examination;
- understand the consequences of not taking the test and be prepared to accept those consequences if they choose not to take it;
- tell the appropriate persons if they believe that the testing conditions adversely affected their performance;
- find out about the confidentiality of the results; and
- present any concerns they have about the testing process or the results to the appropriate persons in a timely manner.

Conclusions

This chapter has provided a general introduction on key concepts about educational decision making, assessment as information for teachers and for students, high-stakes assessments, teachers' professional responsibilities in assessment, and students' rights and responsibilities as test takers. The point was to provide an orientation to what assessment is supposed to do (provide information for educational decisions) and describe the current assessment context (the high-stakes testing climate and teachers' and students' responsibilities). You should now understand what assessment is for, why it is important, and why it will be important to read the rest of this book.

Exercises

1. Each of these statements describes a situation in which a teacher uses an assessment procedure. Critique these scenarios. Which practices were sound, which unsound, and why? Discuss your findings with other members of your class.

   a. Mrs. Jones schedules a short quiz in social studies every Friday. She announces this at the beginning of the semester, and every student is aware that this will occur. She jots down the questions on Friday mornings before class and photocopies them to give out during class. She has never taken a course in assessment, nor has she ever read a book on how to improve assessments.

   b. Mr. Mohan teaches science. A deaf student is in his class. When a test is scheduled, Mr. Mohan gives a copy of the test a few days ahead of schedule to the student's sign language interpreter, who simplifies the language of the questions but keeps the technical or scientific terminology. When other students are sitting for the test, the deaf student is in another room being administered the test by the student's sign language interpreter, who signs the questions to the student.

   c. Mrs. Taibbi teaches biology. Her teacher's guide comes with a printed multiple-choice test covering the materials in the chapter she just taught. She gives the test to the office secretary for duplication a few days ahead of schedule. On the day she is to give the test, she goes over it to make an answer key. She discovers that out of 40 items, 10 items cover material she either did not cover or did not thoroughly teach. She spends the first 15 minutes of class teaching these concepts, and then gives the test. All 40 items count toward students' grades.

   d. Mr. Williams teaches history. The authors of the textbook used in his class provide multiple-choice unit tests. One of the students brings the test home after the results are returned. The student's father goes over it and notices that for 5 of the 40 items, his son's answers are correct according to the information in the textbook but were marked wrong by Mr. Williams. He writes a note to Mr. Williams describing the situation and citing the textbook pages to support his claim. Mr. Williams writes back saying the test was written by the textbook authors and is published, so it would be absurd to question the items' correctness. He refuses to reconsider the items or rescore the papers.

2. Each of the following statements describes a situation in which a teacher administers or scores an assessment. Critique these scenarios. Which practices were sound, which unsound, and why? Discuss your findings with other members of your class.

   a. Mr. Gordon likes to give "pop" quizzes or surprise quizzes to keep his students "on their toes."

b. Mrs. Stravinski believed that the standardized test she was requested to give in reading was too speeded. Consequently she gave the students an extra 10 minutes. She did not report this to anyone.

c. Mrs. Appleton is an itinerant teacher of the hearing-impaired who assists with the education of mainstreamed students at Mountain View High School. Billy is a senior deaf student to whom she administers a standardized achievement test battery using an appropriate signed language. She knows that Billy's results will be sent to postsecondary schools for deaf students, and that they will use the results as part of the admission decision. When scoring the test by hand, she noticed that Billy's scores were unexpectedly low. She reviewed the questions he missed and said to herself, "I know he really knows the answers to these." So she changed his answers to about 25% of the questions to give him a higher score. She rationalized her actions by thinking, "He really is a good student, and if I simply sent in the scores he got, he would not be given the chance I know he deserves."

d. Mr. Pennel gives essay questions and performance tasks as a major part of his assessment. He seldom bothers with developing scoring rubrics because he doesn't know how to do so and they take time to develop. He'd rather spend the time teaching.

e. Mrs. Dingle marks the assessments of John and Robert. They both receive the same score, which is on the borderline between an A and a B. She gives John an A and Robert a B. The boys are friends and they compare papers, discovering the different grades for the same score. John goes to Mrs. Dingle and tells her that Robert deserves the A. Mrs. Dingle says, "John, everyone knows that you are an A student, while Robert is a B student. My grades just reflect this fact so I won't change his grade."

Companion Website

Now go to our Companion Website at **www.prenhall.com/brookhart** to assess your understanding of chapter content with multiple-choice and essay questions. Broaden your knowledge of assessment with links to assessment related web sites.

Validity and Reliability

1. Validity is the soundness of your interpretations and uses of students' assessment results.
2. For large-scale assessment, think of validity as an argument with evidence discussed under four principles: interpretations, uses, values, and consequences.
3. For classroom assessment, your major validity concerns are: (a) ensuring that the assessments truly match the learning objectives (as intended and as taught, in both content and process); and (b) ensuring that the consequences serve students and their learning.

4. Reliability is the degree to which students' results remain consistent over replications of an assessment procedure.
5. For large-scale assessment, reliability can be studied with quantitative measures of the consistency across times, items or tasks, forms, or raters.
6. For classroom assessment, your major reliability concerns are: (a) deciding what kind of consistency, dependability, or accuracy is important for the particular assessment; and (b) insuring that particular consistency/dependability/accuracy and appraising evidence of it.

This chapter is about validity and reliability, which are fundamental principles of information quality for assessment results. What follows is a true story. It happened when the first author (the "I" in the story) was a brand-new college professor.

The second author had arranged an assessment symposium at a large university. Four nationally recognized scholars were invited in to talk about national, state, district, and classroom assessment, respectively. I was one of two local people asked to do a "local response" at the end of the session. The audience included about 300 local teachers and school administrators, and a few other professors. I was a little apprehensive about meeting these daunting "big names," and I wondered how I was going to say anything useful beyond what they already had presented. Besides, I had never addressed a group as big as 300 people.

The speeches were great. I learned a lot, and I think the audience did, too, because they listened very quietly. One of the points in the classroom assessment speech really annoyed me, though. The speaker said that while classroom assessments needed to be valid and reliable, there was no real need to teach pre-service teachers about the technical terms "validity and reliability." To me—recently a school teacher myself—this came perilously close to "they don't need to worry their pretty little heads" about such things.

Therefore, I took exception to this point in my response. I pointed out that we don't expect teachers to design good lessons without learning some child development theory and some learning theory. So why would we expect teachers to design and use assessments well without giving them some information about validity and reliability?

To my utter surprise, the audience applauded. They had sat quietly through the previous speeches, but they applauded me! I think that's because they agreed that teachers do need to understand the principles of sound assessment, and because they agreed that underestimating teachers' interests and abilities is a recipe for disaster (and maybe because they were a little insulted about feeling like they'd been treated as "pretty little heads"). I hope the readers of this book agree, too, and read this chapter in that spirit.

Validity is the soundness of your interpretations and uses of students' assessment results

Scores, like any other numbers—or words, for that matter—have to *mean* something to be useful. For example, if I buy new pants that are too long, I can't just say, "I'll shorten them two." I need to say something like, "It will take a two-inch hem to make the pants the right length." Score meaning is even more of an issue for assessments, because you are not measuring concrete things like inches of length but rather increments on some scale you constructed as an indicator of some abstraction you defined (like "achievement of the objectives for this week's math unit"). It doesn't help to say, "Johnny is an 87" or even "Johnny got an 87% on that math test." Until you can say what an 87% on that math test means for Johnny, you haven't really said much. If you *interpret* that 87 as an indicator of Johnny's performance on particular math objectives, and if you *use* that 87 to assign him a grade of B and let him move on to next week's lessons, you need to be sure that interpretation and those uses are reasonable. What if some of the questions on the test weren't relevant to the particular math objectives, or were way too easy or too hard, or had a high reading level? Then maybe the 87% would not really be interpretable as performance on the objectives for this week's math unit.

You should have evidence from a variety of sources to demonstrate that assessment interpretations and uses are appropriate. Your "interpretation" is what you think the assessment results mean. When you use an assessment to talk about Sallie's "reading fluency," for example, you should be interpreting a score that really does measure reading fluency and not something else—interest in the story or bad behavior, for example.

Students should experience no serious negative consequences when assessment results are used as you intend. If you use your "reading fluency" measure to help place Sallie into a reading group, she should end up working on appropriate materials and making progress. If she doesn't, your use of the measure for placement is suspect—apparently it didn't help you place her where she should be. In effect, validating specific interpretations and uses of assessment results requires making a convincing argument that the evidence supports them (Kane, 1992, 2002; Shepard, 1993).

For large-scale assessment, think of validity as an argument with evidence discussed under four principles: interpretations, uses, values, and consequences

Large-scale assessments include district- and state-mandated assessments, standard-ized achievement and aptitude tests, attitude inventories, and individually adminis-tered intelligence tests, to name only a few. Over the course of your teaching career, you will be required to administer and interpret, or maybe even select, some of them. Here we discuss the types of evidence required to support the valid interpre-tation and use of large-scale assessment results.

Four principles for validation (Must have evidence)

Support validity judgments (Messick, 1989, 1994). Base your judgment on all four principles, not just on one of them. Example 2.1 gives an example.

- The *interpretations* (or meanings) of students' assessment results are valid only to the degree that you can point to evidence that supports them.
- The *uses* of assessment results are valid only to the degree to which you can point to evidence that supports them.
- The interpretations and uses of assessment results are valid only when the *values* they imply are appropriate.
- The interpretations and uses of assessment results are valid only when their *consequences* are consistent with appropriate values.

■ **EXAMPLE 2.1. Example of the four principles for validation**

Interpretation

Hiram is a Lincoln School student. He has taken the *ABC Reading Test* each year, but his scores suddenly rose this year. How would you interpret Hiram's sudden score rise? Possibilities include: (a) his reading comprehension has improved; (b) his moti-vation to do well on reading comprehension tests has improved; and (c) his skill in answering multiple-choice reading comprehension test items has improved. These interpretations are not mutually exclusive. Hiram may have improved in one or more of these areas. The Lincoln School staff may like to interpret Hiram's assessments to mean an improvement in his reading comprehension. Before they can claim that such an interpretation has some degree of validity, however, they need to offer evidence. First, they need to show that the *ABC Reading Test* measures reading comprehension in the way reading specialists define comprehension. Second, they need evidence to show that Hiram's increased test performance is due primarily to his improved reading, rather than simply a result of his increased motivation to do well on the test and his improved test-taking skills. Third, they need to use other evidence that exists in the school: Hiram's reading teacher and/or classroom teacher should compare his test performance with his classroom reading performance.

Uses

The Lincoln School staff might want to (a) certify that Hiram is reading at an appropriate level for his grade; (b) diagnose or identify the types of reading comprehension problems Hiram may be experiencing; (c) place Hiram into a remedial, regular, or advanced reading group; and (d) continually monitor Hiram's growth in reading comprehension. They may wish to use Hiram's scores for more than one of these purposes. Evidence should be provided separately for each intended use of assessment results. For example, what evidence can Lincoln School provide to demonstrate that students assigned to remedial reading groups on the basis of their *ABC Reading Test* scores will learn to read better than if they were assigned to the regular reading classes? For published standardized tests, much of this evidence may be available already in the test's technical manual so a school may not need to do its own research. This is not always the case, however.

Values

What values were implied when Lincoln School's staff interpreted Hiram's *ABC Reading Test* scores as measuring reading comprehension and used them to describe and to plan his reading development? First, the very choice of the *ABC Reading Test* implied that the staff valued the format and content of the test items. Suppose that the *ABC Reading Test* consists of several short passages (less than 500 words each), each followed by several multiple-choice questions. Further, suppose the themes of the reading passages ignore (or are irrelevant to) African American, Hispanic, Native American, and/or other minority cultural experiences. Using and interpreting this test as a measure of reading comprehension implies the staff accepted that such cultural and ethnic experiences are unimportant in assessing a student's reading comprehension. Second, using a multiple-choice format for assessing reading comprehension is also a value judgment: Should longer, more "authentic" reading passages and open-ended questions be used instead? Does the cheaper multiple-choice test have more value than the more costly authentic assessment? Third, the staff's use of the test scores to assign students to different reading groups implies that they value homogeneous grouping for reading instruction. This also implies that the benefits received from being taught with others of similar reading ability outweigh the benefits received from being taught in a more mixed reading ability group.

Consequences

Lincoln School's intended consequence for placing children with low *ABC Reading Test* scores into remedial reading groups was to improve their reading ability as rapidly as possible. As the students' reading comprehension improves, the staff believes, so will their other schoolwork and their self-esteem. But suppose something unintended and unvalued happens instead. Suppose the remedial reading students quickly come to see themselves as incompetent, and their self-esteem declines. Suppose, too, that out of frustration their teachers begin drilling them on material the students do not understand (instead of building on what they already know). Suppose that eventually the students never leave the remedial reading track. In the face of these unintended and negative consequences, would Lincoln School's use of the *ABC Reading Test* scores to form remedial groups still be highly valid? Even if the test measured reading comprehension, when such negative consequences occur, its continued use would be devastating to these children. Interpretations and uses of assessment results must have positively valued consequences (and avoid negatively valued consequences) to have a high degree of validity.

The concept of validity applies to the ways we interpret and use the assessment results and not to the assessment procedure itself. Thus, don't say, "Is the *ABC Reading Test* valid?" except as an informal, shorthand way of speaking. Rather, ask more specific questions such as, "Is it valid to interpret the scores from the *ABC Reading Test* as measuring reading comprehension?" or "Is it valid to use *ABC Reading Test* scores to place students into reading groups?" and so on.

Assessment results have different degrees of validity for different purposes and for different situations. The scores from our hypothetical *ABC Reading Test*, for example, may be highly valid when used to evaluate the reading program in your school district because the items on it match the district's reading program objectives quite well. On the other hand, scores from the same test may have poor validity for evaluating your neighboring district's reading program because the items poorly match that district's reading program objectives.

Judge the validity of your interpretations or uses of assessment results only after studying and combining several types of validity evidence. Table 2.1 describes different types of validity evidence, the questions that are asked in validity studies of that type, and the methods used to answer those questions.

Each type of evidence in Table 2.1 has some usefulness for validating the ways you intend to interpret and use assessment results. Identify which types of evidence are more important for your particular case. For example, the *SAT Reasoning Test* is intended to predict first-year college grade-point averages. Thus, a university or college would weigh more heavily the test's predictive powers and its potential for negative consequences, such as reducing the number of men it selects, than evidence that the test matches curriculum objectives and content.

Kane (1992) gives the following example. Suppose that you wanted to validate using an algebra placement test to assign students either to a remedial algebra course or to a calculus course. To validate this assessment practice, you need arguments supported by evidence (such as described in Table 2.1) that the following are reasonable:

- You can appropriately assess students' success in the calculus course (that is, a suitable criterion assessment procedure is available).

- You can identify the algebra concepts and thinking skills that students will use frequently in the calculus course.

Table 2.1 Summary of the Different Types of Validity Evidence for Large-scale Educational Assessments

Type of evidence	Examples of questions needing to be answered	Techniques often used to obtain answers
1. Content representativeness and relevance (called *content evidence*)	a. How well do the assessment tasks represent the domain of important content? b. How well do the assessment tasks represent the curriculum as you define it? c. How well do the assessment tasks reflect current thinking about what should be taught and assessed? d. Are the assessment tasks worthy of being learned? e. How well do tasks align with state standards?	A description of the curriculum and content to be learned is obtained. Each assessment task is checked to see if it matches important content and learning outcomes. Each assessment task is rated for its relevance, importance, accuracy, and meaningfulness. The assessment procedure is viewed as a whole, and judgments are made about representativeness and relevance of the entire collection of tasks.
2. Types of thinking skills and processes required (called *substantive evidence*)	a. How much do the assessment tasks require students to use important thinking skills and processes? b. How well do the assessment tasks represent the types of thinking skills espoused as important curriculum outcomes? c. Are the thinking skills and processes that students actually use to complete the assessment procedure the same ones claimed to be assessed? d. Do thinking skills required by the test align with thinking skills required by state standards?	The assessment procedure is analyzed to reveal the types of cognitions required to perform the tasks successfully. The relationship between the strategies students are taught to use and those they are required to use during the assessment are determined. Students may be asked to "think aloud" while performing the assessment tasks and the resultant protocols analyzed to identify cognitions the students used. Judgments are made about the assessment procedure as a whole to decide whether desirable, representative, and relevant thinking skills and processes are being assessed.
3. Relationships among the assessment tasks or parts of the assessment (called *internal structure evidence*)	a. Do all the assessment tasks "work together" so that each task contributes positively toward assessing the quality of interest? b. If the different parts of the assessment procedure are supposed to provide unique information, do the results support this uniqueness? c. If the different parts of the assessment procedure are supposed to provide the same similar information, do the results support this? d. Are the students' responses scored in a way that is consistent with the constructs and theory on which the assessment is based?	a. If students' performance on each task is quantified, correlations of task scores with total scores from the assessment are studied to decide whether all tasks contribute positively. b. Each part of the assessment may be scored separately and these part scores intercorrelated to see whether the desired pattern of relationships emerges. c. Logic, substantive knowledge, and experience are used to generate explanations for high and low performance on the assessment. Not all hypotheses should be consistent with the intended interpretations of how the parts function. d. Empirical studies, both experimental and correlational, are conducted to support or refute the hypotheses generated in (c) above.
4. Relationships of assessment results to the results of other variables (called *external structure evidence*)	a. Are the results of this assessment consistent with the results of other similar assessment for these students? b. How well does performance on this assessment procedure reflect the quality or trait that is measured by other tests? c. How well does performance on this assessment procedure predict current or future performance on other valued tasks or measures (criteria)? d. How well can the assessment results be used to select persons for jobs, schools, etc.? What is the magnitude of error? e. How well can the assessment results be used to assign pupils to different types of instruction? Is learning better when pupils are assigned this way?	a. The criterion tasks are identified and analyzed. Assessment of their important characteristics is created. b. Scores from the assessment are compared to scores on the criterion to be predicted. c. Studies of various classification and prediction errors are made. d. Studies show whether the results from this assessment converge with or diverge from results from other assessments in the way expected when the proposed interpretation of the students' performance is used (called *convergent and discriminant evidence*).

5. Reliability over time, assessors, and content domain (called *reliability evidence*)	a. Will the same students obtain nearly the same results if the assessment procedure was applied on another occasion? What is the margin of error expected? b. If different persons administered, graded, or scored the assessment results, would the students' outcomes be the same? What is the margin of error? c. If a second, alternate form of the assessment procedure were to be developed, with similar content, would the students' results be very similar? What is the margin of error?	Studies are conducted focusing on the consistency (reliability) of the assessment results.
6. Generalization of interpretations over different types of people, under different conditions, or with special instruction/intervention (called *generalization evidence*)	a. Does the assessment procedure give significantly different results when it is used with students from different socioeconomic and ethnic backgrounds, but of the same ability? If so, is this fair or unbiased? b. Will students' results from the assessment procedure be altered drastically if they are given special incentives are motives? If so, should this change how the assessment results are interpreted? c. Will special intervention, changes in instructions, or special coaching significantly alter the results students obtain on the assessment? If so, should this change how the assessment results are interpreted?	a. Logic, substantive knowledge, and experience are used to generate explanations (hypotheses) about how the interpretation of the assessment results might change when the procedure is applied to different types of people, under different conditions, or with special instruction (intervention). b. Empirical studies, both experimental and correlational, are conducted to support or refuse the hypotheses generated in (a) above.
7. Value of the intended and/or unintended consequences (called *consequential evidence*)	a. What do we expect to happen to the students if we interpret and use the assessment results in this particular way? To what degree do these expected consequences happen, and is that good? b. What side effects do we anticipate happening to the students if we interpret and use the assessment results in this particular way? To what degree are these anticipated side effects occurring, and are they positive or negative? c. What unanticipated negative side effects happened to the students for whom we interpreted and used the assessment results in this particular way? Can these negative side effects be avoided by using other assessment procedures/techniques or by altering our interpretations?	a. Studies are conducted to describe the intended outcomes of using the given assessment procedure and to determine the degree to which these outcomes are realized for all students. b. Studies are conducted to determine whether anticipated or unanticipated side effects have resulted from interpreting and using the given assessment procedure in a certain way.
8. Cost, efficiency, practicality, instructional features (called *practicality evidence*)	a. Can the assessment procedure accommodate typical numbers of students? b. Is the assessment procedure easy for teachers to use? c. Can the assessment procedure give quick results to guide instruction? d. Do teachers agree that the theoretical concepts behind the assessment procedure reflect the key understandings they are teaching? e. Do the assessment results meaningfully explain individual differences? f. Do the assessment results identify misunderstandings that need to be corrected? g. Would an alternative assessment procedure be more efficient?	Logical analyses, cost analyses, reviews by teachers, and field trial data are used to come to decisions about the factors of cost, efficiency, practicality, and usefulness of instructional features.

Note: These types of validity evidence have been suggested by Messick (1989, 1994) and Linn, Baker, and Dunbar (1991).

- The algebra content and thinking skills assessed by the placement test match those frequently used in the calculus course.

- The remedial course to which low-scoring students will be assigned will succeed in teaching students the algebra concepts and skills needed in the calculus course.

- Scores on the placement test are reliable.

- The placement test scores are not affected by systematic errors or biases that would lower the validity of your interpretation that the placement test measures algebra knowledge and thinking skills.

- It is not helpful for students with high ability in algebra to take the remedial algebra course. Students who score high on the placement tests will not significantly improve their chances of success in calculus by first taking this particular remedial algebra course.

Validity arguments become even more complicated when not every student takes exactly the same version of the test, for example when accommodations are made for students with disabilities.

Validity of scores from test accommodations

If a standardized test was administered under accommodating conditions, do the scores mean the same thing as the scores for students who took the test under standard conditions? The validity of interpretations depends on the type of test, the purpose of the testing, the type of accommodation, the type of disability, and the nature of the interpretation itself. For example, if the purpose of testing is to assess a student's knowledge and ability in social studies or mathematics, then it may be appropriate for a student with a severe reading disability to have a reader to read the test questions aloud. If you can reasonably argue that reading is not part of the knowledge and ability being assessed, you could also argue that poor readers who do not have learning disabilities should also have their mathematics and social studies tests read to them.

On the other hand, a student with a severe reading disability may be unable to complete the reading comprehension section of a standardized achievement test. If the purpose of testing were to assess a student's ability to read standard printed English, it would be invalid to provide a reader for the student on such a test.

Suppose a student can read some material if given more time to answer. This accommodation violates the standardization conditions and invalidates the usual norm-referenced interpretations (e.g., grade equivalents, percentile ranks, and standard scores). Nevertheless, by giving the student more time, you discovered what test material he or she could read when the time element was removed. Any norm-referenced interpretation of the results should take the accommodations into account. You would say something like this:

"Here is how Sally compares to other students. The other students took the test under standard conditions and with limited time. However, Sally took the test under nonstandard conditions and with no time limits because [give your rationale]."

The issue of whether to report any norm-referenced information about a student's performance when the test administration violated the standardized testing conditions (e.g., failing to keep to the time limits) remains controversial. If a test's standardized administration conditions are violated, some would view reporting any type of norm-referencing information or including results in school averages as inappropriate (Phillips, personal communication, 2001). Another concern is violation of students' privacy rights. Whether the results for students administered the test under accommodating conditions should be identified or flagged in the record or score report also remains controversial (Sireci, 2005).

A criterion-referenced interpretation (e.g., an interpretation of the type of material read and types of questions answered) is often made for test results. However, speed of reading is also part of this interpretation for standardized achievement tests because of the standard time limits. Therefore, your criterion-referenced interpretation would be something like this:

"These are the types of materials and questions Sally was able to read when she took the test under nonstandard conditions and with no time limits."

Bias in educational assessment

One of the concerns surrounding the suitability of assessments for various decisions is whether a particular assessment is biased against particular groups. Exactly what a "biased assessment" means is not always clear, because many definitions of assessment or test **bias** exist in the media and the professional literature. In this text, we describe test bias as a test used unfairly against a particular group of persons for a particular purpose or decision. Table 2.2 lists definitions of assessment bias adapted from Flaugher (1978).

Most assessment specialists would not subscribe to the mean difference definition of bias because average differences in groups' performances could represent real differences in the level of their attainment, rather than an artificial difference. If one group receives an inferior education or has been socialized away from learning (that is, the social context and not the assessment itself was unfair), a test will likely result in lower average scores for this group than for another group that has had opportunity and encouragement to learn. However, such mean differences in groups may mean that the assessment procedure is biased, too.

Bias considerations have been important in the recent development of state tests for NCLB. The two most common procedures for examining bias are (a) having a content review panel look over draft test items and (b) examining differential item functioning statistics. Items that exhibit bias in the judgment of the panel or in the statistical analysis are usually dropped or edited.

Table 2.2 Different Definitions of Bias in Educational Assessment

Assessment bias as . . .	Definition	Example
Mean Differences	On the whole test, the average (mean) score of that group falls short of the average score of another group.	There is an achievement "gap" between some groups of students on NAEP.
Differential Item Functioning (DIF)	On one item or task, persons of the same ability perform differently on the item.	On one item, African American students and white students with the same total test score performed differently.
Misinterpretation of Scores	Someone makes inappropriate inferences about students' performances that go beyond the content domain of the assessment.	A female has difficulty solving two-step arithmetic word problems involving knowledge of male suburban experiences; her performance is interpreted as an indication that females have lower arithmetic reasoning skills than males.
Sexist and Racist Content: Facial Bias	Offensive, stereotyped language and pictures are used in the assessment tasks and materials.	Story illustrations include a picture of a woman in a pink shirtwaist dress feeding a baby and waving to a man in a suit leaving for work.
Differential Validity	An assessment predicts criterion scores better for one group of persons than for another.	In studies, educational selection tests seem to predict educational success equally well (or equally poorly) for most groups. Therefore there are no real examples.
Content and Experience Differential	The content of the assessment tasks differs radically from a particular subgroup of students' life experiences and the assessment results are interpreted without taking such differences into proper consideration.	A high school vocabulary test is comprised of slang word meanings likely to be learned only by urban, streetwise, African American youths. The test would be biased if used to judge general verbal ability but not if used to gauge knowledge of this culture-specific vocabulary domain.
Statistical Model Used for Selection Decisions	The statistical procedure used to rank candidates for selection is not fair to all persons, regardless of group membership.	For a job selection, interviews and the application blank itself, plus variety of performance assessments and paper-and-pencil tests, are used to calculate a weighted average. All assessments show some positive relationship to job or school success, but certain subgroups score consistently lower on one or more of the assessments used in the selection process.
Wrong Criterion Measure	Selection tests are used to predict success on a second measure called a criterion. But the criterion measure itself may be biased, making the selection process biased, even if the test is unbiased.	A job does not require reading skills; on-the-job performance is the relevant criterion. An employer uses a paper-and-pencil test of job knowledge as a substitute criterion measure instead of using a measure of actual job performance. He erroneously interprets as the "ability to do the job," so it is biased against those who cannot read or who are poor paper-and-pencil test takers but might well be able to perform the job.
Atmosphere and Conditions of Assessment	Basic test-taking stresses, such as test anxiety, feeling unwelcome, or being tested by a member of the opposite gender or another race, can adversely affect the performance of some groups.	It may be unfair to students and teachers in schools serving the impoverished to use an officially mandated test that serves "to inflict on them periodic, detailed documentation of just how very far away from anything approaching the norm they are" (Flaugher, 1978, p. 677).

For classroom assessment, your major validity concerns are:
(a) ensuring that the assessments truly match the learning objectives
(as intended and as taught, in both content and process) and
(b) ensuring that the consequences serve students and their learning

The validity of your classroom assessment results depends on how well your assessment samples the learning targets. This is huge! To create valid assessments, you must (a) clearly identify the important learning targets and (b) be sure they are well sampled by the assessment procedure. Positive consequences for student learning provide further evidence that your interpretation and uses of assessment results were valid. Guideline 2.1 shows some ways to address these concerns.

Content representativeness and relevance

The tasks included on your assessment should reflect the important content and learning outcomes specified in your school's or state's standards. Your assessment procedure—both tasks and scoring procedures—should emphasize what you taught. Revise tests that come with the curriculum materials or the textbook if their items are of poor quality, emphasize low-level thinking skills, or emphasize different content than you emphasized during teaching.

For example, say you taught a unit on the solar system that emphasized the planets. You find a solar system test in a textbook, but its questions are only half "planet" questions—the other half are about the sun. Reduce the number of "sun" questions to the level of emphasis in your unit; eliminate any items that don't cover content that was important in your unit. Review the remaining set of questions and add your own questions if any important content from your unit is not represented.

Thinking skills and processes

Closely related to content representativeness and relevance is whether your assessment method permits you to evaluate students on a sufficiently wide range of thinking skills and processes. Use both a thinking skills taxonomy and a content outline to write an assessment blueprint. This blueprint helps you ensure that your assessment covers the important thinking skills and content.

Allow enough time for students to demonstrate the type of thinking you are trying to assess. Complex thinking, meaningful problem solving, and creative applications require considerable time for most students to demonstrate. See Chapter 5 for more information about planning tests. For now, the point is that good planning strengthens the validity of your test results.

Find out whether students actually use the types of thinking you expect them to use during the assessment. If you are going to interpret students' assessment as reflecting complex thinking skills, then be sure that students are actually using them when completing the assessment. Check this by observing the strategies your students appear to use during the assessment. You may interview a few students, asking them to "think aloud" as they solve assessment tasks.

Guideline 2.1 Validity concerns for classroom assessment	
Assessments must truly match the learning objectives	
Category	**Your assessments should:**
Content representativeness and relevance	• Emphasize what you taught • Represent school's stated curricular content • Represent current thinking about the subject • Contain content worth learning
Thinking skills and processes	• Require students to integrate and use several thinking skills • Represent thinking processes and skills stated in school's curriculum • Contain tasks that cannot be completed without using intended thinking skills • Allow enough time for students to use complex skills and processes
Consistency with other classroom assessments	• Yield patterns of results consistent with your other assessments of the class • Contain individual tasks (items) not too easy or too difficult
Reliability and objectivity	• Use a systematic procedure for every student to assign quality ratings or marks • Provide each student with several opportunities to demonstrate competence for each learning target assessed
Consequences of using assessment results must support student learning	
Category	**Your assessments should:**
Fairness to different types of students	• Contain tasks that are interpreted appropriately by students with different backgrounds • Accommodate students with disabilities or learning difficulties, if any • Be free of ethnic, racial, and gender bias
Economy, efficiency, practicality, instructional features	• Require a reasonable amount of time for you to construct and students to complete • Represent appropriate use of students' class time • Represent appropriate use of your class time
Multiple assessment usage	• Be used in conjunction with other assessment results for important decisions • Be used in summative ways only after appropriate formative assessment
Learning progress	• Provide students with information they can use to improve • Support student motivation for learning • Result in student learning • Avoid negative consequences

Consistency with other classroom assessments

The results of a student's assessment for grading should be consistent with the student's pattern of performance on formative assessments throughout the period. When inconsistencies do arise, they should be interpretable as changes related to student learning. For example, if a student has studied some material carefully, she may do particularly well on an assessment. Some students may perform better or worse than you expect, of course, and you should try to determine why. However, the pattern of assessment results for the entire class should not surprise you.

If the results are a big surprise, there may be a validity problem with your assessment procedure. Perhaps the emphasis of your test, for example, did not match the emphasis of your teaching. Perhaps it did not match the content emphasis of the other assessments on which you based your expectations. If these reasons explain the discrepancy, you may not be able to interpret the assessment results as an indication of learning.

When assessment tasks are too difficult or too easy, the assessment results will not be consistent with your other student observations. All students will attain nearly the same result—either all good scores or all bad, depending on whether the assessment was too easy or too hard. You won't be able to distinguish reliable individual differences among them. This may lower the validity of the results for grading. Also, too difficult an assessment frustrates students, making them feel as if their study time was wasted. Such a situation is a negative consequence and does not reveal students' best performances. Assessment tasks should be challenging, of course, but not so difficult that only one or two students in the class can perform well on them.

Reliability and objectivity

Reliability refers to the consistency of assessment results. If your students' scores on your assessments are so inconsistent as to be essentially random numbers, your assessment cannot be valid. Use a scoring guide for obtaining quality ratings or scores from students' performance on the assessment. Such a guide may be a scoring key, a rubric, or a rating scale with each rating level clearly defined. Apply your scoring guide to every student you are assessing. Your scoring guide should be clear enough that a qualified teaching colleague could use it and obtain the same results as you do.

Your assessment should be long enough to contain several opportunities for students to demonstrate their knowledge and skill for each learning target. If practical constraints do not allow for a more complete assessment in one class period, consider using another class period, a take-home assessment, or a combination of results from several assessments administered over the marking period.

Fairness to different types of students

Your assessment procedures should be fair to students from all ethnic and socioeconomic backgrounds, as well as students with disabilities. Word the problems or tasks on an assessment so all students will interpret them appropriately. Modify the wording or the administrative conditions of assessment tasks to accommodate students with disabilities or special learning problems. Avoid material that is subtly or blatantly offensive to any subgroup of students or that perpetuates ethnic and gender stereotypes. Assessments need not be free of any reference to race, ethnicity, or gender; rather, eliminate stereotypes and balance the references among various groups.

Economy, efficiency, practicality

Assessments should be a good use of your time and your students' time, and should guide your teaching toward important learning goals. An assessment should be relatively easy to construct and use. There will be some trade-offs. It is simpler to develop essay questions than to develop complex problem-solving performance tasks or good multiple-choice items. Once developed, however, multiple-choice items are easier to score and may be reused for next year's class. Problem-solving performance tasks set in real-life settings are difficult to construct properly. However, they let you assess more completely whether students can use what they learned than do either the typical teacher-crafted multiple-choice items or short-answer questions.

Multiple-assessment usage

Multiple assessments give students many opportunities to show what they know. A multiple-assessment strategy will draw a clearer picture of student achievement than one assessment would. Multiple summative assessments should come after the student has also had multiple opportunities for formative assessment, where practice and feedback afford opportunity to learn. Students should have a chance to practice using the knowledge and skills for which you hold them responsible. They should have a chance to see where they need additional work and be given the opportunity to do it.

Learning progress

The main, intended, positive consequence of classroom assessments should be that they help students learn. Assessment results help students learn by giving them information about where their performance stands in relation to the learning target and by supporting their motivation to learn. Information can come to students in the form of teacher feedback, peer feedback, self-evaluation, going over questions, and the like. The important point is that students hear and understand the information and can use it.

Your assessments should in fact result in student learning. Formative assessment is most useful in this regard, but even summative (graded) assessments should be "episodes of genuine learning" (Wolf, 1993). For example, you may use a term paper to see how well students can research a topic; students learn as they work and you both see the results.

Your assessments should also avoid negative consequences. Negative consequences can be cognitive: Poor assessments help students form misconceptions about what is important to learn. For example, we once had a teacher education student in class who called her field site supervising teacher "the ditto queen" (a reference to the old "ditto master" technology the school still used to reproduce worksheets). This teacher's stock-in-trade was worksheets, and she used them for everything. Her students may have concluded that learning how to fill in worksheets was the main purpose of school.

Negative consequences can also be motivational—for example, poor assessments judge students, or confirm prejudgments of them, and encourage them to give up. Assessments that make students feel stupid or give them a sense of hopelessness are counterproductive. However, assessments that give students information they see as useful to them helps them feel in control of their learning, and that is motivating.

Of course, no information can be in any way meaningful or useful (valid) if it isn't also accurate (reliable). For example, if a test inaccurately indicates Johnny's math achievement, you won't be able to base good decisions on its results. Going back to the pants analogy—if I measured inaccurately and specified two inches when the hem really should have been three inches, the pants won't be the right length even after hemming. Because assessment scores refer not to concrete qualities like inches of length, but rather to abstraction like achievement of learning objectives, assuring reliability requires more serious thought than just checking a ruler. We turn to reliability in the next section.

Reliability is the degree to which students' results remain consistent over replications of an assessment procedure

The fact that there is error in measurement—and in particular that scores on educational assessments are not perfect estimates of student achievement—should not surprise you. Have you ever received a test back where you for some reason missed an item about something you really did know (darn it!)? Have you ever received a test back where you guessed right, and "earned" a point for a question that by rights you should have missed? Did you point out the error to your teacher and ask her to remove a point from your score (we thought not!)? These memories illustrate that measurement error happens, and that it happens in both directions. That is, because of measurement error, your true score can be over- or under-estimated.

Reliability and measurement error are complementary ways of speaking about the same assessment phenomenon. The concept of reliability focuses on the consistency of assessment results. The concept of measurement error focuses on their inconsistencies.

You can think of reliability of scores in educational assessment in terms of consistency, dependability, and/or accuracy. This is not the case with physical measurements, where consistency/dependability and accuracy are two different things. I love my consistent but *inaccurate* bathroom scale that always registers two pounds low. I know it's inaccurate because there is such a thing as a "standard pound" against which I can compare it. In educational assessment, we have no such thing. The only way to judge whether an educational assessment result is "accurate" is to see if it is consistent with other results. Thus, reliability is the degree to which students' assessment results are the same when (a) they complete the same task(s) on two or more different occasions, (b) two or more teachers mark their performance on the same task(s), or (c) they complete two or more different but equivalent tasks on the same or different occasions. Consistent scores over repeated assessment is the key to understanding reliability.

As with validity, reliability refers to the students' assessment results or scores, not to the assessment instrument itself. Because consistency and accuracy are confounded in educational measurements, one of the most important reliability judgments you will make is what kind of consistency is most important for a particular kind of scoring, reporting, and usage of assessment results.

■ EXAMPLE 2.2 Examples of the relationship between reliability and validity

Example of how reliability does not guarantee validity

Ms. Cortez teaches seventh-grade arithmetic. She reflects on the kinds of computations that her students will be expected to perform as they go through their daily lives in the local community and lists these skills. She then creates a computation and problem-solving test to assess her students' ability to perform these skills. Because this paper-and-pencil test has a large number of items, Ms. Cortez can be confident that the resulting scores will be very reliable. However, because she wrote long word problems, the test taps both the arithmetic problem solving she intended to assess and also reading ability. Results do not describe what she intended—students' achievement in arithmetic problem solving. They describe arithmetic problem solving and reading together.

Example of how reliability limits validity

Ms. Cortez teaches seventh-grade arithmetic. She reflects on the kinds of computations that her students will be expected to perform as they go through their daily lives in the local community and lists these skills; this is the *domain* of learning she wishes to assess. She then creates a test to assess her students' ability to perform these skills. The test items are a sample of all the possible questions she could have written. For this example, assume she does write appropriate test items with a low reading load, but that she only writes five 1-point (right/wrong) items. Therefore, reliability will be low. Ms. Cortez decides that students who mastered 80% of the targeted domain should pass. But remember her test items are only a sample from the domain. It is very likely that among all those students who actually mastered 80% or more of the targeted *domain,* some would have *test scores* below 80%. These students would be erroneously classified as failures. On the other hand, among the students who truly know slightly less than 80% of the targeted *domain*, some are very likely to *pass the test*. These students would be erroneously classified as having sufficient competence.

Reliability is necessary for validity; as you saw, we mentioned reliability in the previous validity section. If a student's score or rating is not dependable (accurate, consistent, trustworthy), then it isn't possible to know what it really means. However, the reverse is not true: High reliability does not guarantee validity. Example 2.2 gives two examples of the relationship between reliability and validity.

For large-scale assessment, reliability can be studied with quantitative measures of the consistency across times, items or tasks, forms, or raters

For large-scale assessments, statistical methods indicate the degree of reliability and the approximate size of the measurement errors in the assessment results. These indices can provide guidance on the quality of your assessment results. A low reliability index means that the assessment results are not very consistent. As a result, the quality of your assessment information is poor.

The general strategy to obtain reliability coefficients is to administer the assessment to a group of students one or more times and obtain the scores. Then, one of two approaches is used to examine consistency.

- Correlate the scores from the two administrations. A **correlation coefficient** is an index of whether the relative standing of students in the group (as determined by their scores) differs from one assessment to the next. A correlation used to measure score consistency is called a **reliability coefficient**.

- Estimate the amount by which we can expect a student's score to change from one administration to the next. The index expressing this variation in score consistency is called the **standard error of measurement (*SEM*)**.

Reliability coefficients are most useful when you are comparing assessment procedures that report students' scores on different scales. Standard errors of measurement are more useful than reliability coefficients when you are using a particular instrument and are concerned with interpreting students' scores.

Table 2.3 shows three categories of reliability coefficients and lists several of the coefficients in each category, the major questions for which the coefficients provide answers, and the type of measurement error each addresses. Notice that the question "Are these scores reliable?" has many different answers depending on the types of measurement errors that concern you.

Keep these factors in mind when interpreting reliability and *SEM* information, especially when comparing such information from two or more assessment procedures.

- Longer assessment procedures are more reliable than shorter procedures.

- More objectively scored assessment results are more reliable.

- The reliability coefficients reported in a test manual are based on samples of students. The values will fluctuate. Sampling fluctuations are greater for small samples than for large samples.

- The narrower the range of a group's ability, the lower the reliability coefficient tends to be. It is much easier to distinguish individual differences in ability when students vary widely. Look in test manuals for reliability coefficients calculated on data from students whose ability ranges are similar to your students.

- Students at different achievement levels may be assessed with different degrees of accuracy. The technical manual of a published test should tell you which achievement levels are assessed more reliably.

- The longer the interval between testing, the lower test-retest and alternate-forms reliability coefficients will tend to be (and the shorter the interval, the higher the coefficient).

Table 2.3 Summary of Reliability Coefficients for Large-scale Assessment

Type of coefficient	Major question(s) answered	What is counted as measurement error or inconsistency
	I. Influence of occasions or time	
Test-retest	a. How are scores on the identical content sample affected by testing on another occasion? b. How stable are scores on this particular test form over time?	Time or occasion sampling
Alternate forms (with time interval)	a. How consistent are the test scores regardless of form used or occasion on which it is administered? b. How stable are scores on this trial over time (and content samples)?	Time or occasion sampling and content sampling
	II. Influence of different content samples	
Alternate forms (no time interval)	a. Are scores affected by sampling different content on the same occasion? b. Are two carefully matched test forms interchangeable (equivalent, parallel)?	Content sampling
Split-halves	a. Same as above b. What is an estimate of the alternate-forms reliability coefficient?	Content sampling
Kuder-Richardson formulas 20 and 21, coefficient alpha	a. Same as above, except equivalence or parallelism of forms may not concern the investigator. b. What is a crude estimate of test homogeneity? c. How consistent are responses from item to item? d. Are scores affected by content sampling on the same occasion?	Content sampling and homogeneity
	III. Influence of different scorers	
Scorer reliability, percent agreement	a. To what extent, will the scores be different if different scorers (raters, judges) are used? b. To what extent is the test objective? c. Are the results from different scorers (observers, raters, judges) interchangeable?	Scorer sampling

■ Alternate forms of a test can only be designated "equivalent" or "parallel" if they satisfy specific conditions. In practice, many assessments have no true parallel form.

■ Different methods of estimating reliability will not give the same result. The reliability coefficients differ because they include different sources of error.

Reliability of mastery and pass-fail decisions

We have been discussing consistency of students' scores. This consistency is of concern no matter what type of assessment method you are using. In certain situations, the consistency of the exact score a student receives is less important than the consistency of the decision made about the student. For example, the passing score on a mastery test may be 80% correct. A student who gets 85% receives the same decision (i.e., pass), as does the student who gets 92%. Similarly, two students with 50%

and 65%, respectively, both fail. In this type of assessment interpretation, it makes more sense to speak of *decision consistency* than of score consistency. A **decision consistency index** describes how consistent the classification decisions are rather than how consistent the scores are. For example, suppose you had two forms of a mastery test. Such indexes answer the question, "Would both tests classify the same students as masters and nonmasters?"

A quantitative index of decision consistency can be calculated by administering two parallel forms of a mastery test to the same group of students and studying whether students are consistently classified as masters or nonmasters. Two indices may be calculated: percentage of agreement (P_A) and kappa coefficient (κ) (Cohen, 1960). The **percentage of agreement** is the percentage of students for whom the two judges reached the same decision. The **kappa coefficient** is an index of the consistency of decisions corrected for the amount of agreement expected by chance.

Percentage of agreement is quite a different concept than a correlation-based scorer reliability coefficient. The choice between a percentage of agreement index and a correlation index of inter-rater reliability depends on whether a student's absolute (actual) or relative (rank-order) score level is important for a particular interpretation and use. Percentage of agreement indices measure the reliability of absolute decisions. Correlation-based reliability coefficients measure the reliability of relative decisions.

For classroom assessment, your major reliability concerns are: (a) deciding what kind of consistency, dependability, or accuracy is important for the particular assessment and (b) insuring that particular consistency/dependability/ accuracy and appraising evidence of it

For classroom teachers, the key to reliability is understanding how to decide what sort of consistency is important for different assessment purposes (Parkes & Giron, 2006). You should be confident that your information is solid and trustworthy information, not a fluke or random occurrence. Guideline 2.2 organizes advice for producing reliable results according to type of assessment. For discussion, the table is divided into assessments that are more often summative and those that are more often formative, but in reality the line between the two is fluid. The designation of formative or summative depends on how you and students use the assessment.

All types of assessments should be dependable in the sense that they are achievement information and represent what the student knows or can do, as opposed to representing resistance or lack of attention or motivation. Maintain a classroom environment that encourages students to perform their best. Never punish students for poor performance. Help students see constructive criticism as part of learning. Give them ample opportunities to practice and then to "show what they know." Encourage all students, not just the strong ones.

Match the assessment difficulty to students' ability levels. Students should not have to face an assessment hopelessly—and neither should they be expected to

Guideline 2.2 Reliability concerns for classroom assessment

Reliability for More Summative (Formal, Graded) Assessments

Assessment	Most important type of consistency, dependability, or accuracy	Your assessments should:
All types	Consistency within student [not that they always do the same, but that they consistently try to show what they know]	• Encourage students to perform their best • Match the assessment difficulty to the students' ability levels • Have scoring criteria that are available and well understood by students before they start the assignment
Objective tests (multiple choice, true/false, matching, etc.)	Consistent performance from item to item	• Have enough items • Allow enough time for students
Essays, papers, projects scored with rubrics	Accuracy of rater judgment Consistency across forms (prompts, assignments)	• Have clear enough directions for students that all are likely to produce scorable work • Have a systematic procedure for scoring, including procedures to avoid rater errors • Use multiple markers when possible
Grades	Consistency among assignments Decision consistency	• Use a sufficient number of different procedures to assess all important aspects of learning target(s) • Combine results from several assessments • Differentiate among students
Makeup work	Consistency across occasion (and sometimes form)	• If from absence, use a procedure (usually alternate forms and/or an honors system) to insure equivalence • If from re-dos, performance should show consistency with the last (bad) performance except for changes due to learning progress

Reliability for More Formative (Informal, Ungraded, Practice) Assessments

Assessment	Most important type of consistency, dependability, or accuracy	Your assessments should:
Oral questioning	Dependability of interpretation of answer(s) Accuracy of rater (teacher) judgment	• Use a sufficient number of questions or observations. • Allow enough time for students • Interpret the answers or observed behavior with the most likely and reasonable explanation • Have a systematic procedure to insure questioning or observing all students
Observations	Dependability of interpretation Accuracy of rater (teacher) judgment	
Peer editing, group collaboration ratings, and other peer evaluation techniques	Accuracy of rater (peer) judgment	• Have a systematic procedure for rating and instruct students in its use • Use student procedures that emphasize respect, judging the work not the person, and so on • Use several ratings for the same student and trim extremes if necessary
Self-assessment	Accuracy of rater (self) judgment	• Have a systematic procedure for rating and instruct students in its use

"skate" through questions that are very easy. Either extreme discourages true student engagement.

Scoring criteria should be available and well understood by students *before* they start the assignment. Clear, well-understood criteria are more likely to be used in the same manner by all raters.

Objective tests

For objective tests, students' performance should be consistent from item to item. Have enough items so that the consistency can show itself. For example, suppose you have only one question about a particular kind of math problem, and the student gets it right. How confident would you be in generalizing to say that he has "100% mastery" in this area? Would you be more confident if he got two items in this area correct? How many would it take before you were really comfortable saying "Yes, he can do this"? Also, allow enough time for students to do the items. Performance should indicate achievement and not running out of time.

Essays, papers, and projects scored with rubrics

For tasks scored with partial credit—multipoint items, or tasks scored with rubrics or grades—the major reliability concern is accuracy of judgment. Often one teacher (you!) grades assignments and there is no other rater with whom to compare, although once in a while it's a good thing to get another teacher to double-score as a check on your accuracy.

There are several ways to help make your judgment as accurate as possible. Have clear enough directions that all students are likely to produce scorable work. If every student does something very different, it's hard to score accurately. Use systematic scoring procedures: clear rubrics or scoring guides. Score work without looking at the student's name. Score answers to one question, or one essay or assignment, before moving on to the next, so you are concentrating on one scoring scheme at a time. Use multiple markers when possible.

Grades

For report card (marking period) grades, consistency among assignments and decision consistency ("Would I make the same grading decision about this student again?") are important. Use a sufficient number of different procedures to assess all the important aspects of the learning targets. Combine results from several assessments to arrive at a grade. Combining the results of several assessments increases the reliability of a grade in the same way as having more items increases the reliability of one test score. The more observations, the more stability in judgment.

Use assessments that differentiate among students. If every student is an A, every student looks the same on the scale you're using, which is not likely to be the case. We are not advocating deliberately using assignments that are too hard in order to pass some students and fail others. Rather, make sure that you use assignments that distribute students along the assignments' scoring scales so that you get an accurate picture of their achievement. Then decide on the grades they should receive using procedures that are systematic and fair.

Makeup work

For makeup work, the reliability concern is consistency across occasion, and sometimes form. If the student is making up work missed because of absence, use a procedure to insure equivalence. The procedure could be an honor system in which, for example, students know not to tell their absent friends what questions are on a test. Or the procedure could be to use another form of the same test or assignment.

If the student is redoing work because of poor performance the first time, you should have confidence that any increase in work quality really represents a reliable increase in learning. Changes in the work should be interpretable as changes in learning. For example, if a student neglected to follow certain directions or left something out of an assignment and receives permission to redo it, the changes should reflect this. However, the revisions shouldn't sound like someone else wrote them, or reflect a different approach or information that isn't consistent with that student's work as you know it.

Oral questioning and observations

Reliability concerns for oral questioning and for observations of students include the dependability of your interpretations and the accuracy of your judgment. Use a sufficient number of questions or observations. This is easiest to illustrate in the negative. If you only ask a student one question about a chapter she read, how sure are you that you can interpret a correct answer to mean she read and understood the whole chapter? The number of questions or observations needed depends on the judgment to be made. If you see a kindergartner tie his shoes properly twice, you might conclude he knows how to tie his shoes. But you would want more than two observations to conclude that a student knew how to graph a straight line function in algebra.

Allow enough time for students to answer oral questions, or to do whatever you're observing. As with tests and assignments, oral or observed performance should indicate achievement and not lack of time. Interpret answers or observed behavior with the most likely and reasonable explanation (not the explanation you want to be true, or hope is true). Have a systematic procedure to ensure that you observe or call on all students. It's easy to call on students whose hands are waving wildly and ignore the rest. It's difficult to remember which students you called on from day to day. A class roster check sheet can be helpful to keep you organized.

Peer editing, group collaboration ratings, and other peer evaluation techniques

For peer evaluation, the most important reliability concern is accuracy of judgment. Have a systematic procedure for rating and instruct students in its use. The clearer directions or rubrics are, the more likely students are to use them in the same way. Use student procedures that emphasize respect, judging the work and not the person, and so on. The aim is to have peers judge student achievement against criteria, not to give personal or social opinions.

Use several ratings for the same student, and trim extremes if necessary. For example, you may engage members in rating others' contributions to small-group work. In a group of four, you would have three ratings of each student, which should more or less agree if they were all rating the same work. You may decide to disregard ratings that differ from the rest by more than an expected amount.

Self-evaluation

For self-evaluation, the most important reliability concern is accuracy of self-judgment. Have a systematic procedure for rating and instruct students in its use. Give them lots of opportunity to practice evaluating their work. You also need to create a classroom environment where it is safe for a student to describe his needs for improvement, and where mistakes are interpreted as opportunities to learn and not cause for penalty.

Conclusions

Validity and reliability are foundation topics for the rest of this book. The quality of information received from assessments must be high enough that it is just that—information that supports your classroom decisions—and not random numbers or stray thoughts. Chapters 1 discussed classroom decisions. Chapter 2 provided the foundation concepts that ensure information is of high enough quality to support decisions. Chapters 3 will turn to the topic most of those decisions will be about: learning goals.

Exercises

1. Each of the following questions is one an educator asks about an assessment procedure external to the classroom. Using Table 2.1, identify for each statement the type(s) of validity evidence that is (are) most important to answering the question directly. Then briefly explain your choice.

   a. "Is this spelling test representative of the type of spelling patterns we teach our sixth graders?"

   b. "Can scores on this reading test help me to assign students to different instructional groups?"

   c. "I'm using this performance assessment to select persons for a special training program. I wonder if the results are significantly influenced by the personality of the person administering the assessment?"

   d. "Does this mathematics performance assessment really assess the mathematics ability of these students?"

e. "We now use a procedure to rate student teachers. Does this procedure permit the student teacher to be observed in the broad range of classroom situations likely to be encountered when teaching in this state?"

2. For each of the following types of assessment procedures, explain what is(are) the most important type(s) of consistency, dependability, or accuracy contributing to reliability of scores, and tell why. You may use Guideline 2.2 to help you.
   a. Student essays in social studies exams
   b. Science projects
   c. Grades on art projects
   d. True-false tests in science
   e. Portfolios in English courses
   f. Mathematics homework problems
   g. A teacher's marks for students' daily participation in class
   h. A paper-and-pencil test for a unit in social studies consisting of multiple-choice, matching, and short-answer questions

Companion
Website

Now go to our Companion Website at **www.prenhall.com/brookhart** to assess your understanding of chapter content with multiple-choice and essay questions. Broaden your knowledge of assessment with links to assessment related web sites.

3

Learning Goals

KEY CONCEPTS

1. Learning targets focus instruction and assessment, and they also focus students and teachers on the knowledge and skills intended for learning.
2. Learning goals, state standards, content and performance standards, general and specific learning targets, and developmental and mastery learning targets work together and are stated at different levels of specificity.
3. Taxonomies of thinking skills help you get the most out of your learning targets and assessment tasks.
4. Specific learning targets should be student centered, performance centered, and content centered.
5. Align both instruction *and* assessment to your learning targets.

Three little boys played together sometimes, although it was more like two of them played together and picked on the third. They called him "the fat kid." He didn't like it much, but he felt being picked on was better than being lonely. Usually they played catch or hide-and-seek. One day, though, they decided to play on the railroad tracks. They thought it might be fun to balance on the rails, and there was the added excitement of doing something forbidden.

So off they went. The two bullies went first, of course. They each walked the rails slowly, and when they wobbled, they stuck out their arms to help keep their balance. Neither got far before he fell off. Then it was the fat kid's turn. He stepped up, put his arms out, and walked slowly but smoothly forward until the two yelled at him to come back.

"Nuh-uh!" said the one. "How did you do that?"

"Well," said the fat kid, "I was watching you guys. You were both looking at your feet." Then he paused, deciding something, and finally said, "I can't see my feet. I have to look along the rail ahead, and see where I'm going." He paused again, and smiled. "It works."

Learning targets focus instruction and assessment, and they also focus students and teachers on the knowledge and skills intended for learning

Teachers and students are most successful when they focus on where they're going, as the fat kid did. A **learning objective** specifies what you would like students to achieve when they have completed an instructional segment. We use the term *objective* to emphasize that the goal of teaching involves more than "covering the material" and "keeping students actively engaged." The focus of your teaching should be on student achievements as well as on the learning process. A learning objective states what students should be able to do, value, or feel after you have taught them. Although the formal term is *learning objective*, we will use the informal term *learning target*.

Deciding the specific targets you expect students to learn is an important step in the teaching process. Think of instruction as involving three fundamental but interrelated activities. These activities are interactive rather than a straight one-two-three process.

1. *Decide what the student is to learn.* State what you expect students to be able to do after you have taught them. Usually, you do this by specifying learning targets or by providing several concrete examples of the tasks students should be able to do to demonstrate that the learning targets have been reached. Your understanding of the learning targets guides your teaching and provides a criterion for evaluating student achievement.

2. *Carry out the actual instruction.* Communicate to students what the goal is. Provide the conditions and activities for students to learn. Monitor students' progress and give them feedback on what they need to improve their achievement of the learning targets.

3. *Evaluate the learning.* Through evaluation you and your students come to know how well the learning targets have been reached. The more clearly you specify the learning targets, the more unambiguously you can evaluate your teaching and your students' learning.

The three activities are a simplified description of the teaching process. They do, however, illustrate that teaching can be easier when a teacher has clear learning targets in mind. Learning targets do the following things (Gow, 1976; Nitko & Brookhart, 2007):

- Help teachers and/or curriculum designers make their own educational goals explicit.
- Communicate the intent of instruction to students, parents, other teachers, school administrators, and the public.
- Provide the basis for teachers to analyze what they teach and to construct learning activities.
- Describe the specific performances against which teachers can evaluate the success of instruction.
- Help educators to focus and to clarify discussions of educational goals with parents (and others).
- Communicate to students the performance they are expected to learn. This may empower them to direct their own learning.

- Make individualizing instruction easier.
- Help teachers evaluate and improve both instructional procedures and learning targets.

Learning targets come in a variety of sizes. Some are broad (e.g., "become a good problem solver") and require years of work, in many classes, to attain. Others are more narrow (e.g., "solve word problems involving two-digit subtraction"), narrow enough to use with individual classroom lessons. These targets must all work together toward coordinated ends if they are to lead students' learning.

Learning goals, state standards, content and performance standards, general and specific learning targets, and developmental and mastery learning targets work together and are stated at different levels of specificity

Schooling and other organized instruction help students attain educational goals. Educational goals are broad statements of activities that contribute to individual and societal health—and that can be learned (Gagné, Wager, Golas, & Keller, 2005). Figure 3.1 shows the relationships among standards, goals, and learning targets.

Educational goals give direction and purpose to planning overall educational activities. Examples of statements of broad educational goals appear in reports prepared by state departments of education, local school systems, and associations such as the National Council of Teachers of Mathematics, the American Association for the Advancement of Science, and the Association of American Geographers.

■ **Example of an educational goal**

Every student should acquire skills in using scientific measurement.

These types of broad goals are organized into subject-matter areas such as mathematics and history. The broad goals and statements of subject-matter area and content-specific thinking processes serve as a curriculum framework within which educators can define specific learning targets. State education agencies take the process further by publishing expected learning outcomes or *standards*. In such cases, your school is held accountable for students achieving these particular standards. Obtain a copy of your state's standards from your school principal or central administration office, or check your state's education department web site.

Teachers cannot use broad goals for developing lesson plans and assessments. "Acquiring skills in scientific measurement," for example, communicates a general educational aim but is too broadly stated to be immediately useful for instruction and assessment.

A **general learning target** is a statement of an expected learning outcome that is derived from an educational goal. General learning targets are more specific than educational goals and usually clear enough for general planning of

Figure 3.1 Relationships among the concepts of standards, goals, and learning targets.

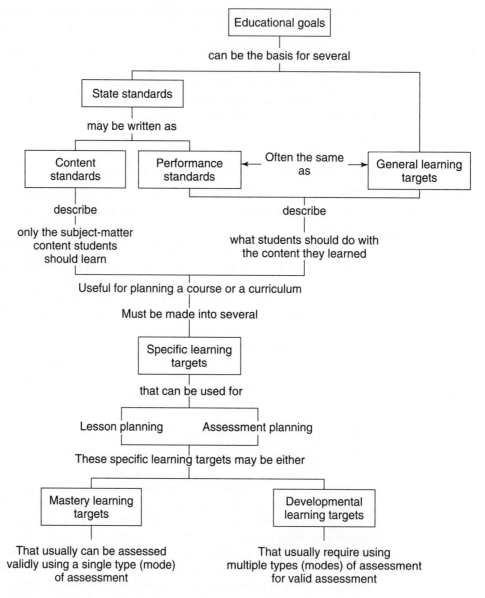

a course or unit. So for a primary school science unit on measurement in the metric system, we might have:

■ **Example of a general learning target**

Acquire the skills needed to use common instruments to measure length, volume, and mass in metric units.

Break this general learning target down into even more specific learning targets in order to plan lessons and assessments. A **specific learning target** is a clear statement about what students are to achieve at the end of a unit of instruction. Here are three examples of specific learning targets derived from the preceding general learning target:

■ **Example of specific learning targets**

The student is able to:

1. Measure the length of objects to the nearest tenth of a meter using a meter stick.
2. Measure the mass of objects to the nearest tenth of a kilogram using a simple beam balance and one set of weights.
3. Measure the volume of liquids to the nearest tenth of a liter using a graduated cylinder.

When learning targets are made more specific, the achievement you are to teach and to assess becomes clear. But beware of overspecificity. Long lists of very narrow "bits" of behavior can fragment the subject to be taught or become too long and be ignored. Identify a few of the most important learning targets for each instructional unit and focus on these. The following example shows a learning target that is too specific, along with a suggested revision.

■ **Example**

The student is able to:

Too specific:	Estimate the number of beans in a jar.
Better:	Solve practical problems using calculations and estimation.
Rationale:	"Beans-in-a-jar" is not the real target of learning. Rather, it is but one of the many possible tasks that a student should complete to demonstrate achievement of estimation and calculation. The learning target statement should describe this desired achievement.

Your state may have mandated that students meet a set of educational standards that you will need to take into account when developing learning targets. **Standards** are statements about what students are expected to learn. Some states call these statements *essential skills, learning expectations, learning outcomes, achievement expectations,* or other names. The NCLB Act requires all states to specify standards and to assess students' achievement of them.

Often there are two sets of standards. Content standards are statements about the subject-matter facts, concepts, principles, and so on that students are expected to learn. For example, a standard for life science might be, "Students should know that the cell nucleus is where genetic information is located in plants and animals." Ideally, performance standards are statements about the things students can perform or do once the content standards are learned. For example, "students can identify the cell nucleus in microscopic slides of various plant and animal cells." However, some states define performance standards (or simply "standards") as certain ranges of test scores and then give these labels. For example, a student whose score is between 20 and 40 may be said to have reached the "basic level" of the standards; between 41 and 60 may be at the "proficient level"; and above 60 at the "advanced level."

State education departments prepare standards used in schools. Local school districts are required to teach students to achieve these standards; the state's assessment system is the accountability mechanism for that requirement. Professional organizations can prepare standards, too. These organizations try to influence what is taught by publicly promoting their own standards. Examples of professional organizations with published standards are the National Academy of Science, National Council of Teachers of English, and National Council of Teachers of Mathematics. Most standards from professional organizations can be found on the organizations' web sites.

States' standards vary greatly in their quality and degree of specificity. Not all states have done a good job of writing standards. There seems to be no standard way (pun intended!) to write standards. In the past, some states have established standards for only some grade levels (e.g., 4th, 8th, 10th, and 12th grades). Under the NCLB Act states must have standards for Grades 3 through 12 in reading/language arts, and in science by 2007. In response to this requirement, most states have prepared many standards for each grade level. Others, however, are experimenting with writing a few select standards for each grade and focusing assessment and teaching on these (Popham, 2005).

The example below shows how specific learning targets are developed from a state standard and compares statements of standards, general learning targets, and specific learning targets for third-grade reading in one school district.

■ Example

State standard
- Communicate well in writing for a variety of purposes.

General learning target
- Write for narrative, persuasive, imaginative, and expository purposes.

Specific learning targets
- Explain the difference between narrative, persuasive, imaginative, and expository writing purposes.
- Apply prewriting skills and strategies to generate ideas, clarify purpose, and define audience before beginning to write.
- After receiving feedback on the first draft in the areas of ideas, organization, voice, word choice, and sentence fluency, use the feedback to revise the draft.
- Review and revise the second draft for grammatical correctness and proper use of standard writing conventions.

Notice that assessment focuses on what you can see students doing. From this observation you will infer whether they have attained the learning targets. For example, a high school biology unit on living cells may have as a general learning target that students should "learn the organizations and functions of cells." But what can the student do to demonstrate learning of this general target? There may be several answers to this question, each phrased as a specific instructional objective and each describing what a student "can do."

■ **Examples of observable instructional objectives**

1. The student can draw models of various types of cells and label their parts.
2. The student can list the parts of a cell and describe the structures included in each.
3. The student can explain the functions that different cells perform and how these functions are related to each other.

Statements of what students can do at the end of instruction may be called **mastery learning targets**. Robert Forsyth (1976) called them "can do" statements. They have also been called *specific learning outcomes* and *behavioral objectives*.

Some skills and abilities are more aptly stated at a somewhat higher level of abstraction than mastery learning targets to communicate that they are continuously developed throughout life. Consider the following examples.

■ **Examples of developmental learning targets**

1. Combine information and ideas from several sources to reach conclusions and solve problems.
2. Analyze and make critical judgments about the viewpoints expressed in passages.
3. Write several paragraphs that explain the author's point of view.
4. Use numerical concepts and measurements to describe real-world objects.
5. Interpret statistical data found in material from a variety of disciplines.
6. Write imaginative and creative stories.
7. Use examples from the materials you read to support your point of view.
8. Communicate your ideas using visual media such as drawings and figures.

Because of the lifelong nature of these targets, they may be called *developmental objectives* (Linn & Miller, 2005) or **developmental learning targets**.

At first glance, it might seem that all one needs to do is to insert a "can do" phrase in front of each of the preceding statements to transform them to mastery learning targets. However, it is not that simple. First, each statement represents a broad domain of loosely related performances. Second, each statement represents skills or abilities typically thought of as developing continuously to higher levels rather than the all-or-none dichotomy implied by the mastery learning targets.

One way to begin designing instruction and assessing progress toward developmental objectives is to list several specific learning targets for each one. They should represent the *key* performances expected of a student at a particular *grade* or *age level*. This is illustrated in the following, which clarifies a broad instructional objective in science by listing several specific learning targets that support it:

■ **Example***

| Developmental learning target: | Interprets and uses Boyle's Law to explain phenomena and solve problems. |

Specific learning targets clarifying this developmental target:

1. States a definition of Boyle's Law.
2. States the domain to which Boyle's Law applies.
3. Describes the relationship between Boyle's Law and Charles' Law.
4. Uses Boyle's Law to explain an observation in a lab experiment.
5. Appropriately analyzes a new (to the student) situation in terms of Boyle's Law.
6. Solves a new problem or makes an appropriate choice for a course of action, taking into account the implications of Boyle's Law.

Although this list of six specific objectives might be made longer, the six objectives would likely be considered adequate for describing what is meant by "interpreting and using Boyle's Law" at the end of a first course in high school physics. Specific tasks could then be prepared for assessing achievement of the six specific objectives. Some tasks could assess only one of these learning targets; others could require a student to use several of these learning targets in combination. A student's overall score could be interpreted as indicating the degree to which a student has acquired the ability to interpret and use Boyle's Law, rather than as a "mastery/nonmastery" description.

Taxonomies of thinking skills help you get the most out of your learning targets and assessment tasks

Simply writing specific learning targets "off the top of your head" can be frustrating because a seemingly endless number of possible targets exist. Further, the first targets you think of will usually be narrow statements about students recalling certain facts or concepts. A **taxonomy** can help you bring to mind the wide range of important learning targets and thinking skills relevant to a particular general learning target.

Taxonomies of instructional learning targets are highly organized schemes for classifying learning targets into various levels of complexity. Generally, educational

---

*Based on Klopfer (1969).

learning targets fall into one of three domains, although a single, real-life, complex performance will likely involve components of more than one domain:

1. **Cognitive domain**: Targets focus on knowledge and abilities requiring memory, thinking, and reasoning processes. For example, you may want students to read a claim made by a political figure and determine whether there is evidence available to support that claim.

2. **Affective domain**: Targets focus on feelings, interests, attitudes, dispositions, and emotional states. For example, you may want students to value the right to vote in elections over other activities competing for their time.

3. **Psychomotor domain**: Targets focus on motor skills and perceptual processes. For example, you may want students to set up, focus, and use a microscope properly during a science investigation of pond water.

Learning targets within each domain may be classified by using a taxonomy for that domain. Several different taxonomies have been developed for sorting learning targets. The *Taxonomy of Educational Objectives, Handbook I: Cognitive Domain* (Bloom, Engelhart, Furst, Hill, & Krathwohl, 1956) has proved to be of considerable value. The taxonomy classifies cognitive performances into six major headings arranged from simple to complex.

1. **Knowledge** involves the recall of facts and concepts.
2. **Comprehension** involves basic understanding. Students who comprehend a concept or story can restate it in their own words.
3. **Application** involves using facts and concepts to solve new or novel problems. Application-level problems usually have one correct answer.
4. **Analysis** involves breaking down information into parts to facilitate reasoning with that information. Analysis-level tasks may have more than one good answer.
5. **Synthesis** involves putting parts together to form a new whole. Synthesis-level tasks require arranging ideas in a new or original way.
6. **Evaluation** involves judging the value of material and methods for given purposes. Evaluation-level activities usually ask students to make a claim about the worth of something and explain their reasons.

Example 3.1 gives an example of a learning target and a corresponding assessment item for each main heading as they may apply to teaching a language arts unit on short stories. Example 3.2 shows how learning targets in science and social studies may be classified in the *Taxonomy*. The taxonomy calls your attention to the variety of abilities and skills toward which you can direct instruction and assessment.

Note that learning targets classified in the first three cognitive categories are more easily assessed with short-answer, true-false, multiple-choice, or matching test items. Learning targets classified in the last three cognitive categories might be partially tested by such item formats, but their assessment usually requires a variety of other procedures such as essay questions, homework, class projects, observing

■ **EXAMPLE 3.1 Examples of learning targets and assessment items at different levels of Bloom's Taxonomy**

Level	Sample learning target	Sample assessment item
Example: You are teaching students to understand the elements that authors use when writing short stories. The short stories you select all concern people's personal problems, and that the characters in these stories handle their personal problems inappropriately.		
Knowledge	Recall the main characters in each of the short stories read and what they did.	• List the names of all of the characters in the *Witch's Forest*. • In the *Witch's Forest*, what did Sally do when her mother refused to let her go into the forest?
Comprehension	Explain the main ideas and themes of the short stories that we read.	Write using your own words what the *Witch's Forest* was all about.
Application	Relate the personal problems of the characters in the short stories that were read to problems that real people face.	Are the problems Sally had with her mother in the story similar to the problems you or someone you know have with their mother? Explain why or why not.
Analysis	Identify the literary devices that authors use to convey their characters' feelings to the reader.	In *Witch's Forest*, Sally was upset with her mother. In *Dog Long Gone*, Billy was upset with his brother. What words and phrases did the authors of these two stories use to show how upset these characters were? Explain and give examples.
Synthesis	Describe, across all of the stories read, the general approach that the characters used to resolve their problems unsuccessfully.	So far we have read *Witch's Forest*, *Dog Long Gone*, *Simon's Top*, and *Woman With No Manners*. In every story one character was not able to solve the personal problem he or she faced. What were the ways these characters tried to solve their problems? What do these unsuccessful ways to solve problems have in common?
Evaluation	Develop one's own set of three or four criteria for judging the quality of a short story. Use the three or four criteria to evaluate several new stories that were not read in class.	• So far we have read four short stories. What are three or four different traits that make a story high quality? Use these traits to develop three or four criteria that you could use to evaluate the quality of any short story. • Read the two new short stories assigned to you. Use the criteria you developed to evaluate these two stories. Evaluate each story on every criterion. Summarize your findings.

■ **EXAMPLE 3.2 Classifying science and social studies outcomes using the Bloom et al. *Taxonomy***

Bloom et al. category	Science	Social studies
Knowledge	• Recall the names of parts of a flower • Identify and label the parts of insects • List the steps in a process	• List known causes of the Civil War • Recall general principles of migration of peoples of Africa
Comprehension	• Find real examples of types of coleoptera • Find real examples of igneous rock and mineral formations • Explain the digestive processes in one's own words	• Explain the meaning of technical concepts in one's own words • Give examples of propaganda usage from current events
Application	• Use scientific principles to make a simple machine • Use a learned process to conduct a new experiment	• Use specified critical thinking skills to explain current events • Carry out a survey and collect data from the field
Analysis	• Show how scientific principles or concepts are applied when designing a refrigerator	• Identify the credible and noncredible claims of an advertisement for clothing • Show the different component parts of a political speech
Synthesis	• Determine what the rule is that underlies the result obtained from several experiments or investigations	• Show the similarities among several schools of social thought • Develop plans for peace among two countries
Evaluation	• Use criteria or standards to evaluate the conclusions drawn from the research findings • Use criteria to evaluate the soundness of a research study	• Use a specific set of criteria to evaluate several political speeches

performance in labs, and portfolios. Learning targets at more complex thinking levels (Analysis, Synthesis, and Evaluation) require students to actually produce or create something, rather than simply to answer questions.

This taxonomy is not a teaching hierarchy. Its only purpose is to classify various learning targets and assessment tasks. For example, you should not teach "knowledge" first and "comprehension" second. In fact, this well-intended but misguided idea is part of the reason that some teachers give low-achieving students only knowledge-level drills, thinking they are not "ready" for higher-order thinking. No wonder some say school is "Boring"! Such tedious school experiences may help contribute to dropping out and other unintended negative consequences. Example 3.3 illustrates by example the concept that cognitive level and difficulty level are not the same thing.

Some schools use a shorter version of the Bloom et al. *Taxonomy*. For example, some reduce it to three categories: Knowledge, Comprehension, and Higher-Order Thinking (collapsing Application, Analysis, Synthesis, and Evaluation). Other

■ EXAMPLE 3.3 Examples to illustrate that cognitive complexity and difficulty are not the same thing!

Cognitive level (Bloom)	Example of an "easy" question at that level	Example of a "difficult" question at that level
Knowledge	What is a hare?	In the play *Hamlet*, who was Claudius?
Comprehension	Why were the tortoise and the hare racing?	Why does Hamlet have actors stage a play called "The Mousetrap"?
Application	Why do you think Aesop used a tortoise and a hare as the main characters?	In Act I, scene v, the Ghost of Hamlet's father accuses Claudius of murdering him. Of Claudius he says: Ay, that incestuous, that adulterate beast, With witchcraft of his wit, with traitorous gifts- O wicked wit and gifts, that have the power So to seduce!- won to his shameful lust The will of my most seeming-virtuous queen. Identify at least three figures of speech in this section.
Analysis	In what ways are the fables "The Tortoise and the Hare" and "The Crow and the Pitcher" alike?	Compare the advice Polonius gives to Ophelia and to Laertes in Act I of *Hamlet*.
Synthesis	Write your own fable. Use animals as the main characters, and make sure you have a moral.	Read *Hamlet* and two other non-Shakespearean tragedies of your choice. Write your own answer to the question, "What is tragedy?" and support your answer with examples from the readings.
Evaluation	Do you think "The Tortoise and the Hare" is a good name for the fable? Why or why not?	Was Hamlet mad? Argue "yes" or "no" and support your answer with examples from the play.

schools form three categories somewhat differently: Knowledge (including Comprehension), Application, and Higher-Order Thinking (including Analysis, Synthesis, and Evaluation). The advantage of these condensations is that they eliminate the need for struggling with how to classify learning targets into one of the top three categories of the *Taxonomy*. A disadvantage of using a condensed version of the *Taxonomy* is that teachers may stop trying to teach learning targets in the Synthesis and Evaluation categories.

The original *Taxonomy of Educational Objectives* is still in wide use in schools. However, this taxonomy has now been revised as: *A Taxonomy for Learning, Teaching, and Assessing: A Revision of Bloom's Taxonomy of Educational Objectives* (Anderson, Krathwohl, Airasian, Cruikshank, Mayer, Pintrich, Raths, & Wittrock, 2001). The *revised Taxonomy* improves on the original by giving a two-dimensional framework into which you may classify learning targets and assessment items. The two dimensions, which where derived from the original taxonomy, are Knowledge Dimension and Cognitive Process Dimension. They are related to the original as follows (Anderson, et al., 2001):

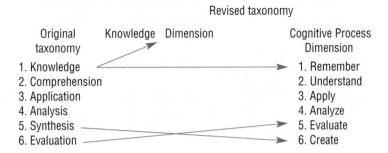

Revised taxonomy

The Knowledge Dimension has four subcategories—Factual Knowledge, Conceptual Knowledge, Procedural Knowledge, and Metacognitive Knowledge— depending on the type of content in the learning target. A two-dimensional table is constructed to describe the location of a learning target and its corresponding assessment on both dimensions simultaneously. Table 3.1 shows this two-dimensional Taxonomy Table. The subcategories of the Knowledge Dimension are lettered, and the subcategories of the Cognitive Process Dimension are numbered. As a short-cut, we can refer to a particular cell in the table by its letter and number. Thus, a learning target that requires students to remember some factual knowledge is placed in cell 1A.

We have discussed one scheme for classifying cognitive learning targets. There are many more taxonomies or schemes that we have not discussed, some of which are in Appendixes D and E of this book (see DeLandsheere, 1988, for a review). Guideline 3.1 presents criteria you can apply to help you choose among the various taxonomies.

Table 3.1 Taxonomy Table from the revised *Taxonomy*

Knowledge dimension	Cognitive process dimension					
	1. Remember	2. Understand	3. Apply	4. Analyze	5. Evaluate	6. Create
A. Factual knowledge						
B. Conceptual knowledge						
C. Procedural knowledge						
D. Metacognitive knowledge						

Source: From Lorin W. Anderson & David R. Krathwohl, *A Taxonomy for Learning, Teaching, and Assessing: A Revision of Bloom's Taxonomy of Educational Objectives, 1e.* Published by Allyn & Bacon, Boston, MA. Copyright © 2001 by Pearson Education. Reprinted by permission of the publisher.

Guideline 3.1	Practical criteria for selecting a taxonomy of cognitive learning targets

Criterion	Key question
Completeness	To what degree can your major learning targets be classified within each taxonomy?
Point of view	To what extent can each taxonomy be used as a platform for explaining your teaching methods or your curriculum characteristics to others?
Reform	To what extent can each taxonomy help you to evaluate your curriculum or your learning targets and lead you to revise the learning targets?
Simplicity	How easy is it for parents, teachers, and education officials to understand each taxonomy?
Reporting	How useful is each taxonomy in organizing reports of assessment results for individual students, educational officials, government officials, or the public?

Now that you have learned about taxonomies to classify your learning targets into various levels of complexity, we turn to writing specific learning targets.

Specific learning targets should be student centered, performance centered, and content centered

Student centered

Because instruction focuses on changes in student performance, learning targets should describe student performances. Consider this example:

■ **Example of what it means for a learning target to be student centered**

Poor: Provide the opportunity for students to express their opinions in classroom discussions about why peace is so difficult to attain.

Better: A student will express his or her opinion in classroom discussions about why peace is so difficult to attain.

The problem with the poor statement is that it is an activity statement *for teachers* rather than a learning target for students. You may "provide the opportunity for students to express their opinions," yet each student may not express his or her opinion. Learning targets need to be student centered if they are to be the basis for assessment procedures that allow you to decide whether the students actually have achieved what you intended.

Performance centered

Not only should a learning target refer to a student, it should state a performance—that is, an observable activity. This can be accomplished by being sure that the statement includes an action verb that specifies a student performance.

■ **EXAMPLE 3.4 Action verbs sometimes used in learning targets**

Specific but acceptable verbs

add, total	describe	match	rename
alphabetize	divide	measure	rephrase
choose	draw	multiply	select
complete, supply	explain	name	sort, classify
construct, make	identify	order, arrange	state
convert	label	pick out	subtract, take away
count	list	regroup	weigh
delete			

Too broad, unacceptable verbs

apply	examine	interpret	respond
deduce	generate	observe	test
do	infer	perform	use

Too specific, essentially indicator verbs

check	draw a line between	put a mark on	underline
circle	draw a ring around	put an X on	write the letter of
color the same as	put a box around	shade	write the number of

Toss-up verbs, requiring further clarification

answer	contrast	differentiate	give
collect, synthesize	demonstrate	discriminate	locate
compare	determine	distinguish	predict

Source: From "Criteria for Stating IPI Objectives" by C. M. Lindvall, 1976, pp. 214–215. In D. T. Gow (Ed.). *Design and Development of Curricular Materials: Intructional Design Articles* (Volume 2). Pittsburgh PA: University of Pittsburgh, University Center for International Studies.

Example 3.4 lists examples of various action verbs to help you write learning targets that describe students' performances. When verbs such as these are used in statements of learning targets, the learning targets will usually satisfy the second criterion of expressing observable student performance. A balance is necessary between verbs that are too broad (and thus imply too many nonequivalent performances) and those that are too specific (and that are often just ways of marking answers). Consider this example:

■ **Example of what it means for a learning target to be performance centered**

Poor. The student is able to put an X on the picture of the correct geometric shape (circle, triangle, rectangle, square, or ellipse) when the name of the shape is given.

Better. The student is able to identify a picture of a geometric shape (circle, triangle, rectangle, square, or ellipse) when the name of the shape is given.

The main intent of the objective is to select or identify the correct shape, not just to make Xs. Any response that indicates the student has correctly identified the required shape is acceptable.

Content centered

A learning target should indicate the content to which a student's performance is to apply. The following poor example lacks a reference to content. To modify this learning target you need to include a reference to a specific list of "important words" or describe them in some way.

> ■ **Example of what it means for a learning target to be content centered**
>
> *Poor*: The student is able to write definitions of the important terms used in the text.
>
> *Better*: The student is able to write definitions of the terms listed in the "Important Terms and Concepts" sections of Chapters 1–5 of the textbook.

If you do not refer to content in your learning target statement, you cannot know with certainty whether an assessment task is valid for evaluating the student. You may not even be able to select an assessment, because you don't know what words should be on it. Or, you may end up with an assessment that requires students to define words that, although in the text, are unimportant. Without knowing the content, it is difficult for anyone to determine what, if anything, was learned.

Align both instruction *and* assessment to your learning targets

The basic purpose of any assessment is to determine the extent to which each student has achieved the stated learning targets. Although this purpose sounds straightforward, it is not always an easy criterion to meet. We discussed matching or aligning assessment tasks to learning targets as a validity issue in Chapter 2.

Aligning assessments to mastery learning targets

The specific tasks or procedures you use in an assessment should require the student to display the skill or knowledge stated in the learning target. For instance, if the main intent of your learning target is for a student to build an apparatus, write a poem, or perform a physical skill, your assessment procedure must give the student the opportunity to *perform*. Assessment procedures that require a student only to name the parts of an apparatus, to analyze an existing poem, or to describe the sequence of steps needed for performing a physical skill, do not require the performance stated in these learning targets. Therefore, they would not be valid for assessing them. Assessment procedures should be aligned with the intentions of the specific learning targets that you include in your assessment plan.

Aligning assessments to developmental learning targets

Developmental learning targets imply a broad domain of performance application. Therefore, you may need to assess the same learning target in several different ways. For example, you might assess knowledge of rules for comma use both by scoring several samples of students' written assignments and by using an objective test. The test provides the opportunity to assess a student's comma use in sentence patterns that might not appear in the natural course of the student's writing, but that may well be part of the learning target. Observing a student's natural writing habits permits you to infer how well the student is likely to use commas in typical writing situations. Using both procedures increases how comprehensively you assess the students' comma use and increases the validity of your evaluation.

Aligning assessments to state standards

Earlier in this chapter we showed how you can derive your learning targets from your state's standards. It is important that you maintain consistency by aligning your classroom assessments with the state's standards, as well. Your assessments should match the span of content covered by the standards, the depth of thinking implied by the standards, the topical emphasis in the standards, and the types of performances specified in the standards.

Aligning assessment to instruction

From a student's point of view, instruction is "practice" on learning targets until they get "good enough" to show what they know on summative assessments. Instruction includes formative assessment, continuous checking of where they are against the target. So misaligned instruction has students "practicing" the wrong thing. You wouldn't have a piano student practice a Mozart sonata and then expect that she play a Chopin waltz in recital. Likewise (but harder to see), you shouldn't ask students to practice understanding Shakespearean English (by giving most of your instructional time to that) and then expect that they analyze MacBeth's character as their main assessment. Maybe some of the lessons in the *MacBeth* unit are about Shakespearean English because it's a tool—and you let students know that. But they also do some character analysis in instruction ("practice") so they know how to do it *and* so they learn that is a main goal of their *MacBeth* unit.

Conclusions

If assessment provides information for educational decisions, the next logical question is "Information about what?" Most often, this means information about student achievement of learning goals. Learning goals (or more specific learning objectives or targets) are the focus for assessment and instruction and the object of attention for students and teachers. They are what unifies formative and summative assessment. Formative assessment gives students information about their progress toward the same learning targets on which they will be evaluated with summative assessment. In the next chapter, we turn to higher-order thinking, a valued learning goal.

Exercises

1. Following are three learning targets. Decide whether each is a mastery learning target or a developmental learning target. Explain your choices.
   a. The student is able to take the square root of any number using a handheld calculator.
   b. The student is able to determine whether the thesis of the argument is supported adequately.
   c. When given data, the student is able to construct a graph to describe the trend in the data.

2. Decide whether each learning target listed here belongs to the cognitive, affective, or psychomotor domain. Does the performance of each learning target require some use of elements from domains other than the one into which you classified it? Which one(s)? Explain why. Does this mean you should reclassify that learning target? Explain.
   a. The student is able to tune a color television set to get the best color resolution.
   b. The student demonstrates knowledge of parliamentary law by conducting a meeting without violating parliamentary procedures.
   c. The student contributes to group maintenance when working with classmates on a science project.
   d. The student makes 5 baskets out of 10 tries on the basketball court while standing at the foul line.

Companion Website

Now go to our Companion Website at **www.prenhall.com/brookhart** to assess your understanding of chapter content with multiple-choice and essay questions. Broaden your knowledge of assessment with links to assessment related web sites.

Higher-Order Thinking

1. To assess higher-order thinking, use tasks that require students to use knowledge or skill in novel situations.
2. Problem solving refers to the kind of thinking required when reaching a goal is not automatic and students must use one or more higher-order thinking processes to do it.
3. Use strategies to assess students' problem-solving skills.
4. Critical thinking is reasonable and reflective thinking focused on deciding what to believe or do.
5. Use strategies to assess students' critical thinking skills.
6. Use checklists or rating scales to assess dispositions toward critical thinking.

McClymer and Knowles (1992, p. 33) tell the following story:

A colleague of ours teaches an introductory calculus section. Early one term, he and his class were working through some standard motion problems: "A boy drops a water balloon from a window. If it takes 0.8 seconds to strike his erstwhile friend, who is 5 feet tall, how high is the window?" On the exam, the problem took this form: "Someone walking along the edge of a pit accidentally kicks into it a small stone, which falls to the bottom in 2.3 seconds. How deep is the pit?" One student was visibly upset. The question was not fair, she protested. The instructor had promised that there would not be any material on the exam that they had not gone over in class. "But we did a dozen of those problems in class," our colleague said. "Oh no," shot back the student, "we never did a single pit problem."

To assess higher-order thinking, use tasks that require students to use knowledge or skill in novel situations

Instruction that leads students to use higher-order thinking results in increased achievement for all students (Wenglinsky, 2004), including educationally disadvantaged students (Pogrow, 2005). Of course, using higher-order thinking in instruction implies that higher-order thinking is the focus of learning targets and assessment, too. Because students have to think *about* something, a focus on higher-order thinking does not mean skimping on content. Rather, it means helping students wrap their minds around that content and do something with it. Not surprisingly, it makes class more fun, too.

The teacher in the story actually did give several different motion problems and encouraged students to understand those problems by drawing them (McClymer & Knowles, 1992). The teacher was right to use novel material to assess understanding. The sad (but valid) interpretation of the assessment results is this student truly did not understand this type of calculus problem. Things would have been different if the instructor had used all "window" problems and had not encouraged strategy use like drawing. Make sure you give students a chance to practice using novel material in instructional activities and in formative assessment before they encounter novel material in summative assessment. This is how to make assessment of higher-order thinking "fair."

If you only assess students' ability to recall what was in the textbook or said in class, you will not assess students' abilities to understand, reason, explain, or interpret on their own. You can use objective or short-answer items with introductory material to assess specific higher-order thinking skills. Use introductory material that was not part of examples in class or the assigned reading. Ask students to explain their reasoning, so you will know whether they have used appropriate criteria and critical thinking to arrive at their answer. You can use more extensive essays or projects to assess combinations of skills.

Higher-order thinking involves a whole set of related thought processes. Concept understanding, rule-governed thinking, problem solving, and critical thinking are all aspects of higher-order thinking and overlap to some extent. For the sake of organization, this chapter is divided into problem solving and critical thinking sections. Use your own critical thinking skills to mix and match assessment strategies as appropriate for the learning targets you assess in your classroom.

Problem solving refers to the kind of thinking required when reaching a goal is not automatic and students must use one or more higher-order thinking processes to do it

A good problem solver defines the problem and identifies obstacles to solving it, identifies alternatives for overcoming the obstacles, and tries at least one of them. A good problem solver can evaluate the relative effectiveness of different solution strategies (Marzano, Pickering, & McTighe, 1993, p. 79). If a procedure is so well known to a student that he can complete the task without having to reason, he does not have to use problem-solving skills. Older students call these kinds of tasks "no-brainers."

Most of the problem tasks in teachers' editions of textbooks and in the end-of-chapter exercises are a few notches above no-brainers. Tasks are clearly laid out. All the information students need is given, the situations are very much the same as you have taught in class, and there is usually one correct answer that students can reach by applying a procedure you taught. These are known as **well-structured problems** (Frederiksen, 1984). Well-structured problems give students opportunities to rehearse the procedures or algorithms you taught.

Most authentic (real-life) problems are **ill-structured** (Simon, 1973). For ill-structured problems, students must (a) organize the information to understand it; (b) clarify the problem itself; (c) obtain all the information needed, which may not be immediately available; and (d) recognize that there may be several equally correct answers. A problem with a single correct answer is called a **closed-response task**; a problem with multiple correct answers is called an **open-response task** (see Collis, 1991).

To solve problems, people use both general and specific problem-solving strategies (Alexander, 1992; Perkins & Salomon, 1989; Shuell, 1990). Experts apply well-known problem-solving strategies in their own field. However, if they work outside their area of expertise, the specific strategies no longer apply. They resort, then, to more general problem-solving strategies. As they develop expertise in an initially unfamiliar area, they drop the general strategies in favor of more area-specific strategies.

Teach students strategies for problem solving and make sure your assessment tasks require students to demonstrate them. The following is a list of 10 general problem-solving strategies (Frederiksen, 1984):

- Try to see the whole picture; do not focus only on details.
- Withhold your judgment; do not rush to a solution too quickly.
- Create a model for a problem using pictures, sketches, diagrams, graphs, equations, or symbols.
- If one way of modeling or representing the problem does not work, try another way.
- State the problem as a question; change the question if the original does not suggest a solution.
- Be flexible; try responding to the situation from a different angle or point of view; think divergently.
- Try working backwards by starting with the goal and going backwards to find the solution strategy.
- Keep track of your partial solutions so you can come back to them and resume where you left off.
- Use analogical thinking: Ask, "What is this problem like?" "Where have I seen something similar to this?"
- Talk about and through a problem; keep talking about it until a solution suggests itself.

Teaching problem-solving strategies can start early. For example, Boyd was a first grader who picked up a purple crayon and tried to do a maze. The object was to get a mouse to some cheese. His purple line ended in a cul-de-sac—no cheese for his mouse. He put his crayon down and made a face, then simply sat for a minute or two. When the teacher arrived at his desk, she said, "What else could you do?" No response. So she said, "Where else does a purple line need to be?" Boyd's eyes lit up. "I could start at the cheese," he said.

Use strategies to assess students' problem-solving skills

Assessing students' problem-solving skills requires set tasks that allow you to systematically evaluate students' thinking about problem solving. Bransford and Stein (1984) organized general problem-solving skills into a five-stage process called the IDEAL Problem Solver:

I   Identify the problem
D   Define and represent the problem
E   Explore possible strategies
A   Act on the strategies
L   Look back and evaluate the effects of your activities

In this section we illustrate 17 assessment strategies that you can use to assess problem-solving skills. Guideline 4.1 presents the assessment strategies grouped according to the IDEAL Problem Solver categories.

The strategies are descriptions of how to approach the assessment, and they suggest the general layout or structure of the tasks. Apply them specifically to your own content area.

Strategy 1: Identify the problem

Ask students to identify the problem to be solved.

Guideline 4.1 Seventeen strategies for assessing problem-solving skills

Problem Solving Category	Strategy
Identifying and recognizing problems	1. Identify the problem
Defining and representing problems	2. Pose questions 3. Demonstrate linguistic understanding 4. Identify irrelevancies 5. Sort problem cards 6. Identify assumptions 7. Describe multiple strategies 8. Model the problem 9. Identify obstacles
Exploring possible solution strategies	10. Justify solutions 11. Justify strategies used 12. Integrate data 13. Produce alternate strategies 14. Use analogies 15. Solve backwards
Acting on and looking back on problem-solution strategies	16. Evaluate the quality of a solution 17. Systematically evaluate strategies

■ **Example of identifying the problem**

Read the description below, and then answer the question.

A young deaf couple has their first child. The infant needs to be fed and changed whenever it cries in the night, but neither parent is able to hear the baby. The couple does not wish to bring the baby into their bed for fear of rolling on it and suffocating it. They also do not wish to put the baby on a strict schedule of changing and feeding at fixed times.

1. Explain the problem that needs to be solved in this situation.

Strategy 2: Pose questions*

Present a statement that contains the problem and ask students to pose the question(s), using the language and concepts of the subject you are teaching, that need(s) to be answered to solve the problem. For example, in mathematics, what mathematical question needs to be answered? In social studies, what political question needs to be addressed?

Strategy 3: Demonstrate linguistic understanding

Present several problems students should be able to solve and underline the key phrases and common vocabulary they need to know to comprehend the context of the problem. Ask students to explain in their own words the meaning of these linguistic features of the problem.

Strategy 4: Identify irrelevancies

Present interpretive materials and a problem statement and ask students to identify all the *irrelevant* information. Be sure the interpretive material contains information that is both relevant and irrelevant to the problem solution.

Strategy 5: Sort problem cards

Presents a collection of two or more examples of each of several *different* types of problem statements and ask students to (a) sort the problems into categories or groups of their own choosing and (b) explain why the problems they put into a group belong together. Put each problem statement on a separate card, but do not specify the type of problem it is. Focus your assessment on whether students are attending to only the wording or other surface features of the problem or, more appropriately, to the deeper features of the problem. For example, students should

---

*Strategies 2, 7, 10, 11, and 12 were adapted from junior high school mathematics performance assessments described by Lane, Parke, and Moskal (1992). We stripped their definitions of mathematical content to suggest the general structure of the strategy. Using this structure, you should be able to create tasks in your own subject area.

group all problems that can be solved using the same mathematical principle, the same scientific law, and so on, even though the problems are worded quite differently or are applied to different content.

Strategy 6: Identify assumptions

State a problem and ask students to state (a) a tentative solution and (b) what assumptions about the current and future problem situation they have made in reaching their solution.

■ **Example of identifying assumptions**

Use the scenario presented for Strategy 1.

2. What assumptions about the couple, their baby, their home life, and so on did you make to come up with the solution to this problem?

Strategy 7: Describe multiple strategies

State a problem and ask students to (a) solve the problem in two or more ways and (b) show their solutions using pictures, diagrams, or graphs.

■ **Example of describing multiple strategies**

Mickey has an album of baseball cards. He has six empty pages. Each page holds nine cards. How many baseball cards does Mickey need to fill his six empty album pages?

1. Show two or more ways to answer the question in the above problem. Use numbers, pictures, drawings, or graphs to show how you arrived at your answer.

Some of the students' responses:

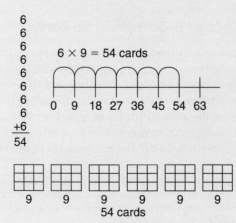

$$6 \times 9 = 54 \text{ cards}$$

Strategy 8: Model the problem

State a problem and ask students to draw a diagram or picture showing the problem situation. Assess how the students represent the problem rather than on whether the problem is correctly solved. Drawings of time problems in mathematics, for example, should depict time lines, not scales.

Strategy 9: Identify obstacles

Present a difficult problem to solve, perhaps one missing a key piece of information, and ask students to explain (a) why it is difficult to complete the task, (b) what the obstacles are, and/or (c) what additional information they need to overcome the obstacles. Assess whether students can identify the obstacle to solving the problem.

Strategy 10: Justify solutions

Present a problem statement along with two or more possible solutions to the problem and ask students to (a) select one solution they believe is correct and (b) justify why it is correct.

Strategy 11: Justify strategies used

State a problem and two or more strategies for solving it, and ask students to explain why both strategies are correct. Be certain both strategies yield the correct solution. In writing an item you might, for example, state that these were different ways that two fictional students solved the problem.

Strategy 12: Integrate data

Present several types of interpretive material (story, cartoon, graph, data table) and a statement of a problem that requires using information from two or more of the interpretive material types. Then ask students to (a) solve the problem and (b) explain the procedure they used to reach a solution. The problem solution must require using information from two or more of the interpretive materials. In science, for example, you might present rainfall tables, soil analyses, temperature tables, tomato nutrition requirements for several varieties, and fertilizer ingredients and require students to select the best variety to plant locally and to develop a plan for watering and feeding the plants based on the information you gave them.

Strategy 13: Produce alternate strategies

Present a problem statement and ask students to state two or more alternative solutions to the problem.

■ **Example of producing alternate strategies**

Use the scenario presented for Strategy 1.

3. Suggest at least three solutions to the problem. Be very specific in describing your proposed solutions.

An alternative approach is to present, along with the problem statement, one strategy that solves the problem, and require students to show you another way the problem could be solved.

Strategy 14: Use analogies

Present a problem statement and a correct solution strategy. Ask students to (a) describe other problems that could (by analogy) be solved by using this same solution strategy and (b) explain why the solution to the problem they generated is like the solution to the problem you gave them. Assess the analogical relationship of the students' solution strategy to the solution strategy you gave them.

■ **Example of using analogies**

Questions 1 and 2 refer to the situation below.

Members of a certain congressional committee talked a lot during committee hearings. Some members talked to explain their own views, some treated a witness as hostile and tried to discredit that witness's testimony, some wanted to prevent their opponents on the committee from speaking, and some wanted to prolong the debate and the hearing to postpone or prolong a committee vote. To solve this problem rules were established to give each committee member a fixed amount of time to speak and to ask questions of a witness. Under these rules, a committee member is allowed to give another member all or part of his allotted time.

1. Describe several other problems in different situations that could be solved by using a set of rules similar to those that the congressional committee used.

2. For each of the problems you listed, explain how the rules might be modified and why this would solve the problem you listed.

Strategy 15: Solve backwards

Present a complex problem situation or a complex (multistep) task to complete, and ask students to work backwards from the desired outcome to develop a plan or a strategy for completing the task or solving the problem. For example, ask students to develop the steps and time frame needed to complete a library research paper. Assess how well students use backward solution strategies.

■ **Example of solving backwards**

A student survey has been completed to determine whether students in a school favor curfews for persons under 18 years old. The results showed that among the girls, 56% favored the curfew (10% did not respond) and among the boys, 48% favored the curfew (9% did not respond). The results were based only on a sample of the students.

1. Working backward from the information above, develop a plan to show how this survey and the results were obtained. Be sure your plan covers all parts of the research.

Strategy 16: Evaluate the quality of the solution

State a problem and ask students to evaluate several different strategies for solving the problem. Ask students to produce several different solutions, or provide several solutions and ask them to evaluate those provided. If you provide solutions to evaluate, be certain to vary their correctness and quality, so that students can display their ability to evaluate. (For example, some may be more efficient, some may have negative consequences, and some may not work at all.) Ask students to determine the best strategy, explain why some strategies work better than others, and why some do not work at all. Assess the students' ability to justify the hierarchical ordering of the strategies' quality.

■ **Example of evaluating the quality of a solution**

Use the scenario from strategy 1.

4. Which of the solutions that you proposed in Question 3 is best? Justify your choice by explaining its advantages and disadvantages.

5. Explain why each of the other solutions is not as good as the one you decided was best.

Strategy 17: Systematically evaluate strategies

Use the same types of tasks as in Strategy 16, but assess the extent to which a student follows systematic *procedures* to evaluate each of the solution strategies you proposed.

Critical thinking is reasonable and reflective thinking focused on deciding what to believe or do

Discussions of critical thinking often use many of the same terms used in discussions of problem solving.

Curriculum frameworks frequently state that developing students' abilities for critical thinking is an important educational goal, although psychologists do not agree on all the skills that constitute it (Woolfolk, 1995; Kuhn, 1999). Critical thinking goals focus on developing students who are fair-minded, are objective, reach sound conclusions, and are disposed toward seeking clarity and accuracy (Marzano et al., 1988).

In this chapter, we adopt Ennis's (1985, p. 54) definition: "**Critical thinking** is reasonable, reflective thinking that is focused on deciding what to believe or do." The ultimate goal of education in critical thinking is to have students use their abilities spontaneously.

A related area of learning is rule-governed or principle-governed thinking. A **principle** is a rule that relates two or more concepts. Students learn abstract principles in later elementary and high school.

■ **Examples of abstract principles learned in high school**

- When performance is followed by a reinforcing event, the probability of that performance reoccurring increases.

- Experimental studies allow conclusions regarding functional relations, whereas correlational studies allow only statements of co-occurrence.

- People tend to immigrate to, and find success in, geographical environments closely resembling those from which they came.

- The status of a group in a society is positively related to the priorities of that society.

- The rate of increase in law enforcement officials is negatively related to the stability of the society.

We say a student uses **principle-governed thinking** when she can apply a principle or rule appropriately in a variety of "new" situations. Assess students' understanding of a principle by asking them to apply it to a new situation rather than by simply mimicking your classroom. Strategies 6, 7, and 8 below are particularly useful for assessing principle-governed thinking.

Use strategies to assess students' critical thinking skills

For the most part, critical thinking abilities are best taught and assessed in the context of individual subjects. Different subject matters have different types of arguments and criteria for verifying truth or credibility. Here we show the *strategies* you could use to assess critical thinking. Apply these strategies to the subject(s) you teach. Guideline 4.2 summarizes assessment strategies for critical thinking.

Strategy 1: Focus on a question

Students who are able to *focus on a question* can critically review an action, a verbal statement, a piece of discourse, a scientific or political argument, or even a cartoon to determine its main point(s) or the essence of the argument. Subskills include

Guideline 4.2 Thirteen strategies for assessing critical thinking skills

Critical Thinking Category	Strategy
Elementary clarification	1. Focus on a question 2. Analyze arguments 3. Ask clarifying questions
Basic support of an argument	4. Judge the credibility of a source 5. Judge observation reports

Inferences	6. Judge deductions by
	   a. comparing different conclusions
	   b. judging the truth of a conclusion
	7. Judge inductions
	8. Make judgments about values

Advanced clarification	9. Judge definitions 10. Identify implicit assumptions
Strategies and tactics	11. Decide on an action 12. Interact with others 13. Identify rhetorical mechanisms and tactics

Source: From *Evaluating Critical Thinking* (Table 1.2, p. 14) by Stephen P. Norris and Robert H. Ennis, 1989, Seaside, CA: The Critical Thinking Co. 800-458-4849/www.criticalthinking.com. Reprinted by permission.

(a) identifying the question or issue being posed, (b) selecting the proper criteria to use in evaluating the material presented, and (c) keeping the issue and its proper context in mind (Ennis, 1985).

Strategy

Strategy 1: How to assess the ability to focus on a question

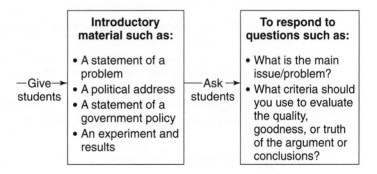

The following example shows two multiple-choice items assessing a student's ability to focus on the main issue in a speech.

■ Example

Strategies applied: Focusing on the main question and drawing conclusions after analyzing

The Gettysburg Address, Abraham Lincoln, November 19, 1863

Four score and seven years ago our fathers brought forth on this continent, a new nation, conceived in Liberty, and dedicated to the proposition that all men are created equal.

Now we are engaged in a great civil war, testing whether that nation, or any nation so conceived and so dedicated, can long endure. We are met on a great battlefield of that war. We have come to dedicate a portion of that field, as a final resting place for those who here gave their lives that that nation might live. It is altogether fitting and proper that we should do this.

But, in a larger sense, we can not dedicate—we can not consecrate—we can not hallow—this ground. The brave men, living and dead, who struggled here, have consecrated it, far above our poor power to add or detract. The world will little note, nor long remember what we say here, but it can never forget what they did here. It is for us the living, rather, to be dedicated here to the unfinished work which they who fought here have thus far so nobly advanced. It is rather for us to be here dedicated to the great task remaining before us—that from these honored dead we take increased devotion to that cause for which they gave the last full measure of devotion—that we here highly resolve that these dead shall not have died in vain—that this nation, under God, shall have a new birth of freedom—and that government of the people, by the people, for the people, shall not perish from the earth.

Questions 1 and 2 refer to the Gettysburg Address.

1. Of the following purposes stated in the speech, which one seems most important to Lincoln?
    a.   To dedicate a cemetery on the Gettysburg battlefield
    b.   To honor the dead soldiers buried in the cemetery
  *c.   To inspire people to continue to work for democracy

2. Why does Lincoln refer to our power as "poor" and say "The world will little note, nor long remember what we say here"?
    a.   He is being modest, so that people will take his speech seriously.
  *b.   He is comparing talking about being brave with actually being brave enough to die for a cause.
    c.   He means that the dedication of a cemetery is not very important, and so it doesn't matter a lot what gets said at the dedication.

Strategy 2: Analyze arguments

Students who can *analyze arguments* are able to analyze the *details* of the arguments presented in verbal statements, discussions, scientific or political reports, cartoons, and so on. The subskills include (a) identifying the conclusions in a statement; (b) identifying the stated and unstated reasons behind an argument; (c) seeing similarities and differences among two or more arguments; (d) finding, pointing out, and ignoring (when appropriate) irrelevancies appearing in an argument; (e) representing the logic or structure of an argument; and (f) summarizing an argument (Ennis, 1985).

Strategy

Strategy 2: How to assess the ability to analyze arguments

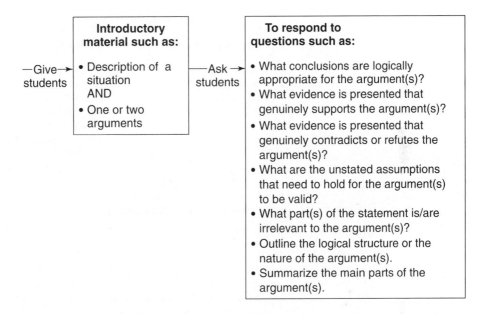

Strategy 3: Ask clarifying questions

Students who are able to *ask clarifying questions* can do two things: (a) ask appropriate questions of someone who is presenting an argument, and (b) answer critical questions appropriately when making an argument themselves. Among the questions that students should ask and be able to answer are: Why? What would not be an example? How does that apply in this situation? What are the facts that support your position? (Ennis, 1985). Probably the best way to assess this ability is to collect information about it over a long period, use a variety of assignments and tasks, and use a systematic procedure for recording your assessments such as a checklist (see Example 4.2) or a rating scale (Example 4.3).

Strategy 4: Judge the credibility of a source

Students can evaluate the quality of the evidence someone uses in supporting a position. Standards or criteria a student should be able to use when *judging credibility* include (a) the expertise of the person giving the evidence, (b) whether the person giving the evidence has a conflict of interest, (c) whether different sources of evidence agree, (d) whether the source of evidence has a reputation for being accurate and correct, (e) whether the evidence was obtained by established procedures that give it validity, and (f) whether there are good reasons for using the evidence under the given circumstances (Ennis, 1985). Each discipline will have specific rules of evidence, too.

Strategy

Strategy 4: How to assess the ability to judge credibility

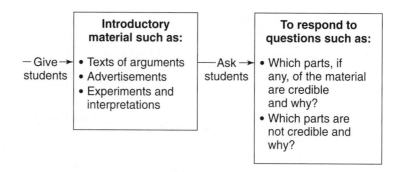

Strategy 5: Judge observation reports

Students should be able to *evaluate the quality of information obtained from eyewitness or direct observation* of an event. They should be able to judge whether (a) an observer reports with minimal referral to others' observations; (b) the time between the event and the report by the observer is short; (c) an observer is not reporting hearsay; (d) an observer keeps records of the observation; (e) the observations reported are corroborated by others; (f) an observer had good access to the event or person so direct observation can be accurate; (g) an observer records the observations properly; and (h) an observer is a credible source (Ennis, 1985). Each discipline may have more specific criteria as well. Newspaper articles related to your subject area may be useful sources for introductory material.

Strategy

Strategy 5: How to assess the ability to judge observation reports

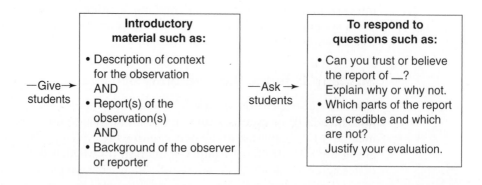

Strategy 6: Judge deductions

Students who can *judge deductions* apply logical thinking when they analyze statements and conclusions. Subskills include (a) using the logic of class inclusion (what elements or members should be logically included in a class or category), (b) using conditional logic (identifying the conditions under which something is true or false), and (c) properly interpreting statements using logical strategies (negatives, double negatives, necessary vs. sufficient conditions, and words such as if, or, some, not, both) (Ennis, 1985).

Strategy

Strategy 6(A): How to assess the ability to make and judge conclusions by comparing different conclusions

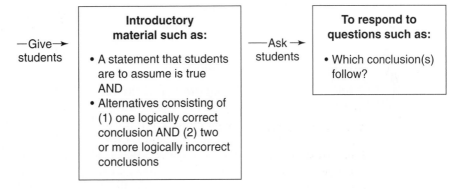

Strategy 6(B): How to assess the ability to make and judge conclusions by judging the truth of a conclusion

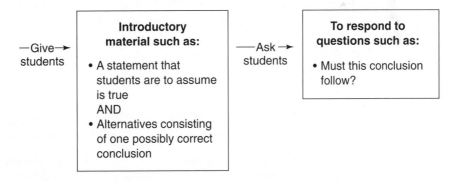

■ **Example**

Examples of items assessing students' ability to judge logical conclusions

Questions 1 and 2 are based on the information below.

If this substance is calcium carbonate, then it will bubble when acid is added. But there were no bubbles when I added the acid.

An item applying Strategy 6(A): Comparing different conclusions

1. Based on the above information, which of the following is correct?
    A   This substance cannot produce bubbles.
    B   This substance is calcium carbonate.
    *C   This substance is not calcium carbonate.
    D   This substance is calcium chloride.

An item applying Strategy 6(B): Judging the truth of one conclusion

2. Based on the above information, is it true that this substance is calcium carbonate?
    A   Yes, it must be true.
    *B   No, it cannot be true.
    C   We cannot be certain it is true from the information given.

Strategy 7: Judge inductions

Students who can *judge inductions* identify the conclusions that best explain the given evidence (Norris & Ennis, 1989). They can (a) identify and use typical features or patterns in the data to make inferences, (b) use appropriate techniques to make inferences from sample data, and (c) use patterns and trends shown in tables and graphs to make inferences (Ennis, 1985). They understand and use (a) different types of hypotheses and explanations (recognizing causal claims, recognizing historical claims, etc.), (b) valid ways of collecting relevant information (designing empirical research studies, methods of seeking evidence and counterevidence, etc.), and (c) criteria to evaluate the extent to which the information (data) supports the conclusion (Ennis, 1985). Both response-choice and constructed-response tasks can assess students' ability to reach a conclusion.

Strategy

Strategy 7(A): How to assess the ability to judge inductions using response-choice items

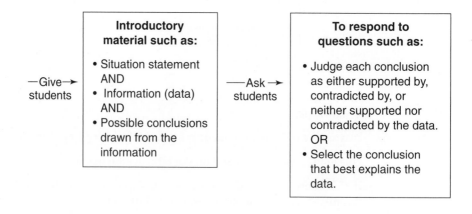

—Give→
students

Introductory material such as:

• Situation statement AND
• Information (data) AND
• Possible conclusions drawn from the information

—Ask→
students

To respond to questions such as:

• Judge each conclusion as either supported by, contradicted by, or neither supported nor contradicted by the data. OR
• Select the conclusion that best explains the data.

Strategy 7(B): How to assess the ability to judge inductions using constructed response items

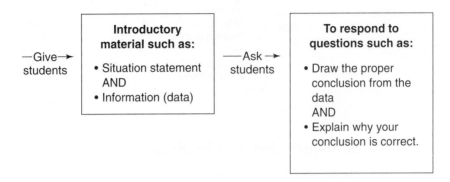

Having students justify their answers is a very important way to assess whether they can make or judge inductions appropriately. Students may choose the correct conclusion for the wrong reasons, or choose an incorrect conclusion because they do not have enough information to interpret the context of the situation you gave them correctly. Probably the single most powerful strategy you can use to both foster and assess your students' critical thinking is also the simplest: get in the habit of asking students "Why do you think that?" every time they make an assertion.

Strategy 8: Make judgments about values

Not all critical thinking inferences are made using data and syllogisms. Some are based on *judging value definitions*. Students with this critical thinking ability are able to identify when inferences have been made on the basis of values, what these values are, and when to use their own values to make inferences. Subskills include (a) gathering and using appropriate background information before judging, (b) identifying the consequences of the inferences that could be drawn and weighing the consequences before drawing conclusions, (c) identifying alternative actions and their value, and (d) balancing alternatives, weighing consequences, and deciding rationally (Ennis, 1985).

To assess this ability, ask students to explain the value, worth, or importance behind their inferences. Also, assess whether they recognize that different inferences or conclusions imply actions that have different consequences. Therefore, the assessment task should ask students to create or judge different courses of action, using different values as criteria, and to explain their reasons.

Strategy

Strategy 8: How to assess the ability to make judgments about values

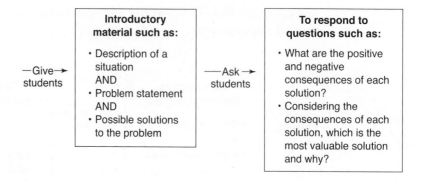

Strategy 9: Judge definitions

Students can *analyze the meanings and definitions of terms* used in the course of arguments, statements, and events to evaluate them critically. Subskills include (a) knowing the various forms that key terms may take and how these forms function in the context of an argument, (b) knowing how different strategies are used to define key terms in arguments, and (c) knowing the validity of the content of the definition itself (Ennis, 1985).

Assessment of this critical thinking ability must go beyond simply asking for definitions. The idea is to assess whether a student can recognize that words may be defined in certain ways to make a point, distort an argument, or deceive a listener or reader. For example, there may be two or more meanings for a key term. In an argumentative presentation, a writer may shift from one meaning to another (Ennis, 1985). Students skilled in this aspect of critical thinking should be able to detect the shift of meaning and describe the impact of the shift on the quality of the argument.

Strategy

Strategy 9: How to assess the ability to judge definitions

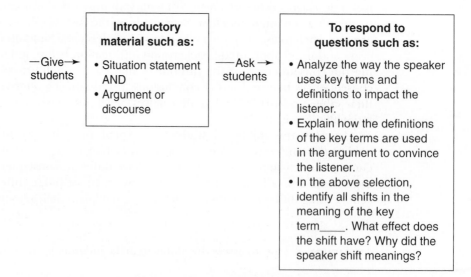

Strategy 10: Identify implicit assumptions

Students can *identify assumption(s)* that are part of someone's reasoning about what
to believe or to do. "Assumption" in this sense means an unstated basis for someone's reasoning.

■ Example

Poor: Confuses assumptions with conclusions

According to the Federal Election Commission, the percentages of the voting population who voted in the presidential election years 1932–1988 were:

Year	%	Year	%	Year	%	Year	%
1932	52.4	1948	51.1	1964	61.9	1980	54.0
1936	56.0	1952	61.6	1968	60.9	1984	53.1
1940	58.9	1956	59.3	1972	55.2	1988	50.1
1944	56.0	1960	62.8	1976	53.5		

1. From the above data you can assume that
   - A   in 1988 most voters were unhappy with the candidates.
   - B   in 1988 voter turnout was at an all-time low.
   - C   voter turnout declined from 1980 to 1988.
   - D   the majority of the voters did not vote.

Better: Gives conclusion and asks for the assumption needed to reach conclusion

Facts: According to the Federal Election Commission, the percentage of the voting
population who voted in the presidential election years 1932–1988 were:

Year	%	Year	%	Year	%	Year	%
1932	52.4	1948	51.1	1964	61.9	1980	54.0
1936	56.0	1952	61.6	1968	60.9	1984	53.1
1940	58.9	1956	59.3	1972	55.2	1988	50.1
1944	56.0	1960	62.8	1976	53.5		

Conclusion: The number of persons voting in national elections in presidential election years 1931–1988 was at its lowest in 1988.

2. For this conclusion to be true, it must be assumed that
   - A   the number of voting-age persons in 1988 was the same as or less than
           each of the other presidential election years in 1932–1988.
   - B   the number of voting-age persons increased from 1932–1988.
   - C   the percentage of voting-age persons who voted in each of the other pres-
           idential election years was less than 50.1%.

The problem with Item 1 is that, even though it uses the word *assume*, it actually requires students to draw conclusions from the given data: A student is not required to identify an implicit or unstated assumption that might be the basis for a conclusion. Item 2 is an improvement because it is rewritten to focus on implicit assumptions.

Strategy

Strategy 10: How to assess the ability to identify implicit assumptions with response-choice items

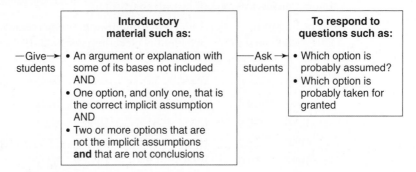

Be sure that the interpretive material you use in fact has an implicit assumption. This means you cannot include passages for which the author makes his or her assumptions explicit. It also means you cannot use material for which no assumptions have been made to reach the conclusion.

Strategy 11: Decide on an action

Students who can *decide on an action* are essentially good problem solvers. The subskills are those we discussed earlier in this chapter on problem solving: defining problems, formulating and evaluating solutions, viewing the total problem and taking action, and evaluating the action taken. The assessment strategies for this ability are the same as those you would use in assessing problem-solving skills.

Strategy 12: Interact with others

Students who are good at *interacting with others* are able to identify and use rhetorical devices to persuade, explain, or argue. Among the rhetorical devices the student should be able to identify and use are (a) argumentative verbal tactics (appeal to authority, strawman, etc.), (b) logical strategies, and (c) skillful organization and presentation (Ennis, 1985).

Assessment of this ability may take several forms. One form is to ask students to present argumentative or persuasive work of their own creation. Use a rating scale for assessment: (a) it makes clear the criteria you use to evaluate students; (b) you can give the scale to students, so they can internalize standards for performance; and (c) it greatly improves the consistency (reliability) of your marking. Example 4.1 shows an example of a rating scale for evaluating an argumentative presentation.

■ **EXAMPLE 4.1 Example of a simple rating scale to use as a scoring rubric for assessing the quality of a student's oral or written presentation of an argument**

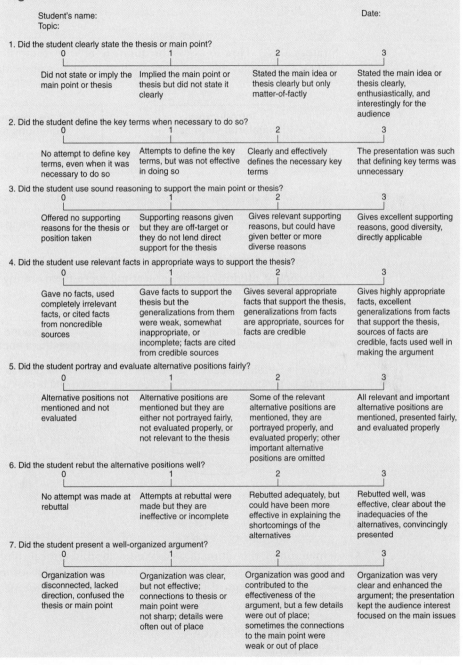

Student's name: Date:
Topic:

1. Did the student clearly state the thesis or main point?

0	1	2	3
Did not state or imply the main point or thesis	Implied the main point or thesis but did not state it clearly	Stated the main idea or thesis clearly but only matter-of-factly	Stated the main idea or thesis clearly, enthusiastically, and interestingly for the audience

2. Did the student define the key terms when necessary to do so?

0	1	2	3
No attempt to define key terms, even when it was necessary to do so	Attempts to define the key terms, but was not effective in doing so	Clearly and effectively defines the necessary key terms	The presentation was such that defining key terms was unnecessary

3. Did the student use sound reasoning to support the main point or thesis?

0	1	2	3
Offered no supporting reasons for the thesis or position taken	Supporting reasons given but they are off-target or they do not lend direct support for the thesis	Gives relevant supporting reasons, but could have given better or more diverse reasons	Gives excellent supporting reasons, good diversity, directly applicable

4. Did the student use relevant facts in appropriate ways to support the thesis?

0	1	2	3
Gave no facts, used completely irrelevant facts, or cited facts from noncredible sources	Gave facts to support the thesis but the generalizations from them were weak, somewhat inappropriate, or incomplete; facts are cited from credible sources	Gives several appropriate facts that support the thesis, generalizations from facts are appropriate, sources for facts are credible	Gives highly appropriate facts, excellent generalizations from facts that support the thesis, sources of facts are credible, facts used well in making the argument

5. Did the student portray and evaluate alternative positions fairly?

0	1	2	3
Alternative positions not mentioned and not evaluated	Alternative positions are mentioned but they are either not portrayed fairly, not evaluated properly, or not relevant to the thesis	Some of the relevant alternative positions are mentioned, they are portrayed properly, and evaluated properly; other important alternative positions are omitted	All relevant and important alternative positions are mentioned, presented fairly, and evaluated properly

6. Did the student rebut the alternative positions well?

0	1	2	3
No attempt was made at rebuttal	Attempts at rebuttal were made but they are ineffective or incomplete	Rebutted adequately, but could have been more effective in explaining the shortcomings of the alternatives	Rebutted well, was effective, clear about the inadequacies of the alternatives, convincingly presented

7. Did the student present a well-organized argument?

0	1	2	3
Organization was disconnected, lacked direction, confused the thesis or main point	Organization was clear, but not effective; connections to thesis or main point were not sharp; details were often out of place	Organization was good and contributed to the effectiveness of the argument, but a few details were out of place; sometimes the connections to the main point were weak or out of place	Organization was very clear and enhanced the argument; the presentation kept the audience interest focused on the main issues

Strategy 13: Identify rhetorical mechanisms and tactics

You may also wish to assess whether students can *identify the rhetorical mechanisms and tactics* that are used in a particular piece of writing, speech, advertisement, or other persuasive material.

Strategy

Strategy 13(A): How to assess the ability to identify rhetorical mechanisms and tactics by analyzing one piece to identify what is misleading

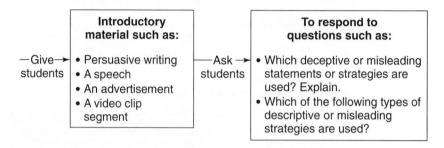

Strategy 13(B): How to assess the ability to identify rhetorical mechanisms and tactics by identifying the misleading piece from among several pieces that are not misleading

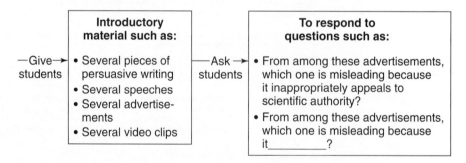

Use checklists or rating scales to assess dispositions toward critical thinking

As we mentioned, the ultimate goal of education in critical thinking is to have students use these skills spontaneously. Dispositions are habits of mind or tendencies to use appropriate critical thinking behaviors often. Students who are disposed toward critical thinking:

■ seek a statement of the thesis or question;

■ seek reasons;

■ try to be well informed;

- use credible sources and mention them;
- take into account the total situation;
- keep their thinking relevant to the main point;
- keep in mind the original or most basic concern;
- look for alternatives;
- are open minded and
  - seriously consider points of view other than their own;
  - reason from starting points with which they disagree without letting the disagreement interfere with their reasoning;
  - withhold judgment when the evidence and reasons are insufficient;
- take a position and change a position when the evidence and reasons are sufficient to do so;
- seek as much precision as the subject permits;
- deal in an orderly manner with the parts of a complex whole;
- employ their critical thinking abilities;
- are sensitive to the feelings, level of knowledge, and degree of sophistication of others.

Source: From *Evaluating Critical Thinking* (Table 1.1, p. 12) by Stephen P. Norris and Robert H. Ennis, 1989, Seaside, CA: The Critical Thinking Co. 800-458-4849/www.criticalthinking.com. Reprinted by permission.

Although you can assess a student's use of a critical thinking ability or skill on one occasion, *assessment of a student's disposition requires you to focus on her long-term habits*. Your assessment should report how frequently over a marking period, term, or year a student uses critical thinking in the curriculum subject matter. Assess dispositions using either a checklist or a rating scale. Chapters 10 discusses how to construct checklists and rating scales. Here we simply give examples (Examples 4.2 and 4.3) of using these tools to assess dispositions toward critical thinking.

Conclusions

If you only remember one idea from this chapter, it should be that novel material is absolutely necessary for assessing higher-order thinking. (Of course, we want you to remember other things, too!). You don't want to assess students' ability to recall the induction *you* made. This concept is absolutely critical. It's easy to feel pressure to be "fair" and not ask students to do anything they haven't done before. Don't let this feeling lead you away from using novel material.

We cannot stress enough that applying skills and concepts to novel materials should not be new to the students at the time of summative assessment. They should be used to handling new materials from their experiences in instruction and

■ **EXAMPLE 4.2 Example of a checklist to keep track of a student's use of critical thinking dispositions throughout a teaching unit**

Individual Student's Critical Thinking Disposition Record

Student's name: **Class period:**   **Dates:**
Student/unit: U.S. History/Unit III.Beginning a Government, 1780–1800

Assignment/activity

Critical thinking dispositions	Class discussion of the Articles of the Confederation	Essay discussing arguments for and against ratification of the Constitution	Scrapbook collecting and analyzing events reported in the newspaper using concepts from the Constitution	Teams debate the issue, "Have political parties made the United States government better?"	Essay evaluating Washington as president
1. Seeks statements of the main point or question	✓	—	✓	✓	NA
2. Looks for explanations and reasons	✓	✓	✓	✓	✓
3. Uses and cites credible sources	—	✓	—	✓	—
4. Keeps to the main and relevant point(s)	—	—	NA	✓	✓
5. Looks for alternatives	—	—	NA	—	NA
6. Open-minded	✓	✓	✓	NA	—
7. Takes a position on an issue		✓	—	✓	—
8. Changes position on an issue with good reason(s)	NA	—	NA	NA	NA
9. Seeks to be accurate and precise in statements and work	NA	—	✓	✓	—
10. Sensitive to the feelings, levels of knowledge of others	✓	NA	—	—	NA

formative assessment. Share with students the reasons for using novel materials. Ask them to reflect on the kind of thinking they do. Help students become your partners in assessing higher-order thinking. What's *really* "not fair" is to let students slip through your classes without the opportunity to learn how to do higher-order thinking.

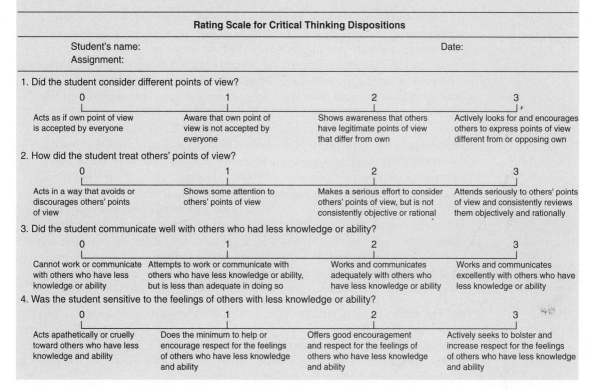

■ **EXAMPLE 4.3 Sample rating scale assessing the quality of some of a student's dispositions toward critical thinking that a teacher might observe as the student completes an assignment**

Rating Scale for Critical Thinking Dispositions

Student's name: Date:
Assignment:

1. Did the student consider different points of view?

0	1	2	3
Acts as if own point of view is accepted by everyone	Aware that own point of view is not accepted by everyone	Shows awareness that others have legitimate points of view that differ from own	Actively looks for and encourages others to express points of view different from or opposing own

2. How did the student treat others' points of view?

0	1	2	3
Acts in a way that avoids or discourages others' points of view	Shows some attention to others' points of view	Makes a serious effort to consider others' points of view, but is not consistently objective or rational	Attends seriously to others' points of view and consistently reviews them objectively and rationally

3. Did the student communicate well with others who had less knowledge or ability?

0	1	2	3
Cannot work or communicate with others who have less knowledge or ability	Attempts to work or communicate with others who have less knowledge or ability, but is less than adequate in doing so	Works and communicates adequately with others who have less knowledge or ability	Works and communicates excellently with others who have less knowledge or ability

4. Was the student sensitive to the feelings of others with less knowledge or ability?

0	1	2	3
Acts apathetically or cruelly toward others who have less knowledge and ability	Does the minimum to help or encourage respect for the feelings of others who have less knowledge and ability	Offers good encouragement and respect for the feelings of others who have less knowledge and ability	Actively seeks to bolster and increase respect for the feelings of others who have less knowledge and ability

Exercises

1. Each of the following items is an attempt to assess problem solving. For each item, identify which strategy or strategies in Guideline 4.1 is intended. Then, compare and contrast the kinds of higher-order thinking students would need to do for each of these three items.

   a. Sam had a dozen cookies. He wanted to share them with Martha, Boyd, and Shirelle so they all got the same amount. How many cookies did each child get?

   b. Sam had a dozen cookies. He wanted to share them with Martha, Boyd, and Shirelle so they all got the same amount. How many cookies did each child get? Draw a picture to illustrate your answer.

   c. Sam had a dozen cookies. He wanted to share them with Martha, Boyd, and Shirelle so they all got the same amount. How many cookies did each child get? Show at least two ways you could use to find the answer.

2. Each of the following questions is based on Aesop's fable "The Eagle, the Cat, and the Wild Sow." For each item, identify which critical thinking strategy or

strategies in Guideline 4.2 is intended. Then, compare and contrast the kinds of higher-order thinking students would need to do for each of these three items.

The Eagle, the Cat, and the Wild Sow

AN EAGLE made her nest at the top of a lofty oak; a Cat, having found a convenient hole, moved into the middle of the trunk; and a Wild Sow, with her young, took shelter in a hollow at its foot. The Cat cunningly resolved to destroy this chance-made colony. To carry out her design, she climbed to the nest of the Eagle, and said, "Destruction is preparing for you, and for me too, unfortunately. The Wild Sow, whom you see daily digging up the earth, wishes to uproot the oak, so she may on its fall seize our families as food for her young." Having thus frightened the Eagle out of her senses, she crept down to the cave of the Sow, and said, "Your children are in great danger; for as soon as you go out with your litter to find food, the Eagle is prepared to pounce upon one of your little pigs." Having instilled these fears into the Sow, she went and pretended to hide herself in the hollow of the tree. When night came she went forth with silent foot and obtained food for herself and her kittens, but feigning to be afraid, she kept a look-out all through the day. Meanwhile, the Eagle, full of fear of the Sow, sat still on the branches, and the Sow, terrified by the Eagle, did not dare to go out from her cave. And thus they both, along with their families, perished from hunger, and afforded ample provision for the Cat and her kittens.

a. "The Eagle, the Cat, and the Wild Sow" is mainly a story about some things the Cat did. What do her actions tell you about what she thinks is important and what she thinks is not important?
b. Read the fable, "The Eagle, the Cat, and the Wild Sow." What do you think is the moral of the story? Explain why you think so.
c. Read the fable, "The Eagle, the Cat, and the Wild Sow." Which of the following do you think is the best statement of the moral of the story? Explain your choice.
    i. "Gossips are to be seen and not heard."
    ii. "Beware of the Cat."

Companion
Website

Now go to our Companion Website at **www.prenhall.com/brookhart** to assess your understanding of chapter content with multiple-choice and essay questions. Broaden your knowledge of assessment with links to assessment related web sites.

5

Planning Assessment and Instruction

KEY CONCEPTS

1. Good assessment planning and good instructional planning are two sides of the same coin; do them together.
2. Formative and summative assessment both require planning.
3. A wide array of assessment options are available: paper-and-pencil, performance, long-term assignment, and personal communication formats.
4. Plan assessment directions, length, and difficulty.
5. Assessment planning for a marking period should be based on learning goals and outline the main instructional and assessment strategies you will use.
6. Assessment planning for a unit of instruction should be based on learning goals and objectives and detail the instructional and assessment strategies you will use. Use a pretest to help plan your teaching.
7. Use a blueprint to plan individual summative assessments.

There are many story possibilities for a unit on planning: from Aesop's Fables ("The Ant and the Grasshopper") to the Boy Scouts of America (Be prepared) or the U.S. Coast Guard (*Semper paratus*). We have chosen a true story that, unfortunately, really happened to the first author (the "I" in the story).

> In my early career, I did quite a lot of substituting. Some classrooms had detailed plans, but I never knew where they fit with the bigger educational goals. Thus the students and I tended to concentrate on "right" and "wrong" answers to individual assignments. It was hard to know what to emphasize or why something was important.
>
> For the same reason, if I "ran out" of plans before I ran out of time, it was hard to know what to do. Probably the worst day in this regard was one time I was substituting in a kindergarten class, had accomplished everything in the plans the teacher had left for me, and still had a half hour left in the morning. I had to come up with something that would last a half hour but that I could plan in a few minutes while also teaching the class.
>
> I noticed there was a good supply of construction paper and some blunt scissors, so I decided the children could make fantasy animals (head of a dog, body of a snake, tail of a rabbit, that sort of thing). Creative, fun, and time-consuming, right? Well, as it turns out, wrong. In my haste, I forgot a principle of child development that I actually did know. Many kindergarten

children do not yet have sufficient small muscle coordination to use scissors to cut with much detail. So we had a half hour filled with lots of frustration, noise, ripped paper, and one very chagrined substitute teacher!

The planning errors here are legion. First, the "objective" was "to fill half an hour." Second, the activity was selected under pressure at the last minute, which caused me to forget basic information about children. Third and as a result, an assessment (for example, children showing and describing their fantasy animals) did not even happen. This is probably just as well, because it would have given many of the children evidence that they couldn't do a very good fantasy animal, and that was my fault.

Good assessment planning and good instructional planning are two sides of the same coin; do them together

Plans for teaching are incomplete unless they contain plans for assessment. Good assessment planning benefits your teaching in several ways.

- When you monitor and evaluate student progress with quality assessment, you can plan better teaching.

- What and how you assess communicates in a powerful way what you really value in your students' learning. No matter what you *say* you want students to learn or do, they will conclude that what is assessed is what "counts" and is what is really important to you.

- Carefully defined assessment tasks clarify what you want students to learn.

- Knowledge of assessment will help you become a critical consumer of assessment procedures, whether they are part of your curriculum materials or are imposed by or on your school district, such as standardized achievement tests and state-mandated assessments.

- Knowing how to plan your own assessment tasks increases your freedom to design lessons (Stiggins, 2005). You are not chained to the assessment procedures prepared by textbook publishers and others.

- Careful planning improves the validity of your interpretations and uses of assessment results.

- Planning allows you to appreciate and leverage the strengths and limitations of each type of assessment procedure.

Formative and summative assessment both require planning

A major point to keep in mind is that you must assess for both formative and summative purposes, which requires planning. Table 5.1 shows common uses for classroom assessment results, organized into formative and summative categories to

Table 5.1 Examples of classroom assessment purposes

Formative uses—to monitor or guide student learning while it is still in progress	
Assessment Purpose	Using assessment to
Sizing-up	Form initial impressions of students' strengths, weaknesses, learning characteristics, and personalities at the beginning of the year or course.
Communicating achievement expectations	Clarify for students exactly what they are expected to be able to perform when their learning is complete. This may be done by showing the actual assessment tasks or by reviewing the various levels or degrees of performance of previous students on specific assessment tasks so that current students may be clear about expectations.
Teaching	Be a teaching strategy. For example, a teacher may give practice tests or "mock exams" to help students understand the types of tasks used on the assessment, to practice answering and recording answers in the desired way, or to improve the speed at which they respond. In some cases, the performance assessed is identical or nearly identical to the desired learning target so that "practicing the assessment" is akin to teaching the desired learning target.
Diagnosing individual learning needs	Identify what the student has learned and what still needs to be learned, to decide how instruction needs to be adapted, and to decide what feedback the student needs about how to improve.
Diagnosing group learning needs	Identify how the class as a whole has progressed in its learning, what might need to be reinforced or re-taught, and when the group is ready to move on to new learning.
Providing specific feedback	Give students information about how to improve.
Planning instruction	Design and implement appropriate learning and instruction activities, to decide what content to include or emphasize, and to organize and manage the classroom as a learning environment.
Summative uses—to evaluate student learning after teaching one or more units of a course of study	
Assessment Purpose	Using assessment to
Assigning grades for report cards	Communicate evaluations to students, their parents, and responsible educational authorities.
Placing students into remedial and advanced courses	Adapt instruction to individuals' needs when teaching is group-based: placing students into remedial classes for alternate or supplemental instruction, or into a higher level or more enriched class.
Evaluating one's own teaching	Identify which lessons were successful with which students, and to formulate modifications in teaching strategies that will lead to improved student performance the next time the lessons are taught.

make discussion easier. In reality, the boundary between formative and summative assessment is fluid. Plan for all types of assessment.

Formative uses of assessment help you to guide or monitor student learning while it is still in progress. High-quality formative assessment and **feedback** increases student learning (Black & Wiliam, 1998). Use a variety of formal and informal assessment results to make instructional decisions and to provide formative feedback to students. Record the results of these assessments to help your memory, but do not use them for grading.

Summative uses of assessment help you evaluate your students and your own teaching after you finish teaching one or more units. Summative information about students' achievement usually counts toward their grades for a marking period. Parents and school authorities interpret those grades as the progress students have made toward achieving the curriculum's learning targets. Often this reporting is done through a home report or a report card. Keep records of students' results on those assessments that will be used in the grades.

Some teachers use classroom assessment to control students' behaviors. We note this only for the sake of completeness of our treatment of "uses" of assessment. However common a practice, using assessments to control students' behaviors is usually unwise and sometimes unethical. This practice turns a process of information gathering into a process of threatening and punishing students, which has negative consequences for their learning and motivation.

A wide array of assessment options are available: paper-and-pencil, performance, long-term assignment, and personal communication formats

To decide which assessment option to use, you need to know three things: (a) the learning targets students should achieve, (b) the purpose for which you want to use the assessment results, and (c) the advantages of an assessment technique for the specific purpose you have in mind. We have already discussed the first two items in Chapters 1 and 3. This section discusses the general advantages and disadvantages of the many assessment options available to you.

Researchers have identified the most commonly used types of classroom assessment procedures (Airasian, 2005; Stiggins, Conklin, et al., 1992). These are listed in Table 5.2 along with their advantages, their limitations, and brief suggestions for improved use. The techniques are grouped into two categories: formative assessment techniques and summative assessment techniques. Again, remember in reality the distinction is not quite that neat.

Formative assessment options

Choose from among formative assessment options when you are gathering information to plan your next teaching activities, to diagnose the causes of students' learning difficulties, and especially to give students information about how to improve. In fact, it is questionable whether we should call assessment "formative" unless students actually use the information for improvement. Gather this information while you are still teaching the material and while students are still learning it. Table 5.2 summarizes eight categories of formative assessment options, discussed in three groups below.

Oral assessments

Conversations with teachers who have taught a student may give you insight into the student's background and which approaches have worked in the past. These conversations may also help as you size up the class at the beginning of the term. Conversations with students give you additional insight into their feelings, attitudes, interests, and motivations.

As you teach a lesson, you question students about the material. These questions should encourage students to think about the material and to reveal their understandings, including misconceptions. This will help guide your teaching. Avoid "recitation" type questioning in which you seek short answers to your questions. This style of questioning provides little insight into students' thinking and, therefore, provides little formative information. Avoid the tendency to ignore or ask only simple questions of the shy and less verbal students (Good & Brophy, 2003). A good way to plan your oral questioning is to use a thinking skills taxonomy (see Chapter 3). In every lesson, plan to ask several questions from the higher-order thinking categories of the taxonomy.

Paper-and-pencil assessments

Each day you give students seatwork and homework. These **paper-and-pencil assessments** let students practice and perhaps extend their learning. Review the results of seatwork and homework not just for correctness, but for what the work reveals about students' thinking. For example, a pattern of errors may indicate a misconception or misuse of a rule or principle. Providing that specific information as feedback to students who need it is a powerful way of personalizing learning and helps students change.

You also periodically give short quizzes and tests to monitor students' progress toward achieving learning targets. Tests tend to be somewhat formal and are more useful for summative evaluation of students than for formative evaluation. However, if you use open-ended response items and carefully review students' responses for insights into their thinking, you can get some diagnostic information.

Portfolios

A **growth and learning progress portfolio** is a selected sequence of a student's work that demonstrates progress or development toward achieving the learning target(s). It contains "not-so-good works," "improved works," and "best works" in order to show progress and learning.

Typically, both the teacher and the student decide what a portfolio should include. Further, students are usually asked to describe the work they included, why they selected it, what it demonstrates about their learning, and their reflections on the material and their learning experiences. Because a portfolio is built up over time, it permits closer integration of assessment with instruction than some of the other techniques.

Table 5.2 Advantages and limitations of alternative types of classroom assessment techniques.

Assessment alternatives	Advantages for teachers	Disadvantages for teachers	Suggestions for improved use
	Formative assessment techniques		
1. Conversations and comments from other teachers	(a) Fast way to obtain certain types of background information about a student. (b) Permit colleagues to share experiences with specific students in other learning contexts, thereby broadening the perspective about the learners. (c) Permit attainment of information about a student's family, siblings; or peer problems that may be affecting the student's learning.	(a) Tend to reinforce stereotypes and biases toward a family or social class. (b) Students' learning under another teacher or in another context may be quite unlike their learning in the current context. (c) Others' opinions are not objective, often based on incomplete information, personal life view, or personal theory of personality.	(a) Do not believe hearsay, rumors, biases of others. (b) Do not gossip or reveal private and confidential information about students. (c) Keep the conversation on a professional level focused on facts rather than speculation and confidential so it is not overheard by others.
2. Casual conversations with students	(a) Provide relaxed, informal setting for obtaining information. (b) Students may reveal their attitudes and motivations toward learning that are not exhibited in class.	(a) A student's mind may not be focused on the learning target being assessed. (b) Inadequate sampling of students' knowledge; too few students assessed. (c) Inefficient students' conversation may be irrelevant to assessing their achievement.	(a) Do not appear as an inquisitor, always probing students. (b) Be careful not to misperceive a student's attitude or a student's degree of understanding.
3. Questioning students during instruction	(a) Permits judgments about students' thinking and learning progress during the course of teaching; gives teachers immediate feedback. (b) Permits teachers to ask questions requiring higher-order thinking and elaborated responses. (c) Permits student-to-student interaction to be assessed. (d) Permits assessment of students' ability to discuss issues with others orally and in some depth.	(a) Some students cannot express themselves well in front of other students. (b) Requires education in how to ask proper questions and to plan for asking specific types of questions during the lesson. (c) Information obtained tends to be only a small sample of the learning outcomes and of the students in the class. (d) Some learning targets cannot be assessed by spontaneous and short oral responses; they require longer time frames in which students are free to think, create, and respond. (e) Records of students' responses are kept only in the teacher's mind, which may be unreliable.	(a) Be sure to ask questions of students who are reticent or slow to respond. Avoid focusing on verbally aggressive and pleasant "stars." (b) Wait 5–10 seconds for a student to respond before moving on to another. (c) Avoid limiting questions to those requiring facts or a definite correct answer, thereby narrowing the focus the assessment inappropriately. (d) Do not punish students for failing to participate in class question sessions or inappropriately reward those verbally aggressive students who participate fully. (e) Students' verbal and nonverbal behavior in class may not indicate their true attitudes/values.

Method		
4. Daily homework and seatwork	(a) Provide formative information about how learning is progressing. (b) Allow errors to be diagnosed and corrected. (c) Combine practice, reinforcement, and assessment.	(a) Tend to focus on narrow segments of learning rather than integrating large complexes of skills and knowledge. (b) Sample only a small variety of content and skills on any one assignment. (c) Assignment may not be complete or may be copied from others.	(a) This method assesses learning that is only in the formative stages. It may be inappropriate to assign summative letter grades from the results. (b) Failure to complete homework or completing it late is no reason to punish students by embarrassing them in front of others or by lowering their overall grade. Learning may be subsequently demonstrated through other assessments. (c) Do not inappropriately attribute poor test performance to the student not doing the homework. (d) Do not overemphasize the homework grade and overuse homework as a teaching strategy (e.g., using it as a primary teaching method.)
5. Teacher-made quizzes and tests	(a) Although primarily useful for summative evaluation they may permit diagnosis of errors and faulty thinking. (b) Provide for students' written expression of knowledge.	(a) Require time to craft good tasks useful for diagnosis. (b) Focus exclusively on cognitive learning targets.	(a) Do not overemphasize lower level thinking skills. (b) Use open-ended or constructed-response tasks to gain insight into a student's thinking processes and errors. (c) For better diagnosis of a student's thinking, use tasks that require students to apply and use their knowledge to "real-life" situations.
6. In-depth interviews of individual students	(a) Permit in-depth probing of students understandings, thinking patterns, and problem-solving strategies. (b) Permit follow-up questions tailored to a student's responses and allow a student to elaborate answers. (c) Permit diagnosis of faulty thinking and errors in performances.	(a) Require a lot of time to complete. (b) Require keeping the rest of the class occupied while one student is being interviewed. (c) Require learning skills in effective educational achievement interviewing and diagnosis.	(a) If assessing students' thinking patterns, problem-solving strategies, etc., avoid prompting student toward a prescribed way of problem solving. (b) Some students need their self-confidence bolstered before they feel comfortable revealing their mistakes.

(Continued)

Table 5.2 Continued

Assessment alternatives	Advantages for teachers	Disadvantages for teachers	Suggestions for improved use
Formative assessment techniques			
7. Growth and learning-progress portfolios	(a) Allow large segments of a student's learning experiences to be reviewed. (b) Allow monitoring a student's growth and progress. (c) Communicate to students that growth and progress are more important than test results. (d) Allow student to participate in selecting and evaluating material to include in the portfolio. (e) Can become a focus of teaching and learning.	(a) Require a long time to accumulate evidence of growth and progress. (b) Require special effort to teach students how to use appropriate and realistic self-assessment techniques. (c) Require high-level knowledge of the subject matter to diagnose and guide students. (d) Require the ability to recognize complex and subtle pattern of growth and progress in the subjects. (e) Results tend to be inconsistent from teacher to teacher.	(a) Be very clear about the learning targets toward which you are monitoring progress. (b) Use a conceptual framework or learning progress model to guide your diagnosis and monitoring. (c) Coordinate portfolio development and assessment with other teachers. (d) Develop scoring rubrics to define standards and maintain consistency.
8. Attitude and values questionnaires	(a) Assess affective characteristics of students (b) Knowing student's attitudes and values in relation to a specific topic or subject matter may be useful in planning teaching. (c) May provide insights into students' motivations.	(a) The results are sensitive to the way questions are worded. Students may misinterpret, not understand, or react differently than the assessor intended. (b) Can be easily "faked" by older and testwise students.	(a) The way questions are worded significantly affects how students respond. (b) Attitude questionnaire responses may change drastically from one occasion or context to another. (c) Your personal theory of personality or personal value system may lead to incorrect interpretations of students' responses.
Summative assessment techniques			
1. Teacher-made tests and quizzes	(a) Can assess a wide range of content and cognitive skills. (b) Can be aligned with what was actually taught. (c) Use a variety of task formats. (d) Allow for assessment of written expression.	(a) Difficult to assess complex skills or ability to use combinations of skills. (b) Require time to create, edit, and produce good items. (c) Class period is often too short for a complete assessment. (d) Focus exclusively on cognitive outcomes.	(a) Do not overemphasize lower level thinking skills. (b) Do not overuse short-answer and response-choice items. (c) Create tasks requiring students to apply knowledge to "real life."

2. Task focusing on procedures and processes	(a) Allow assessments of nonverbal as well as verbal responses. (b) Allow students to integrate several simple skills and knowledge to perform a complex, realistic task. (c) Allow for group and cooperative performance and assessment. (d) Allow assessment of steps used to complete an assignment.	(a) Focus on a narrow range of content knowledge and cognitive skills. (b) Require a great deal of time to properly formulate, administer, and rate. (c) May have low interrater reliability unless scoring rubrics are used. (d) Results are often specific to the combination of student and task. Students' performance quality is not easily generalized across different content and tasks. (e) Tasks that students perceive as uninteresting, boring, or irrelevant do not elicit the students' best efforts.	(a) Investigate carefully the reason for student's failure to complete the task successfully. (b) Use a scoring rubric to increase the reliability and validity of results. (c) Do not confuse the evaluation of the process a student uses with the need to evaluate the correctness of the answers. (d) Allow sufficient time for students to adequately demonstrate the performance.
3. Projects and tasks focusing on products	(a) Same as 2(a), (b), and (c). (b) Permit several equally valid processes to be used to produce the product or complete the project. (c) Allow assessment of the quality of the product. (d) Allow longer time than class period to complete the tasks.	(a) Same as 2(a), (b), (c), (d), and (e). (b) Students may have unauthorized help outside class to complete the product or project. (c) All students in the class must have the same opportunity to use all appropriate materials and tools in order for the assessment to be fair.	(a) Same as 2(a), (b), (c), and (d). (b) Give adequate instruction to students on the criteria that will be used to evaluate their work, the standards that will be applied, and how students can use these criteria and standards to monitor their own progress in completing the work. (c) Do not mistake the aesthetic appearance of the product for substance and thoughtfulness. (d) Do not punish tardiness in completing the project or product by lowering the student's grade.
4. Best works portfolios	(a) Allow large segments of a student's learning experience to be assessed. (b) May allow students to participate in the selection of the material to be included in the portfolio. (c) Allow either quantitative or qualitative assessment of the works in the portfolio. (d) Permit a much broader assessment of learning targets than tests.	(a) Require waiting a long time before reporting assessment results. (b) Students must be taught how to select work to include as well as how to present it effectively. (c) Teachers must learn to use a scoring rubric that assesses a wide variety of pieces of work. (d) Interrater reliability is low from teacher to teacher. (e) Require high levels of subject-matter knowledge to evaluate students' work properly.	(a) Be very clear about the learning targets to be assessed to avoid confusion and invalid portfolio assessment results. (b) Teach a student to use appropriate criteria to choose the work to include. (c) Do not collect too much material to evaluate. (d) Coordinate portfolio development with other teachers. (e) Develop and use scoring rubrics to define standards and maintain consistency.

(Continued)

Table 5.2 Continued

Assessment alternatives	Advantages for teachers	Disadvantages for teachers	Suggestions for improved use
		Formative assessment techniques	
5. Textbook-supplied tests and quizzes	(a) Allow for assessment of written expression. (b) Already prepared, save teachers' time. (c) Match the content and sequence of the textbook or curricular materials.	(a) Often do not assess complex skills or ability to use combinations of skills. (b) Often do not match the emphases and presentations in class. (c) Focus on cognitive sills. (d) Class period is often too short for a complete assessment.	(a) Be skeptical that the items were made by professionals and are of high quality. (b) Carefully edit or rewrite the item to match what you have taught.
6. Standardized achievement tests	(a) Assess a wide range of cognitive abilities and skills that cover a year's learning. (b) Assess content and skills common to many schools across the country. (c) Items developed and screened by professionals, resulting in only the best items being included. (d) Corroborate what teachers know about pupils; sometimes indicate unexpected results for specific students. (e) Provide norm-referenced information that permits evaluation of students' progress in relation to students nationwide. (f) Provide legitimate comparisons of a student's achievement in two or more curricular areas. (g) Provide growth scales so students' long-term educational development can be monitored. (h) Useful for curriculum evaluation.	(a) Focus exclusively on cognitive outcomes. (b) Often the emphasis on a particular test is different from the emphasis of a particular teacher. (c) Do not provide diagnostic information. (d) Results usually take too long to get back to teachers, so are not directly useful for instructional planning.	(a) Avoid narrowing your instruction to prepare students for these tests when administrators put pressure on teachers. (b) Do not use these tests to evaluate teachers. (c) Do not confuse the quality of the learning that did occur in the classroom with the results on standardized tests when interpreting them. (d) Educate parents about the tests, limited validity for assessing a student's learning potentials.

Interviews

In addition to portfolios, you may conduct *interviews with individual students*. Interviews can give you additional insights into students' thinking and learning difficulties. Interviews are more effective if you organize them around key concepts or specific problem-solving tasks. For example, you could work with the student to create a mental map of the relevant concepts in a unit and discuss with the student how he believes the concepts to be related to one another. You may also administer a simple questionnaire to your class to gain insight into the attitudes and values students associate with the concepts you are about to teach.

Summative assessment options

Summative assessment techniques are usually more formal than formative assessment techniques. Keep in mind, however, that formative and summative are not always distinct. For example, after you teach a unit, you may give a summative unit test. However, you may find students who have not achieved the learning targets. This will usually require you to reteach the students or provide remedial instruction. Because you have used the summative assessment to guide your teaching, it has provided formative assessment information.

For summative assessment, use the mixture of assessment options that *most directly assesses the intents* of the stated learning targets. Different assessment options are more valid for some purposes than for others. Because no single assessment method gives perfectly valid results, more than one method should be used to assess achievement of important learning targets. Table 5.2 shows six categories of summative assessment options. We discuss these in two groups: teacher-made techniques and external (extra-classroom) techniques.

Teacher-made assessments

We have already mentioned tests and quizzes. These paper-and-pencil assessments may include open-ended questions (such as essays and other constructed-response formats), multiple-choice, true-false, and matching exercises. Paper-and-pencil techniques are limited primarily to verbal expressions of knowledge. Students must read and respond to the assessment materials using some type of written response, ranging from simple marks and single words to complex and elaborated essays. Students' abilities to carry out actual experiments, to carry out library research, or to build a model, for example, are not assessed directly with paper-and-pencil techniques. Further, it is usually difficult for teachers to design paper-and-pencil tasks that require students to apply knowledge and skills from several areas to solve real-life or "authentic" problems.

Performance assessment techniques require students to physically carry out a complex, extended *process* (e.g., present an argument orally, play a musical piece, or climb a knotted rope) or produce an important *product* (e.g., write a poem, report on an experiment, or create a painting). Projects, extended written assignments, and laboratory exercises result in products. The performances you assess should (a) be very close to the ultimate learning targets, (b) require students to use combinations of many different abilities and skills, and (c) require students to perform under "realistic conditions" (especially requiring student self-pacing, self-motivation, and self-evaluation). Some performance assessments require paper-and-pencil as a medium for expression (e.g., writing a research paper or a short story), but the emphasis in these performances is on the complexity of the product, and students are allowed appropriate time limits. This distinguishes such performance assessments from the short answers, decontextualized math problems, or brief (one class period) essay tasks found on typical paper-and-pencil assessments.

Because some performance assessments very closely measure the ultimate learning targets of schooling, they may be used as instructional tools. For example, you may instruct a student on presenting arguments orally and require the student to perform the task several times over the course of the term. You might repeat the teaching-performance combination several times until the student has learned the technique to the degree of expertise appropriate to the student's level of educational development.

Principal disadvantages are that a great deal of time is required to create appropriate tasks, to prepare marking schemes or rating scales, to carry out the assessment itself, and to administer several tasks. For performance assessment, you need several tasks to make a valid interpretation of students' results. Seldom can you generalize a student's performance on one task to performance on another. That is, how well a student performs depends on the specific content and task to which the performance is linked (Baker, 1992; Linn, 1994). A student may write a good poem about the people in her neighborhood but an awful poem about the traffic in Los Angeles. How good is the student as a poet in such cases? Quality performance assessment requires a very clear vision of an important learning target and a high level of skill to translate that vision into appropriate tasks and grading criteria (Arter & Stiggins, 1992).

We discussed the growth and learning progress portfolio as a formative assessment tool. Portfolios may also be used for summative evaluation. The **best works portfolio** is a representative selection of a student's best products that provides evidence of the degree to which the student has achieved specified learning targets. In an art course it might be the student's best works in drawing, painting, sculpture, craftwork, and, perhaps, a medium chosen by the student. In mathematics it might include reports on mathematical investigations, examples of how the student applied mathematics to a real problem, writings about mathematics or mathematicians, and examples of how to use mathematics in social studies, English, and science. Best works portfolios focus on summative evaluation. To improve reliability of portfolio evaluations, use scoring rubrics. Share the rubrics with students and teach them how to select their best work in light of those rubrics.

External (extra-classroom) assessments

Teachers often use two other techniques. One is the quizzes and tests supplied by textbook publishers. These are convenient because you don't have to write them yourself, and they match the book you are using. However, they may not match local learning targets very well, focus on low-level thinking skills, and/or be poorly constructed. Review these assessment materials before using them, and improve them if necessary. Remove or add items to make a better match with your classroom learning targets. Edit items that do not have the properties good items should have (see the guidelines for different item types in Chapters 7 and 8).

Standardized achievement tests also provide summative assessment information. Unlike textbook tests, these materials are usually very well written and supported by research on the validity of the scores. The tests consist of a battery of subtests, each covering a different curriculum area. Because the same group of students (norm group) took all subtests, the publisher's norms allow you to compare a student's development in two or more curricular areas, and the publisher's score scales allow you to monitor a student's growth over time. Your own tests or your school district's tests cannot provide these types of information. A standardized test battery does not match your curriculum or your teaching goals exactly. Therefore, use it to assess broad goals (e.g., reading comprehension) rather than to grade students on your specific classroom learning targets.

Now that we have discussed various assessment options that are available, we turn to specifics of planning assessments for students.

Plan assessment directions, length, and difficulty

As you plan your assessments, it is important to also plan ways to make clear to students how and when they will be assessed and what they will be required to do. All students should understand the directions, the assessment tasks (e.g., your test questions), and the scoring rubrics (e.g., criteria for full marks).

Plan the length of your assessment considering three major factors: (a) the amount of time you have available for assessment, (b) the students' educational development, and (c) the level of reliability you want the results to have (longer assessments are more reliable than shorter assessments). Classroom assessments should be power assessments: Every student who has learned the material should have enough time to perform each task. Your experience with the subject matter and the students you teach will help you decide on how long to make the assessment.

As practical guidelines, use the time suggestions in Table 5.3 for students in junior and senior high school. In 40 minutes of assessment, for example, you can administer a test with a short essay and 15 to 20 complex multiple-choice items. Modify these time suggestions to suit your students as your experience deepens.

Remember, too, that students will be taking state-mandated and other standardized tests: These tests are typically 40 to 60 minutes in length, even for elementary students. Your classroom assessments should give students the opportunity to practice taking longer assessments. You do not want the mandated assessment to be the first long test students take each year. That wouldn't be fair to your students.

The tasks on your assessment should match the conditions stated in the learning targets. Altering the "givens" or conditions under which you expect the students to perform alters the complexity of a task. For example, consider the difference in

Table 5.3 Time requirements for certain assessment tasks.

Type of task	Approximate time per task (item)
True-false items	20–30 seconds
Multiple-choice (factual)	40–60 seconds
One-word fill-in	40–60 seconds
Multiple-choice (complex)	70–90 seconds
Matching (5 stems/6 choices)	2–4 minutes
Short-answer	2–4 minutes
Multiple-choice (w/calculations)	2–5 minutes
Word problems (simple arithmetic)	5–10 munutes
Short essays	15–20 minutes
Data analyses/graphing	15–25 minutes
Drawing models/labeling	20–30 minutes
Extended essays	35–50 minutes

complexity when students are and are not allowed to use calculators to solve mathematics word problems, or when translating a French passage from memory versus using a dictionary and idiom list.

Plan the difficulty level of your assessment, considering three things: (a) the complexity of the task, (b) the ability of the students responding to it, and (c) the nature (or quality) of instruction preceding the task administration. The combination of these three factors raises or lowers the percentage of students correctly completing a task. Also, when students perceive that an assessment task is too complicated or too difficult, they skip it. As a result, the percentage of students answering it correctly is lower.

Assume you are planning your assessment method, tasks, directions, length, and difficulty as suggested. What should you do if you create or identify a "great" task that does not match the stated learning target? You have only three choices: Disregard the task, modify the task so it matches the learning target, or modify the learning target so it matches the task. Often, creating an excellent assessment task helps further clarify a learning target. If this is the case, then modify the stated learning target so it more clearly expresses what you intend. Make sure to communicate this to students. Don't "surprise" them with a more complex or difficult task than the type for which they are preparing themselves.

Assessment planning for a marking period should be based on learning goals and outline the main instructional and assessment strategies you will use

You may plan for a year, a semester, a marking period, a unit, or a lesson. Plans for a year or a semester set out the general approaches and strategies you will use to teach and to assess. Such a plan contains an outline of the topics you will teach, the general learning targets your students will achieve, and the main strategies you will use to assess them.

Plans for a marking period usually apply to two or three units of instruction. A **marking period** is the number of weeks you must teach before you need to prepare a grade for each student's report card. In a typical academic year a marking period consists of nine weeks. A **unit of instruction** is a teaching sequence covering from one to seven weeks of lessons, depending on the students and topics you are teaching. You use plans for instructional units to break down and organize the larger curriculum into manageable teaching, learning, and assessment sequences. Planning for several units at one time allows for sequencing the units and for keeping your teaching and assessment approaches consistent. It also allows you to describe your plans for formative and summative assessment.

Plans for only one unit will be more detailed. Describe the specific content, concepts, procedures, terminology, and thinking skills your students will learn and use. Identify the learning targets for individual lessons. Describe your teaching activities and your students' learning activities. Identify the specific formative and summative assessments you will use and when you will use them.

The shortest term for planning is for one day or one lesson. As you teach, reflect on what you have previously taught and how well your students have achieved the unit's learning targets to date. This reflection is an opportunity for you to adjust your unit plan. Your teaching and assessment strategies become more fine-tuned, adapting to your students' abilities. Teaching and assessment plans are guidelines, subject to change as new information about your students' achievements accumulates.

Let's look at an example. Because this is an assessment book we emphasize the assessment aspects of planning, but you will also plan instructional activities. Suppose you are teaching middle school science. Suppose, further, that you are planning for a nine-week marking period. Perhaps you plan to teach two units: one on the water cycle and one on weather. For each unit you would outline the major points of content you will cover, the general sequence and timing of the units, and, most importantly, the learning targets your students will achieve from each unit. Your plan is beginning to take shape.

You will need to answer questions such as the following. What overall approach and teaching strategy will you adopt? The water cycle and weather units are related; how will you make that clear to students? What kinds of learning activities will you need to create and use (e.g., creating a demonstration of condensation, cloud simulation, building a diorama of the water cycle, drawing weather maps, measuring variables related to weather such as wind speed and precipitation, collecting and reading weather maps, or conducting a weather prediction activity)? How will you evaluate students' achievement of the learning targets? What are your general strategies for formative evaluation? When you use oral questioning, what levels of the taxonomy will you emphasize most? How will you build formative assessment opportunities into intermediate steps toward larger projects (plans, outlines, drafts, etc.)?

Perhaps you plan for some in-class activities and exercises that will allow you to evaluate how well students are progressing. These also allow you to give students appropriate feedback. Will students' peers evaluate performance? If so, students will need evaluation criteria and scoring rubrics. Perhaps you plan homework exercises. These allow you to evaluate whether students have mastered the basic concepts. Your

■ **EXAMPLE 5.1 A long-term plan for a marking period in which two elementary science units will be taught**

Unit 1. The Water Cycle

General learning target:	Understanding what the water cycle is, how it works, and how it helps living things. Ability to explain the water cycle and apply it to real life.
Time frame:	It will take 2 weeks to complete.
Formative assessment:	(a) Three homework assignments (taken from Chapter 8). (b) Condensation demonstrations (Group activity; I will ask students to explain what they are doing, how it relates to the water cycle, and how it relates to real life.) (c) Short quiz on the basic concepts at the end of Week 1
Summative assessment:	A written test at the end of the unit (short-answer and an essay)
Weights:	(a) Homework 10% (b) Quiz 10% (c) End-of-unit test 80%

Unit 2. Weather Systems and Predicting Weather

General learning target:	Understanding basic weather patterns, their movements, and their influence on local climate. Ability to understand weather maps, weather forecasts; ability to collect weather data and use them to make simple predictions.
Time frame:	It will take 7 weeks to complete.
Formative assessment:	(a) Seven homework assignments (taken from Chapter 8 and my own) (b) Seatwork on drawing a simple weather map with symbols (I will circulate among students and ask questions to check their understanding.) (c) Correct use of simple instruments to gather weather-related data (I will have each students demonstrate each instrument's use and give them feedback when necessary.) (d) Collection of weather maps and forecasts (I will discuss with students what the maps and forecasts mean and be sure they understand them.) (e) Four quizzes on the major concepts and a performance activity (Week 1, Week 3, Week 4, and Week 5)
Summative assessment:	(a) Map drawing (I will provide weather information; students will draw corresponding maps independently. This will be Quiz 4.) (b) End-of-unit test (short-answer, matching, map identification, essay question) (c) Independent investigation (Collect weather data for 2 weeks and make daily 2-day weather predictions. I will structure this activity. It will be done toward the end of the unit.)
Weights:	(a) Homework 10% (b) Quizzes 10% (c) Independent investigation 30% (d) Map drawing 20% (e) End-of-unit test 30%

Marking Period Grade

Unit 1 marks count 30%

Unit 2 marks count 70%

thinking should include planning for how often you assess. At what points in the lessons will homework or quizzes be appropriate, for example?

Plan to use the formative feedback to help students improve their learning. In order for formative feedback to be effective, you will probably have to teach your students how to use this feedback in their learning. You may also need to teach them how to review and evaluate their own work as they proceed through the lessons. Some strategies for doing this differ by subject. Others are more general (for example, students should get in the habit of asking themselves "Do I understand this?" as they work).

Plan your summative evaluation strategy also. Not all assessment options are equally valid for your specific learning targets. Think ahead, so that you can evaluate students on what you taught them and on the learning targets they should achieve. You might use a paper-and-pencil test at the end of each unit. You might use a project for one unit and a performance activity for another. For example, students may collect weather data and use them to predict the weather. For some other subjects, term papers, independent investigations, or portfolios might prove useful for summative evaluation.

Your plan must include the weighting of each component as part of a final grade: How much will the tests, homework, projects, and so forth count toward the grade? Will each count equally, or will some weigh more heavily than others? To be fair, you will need to explain the weighting to students in advance.

Example 5.1 shows an assessment plan that a hypothetical teacher created when teaching the two science units referred to in the preceding paragraphs. Your own plan may be handwritten, put into your teaching folder, and used as a working document as you teach. The main points are that by planning (a) you have decided ahead about when and how you will assess, (b) recorded this thinking so that you do not forget, and (c) followed a systematic plan to achieve your assessment goals.

Assessment planning for a unit of instruction should be based on learning goals and objectives and detail the instructional and assessment strategies you will use. Use a pretest to help plan your teaching

Designing an assessment plan for one unit is a bit more detailed. Lay out the lesson sequences, the learning targets, and the instructional activities. Choose the assessment methods you will use. Identify why you need to use each type, how the assessments are related to the lessons, and what actions you will take once you have information about the students' achievement.

Example 5.2 shows an example of an assessment plan for one of the science units in Example 5.1. It includes all the thinking a teacher might use when deciding what assessments to conduct. The important points are that you can explain when and why you are using different assessment methods, that you match the assessment methods with the learning target(s) for which they are appropriate, and that you can state what teaching action you will take once the information is gathered.

More Formative in Nature →

Assessment techniques	Description of assessment purpose, activity, and follow-up action (use)						
Pretest	About a week before beginning this unit, I will give a very brief pretest to get a sense of students' attitudes, experiences, knowledge, and belief about weather. (See Figure 6.4). *Action:* I will use this information to help me develop discussions in class, to develop lessons that overcome students' misconceptions and fears about the weather, and to build on what students already know.						
	Lesson 1 Comprehending basic weather concepts	**Lesson 2** Distinguishing weather patterns and systems	**Lesson 3** Identifying local weather conditions and patterns	**Lesson 4** Using basic tools for measuring weather	**Lesson 5** Understanding and making weather maps	**Lesson 6** Collecting and recording local weather data	**Lesson 7** Using data to predict local weather
Observation and oral questioning	In every lesson, I will observe students and ask questions during the lesson to assess how well they are responding to the material, how well they seem to understand the daily activities and assignments, and whether they have any misconceptions about the weather concepts we are studying. *Action:* I'll adjust my teaching if most of the class is having difficulty. If only a few are experiencing difficulty, I'll work with them individually, in small groups, or ask another student to teach the concept.						
Homework	I will assign homework after every lesson. Homework activities will focus on observing and discovering real-world examples of the weather concepts we learn in class. Students will record their observations and write explanations of them using proper scientific language learned in the unit. *Action:* As I read students' homework responses, I will note for each students how accurately and fluently the student uses scientific language to discuss the weather. I will also evaluate their observational and recording skills. I will reteach those materials for which many students experience difficulty. If only a few are having difficulty, I will work with them individually.						
Quizzes	**Quiz 1** (covers Lesson 1): Short-answer questions testing basic vocabulary *Action:* Students not mastering the basic concepts will be retaught.	**Quiz 2** (covers Lessons 2 and 3): Short-answer questions with some diagrams. Focuses on weather patterns: local, national, and international. *Action:* I will use this quiz to monitor students' understanding of weather patterns and systems. I'll reteach or move on, depending on the outcomes.		**Quiz 3** (covers Lesson 4): This will be a performance activity. I want to be sure each student can use with accuracy the weather-measuring tools and can record data property. *Action:* I will correct errors on the spot.	**Quiz 4** (covers Lesson 5): I want students to read, interpret, and draw simple weather maps. I will give weather data to the students and ask them to draw an appropriate map using the weather data. I will also give maps already drawn and ask students to interpret them. *Action:* I will reteach if there are problems.		
Independent Investigation (performance assessment)				**Predicting the Weather** (begins after Lesson 4, and includes Lessons 5 and 6): This performance assessment will help me evaluate whether students can apply the concepts from the lessons to the real world. It will help me evaluate whether they can synthesize and use criteria to evaluate the data they collect. Students will collect and measure weather data, record it, and use it to predict the local weather for 2 days in advance. They will repeat the exercise every day for at least 2 weeks. They will work independently. They will prepare a report describing what they did and evaluating their investigation and its accuracy. *Action:* This is a type of summative evaluation. I will use the exercise to help me decide how well the students have learned the concepts and principles in this unit. I should have a pretty good idea whether students can apply what they learned in class.			
End-of-unit test							**Unit Test** (covers all lessons): This will come at the end of all the lessons. It will be a paper-and-pencil test given in class. (I may give it over 2 days.) It will be comprehensive, covering most of the important learning targets in the unit.) *Action:* I will use the results of this test along with the results from homework, quizzes, drawing, and the independent investigation to assign a grade to the students for the unit. (Weights are given in Figure 6.2.)

← More Summative in Nature

In this example seven lessons are planned. Directly below each lesson is a brief statement of the lesson's main learning target. The various types or methods of assessment (pretest, observation, homework, quizzes, independent investigations, end-of-unit test) are listed in the leftmost column. Notice that as you go down the column, the purposes of assessment become more summative and the assessment procedure becomes more formal. The statements written in the body of the figure describe the purpose, procedure, and action to be taken for each assessment. These actions are steps the teacher will take to improve students' achievement based on the assessment results.

When the statements in this figure are spread across the page, that means that the assessment's purpose, procedure, and actions apply to all of the lessons. In the figure, observation, oral questioning, and homework are of this type. Statements that appear directly below one or two lessons mean that the assessment applies to only those one or two lessons. The quizzes, independent investigation, and end-of-unit test are of this type. Because the seven lessons are spread out in sequence over time, the plan shows that some assessments occur at different times throughout the unit.

Example 5.2 shows the teacher gave a pretest about a week before teaching this unit. She did not use the pretest results to grade students. She used them to help her understand the students' attitudes, knowledge, beliefs, and experiences about the weather so she could teach the unit better. The "pretest" does not need to be a formal test. You may, for example, have a class discussion about some of the topics that you will be teaching in an upcoming unit. From this discussion you can gauge how much the class already knows about the topics and what kinds of misconceptions they may have. Use this information to plan your teaching of the unit.

Often students' beliefs about a topic are contrary to what you will teach. If students do not believe what you are teaching, then they do not integrate new concepts into their existing ways of thinking, and they will be unable to apply that information in the future. For example, children know that wearing sweaters keeps them warm. When teaching a science unit on insulating properties, you may teach that air has insulating properties. If you ask children what happens to the temperature of a cold bottle of soft drink when you wrap it in a sweater, many may say it gets very warm. If you tell them it will stay cold, many will not believe you because they know sweaters keep them warm. Knowing this, your teaching will have to include activities that change students' beliefs by building on their prior experiences and knowledge. Your instruction will have to offer a real demonstration and comprehensive explanation—for example, why a sweater keeps the student warm *and* the soft drink cool—before that instruction can alter their beliefs.

A **preinstruction unit assessment framework** is a plan you use to help you to assess cognitive and affective learning targets of an upcoming unit. Preinstruction assessments should be relatively short, however, so focus your assessment on only a few core elements. Do a written assessment so you can easily summarize the information and use it to make your planning decisions. You could also organize a class discussion around the results.

It is especially helpful if you adopt a set framework and use it to generate assessment questions for every unit you teach. This establishes a comprehensive and consistent approach to gathering and using information. The framework in Example 5.3

■ **EXAMPLE 5.3 Framework for creating a written assessment of students' attitudes, knowledge, beliefs, and experiences about a topic**

Area assessed	Example question
1. Student's attitudes about the topic.	"I think meteorology is *boring, interesting*, etc."
2. Student's school experiences with the topics.	"Have you ever studied meteorology of the weather? When?"
3. Students' knowledge of an explanatory model centrally important in the unit.	"Explain what makes it rain. Include a diagram if you wish."
4. Students' awareness of common knowledge associated with the topic.	"Imagine you are a TV or radio weather announcer. Write a forecast for what the weather will be tomorrow."
5. Students' knowledge of technical terms associated with the topic.	"Describe what each of these instruments does or is used for: barometer, thermometer, and weather vane."
6. Students' personal experiences with some aspect of the topic.	"Describe your most unusual or scary experience involving weather."

Source: Adapted from "Instructional Assessments: Lever for Systematic Change in Science Education Classrooms," by B. Gong, R. Venezky, and D. Mioduser, 1992. *Journal of Science Education and Technology, 1*(13), pp. 164–165. With kind permission of Springer Science and Business Media and the author.

is useful to follow for several subject matters. It uses six categories of information. It was originally developed for middle school science.

Use a blueprint to plan individual summative assessments

Use a blueprint to develop a plan for one formal assessment instrument you will use to help assign grades to students (e.g., a unit test). The same kind of blueprint can be used more generally to plan for assessing performance learning targets with rubrics, or even for assessing a set of objectives with several assessments.

A **blueprint** describes both the content the assessment should cover and the performance expected of the student in relation to that content. Some authors call the blueprint a **table of specifications**. The blueprint serves as a basis for setting the number of assessment tasks and for ensuring that the assessment will have the desired emphasis and balance. Thus, the elements of a complete test plan include (a) content topics to assess, (b) types of thinking skills to assess, (c) specific learning targets to assess, and (d) emphasis (number of item or points) for each learning target to be assessed. Example 5.4 illustrates such a blueprint for a middle school science unit on cells. It is possible to create other useful but less complete specifications. See Appendix F for examples of alternate procedures for test blueprints.

The row headings along the left margin list the major topics the assessment will cover. You can use a more detailed outline if you wish. The column headings across the top list three major classifications of Bloom's *Taxonomy* of cognitive educational objectives. You may use one of the other taxonomies, described in more detail in Appendixes D and E, if you prefer. From left to right the types of performances

■ **EXAMPLE 5.4 Example of a blueprint for summative assessment of a middle school science unit**

Content Outline	Knowledge	Comprehension	Application	Total Points	%
Basic Parts of Cell	Name and tell function of nucleus, cytoplasm, cell membrane; Label parts of a cell on a line drawing *(12 points)*		Given photos of actual plant and animal cells, label the parts *(4 points)*	16	40
Plant vs. Animal Cells		Explain differences between plant and animal cells; describe cell walls and cell membrane *(4 points)*		4	10
Cell Membrane	Define diffusion; list substances diffused and not diffused by cell membrane *(6 points)*		Distinguish between diffusion and oxidation *(2 points)*	8	20
Division of Cells	Define division, chromosomes, and DNA *(4 points)*	Explain differences between plant and animal cell division *(4 points)*	Given the numbers of chromosomes in a cell before division, state the number in each cell after division *(4 points)*	12	30
Total Points	**22**	**8**	**10**	**40**	
%	**55**	**20**	**25**		**100**

implied by the column headings are increasingly complex. This blueprint only uses three levels of the taxonomy because there will be no questions on the test that require Analysis, Synthesis, or Evaluation. A project might be assigned to address one or more of these higher cognitive levels and combined with the test score in the final grade for the unit.

The body of the blueprint lists the specific learning targets. A content topic and a level of complexity of the taxonomic category thus doubly classify the learning targets. Points are allocated to each cell and totaled across rows and down columns. The totals will tell you what percent of the test score is dedicated to each content area and to each cognitive level.

A blueprint allows you to view the assessment as a whole and the overall distribution of points. You can use the blueprint to identify cells in which to write other objectives to assess. Usually, not all cells will be filled, but the overall distribution should match your intentions for student learning. Thus, you can maintain whatever

Guideline 5.1 A checklist for judging the quality of a plan for a summative unit assessment.

1. Does your plan clarity the purpose(s) of the assessment and what you expect it to tell you about each student?	Yes	No
2. Does your plan indicate the main subject-matter topics and performances you want to assess?	Yes	No
3. Will your plan help you to judge whether the assessment tasks match the major content topics and learning targets you have specified?	Yes	No
4. Have you clearly identified the elements of knowledge and performance that *all* students need to know?	Yes	No
5. Does your plan give the most important learning targets the heaviest weights in the total score? Are the least important learning targets given the least weight? (You may wish to give certain tasks more weight than others.)	Yes	No
6. Do you know what kind(s) of assessment tasks should be used to assess each content-thinking skill combination? Are these tasks the best ways to assess the combination?	Yes	No
7. Have you estimated the amount of time students need to complete this assessment? Is this estimated time realistic?	Yes	No
8. Have you estimated the amount of time you will need to evaluate the students' responses? (Consider how this time might be shortened, without reducing the validity of the results; by changing some of the tasks, rearranging tasks on a page, or using the capabilities of a microcomputer or other scoring device.)	Yes	No

Note: Revise your assessment plan if you answered no to one or more of the questions in the checklist.

Source: Adapted from *Teacher's Guide to Better Classroom Testing: A Judgmental Approach* (p. 26), by A. J. Nitko and T. C. Hsu, 1987. Pittsburgh, PA: Institute for Practice and Research in Education, School of Education, University of Pittsburgh. Adapted by permission of the authors.

balance or emphasis of content coverage and whatever complexity of performance you believe is necessary to match your teaching, and the assessment will neither be too easy nor too hard for your students. This helps assure the validity of your results. Plus, it simplifies the task of writing the test. It is easier to do that when a blueprint tells you exactly what kind of tasks and items you need.

Blueprints are useful instructional tools, especially with students in junior and senior high school. The blueprint is a concise way to explain what is important for students to learn. Share your assessment blueprints with your students. Ideally, you should do this sharing when you begin the unit. Review and discuss the blueprint thoroughly with the students to ensure that they (a) have no misunderstandings, (b) understand the unit's emphasis, (c) understand what they will be held accountable for performing, and (d) see how the summative assessment factors into their overall grades. Older students may offer suggestions for changing the emphasis or manner of assessment, thus more fully engaging in their own learning and evaluation. Students can write test questions for each blueprint cell. Use them for a practice test.

Guideline 5.1 is a checklist for judging the quality of your plan for a summative assessment, including the blueprint.

If you develop a blueprint for a few units each year, after a few years you will have blueprints for most of your units. As learning targets change, you can update these blueprints with less work than it took to develop them originally. If your content has remained essentially the same since the last time you taught the unit, your summative assessment instruments on the two occasions should be equivalent. **Equivalence** means that students past and present are required to know and perform tasks of similar complexity and difficulty to earn the same grade. Building this year's assessment instruments to last year's blueprints increases the likelihood the two will be equivalent. Even with different questions, both years' assessments should cover the same content and thinking skills with the same emphases. Equivalent instruments are fairer to students. Of course, if you changed the content or learning targets of the unit, the blueprints and the assessment should change, too.

Any modifications you have made to the items on the test, conditions of administration, or student response modes in order to accommodate students with disabilities must give you assessment information that is valid. For example, if you are using a modified set of learning objectives for a student, consistent with the IEP, then a modified blueprint should be used to assure the test reflects those learning objectives. If a student's IEP specifies that test items should be read to her, then (unless the test is a reading test) you should plan the logistics (the reader, a quiet location, etc.) to allow this to happen.

Conclusions

This chapter has been about how and why to plan assessments. Therefore, it has necessarily also been about learning targets, validity, and planning instruction, as well as using assessment options. The next several chapters describe in more detail how to prepare formative assessments, various kinds of tests, and performance assessments. Keep the big picture firmly in mind—especially the learning targets—as you drill down into the detail, both as you read this book and as you actually plan assessments for your classroom.

Exercises

1. The teacher in each of the situations below wants some information. For each situation, identify from the assessment options in Table 5.2 the technique most likely to be useful.
   a. At the beginning of a unit on the weather, the teacher wants to ascertain what students' former experiences with this topic have been.
   b. The teacher wants to find out why Janis is not doing her homework.
   c. At the end of a unit on weather, the teacher wants to find out how students understand the information about U.S. weather presented on the TV Weather Channel.
   d. Over the course of a year, the teacher wants to discover—and wants the students to realize, too—how much progress they have made in learning to solve math problems.
2. A teacher is teaching a unit on poetry. Two of her learning goals for the unit are: (1) The student will read and respond to poems from a variety of historical and cultural settings. (2) The student will explain the effects of common literary devices (e.g., symbolism, imagery, metaphor) in a variety of poems. Discuss the issues you would deal with in making the assessment plan for the unit.

Now go to our Companion Website at **www.prenhall.com/brookhart** to assess your understanding of chapter content with multiple-choice and essay questions. Broaden your knowledge of assessment with links to assessment related web sites.

6

Formative Assessment

KEY CONCEPTS

1. Formative assessment is a loop: Students and teachers focus on a learning target, evaluate current student work against the target, act to move the work closer to the target, and repeat.
2. Cognitive benefits of formative assessment include providing the information students need in order to improve and giving the student practice at "learning how to learn."
3. Motivational benefits of formative assessment include helping students feel in control of their own learning and supporting self-regulation.
4. A system of good assignments, formative feedback and self-assessment, summative assessments, and scoring criteria that all match the learning targets add up to support learning.
5. Formative assessment information for the teacher can come from talking with students, observing them working, or looking at the work itself.
6. Formative assessment information for the student comes mainly in the form of feedback. Good feedback is descriptive, specific, and contains information for improvement.
7. Record the results of formative assessments, look for patterns, and share your insights with students.

Ellen (a real teacher—only her name has been changed) is a Title I reading specialist in a rural elementary school with a high proportion of economically disadvantaged students. She wanted to become more aware of her own use of formative assessment. She began by experimenting simply with keeping records. During weekly reading assessments she began to make notes of students' progress. In her journal, she wrote that she tried to make her notes very specific (example: Student had trouble with /sh/ sound today), and took time to both reteach and also to make the students aware of what they needed to work on to become better readers.

Telling the students what she had noted about their reading worked so well to focus their efforts that she tried a next step. To involve the students with their progress, she filled out weekly progress cards for each student and sent them home for their parents to see. The progress card would have a reading strength and a reading goal on it. After she observed (in her journal, she wrote "caught," as in "catch them being good") the student working on a goal five times, she would give the student a new goal.

She found that third graders were very involved with the progress cards. They reminded her to tally when they worked towards their goal, and got excited when they met those goals. Her first-grade students responded better to the specific oral feedback that she gave them during the weekly assessments. This makes sense, because students had to read at least a little to use the progress cards.

An excerpt from her journal reads: "I have learned that my use of formative assessment can be a powerful tool to help my students make reading progress. I have also learned that if I want my instruction to be more effective that I need to keep notations of student progress. I need to review these notations on a consistent basis, and then make observations of my students with these thoughts in mind. And because formative assessment is done on an ongoing basis, I need to take notes regularly, not just on the days that I do my more formal assessments (a thought for next year)!"

Chapter 5 listed formative assessment options. Here we present more details. The reason formative assessment is so powerful is that it is the only strategy we know that packs a "one-two punch." As we can see in Ellen's class, formative assessment supports both the cognition and the motivation students need in order to learn. That is why we devote a whole chapter to it.

Formative assessment is a loop: Students and teachers focus on a learning target, evaluate current student work against the target, act to move the work closer to the target, and repeat

This three-step process is an oversimplification, but it is a useful pattern to keep in mind for teaching and assessment (Sadler, 1983, 1989). In fact, if you had to only learn one thing about teaching, you might choose this cycle. From a student's point of view, the cycle is:

- What am I aiming for?
- How close am I now?
- What else do I have to do to get there?

The best formative assessment is student-centered, but it starts with the teacher's vision. You are the one who "understands" the learning target at first, when the students don't. Your first task is to make the target clear to the student. Typically, writing your objective on the board is not enough. If the student knew what that meant, you wouldn't have to teach the lesson!

First, you have to have the learning target clear in your own mind. This is not always as straightforward as it sounds. We once did an evaluation of a professional development program to teach middle school teachers how to assess reading. The middle school teachers had all been trained as English teachers, and their main areas of study had been literature and writing. Of course they knew what "reading" was, but they didn't understand that target well enough to help the students who reached middle school needing basic reading instruction. Without a detailed understanding of the target themselves, what they did with poor readers in their classroom was just "make them read" more, and their assessments indicated the students were—surprise—poor readers. The professional development program divided reading targets into five areas: oral fluency, comprehension, strategy use, higher-order thinking, and motivation. The idea was that the program could then offer assessment techniques for each of the five areas. According to teachers' evaluation interviews, the single best thing the program gave them was not the assessment techniques, but a clearer definition of what it meant to be a good reader. Students began to improve as their teachers became better able to show them what they needed to work on (fluency, comprehension, and so on).

Second, you have to communicate the target to students in ways that they understand. Sometimes this will involve showing them instead of telling them. For example, silent reading works better in elementary classrooms in which the teacher models silent reading, shares the books she reads, and talks about why she liked them than in classrooms in which the teacher uses silent reading time to catch up on paperwork. During the course of learning, ownership of the learning target shifts. What began as the teacher's vision, or at least her responsibility, is transferred to the student's repertoire.

Third, the students have to buy in. If you have been successful at communicating the target, you will have also helped students see why it is important for them to expend effort to reach it. This can be because of interest ("this topic is cool!") or academic, for example, when students are convinced to learn to write term papers in high school so they can do what is required in college. It can be because students want to be able to do something you or other adults can do, or something their older peers can do. Sometimes several of these motivations occur at the same time. For any given learning target, there will be a mixture of motivations in your class. For example, one student may be interested in a particular topic and another simply convinced that it is an important school target.

To properly communicate a target, you also need to share the criteria for good work. Otherwise, you and the students have no way to evaluate how close their work comes to being "good." You can do this by sharing criteria, for example, giving students a copy of the scoring rubrics you will use to evaluate their final work. You can also show some examples of good work. Or, show some examples over a range of quality levels and let the students figure out what is "good" about the good work.

For some important assignments that you plan to use other years, ask some students if you can save a copy of their work to use in future classes. Most will be delighted. We know one teacher in Nebraska who saved "good example" copies of science notebooks each year to use with future students. She found that the quality level rose each year. Succeeding classes were able to grasp and meet, and then improve on, the standards of achievement shown in the notebooks.

Students can evaluate their own or peers' work against criteria you provide or criteria they deduce from examples, and provide feedback. Some research suggests that self-evaluation leads more directly to improvement than peer evaluation (Sadler & Good, 2006). You also should provide feedback, and we discuss particular ways to do that below.

Armed with appropriate feedback, students should have what they need to improve. For mastery learning targets, this is a more short-term and immediate process. (Practice today, find out what you need to work on, do better tomorrow.) For developmental learning targets like becoming a good writer, the process is longer. Students can take into account feedback on today's writing, but also on previous writing, when they write tomorrow.

Students should have the opportunity to evaluate their own learning. This is known as student **self-assessment**. Teach students effective self-assessment techniques; for many students, they don't come naturally.

Start with simple self-assessment techniques. When you offer opportunities for students to apply criteria to their own work in progress, show them how to take one criterion at a time, asking "Does this describe my work—why or why not?" Then show them how to rephrase the "why nots" as strategies for improvement. If a criterion says there should be details from a story to support a point, for example, and the details the student wrote about don't really pertain to the point, the improvement strategy becomes "Add more details from the story that support this point." Sounds obvious—but it isn't obvious to some students. Other simple self-assessment techniques include having students discuss their work with peers or having them reflect on their work after its completion before turning it in.

During an evaluation project in a school district in Pennsylvania, we had the opportunity to look at reflection sheets elementary students wrote to include in portfolios. Even the first graders did this. There were two first-grade teachers. One saw her students had just filled in blanks on the reflection sheet; for example, writing "Adding 5s" in the blank after "What did you learn?" because that was the title of the assignment sheet. She asked her students follow-up questions to stimulate further thinking (questions like "What did you learn to do when you add 5s?") and gradually got more reflective answers (like "You get 5 or 0 in the ones place" or "I learned I [already] know it"). The other first-grade teacher just passed out the reflection sheets like worksheets, because the evaluation required it. Most of her students stayed in the "copying" phase. The difference between these classes was very apparent to those of us who got to see both.

Cognitive benefits of formative assessment include providing the information students need in order to improve and giving the student practice at "learning how to learn"

The effects of good formative assessment on achievement can be as much as 0.4 to 0.7 standard deviations—the equivalent of moving from the 50th percentile to the 65th or 75th percentile on a standardized test (Black & Wiliam, 1998). These effects exist at all levels—primary, intermediate, and secondary—and are especially noticeable among lower achievers. There are many reasons for these effects.

- Formative assessment helps teachers and students identify what students can do with help and what they can do independently.
- Participating in formative assessment is active learning, keeping students on task and focused on learning goals.

- Formative assessment, especially peer- and self-evaluation, help students with the social construction of knowledge.
- Formative assessment allows students to receive feedback on precisely the points they need in order to improve. It shows them what to do next to get better.

The latter reason is probably the most important.

Motivational benefits of formative assessment include helping students feel in control of their own learning and supporting self-regulation

Motivational benefits of formative assessment are a little more complicated. Different students respond differently to the various aspects of the formative assessment process.

Student self-assessment fosters both motivation and achievement. Students who can size up their work, figure out how close they are to their goal, and plan what they need to do to improve are, in fact, learning as they do that. Carrying out their plans for improvement not only makes their work better, but it helps them feel in control, and that is motivating. This process, called self-regulation, has been found to be a characteristic of successful, motivated learners.

Regulation of learning can be internal, as when a student uses self-assessment information to improve, or external, as when student uses teacher feedback to improve. Either can support learning. Ideally, the internal and external work together.

Some students will need instruction about how to use feedback and especially about how to do self-assessment. Some may at first claim that feedback is solely "the teacher's job." Once students learn that information from both teacher feedback and their own self-assessment helps them improve, research suggests that they will process material more deeply, persist longer, and try harder. They will become more self-regulated learners (Butler & Winne, 1995).

The effects of feedback depend not only on the information itself, but also on the characteristics of the people who send (teacher) and receive (student) the message. Whether students hear feedback as informational or controlling depends in part on them. One student may hear a helpful, clear description of how to improve a paper with gratitude, while another may hear the same feedback as just another confirmation of how stupid he is. Covington (1992) wrote that while no two children come to school with equal academic abilities and backgrounds, there is no reason that they should not all have access to equally motivational feedback. He called this "motivational equity."

There is some evidence that good students use all information, including graded work, formatively (Brookhart, 2001). This is not the case for students who experience negative feelings after failure. These feelings get in the way of processing additional information about their learning. For them, the value of feedback is lost, overshadowed by the low grade. For unsuccessful and unmotivated students, deal with negative feelings first, before providing other formative assessment information, in order to break the cycle of failure (Turner, Thorpe, & Meyer, 1998). For these students, formative feedback should begin with statements of accomplishment and suggest small, doable steps for improvement. And even such careful efforts don't always work, as the following true story shows.

Kasim was a poster child for the cycle of failure. Fifteen and in my seventh-grade English class, he never completed any assignment. He would write a line or two of an exercise or assignment, and then simply stop. Most of his teachers—including myself, I'm ashamed to admit—worked on getting him to "behave" first and learn second, so the class was not disrupted for the other students. Kasim lived in a foster home, had been abused as a child, and had the scars to prove it.

One day, in response to a brief writing assignment, Kasim brought me a three-page story, printed in tiny, cramped letters. It was an autobiographical story about how he had been separated from his sister, did not know where she was, and missed her terribly. It had a strong voice, expressive vocabulary, and readable (if not perfect) mechanics. I was excited. He could write! (I really hadn't been too sure about that.) More than that, he had wanted to write. However, perhaps I got too excited. Or maybe it wasn't me, but for whatever reason, when I tried to encourage him and talk about his story, he appeared embarrassed to have written it and shut down. That was the first and last complete piece he ever did in a whole year.

Kasim would be a grown man now. When I think of him, I hope he's alive, I hope he's not in jail, and I hope he has found his sister. I'm not sure what could have broken his failure cycle or changed his negative attitude toward school. If I had it to do all over again, especially knowing what I know now about students like Kasim, I would have done things differently. I would have given him short assignments with more opportunities for peer and teacher feedback, and given him a whole lot more choice. Kasim's life was full of circumstances beyond his control, and with hindsight that included my class.

All students, from those enmeshed in a cycle of failure to self-regulated learners, have a better chance of achieving if their learning experience as a whole makes sense to them. Clear learning targets keep what students will perceive as "your class"—which includes what you say and what you ask them to do—coherent. The next section shows you how this works.

Good assignments, formative feedback and self-assessment, summative assessments, and scoring criteria that all match the learning targets add up to support learning

Learning targets are the hub that connects

- assignments (which in embodying the learning targets serve to communicate them to students and to afford practice on them),
- teacher formative feedback and student self-assessment (which apprises the student of where he stands in relation to the learning targets and what he should do next),

- summative assessment (which evaluates the results of student efforts against the learning targets), and
- scoring criteria (which express the results of assessment in a symbol system designed to describe quality levels on the learning targets).

In Chapters 2 and 5, we discussed the importance of assessments and scoring criteria matching learning targets, in both content and cognitive level, as a validity issue. The same principle of alignment holds for any classroom assignment. Students will interpret what you ask them to "do" (their assignments) as what you want them to learn. Thus, all assignments, not just assessments, must embody the learning targets.

So, for example, if the learning target is for students to write descriptive paragraphs, the assignments should include practice writing descriptive paragraphs. Formative feedback on these should be based on your criteria for "good" descriptive paragraphs. Students should have the opportunity to use the feedback. Finally, they write a descriptive paragraph that is graded according to those same criteria.

Formative assessments give you information about how long to "form" and when to "sum." When students' work gets close to the learning target, they are ready to demonstrate achievement on summative assessment. Students whose formative assessments show they don't need more practice, when classmates still do, can do enrichment work related to the learning target or use their time for some other work.

Example 6.1 presents some examples of formative assessment. We present this with a big caution statement. Whether an assessment is "formative" depends on what you or the students do with the information from it. Any assessment can be used formatively, and doing something you call a "formative assessment" without using the information to improve learning isn't formative at all.

Perhaps the most powerful general formative assessment strategy is simply to get in the habit of asking students to give reasons for all their answers ("Why do you say that?"), whether correct or incorrect, and getting students in the habit of articulating what they know and where they think they're stuck.

Formative assessment information for the teacher can come from talking with students, observing them working, or looking at the work itself

Students and teachers should routinely share information about the quality of student work. Formative assessment activities typically allow an exchange of information by focusing on criteria for good work for a particular target. Conversations and observations can be just as important a source of information as finished work. For example, if you observe a student having trouble working at her desk, you know there is some problem. If you ask her where she is stuck, she may be able to give you enough information about her thinking that you can help her move along.

Type of Learning Target	Formative Assessment(s)	Use of Results
Learning targets involving concepts	Students reflect on previous learning, attitude, and interest	Extending class discussion Selecting appropriate and interesting class activities Identifying and correcting misconceptions Building on previous knowledge (using no more review than is necessary)
Writing (e.g., descriptive, narrative, persuasive, or expository paragraph)	Peer editing Self-assessment and teacher conference	Revising Future writing Reflecting on why the revision is better than the first draft
Learning math tables, spelling words, and other "facts"	Students predict what study strategies (e.g., flash cards) will work best for them, and keep track of what works for them quiz by quiz Students record what they "know" and "don't," gradually moving the "don'ts" into the "know" category as they progress	Students adjust own study strategies Students see exactly what they know and don't, and have control over moving their own knowledge
Science or social studies content from textbooks	Students summarize reading in their own words, meet with a peer, and discuss how their summaries are alike/different Students make lists of vocabulary or concepts they feel they understand and those they find difficult	Extending class discussion Focus studying for unit test
Learning targets involving seatwork	Students have a "teacher alert" on their desks, turned to the happy face or the green light when they're understanding and the sad face or red light when they need teacher help	Individual assistance in a "just-in-time" fashion, focused on the student-perceived source of difficulty
Learning targets involving classwork	Instead of questioning individual students, all students "vote" their answer so you can scan the class for understanding Younger children can answer yes/no questions as a group by standing ("Stand up if you think that a soda wrapped in a sweater will get warm") Older students can use answer cards for multiple-choice questions, or use electronic answer pads, or write one-minute responses on 3 × 5 cards	Adjust pacing of class instruction Adjust content of class instruction Extending class discussion Identifying and correcting misconceptions Building on previous knowledge (using no more review than is necessary) Understanding where all or most of the class is, not just a few students who have been called on
Learning targets involving projects or assignments graded with rubrics	Students look at examples of previous students' work across a range of quality levels and discuss what makes the work of that quality Students "translate" the rubrics into their own words to make them "kid-friendly" evaluation tools Peer assessment of drafts or partial products Self-assessment and teacher conference	Improved understanding of the qualities of good work Revising and finishing the project or assignment Reflecting on the qualities of one's own work for use in future work
Learning targets involving skills (e.g., reading aloud, using the library or computer, writing)	Students set and record a goal and work toward it Teacher suggests a goal, shares with student Observe students in the process of working (e.g., using a microscope) as well as the finished assignment	Student either realizes goal (and sets another) or can state how far she/he has come and what still needs work Adjust instruction at the individual or group level, as needed

Note: These are examples. Your use of formative assessment should start with, and use results for, your own learning targets. You will think of many more formative assessment methods.

Many formative assessment activities involve putting student or teacher observations on paper where they are easy to see and then discuss. For example, some teachers routinely use reflections sheets. Or, some have students indicate by red light/green light or happy/sad faces on their work whether they are certain or uncertain about their understanding. It is easier to see and interpret a red light than to try to guess from students' expressions that they don't understand.

Formative assessment is not used for grading. Students need—and deserve—an opportunity to learn before they are graded on how well they have learned. Formative assessment is used before instruction, to find out where students are, and during instruction, to find out how they are progressing. The assessment is informational, not judgmental. Students are free to pay attention to figuring out how they are doing and what they need to work on without worrying about a grade.

Make formative assessment a part of your teaching. Plan your instruction in ways that provide opportunities for individual students to make formative decisions about their own learning. For example, provide self-assessment opportunities in your lesson plans. You also make formative decisions about the group's learning needs and provide group feedback. For example, you may return an assignment on which a large number of students demonstrated a misconception, and use the opportunity to reteach the material.

Teach students how to compare their performance with the learning target. Most students will not automatically reflect on their own work in the manner that you intend. For example, if you ask a student, "What did you learn?" without providing any guidance on what to do, many will copy the title of the assignment: "I learned two-digit subtraction" or "I learned how a bill becomes a law." Remember the first graders in our evaluation project.

Rubrics with clear performance level descriptions are helpful in this process. Even with good rubrics, however, students need instruction and practice in comparing their own work with the description in the rubric. Students can work together to compare their work to the learning targets. Teachers should provide a "safe" atmosphere for this, where criticism is seen as constructive and part of the learning process. That is an important lesson in itself.

There are some developmental differences in student use of self-evaluation. Younger children may focus on neatness and other surface characteristics of work when they first do self-evaluation (Higgins, Harris, & Kuehn, 1994). With instruction and practice, children can learn to focus on the learning target (Ross, Rolheiser, & Hogaboam-Gray, 2002).

Your professional knowledge is important, too. Experience or study will teach you the common misconceptions your students are likely to have along the way as they learn a particular concept. Knowing these, you will be able to more meaningfully evaluate performance levels and suggest next steps.

Narrowing the gap between the student's performance and the learning goal may not be a smooth process. Depending on the scope of the learning goal, there may be additional rounds of the formative assessment process for the same goal. For example, students may write a series of essays in high school, each one benefiting from preceding teacher feedback and self-evaluations. No matter the scope of the accomplishment, students should be able to see their work getting closer to the goal, and should understand what specific feedback insights and learning strategies they used helped them close the gap. This is an empowering cycle.

Formative assessment information for the student comes mainly in the form of feedback. Good feedback is descriptive, specific, and contains information for improvement

The type of feedback you give should match the purpose you have for giving it. We illustrate different types of feedback here, so you will be better able to control the kind of feedback you give.

Feedback can vary according to the *kind of comparison* it makes.

- *Norm-referenced* feedback compares performance to other students. ("Your paragraph was the best in the class.")
- *Criterion-referenced* feedback compares performance to a standard and describes what students can or cannot do. ("You are particularly good at using a variety of descriptive adjectives.")
- *Self-referenced* feedback compares a student's performance to his own past performance, or sometimes to expected performance. ("This paragraph is better than the last one you wrote.")

The best formative feedback for practice work is criterion-referenced or self-referenced feedback. For students whose beliefs about their own capabilities are low, use self-referenced feedback to show them how they are improving.

Feedback can vary according to whether it describes *results* or *processes* underlying results.

- **Outcome feedback** is knowledge of results. ("You got a B on that paper.")
- **Cognitive feedback** describes the connections between aspects of the task and the student's achievement. ("It doesn't seem like you used the study guide very much.")

Cognitive feedback helps the student know what to do to improve. Outcome feedback only supports improvement if the student can internally generate the cognitive feedback (Butler & Winne, 1995). For example, a student may get back a paragraph where the teacher marked three comma faults and conclude on his own, "I should study comma use." However, many students need the scaffolding provided when the teacher explicitly provides cognitive feedback. Suggest a short-term learning goal (what to aim for next), and suggest specific strategies the student can use to get there.

Feedback can vary according to its *functional significance* (Ryan, Connell, & Deci, 1985).

- **Descriptive feedback** gives information about the work. ("I like the way you developed your main character.")
- **Evaluative feedback** passes judgment on the work. ("A" or "Good job!")

Descriptive feedback is more useful for formative assessment than evaluative feedback, because it has the potential to give students information they can use to improve. Check that the feedback you give students not only *is* descriptive, but that the descriptions are statements of how the work relates to criteria you have shared with students.

Verbal feedback, whether oral or written, also varies in other ways that any verbal communication can vary.

- Feedback varies in *clarity*. Students have to clearly understand what your feedback means if it is to be useful to them.

- Feedback varies in *specificity*. General statements are usually less helpful for improvement than specific descriptions and suggestions.

- Feedback varies in *person*. First-person ("I" statements) feedback works for some formative feedback (e.g., "I don't understand what you mean here."). Third-person statements can help you describe the work, not the student (e.g., "This paragraph doesn't have supporting details" is better than "You didn't use supporting details."). Avoid the second person. "You" did this or that comes out sounding like finger-wagging.

- Feedback varies in *tone*. Keep the tone supportive. We know, for example, of one teacher who wrote, "You think like a chicken!" That's not helpful.

Not all students will hear feedback in the way you intend. For example, some students who have low self-efficacy or who are fearful may hear feedback you intended to be descriptive as evaluative. They may simply hear in your description a judgment that their work is "no good." Observe how students hear and respond to your feedback and what they do as a result.

Tunstall and Gipps (1994) developed a typology of teacher feedback from their research in primary schools. Figure 6.1 presents the achievement portion of the typology (they also noted that some feedback is for socialization). Generally, more descriptive feedback is better for formative assessment. If the description only affirms what is good, however, it may not help students improve in the future. A good plan for written feedback on a student's paper is to describe a couple of positive aspects of the work and one aspect that needs improvement.

Figure 6.2 presents a "Dogs and Cats" essay, written by a fourth grader, in response to this assignment: "Do dogs or cats make better pets? Choose one and give three reasons. Write a paragraph that has a topic sentence, three supporting details, and a concluding sentence." Example 6.2 shows potential feedback, any one or several of which might be used, and identifies its type. Notice that, in general, the most helpful type of feedback seems to be "constructing the way forward." However, without knowing the classroom context, we can't say for sure which of the other comments might be helpful, too. For example, the comment about spelling might be seen as trivial—or it could be helpful and right on target for a student who had been working hard on spelling.

Figure 6.1 Typology of Teacher Feedback

	Type A	Type B	Type C	Type D	
1 **Positive feedback**	**Rewarding**	**Approving**	**Specifying attainment**	**Constructing achievement**	**1** **Achievement feedback**
	Rewards	Positive personal expression	Specific acknowledgement of attainment	Mutual articulation of achievement	
		Warm expression of feeling	Use of criteria in relation to work behavior; teacher models	Additional use of emerging criteria; child role in presentation	
		General praise	More specific praise	Praise integral to description	
		Positive nonverbal feedback			
2 **Negative feedback**	**Punishing**	**Disapproving**	**Specifying improvement**	**Constructing the way forward**	**2** **Improvement feedback**
	Punishments	Negative personal expression	Correction of errors	Mutual critical appraisal	
		Reprimands; negative generalizations	More practice given; training in self-checking	Provision of strategies	
		Negative nonverbal feedback			
	Evaluative		Descriptive		

Source: Adapted from "Teacher Feedback to Young Children in Formative Assessment: A Typology," by Pat Tunstall and Caroline Gipps, 1996, *British Educational Research Journal, 22*, p. 394. Used by permission of the publisher, Taylor & Francis Ltd: http://www.tandf.co.uk/journals.

Figure 6.2 Fourth-Grade "Dogs vs. Cats" Essay

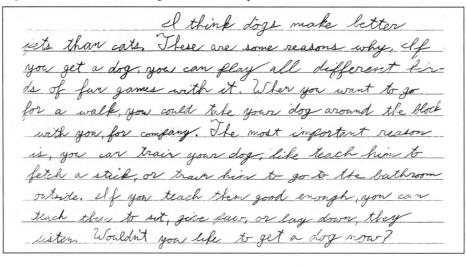

I think dogs make better pets than cats. These are some reasons why. If you get a dog, you can play all different kinds of fun games with it. When you want to go for a walk, you could take your dog around the block with you, for company. The most important reason is, you can train your dog, like teach him to fetch a stick, or train him to go to the bathroom outside. If you teach them good enough, you can teach them to sit, give paw, or lay down, they listen. Wouldn't you like to get a dog now?

■ **EXAMPLE 6.2 Different kinds of feedback teachers might give to the student who wrote the "Dogs vs. Cats" essay in Figure 6.2**

Feedback (written or oral)	Type	Comments
A—Great job.	Evaluative, Positive, Approving	These give outcome feedback (knowledge of results). This information would only be formative if the student figures out the reasons for the results himself.
C—You can do better.	Evaluative, Negative, Disapproving	
Your topic sentence and concluding sentence are clear and go together well.	Descriptive, Positive, Specifying attainment	These comments affirm and describe achievement in terms of the criteria for the assignment. They communicate to students that you noticed these specific features and tied them to the criteria for good work. You might use a couple of these in combination with the constructive criticism below.
I like the way you have used complicated sentences to describe your reasons.	Descriptive, Positive, Specifying attainment	
Nice use of details. For example, I count five different things you can train a dog to do.	Descriptive, Positive, Specifying attainment	
Your reasons are all about dogs. Readers would already have to know what cats are like. They wouldn't know from your paragraph whether you can walk or train or play with a cat. When you "compare and contrast," make sure you talk about both of the things you are comparing.	Descriptive, Negative, Constructing the way forward	This is potentially the most constructive feedback in the table. It criticizes a specific feature of the work, explains the reason for the criticism, and suggests what to do about it.
Don't divide one-syllable words like "kind."	Descriptive, Negative, Specifying improvement	These descriptive comments affirm or critique achievement in terms of general criteria that are not specific to the learning target for the assignment. Their value would depend on how syllabication, format, or spelling, respectively, have figured in to the developmental learning targets in the classroom in which they are used.
Use bigger margins.	Descriptive, Negative, Specifying improvement	
Every word is spelled correctly!	Descriptive, Positive, Specifying attainment	
What does "give paw" mean?	Descriptive, Could be positive or negative depending on context	Depending on the tone (of voice, or in written comments), this comment could communicate either criticism or curiosity.

Record the results of formative assessments, look for patterns, and share your insights with students

Keep records of the important results of formative assessment, not for grading, but to keep yourself organized. For example, you should know what sort of feedback you have given, over time, to a student on a particular skill (e.g., writing). You can design your own class, individual, or group record-keeping sheets for specific purposes. You may wish to use a computer spreadsheet or database program.

Keeping records will help ensure that you are systematic and have an opportunity to observe all students on all the behaviors or skills you have decided are important. You will be able to see for which students you have observed which target behaviors or skills, and make a point to observe the rest of them. Also, making notes will result in more complete and organized information than if you relied on your memory. Use patterns of observations to decide what each student needs, or what the group needs. If no natural opportunity to observe a skill presents itself, you may have to create one.

How many observations you want to see before you identify a pattern or draw conclusions will vary. For example, a kindergarten teacher might want to make sure she observes each child holding a pencil correctly at least five different times. Or a high school biology teacher might want to observe each student preparing a slide correctly at least twice.

Conclusions

Formative assessment loops assessment information back into the learning process itself. This chapter has described good formative assessment as based on learning goals and highlighted the importance of appropriate teacher feedback and student self-assessment. Helping teachers develop effective formative assessment skills is the most effective, and cost-effective, strategy for raising student achievement known today (Wiliam & Leahy, in press). We have explained this in terms of its "one-two punch," namely, that formative assessment addresses student cognitive and motivational needs at the same time.

Exercises

1. For each of the following assessment activities, identify at least one formative use for the information the teacher will get from it. You may use Example 6.1 to help you.
   a. Students set a "help" button on their desk to let the teacher know they're having trouble during math practice.
   b. Students get together in pairs to read and critique each others' reports on a planet.
   c. Students write new vocabulary words on flash cards and use a recipe box to file words into three categories: "know cold," "know most of the time," and "don't know."
   d. At the end of each social studies class, students write "one question I still have" on a 3×5 card and turn it in as their "ticket" out of class.

2. Using the typology in Figure 6.1, identify the kind of feedback in each of the examples below.
   a. "I never want to see such sloppy work again!"
   b. "Use a capital A for Anne's name."
   c. "It was so wonderful to read your insightful description of Captain Ahab; I feel you really understand his motives."
   d. "All your spelling words were correct, so you get an extra 5 minutes at the computer."

Now go to our Companion Website at **www.prenhall.com/brookhart** to assess your understanding of chapter content with multiple-choice and essay questions. Broaden your knowledge of assessment with links to assessment related web sites.

Companion
Website

7

Completion and Selected Response Test Items

1. Align assessments to the content and performance requirements of your learning targets.
2. Short-answer items require a word, short phrase, number, or symbol response.
3. A true-false item consists of a statement or a proposition that a student must judge and mark as either true or false.
4. A multiple-choice item consists of one or more introductory sentences followed by a list of two or more suggested responses. The student must choose the correct answer.
5. Introductory materials (readings, graphs, tables, and maps) used in context-dependent item sets can help assess higher order thinking.
6. A matching exercise presents a student with three things: (1) directions for matching, (2) a list of premises, and (3) a list of responses.

I have done a lot of surveys, of one kind or another, for research or evaluation. What I have learned is—if you want your questions answered, make them multiple choice if you can. Most people will give much more complete answers if all they have to do is choose one. If you write open-ended questions and give them space to write, many will write a couple sentences (or even a couple sentence fragments) and let it go at that. If most adults tend to be like that, what do you think children in K–12 classrooms will do?

Of course, you should ask students to write their own answers to questions where knowing that they can articulate an answer is important. When you ask students to write, it should be clear to students why it's important to write—and the reason should have to do with what they are supposed to have learned. For checking understanding, simple application, and problem solving, selected response items are a way to get more information "out" of the kids' heads more efficiently for both the teacher who gives the assessment and the kids who take it. And if they're anything like the people I've surveyed, they'll even prefer it some of the time.

Align assessments to the content and performance requirements of your learning targets

Assessments should follow three fundamental principles. First, match each assessment task with the content and performance levels for important learning targets. Second, create each assessment task to elicit from students *only* the knowledge and performance that are relevant to those learning targets. Finally, assessment tasks should make the connection clearly and unambiguously so students can demonstrate their levels of attainment of the learning targets.

For example, suppose a learning target is that students will be able to interpret imagery in short poems. An assessment that asks them to interpret a poem already discussed in class doesn't match—that's about short-term memory of class discussion. An assessment that asks students to interpret imagery in a narrative passage doesn't match, either. An assessment that asks students to interpret the imagery and presents a new poem does match.

Review and revise the first drafts of all your assessment tasks, applying these principles. Make sure each item is clearly and accurately worded and taps only the learning target. If clues and other item flaws slip through, your items will tap test-wiseness or other skills irrelevant to the learning target you are trying to measure. Editing assessment tasks is an important step in the assessment development process.

In this chapter we will discuss short-answer, true-false, multiple-choice, and matching items.

Short-answer items require a word, short phrase, number, or symbol response

There are three types of **short-answer items**: question, completion, and association (Odell, 1928; Wesman, 1971). The **question variety** asks a direct question and the students give short answers.

> ■ **Examples of the question variety of short-answer item**
>
> 1. What is the capital city of Pennsylvania?   (Harrisburg)
> 2. How many microns make up one millimeter?   (1000)

The **completion variety** presents a student with an incomplete sentence and requires the student to add one or more words to complete it.

> ■ **Examples of the completion variety of short-answer item**
>
> 1. The capital city of Pennsylvania is   (Harrisburg)
> 2. $4 + (6 \div 2) =$ (7)

The **association variety** consists of a list of terms or a picture for which students have to recall numbers, labels, symbols, or other terms. This type of question is also called the *identification* variety.

■ **Example of the association variety of short-answer item**

On the blank next to the name of each chemical element, write the symbol used for it.

Element	Symbol
Barium	_(Ba)_
Calcium	_(Ca)_
Chlorine	_(Cl)_
Potassium	_(K)_
Zinc	_(Zn)_

Short-answer items can assess students' recall and comprehension of information. The short-answer format also can be used to assess higher level abilities (Linn & Miller, 2005), such as solving simple problems, interpreting basic data, or applying rules (e.g., counting the number of syllables in a word).

Example 7.1 lists examples of strategies that you may adapt to write short-answer items for some of your learning targets.

Short-answer items are relatively easy to construct and can be scored more or less objectively. However, short-answer items are not completely free of subjectivity in scoring. You cannot anticipate all possible responses students will make. For example, to the question, "What is the name of the author of Alice in Wonderland?" students may respond Carroll Lewis, Louis Carroll, Charles Dodgson, Lutwidge Dodgson, or Lewis Carroll Dodgson. Which, if any, should be considered correct? These judgment calls slow down the scoring process and tend to lower the reliability of the obtained scores.

An advantage of the short-answer format is that it lowers the probability of getting the answer correct by random guessing. Short-answer items do not prevent students from attempting to guess the answer—they only lower the probability of the students guessing correctly. In principle, guessing can be distinguished from using one's partial knowledge to help formulate an answer. Partial knowledge is not likely to result in the (exact) correct answer in short-answer items. Teachers, however, often give **partial credit** for responses judged to be partially correct. This is an appropriate practice and can result in more reliable scores *if* you use a **scoring key** that shows the kinds of answers eligible for partial credit. Using such a scoring key makes your assignment of partial credit more consistent from student to student, improving reliability.

To create short-answer items, follow the guidelines in the left column of Guideline 7.1. Use this as a checklist to review items before you put them on your test. A no answer to any one question is sufficient reason for you to omit an item from tests until you correct the flaw.

A true-false item consists of a statement or a proposition that a student must judge and mark as either true or false

There are at least six varieties of **true-false item**: true-false, yes-no, right-wrong, correction, multiple true-false, and yes-no with explanation. The true-false variety presents a **proposition** that a student judges true or false.

■ **EXAMPLE 7.1 Examples of short-answer items assessing different types of lower order thinking skills**

	Examples of generic questions*	Examples of actual questions
Knowledge of terminology	What is a ____? What does ____ mean? Define the meaning of ____?	What is a *geode*?
Knowledge of specific facts	Who did ____? When did ____? Why did ____ happen? Name the causes of ____.	What is the title of the person who heads the executive branch of government?
Knowledge of conventions	What are ____ usually called? Where are ____ usually found? What is the proper way to ____? Who usually ____?	What are magnetic poles usually named?
Knowledge of trends and sequences	In what order does ____ happen? Name the stages in ____. After ____, what happens next? Over the last ____ years, what has happened to ____? List the causes of the ____.	Write the life cycle stages of the moth in their correct order. 1st ____ 2nd ____ 3rd ____ 4th ____
Knowledge of classifications and categories	To what group do ____ belong? In what category would you classify ____? Which ____ does not belong with the others? List the advantages and disadvantages of ____.	Mars, Earth, Jupiter, and Venus are all ____
Knowledge of criteria*	By what criteria would you judge ____? What standards should ____ meet? How do you know if ____ is of high quality?	What is the main criterion against which an organization such as Greenpeace would judge the voting record of a congressional representative?
Knowledge of methods, principles, techniques	How do you test for ____ When ____ increases, what happens to ____ What should you do to ____ to get the ____ effect?	Today the sun's rays are more oblique to Centerville than they were 4 months ago. How does Centerville's temperature today compare with its temperature 4 months ago?
Comprehension	Write ____ in your own words. Explain ____ in your own words. Draw a simple diagram to show ____	What do these two lines from Shakespeare's Sonnet XV mean? "When I consider everything that grows, Holds in perfection but a little moment. . . ."
Simple interpretations	Identify the ____ in the ____ How many ____ are shown below? Label ____ What is the ____ in ____	In the blank, write the adjective in each phrase below *Phrase* 1. A beautiful girl ____ 2. A mouse is a small rodent ____ 3. John found the muddy river ____
Solving numerical problems	(Problem statement or figures to calculate would be placed here.) Use the data above to find the ____	Draw a graph to show John's activities between 2:00 p.m. and 2:45 p.m. • John left home at 2:00 p.m. • John ran from 2:00 p.m. to 2:15 p.m. • John walked from 2:15 p.m. to 2:30 p.m. • John sat from 2:30 p.m. to 2:45 p.m.
Manipulating symbols, equations	Balance these equations. Derive the formula for ____ Show that ____ equals ____ Factor the expressions below.	Balance this equation ____ Cu + ____ H_2SO_4 = ____ $CuSO_4$ + ____ H_2O + SO_2

*The "blanks" in the generic items are for you to fill in. The generic items are simply suggestions to get you started. You generate your own items suitable for testing your students. Your items must match your learning targets to be valid.

Guideline 7.1 Guidelines for writing short-answer items

Guideline—Your short-answer item should	Negative Example—Poor Item	Good Example—Revised Item
Assess an important aspect of the unit's instructional targets.	We can't give examples without knowing your learning targets and your test blueprint. However, these are basic validity criteria. Evaluate every test item using these two criteria.	
Match your assessment plan in terms of performance, emphasis, and number of points.		
Be written in question format if possible.	The author of _____ Alice in Wonderland was _____. *Because this is not written in a question format, many correct answers are possible, including "a story writer," "a mathematician," "an Englishman," and "buried in 1898."*	What is the pen name of the author of (Lewis Carroll) *Alice in Wonderland?*
Have an answer that is a brief phrase, single word, or single number.	Where is Pittsburgh, Pennsylvania located? _____ *Several answers are possible: "Western Pennsylvania," "southwestern corner of Pennsylvania," "Ohio River," "Monongahela and Allegheny Rivers," and so on are all correct. If you want to focus on the rivers, use the first rephrased version. To focus on the city, use the second rephrased version.*	Pittsburgh, Pennsylvania is located at the confluence of what two rivers? (Allegheny and Monongahela) Or. What city is located at the confluence of the Allegheny and Monongahela rivers? (Pittsburgh, PA)
Have the blank toward the end of the sentence.	_____ is the name of the capital city of Illinois. *The student has to mentally rearrange the item as a question before responding.*	The name of the capital city of Illinois is (Springfield)
Avoid textbook wording.	In general the more common punctuation marks—periods, question marks, commas, semicolons, and so on—indicate intonation and degrees of (interruption) that would occur if the material was read aloud. *When you copy material, you encourage students' rote memorization rather than their comprehension and understanding.*	The main function of common punctuation marks is to control the flow of (reading) .
Omit an important (not a trivial) word.	The name of the capital (city) of Illinois is Springfield.	The name of the capital city of Illinois is (Springfield) .
Have only one or two blanks.	_____ and _____ are two examples of _____. *Who knows? Many things would fit here.*	Iambic and anapestic are two examples of (meter) .
Have blanks the same length, and in the same format, as all items.	*For example, the items in the "good examples" column of this table are all in the same format.*	
Have directions for students on the amount of precision you want in the answer, if appropriate.	If each letter to be mailed weighs 1 1/8 oz., how much will 10 letters weigh?	If each letter to be mailed weighs 1 1/8 oz., how much (to the nearest whole oz.) will 10 letters weigh? (11 oz.)
Avoid grammatical or other clues.	A specialist in urban planning is called an (urbanist) .	A specialist in city planning is called a(n) (urbanist) .

Sources: Based on guidelines in Nitko & Brookhart, 2007.

■ Example of a true-false item

The sum of all the angles in any four-sided closed figure equals   T   F
360 degrees.

The **yes-no** variety asks a direct question, to which a student answers yes or no.

■ Example of a yes-no item

Is it possible for a presidential candidate to become president of   Yes   No
the United States without obtaining a majority of the votes cast
on election day?

The **right-wrong** variety presents a computation, equation, or language sentence that the student judges as correct or incorrect (right or wrong).

■ Examples of right-wrong items

Example assessing an arithmetic principle

$5 + 3 \times 2 = 16$ R   W

Example assessing grammatical correctness

Did she know whom it was?   C   I

The **correction** variety requires a student to judge a proposition, as does the true-false variety, but the student is also required to correct any false statement to make it true.

■ Example of a correction item

Read each statement below and decide if it is correct or incorrect. If it is incorrect, change the <u>underlined word</u> or phrase to make the statement correct.
The new student, <u>who</u> we met today, came from Greece.   C   I

The **multiple true-false** variety looks similar to a multiple-choice item. However, instead of selecting one option as correct, the student treats every option as a separate true-false statement. (More than one choice may be true.) Each choice is scored as a separate item. Multiple true-false items are a somewhat neglected but very useful format (Haladyna, Downing, & Rodriguez, 2002).

■ Example of a multiple true-false item

Under the Bill of Rights, freedom of the press means that newspapers:

1. have the right to print anything they wish without restrictions.   T   F
2. can be stopped from printing criticisms of the government.   T   F
3. have the right to attend any meeting of the executive branch of
   the federal government.   T   F

One advantage of true-false items is the fact that some subject matter readily lends itself to verbal propositions that can be judged true or false. True-false items are relatively easy to write, are easily scored, are objective, and cover a wide range of content quickly. Criticisms of true-false items are especially true of *poorly constructed* true-false items. True-false items frequently assess trivia, can be ambiguously worded, have a 50% chance (random guessing) score, and can encourage students to study and accept only oversimplified statements of truth and factual details.

True-false items *can* assess more than simple recall. Well-written true-false items can assess a student's ability to identify the correctness or appropriateness of a variety of meaningful propositions. Examples are shown in Example 7.2. Adapt these strategies to assess some of your intended learning targets.

To write good true-false items, you must be able to identify propositions that (a) represent important ideas, (b) can be defended by competent critics as true or false, and (c) are not obviously correct to persons with general knowledge or good common sense who have not studied the subject (Ebel & Frisbie, 1991). These propositions are then used as starting points to derive true-false items.

Frisbie and Becker (1990) offer these additional suggestions for getting started:

■ Create pairs of items, one true and one false, related to the same idea, and use one from each pair. If all you can do to write a false statement is to insert "not" into your true one, the true statement isn't good, either.

■ If your statement asks students to make evaluative judgments ("The best ... is ...," "The most important ... is ...," etc.), try to rephrase it as a comparative statement ("Compared to ..., A is better than ...").

■ Write false statements that reflect the actual misconceptions held by students who have not achieved the learning targets.

■ You may wish to convert a multiple-choice item into two or more true-false items.

Guideline 7.2 summarizes principles for improving the quality of true-false items. Use the guidelines to review true-false items that come with your textbook and curriculum materials or to write your own.

A multiple-choice item consists of one or more introductory sentences followed by a list of two or more suggested responses. The student must choose the correct answer

There are many types of multiple-choice items. Teachers usually find the correct-answer, best answer, incomplete-statement, and negative varieties of **multiple-choice** item (Example 7.3) most useful.

Multiple-choice items consist of a stem, alternatives, and distractors. The **stem** is the part of the item that asks the question, sets the task a student must perform, or states the problem a student must solve. You write the stem so that a student understands what task to perform or what question to answer. Teachers call the list of suggested responses by various names: **alternatives**, **responses**, and **options**. The

■ **EXAMPLE 7.2 Types of statements that could form the basis for your true-false items**

Type of statement	Examples of introductory words or phrases	Examples of true-false items
Generalization	All . . . Most . . . Many . . .	All adverbs modify verbs. (F).
Comparative	The difference between . . . is . . . Both . . . and . . . require . . .	Both dependent and independent clauses contain subjects and verbs. (T)
Conditional	If . . . (then) . . . When . . .	When there is no coordinating conjunction between two independent clauses, they should be separated by a colon. (F)
Relational	The larger . . . The higher . . . The lower . . . Making . . . us likely to . . . Increasing . . . tends to . . . How much . . . depends on . . .	The amount of technical vocabulary you should include in an essay depends on your intended audience. (T)
Explanatory	The main reason for . . . The purpose of . . . One of the actors that adversely affect . . . Since . . . Although . . .	One of the factors affecting changes in rules governing English grammar and style is changes in how people use the language. (T)
Exemplary	An example of . . . One instance of . . .	The movie title *The Man Who Came to Dinner* contains a nonrestrictive clause. (F)
Evidential	Studies of . . . reveal . . .	Studies of contemporary literature show that some authors deliberately violate style and usage rules to create literary effects. (T)
Predictive	One could expect . . . Increasing . . . would result in . . .	Increasing the number of clauses in sentences usually increases the reading difficulty of a passage. (T)
Procedural	To find . . . one must . . . In order to . . . one must . . . One method of . . . is to . . . One essential step . . . is to . . . Use . . . of . . . The first step toward . . .	The first step toward composing a good essay is to write a rough draft. (F)
Computational	(Item includes numerical data and requires computation or estimation.)	There are two adjectives in the sentence "The quick brown fox jumped over the lazy dog." (F)
Evaluative	A good . . . It is better to . . . than . . . The best . . . is . . . The maximum . . . is . . . The easiest method of . . . is to . . . It is easy to demonstrate that . . . It is difficult to . . . It is possible to . . . It is reasonable to . . . It is necessary to . . . in order to . . . The major drawback to . . . is . . .	It is generally better to express complex ideas as two or more shorter sentences rather than one longer sentence. (T)

Note: To be valid, the items must match specific learning targets.

Source: Adapted from *Essentials of Educational Measurement* by R. L. Ebel, 1991 & D. A. Frisbie, Upper Saddle River, NJ: Prentice Hall. Adapted by permission of the copyright holder.

Guideline 7.2 Guidelines for writing true-false items

Guideline—Your true-false item should	Negative Example—Poor Item	Good Example—Revised Item
Assess an important aspect of the unit's instructional targets.	*We can't give examples without knowing your learning targets and your test blueprint. However, these are basic validity criteria. Evaluate every test item using these two criteria.*	
Match your assessment plan in terms of performance, emphasis, and number of points.		
Assess important ideas (not trivia or common sense).	George Washington had wooden teeth.　　T　F	George Washington actively participated in the Constitutional Convention.　　T　F
Be definitely true or definitely false.	The US national debt is around 8 trillion dollars.　　T　F	The US national debt in 2006 was between 8.2 and 8.4 trillion dollars.　　T　F
Avoid textbook wording.	A scarab is an ancient Egyptian seal or amulet made of stone or faience in the shape of a dung beetle; associated with the sun's regenerative powers, scarabs were often buried with the dead.　　T　F	A scarab is a likeness of a dung beetle.　　T　F
Be about the same length as other items, whether true or false.	*Teachers tend to make true statements more qualified and wordy than false statements. Test-wise students can pick up on this irrelevant clue and get the item right without achieving the learning target.*	
Avoid a repetitive pattern of answers.	TFTF …, or TTFFTT …, or TFFTFF …	FFTFTFFFT…
Avoid verbal clues.	Dome A in the Antarctic Plateau is always the coldest place on earth.　　T　F	Dome A in the Antarctic Plateau is thought to be the coldest place on earth.　　T　F
State the source of the opinion, if your item presents an opinion.	Beethoven was the most important composer In the 19th century.	According to your textbook, Beethoven was the most important composer in the 19th century.　　T　F
		This referencing reduces ambiguity in two ways: (a) it makes clear that the statement is not to be judged in general, but rather in terms of the specific source; and (b) it makes clear that you are not asking for the student's personal opinion.
Focus on only one important idea or on one relationship between ideas.	The Monongahela River flows north to join the Allegheny River at Columbus, where they form the Ohio River.　　T　F	The Monongahela River and the Allegheny River join to form the Ohio River.　　T　F
	A student may respond with the correct answer, F, for an appropriate reason: The student may think (erroneously) that the Monongahela River does not flow north, may be unaware that the confluence of the rivers is at Pittsburgh, or may not know anything about the three rivers. Thus, the student would get the item right without having the knowledge that getting the item right without having the knowledge that getting the item right implies.	

Sources: Based on guidelines in Nitko & Brookhart, 2007.

137

■ EXAMPLE 7.3 Varieties of multiple-choice items

A. *The correct-answer variety*

Who invented the sewing machine?

  A. Fulton

*B. Howe

  C. Singer

  D. White

  E. Whitney

B. *The best-answer variety*

What was the basic purpose of the Marshall Plan?

  A. military defended western Europe

*B. reestablish business and industry in western Europe

  C. settle United States' differences with Russia

  D. directly help the hungry and homeless in Europe

C. *The multiple-response variety*

What factors are principally responsible for the clotting of blood?

  A. contact of blood with a foreign substance

*B. contact of blood with injured tissue

  C. oxidation of hemoglobin

  D. presence of unchanged prothrombin

D. *The incomplete-statement variety*

Millions of dollars of corn, oats, wheat, and rye are destroyed annually in the United States by

  A. mildews.

  B. molds.

  C. rusts.

*D. smuts.

E. *The negative variety*

Which of these is NOT true of viruses?

  A. Viruses live only in plants and animals.

  B. Viruses reproduce themselves.

*C. Viruses are composed of very large living cells.

  D. Viruses can cause diseases.

F. *The substitution variety*

Passage to be read

Surely the forces of education should be fully utilized to acquaint youth with the real nature of the dangers to democracy, <u>for</u> no other place

1

offers <u>as good or better opportunities than</u> the

2

school for a <u>rational</u> consideration of the prob-

3

lems involved.

Items to be answered

1. *A. for

  B. For

  C. for

  D. no punctuation needed

2. A. As good or better opportunities than

  B. as good opportunities or better than

  C. as good opportunities as or better than

*D. better opportunities than

3. *A. rational

  B. radical

  C. reasonable

  D. realistic

G. *The incomplete-alternative variety*[a]

An apple that has a sharp, pungent, but not disagreeably sour or bitter, taste is said to be (4)

  A. p

  B. q

*C. t

  D. v

  E. w

H. *The combined response variety*

In what order should these sentences be written in order to make a coherent paragraph?

a. A sharp distinction must be drawn between table manners and sporting manners.

b. This kind of handling of a spoon at the table, however, is likely to produce nothing more than an angry protest against squirting grapefruit juice about.

c. Thus, for example, a fly ball caught by an outfielder in baseball or a completed pass in football is a subject for applause.

d. Similarly, the dexterous handling of a spoon in golf to release a ball from a sand trap may win a championship match.

e. But a biscuit or a muffin tossed and caught at table produces scorn and reproach.

  A. a, b, c, d, e

*B. a, c, e, d, b

  C. a, e, c, d, b

  D. b, e, d, c, a

[a] The numeral in parentheses indicates the number of letters in the correct answer (which in this case is "tart"). Using this number rules out borderline correct answers.

alternatives should always be arranged in a meaningful way (logically, numerically, alphabetically, etc.).

The alternative that is the correct or best answer to the question or problem you pose is called the keyed answer, keyed alternative, or simply the **key**. The remaining incorrect alternatives are called **distractors** or **foils**. The purpose is to present plausible (but incorrect) answers to the question or solutions to the problem in the stem. These foils should be plausible only to students who do not have the level of knowledge or understanding required by your learning target.

Advantages of multiple-choice items include the following.

- The multiple-choice format can be used to assess a greater variety of learning targets than other formats of response-choice items.

- Multiple-choice items do not require students to write out and elaborate their answers and thus minimize the opportunity for less knowledgeable students to "bluff" or "dress-up" their answers (Wood, 1977).

- Multiple-choice tests focus on reading and thinking.

- Students have less chance to guess the correct answer to a multiple-choice item than to a true-false item or to a poorly constructed matching exercise. The probability of a student blindly guessing the correct answer to a three-alternative item is 1/3; to a four-alternative item it is 1/4; and so on.

- The distractor a student chooses may give you diagnostic insight into difficulties the student is experiencing.

- If your students will be administered a standardized achievement test (either by your school district or by the state), it will be to their advantage to have experience answering multiple-choice items.

Wood (1977) has summarized several criticisms of multiple-choice tests.

- Students do not have the opportunity to create or express their own ideas or solutions.

- Poorly written multiple-choice items can be superficial or trivial. Further, if you use multiple-choice tests that do not use items linked to realistic interpretive materials, tests may not assess whether students can use what they have learned in a meaningful and authentic context.

- Bright students may detect flaws in multiple-choice items due to ambiguities of wording, divergent viewpoints, or additional knowledge of the subject, and be penalized for choosing the wrong answer on that basis.

- The problems students solve on multiple-choice items tend to be very structured and closed (having one correct answer). This gives the impression that all problems in a subject area have a single correct answer, which may encourage students to place too much faith in an authority figure's correctness or may misrepresent a subject area as having a fixed and limited knowledge base.

- Exclusive use of multiple-choice testing for important or high-stakes assessments may shape education in undesirable ways. If a high-stakes assessment's multiple-choice items focus on factual knowledge, teachers tend to use drill-and-practice techniques to prepare students for it.

Another advantage of multiple-choice items is that you can construct a test item for students at various difficulty levels. Consider the following items:

■ **Example of varying the difficulty level of an item**

1. In what year did the United States enter World War I?
   - A.   1776
   - B.   1812
   - *C.   1917
   - D.   1981

2. In what year did the United States enter World War I?
   - A.   1901
   - *B.   1917
   - C.   1941
   - D.   1950

3. In what year did the United States enter World War I?
   - A.   1913
   - B.   1915
   - C.   1916
   - *D.   1917

All three items ask the same question, but the specificity of knowledge that is required to answer that question increases from Item 1 to Item 3. In this example, you can easily see how the *alternatives operate to make the item easy or difficult.* The alternatives require the students to make finer distinctions among the dates. Although in our example we use numbers, similarity also applies to alternatives that use words. Some research supports the idea that similarity among the alternatives increases the difficulty of an item (Green, 1984). Of course, manipulating the alternatives is not the only way to create more difficult items.

You will craft useful multiple-choice items if you learn how to do five things: (a) focus items to assess specific learning targets; (b) prepare the stem as a question or problem to be solved; (c) write a concise, correct alternative; (d) write distractors that are plausible; and (e) edit the item to remove irrelevant clues to the correct answer. Guideline 7.3 presents guidelines and examples for writing multiple-choice items.

Introductory materials (readings, graphs, tables, and maps) used in context-dependent item sets can help assess higher order thinking

To assess higher-order thinking, you may need to add information to present students with information to think about. You may wish to assess a learning target, for example, that requires students to apply their knowledge to a situation described in a paragraph. Assessment strategies for problem solving and critical thinking require presenting students with novel material. One way to do that is in **context-dependent item sets.** These consist of introductory material followed by several items for which introductory material is necessary to answer the questions.

Guideline 7.3 Guidelines for writing multiple-choice items

Guideline—Your multiple-choice item should	Negative Example—Poor Item	Good Example—Revised Item
Assess an important aspect of the unit's instructional targets.	*We can't give examples without knowing your learning targets and your test blueprint. However, these are basic validity criteria. Evaluate every test item using these two criteria.*	
Match your assessment plan in terms of performance, emphasis, and number of points.		
Ask a direct question or set a specific problem.	W. E. B. DuBois *A Actively pressed for complete political participation and full rights for African Americans. B Taught that the immediate need was for African Americans to raise their economic status by learning trades and crafts. C Emphasized helping African Americans through the National Urban League. D Founded the Association for the Study of Negro Life and History.	Which of the following comes closest to expressing W. E. B. DuBois's ideas about priorities of activities of African Americans during the early 20th century? A African Americans should first improve their economic condition before becoming fully involved in politics. B African Americans should postpone the fight for equal access to higher education until their majority acquire salable trade skills. C African Americans should withdraw from white society to form a separate state in which they have complete political and economic control. *D African Americans should become active, seeking out complete citizenship and full political participation immediately.
Put the alternatives at the end.	Before the Civil War, the South's _____ was one of the major reasons manufacturing developed more slowly than it did in the North. *A emphasis on staple-crop production B lack of suitable supply of raw materials C short supply of personnel capable of operating the necessary machinery	Before the Civil War, why did manufacturing develop more slowly in the South than in the North? *A The South emphasized staple-crop production. B The South lacked a suitable supply of raw materials. C The South had a short supply of people capable of operating the necessary machinery.
Put repeated words in the stem.	Which of the following is the best definition of *seismograph?* A an apparatus for measuring sound waves B an apparatus for measuring heat waves *C an apparatus for measuring earthquake waves D an apparatus for measuring ocean waves	What type of waves does a *seismograph* measure? *A earthquake waves B heat waves C ocean waves D sound waves
Place the word in the stem and definitions in the alternatives, if testing definitions.	The increase in length per unit of length of a metal rod for each degree rise in temperature (Centigrade) is known as the *A coefficient of linear expansion of the metal. B elasticity of the metal. C specific heat of the metal. D surface tension of the metal.	What is the *coefficient of linear expansion* of a metal rod? A the increase in length of the rod when its temperature is raised 1°C *B the increase in length when the temperature is raised 1°C divided by the total length of the rod at its original temperature C the ratio of its length at 100 to its length at 0°C D the rise in temperature (degrees Centigrade) which is necessary to cause the length of the rod to expand 1 percent

Guideline—Your multiple-choice item should	Negative Example—Poor Item	Good Example—Revised Item

Avoid "cluing" and "linking" (where the correct answer of one item depends on another item).	*Preceding item*
	1. The perimeter of a rectangle is 350 centimeters. The length of the rectangle is 3 centimeters longer than the width. What is the width?
	
	  A 18.7 cm. C 89.0 cm.
	  *B 86.0 cm. D 116.7 cm.
	
	Subsequent item: Linked to Item 1
	2. What is the area of the rectangle described in Question 1?
	
	  A 1050 sq. cm. *C 7654 sq. cm.
	  B 7396 sq. cm. D 8188 sq. cm.
		Better subsequent item: Independent of Item 1
		2. The width of a rectangle is 4 centimeters and the length is 3 centimeters. What is the area?
		
		    A 9 sq. cm.
		   *B 12 sq. cm.
		    C 16 sq. cm.
		    D 17 sq. cm.
		
		A mistake in Item 1 would not now guarantee the student would get Item 2 wrong also.

Avoid textbook wording.	A scarab is an ancient Egyptian seal or amulet made of stone or faience in the shape of a dung beetle and is associated with the
	
	   A moon.
	   B stars.
	  *C sun.
		With what force of nature did the ancient Egyptians associate the scarab?
		
		   A Moon
		   B Stars
		  *C Sun

Use simple vocabulary and sentence structure.	Given the present day utilization of the automobile in urban settings, which of the following represents an important contribution of Garrett A. Morgan's genius?
	
	  A automobile safety belts
	  B crosswalk markers
	  *C traffic lights
	  D vulcanized rubber tires
		Which of the following did Garrett A. Morgan invent?
		
		  A automobile safety belts
		  B crosswalk markers
		  *C traffic lights
		  D vulcanized rubber tires

Use consistent, correct punctuation and grammar relative to the stem.	Green plants may lose their color when
	
	  A are forming flowers.
	  *B grown in the dark.
	  C are placed in strong light.
	  D temperature drops.
		When may green plants lose their color?
		
		  A when they form flowers
		  *B when they are grown in the dark
		  C when they are placed in strong light
		  D when the surrounding temperatures drop

Avoid phrasing the item so the student's personal opinion is an option.	Which of the following men contributed most toward the improvement of the self-confidence of African Americans?
	
	  A W. E. B. DuBois C Booker T. Washington
	  B Eugene K. Jones D Carter G. Woodson
		Use an essay or paper assignment. Ask students to select a person and argue the importance of his contributions.

Guideline	Poor example	Better example
Arrange alternatives in a logical order.	In what year was the Magna Carta signed? *A 1215 B 1220 C 1205	In what year was the Magna Carta signed? A 1205 *B 1215 C 1220
Have distractors that would be plausible to nonknowledgeable students.	What is the official state bird of Pennsylvania? A mountain laurel B Philadelphia *C ruffed grouse D Susquehanna River	What is the official state bird of Pennsylvania? A goldfinch B robin *C ruffed grouse D wild turkey
Have homogenous alternatives.		
Have distractors based on common errors or misconceptions if possible.	$310 - 189 =$ A 89 *B 121 C 200	$310 - 189 =$ *A 121 B 210 C 230
Have 3 to 5 functional alternatives. Three is enough (Rodriguez, 2005) unless there is a compelling reason to have 4 or 5 (for example, a set of choices that represents common errors).	Which president of the United States was elected to four terms? A Abraham Lincoln B Theodore Roosevelt *C Franklin D. Roosevelt D Mickey Mouse	Which president of the United States was elected to four terms? A Abraham Lincoln B Theodore Roosevelt *C Franklin D. Roosevelt
Have one correct or best answer.	A *linear function* is *A completely determined if we know two points. B completely determined if we know one point. C unrelated to the point-slope formula. D related to the y intercept.	In which of the following situations would it be possible to write the *equation for a linear function?* *A We know the line passes through the points (3,5) and (4,6). B We know the slope is 1. C We know the y intercept is (0,2).
Avoid "all of the above" and use "none of the above" sparingly.	*Never use "none of the above" with the best-answer variety of multiple-choice items. The very nature of a best-answer question requires that all of the options are to some degree incorrect, but one of them is "best." It seems illogical to require students to choose "none" under these conditions. It does make sense to use "none of the above" with some correct-answer questions. In areas such as arithmetic, certain English mechanics, spelling, and the like, a single, completely correct answer can be definitely established and defended. Some assessment experts recommend using "none of the above" only when students are more likely to solve a problem first before looking at the options, as opposed to searching through the distractors before proceeding with the solution to the problem.*	

Source: Adapted from *Teacher's Guide to Better Classroom Testing: A Judgmental Approach* (p. 35), by A. J. Nitko & T-C Hsu, 1987, Pittsburgh, PA: Institute for Practice and Research in Education, School of Education, University of Pittsburgh. Adapted by permission of the copyright holders.

Context-dependent item sets are sometimes called **interpretive exercises**. The introductory material may be extracts from reading materials, pictures, graphs, drawings, paragraphs, poems, formulas, tables of numbers, lists of words or symbols, specimens, maps, films, sound recordings, and so on.

Item 1 of Example 7.4 requires a student to read the table and locate the information in a cell and to compare several values read from the table to determine which is largest. Item 2 requires a student to make an inference concerning the likelihood of an event based on understanding the trends and facts presented.

A context-dependent item set has these advantages: (a) it provides an opportunity to assess students on materials that are relatively close to the real-world contexts; (b) it provides, through the introductory material, the same context for all students; (c) its introductory material lessens the burden of memorizing and may moderate the effects of prior experience with the specific content; and (d) frequently it is the only means to test certain intellectual abilities.

Some disadvantages of a context-dependent item set are (a) the set may be difficult to construct, (b) you must carefully create the introductory material to assess higher-order thinking skills, (c) a student's performance on one context-dependent item set may not generalize well to performance on another similar set, (d) the set often requires students to use additional abilities (such as reading comprehension and writing skills) that may go beyond the major focus of the assessment tasks, and (e) you may need special facilities (such as copying machines and/or drawing skill and equipment) to produce them that may not be available.

■ **EXAMPLE 7.4 Examples of items written to assess graph and table reading skills**

Use the table below to answer Questions 1 and 2

	Average Temperature and Rainfall at Windy Hill Town							
	2000		2001		2002		2003	
	Temp	Rain	Temp	Rain	Temp	Rain	Temp	Rain
September	64°	0.1 in	63°	0.2 in	66°	0.0 in	64°	0.3 in
October	72°	0.4 in	71°	0.5 in	74°	0.4 in	71°	0.6 in
November	77°	0.9 in	75°	1.0 in	78°	0.8 in	76°	0.7 in
December	81°	2.0 in	80°	2.7 in	85°	1.5 in	80°	2.1 in

Example of assessing the ability to locate and compare information from a table

1. When did the highest average rainfall occur?
   - A. November of 2000
   - B. November of 2001
   - *C. December of 2001
   - D. December of 2003

Example of assessing the ability to draw inferences based on trends and other information in a table

2. Which of the following events is most likely to have occurred between September and December of 2002?
   - A. The roads were covered with ice and snow.
   - *B. The town's water reserves were very low.
   - C. The river flowing through the town overflowed its banks.

You may have to rewrite or modify reference materials before they are suitable for use in assessment, because (a) they contain material irrelevant or extraneous to assessing the objective at hand, (b) they are too long, or (c) the extract is out of context and is therefore not clear to students. You may need to obtain written permission to reproduce copyrighted materials. You may, of course, use entire volumes or take students to the library for the assessment. To do so, you will need sufficient materials (or computers) for all students, as well as sufficient uninterrupted time to administer this type of performance assessment.

A matching exercise presents a student with three things: (1) directions for matching, (2) a list of premises, and (3) a list of responses

In a matching exercise, the student's task is to match each **premise** with one of the **responses**, using as a basis for matching the criteria described in the directions. Example 7.5 shows a **matching exercise** with its various parts labeled.

Study the example. Premises are listed in the left column and responses in the right column. Each premise is numbered because each is a separately scorable item. You can

■ **EXAMPLE 7.5 Example of a matching exercise.**

Directions: In the left column below are descriptions of some late 19th century American painters. For each description, choose the name of the person being described from the right column, and place the letter identifying it on the line preceding the number of the description. Each name in the right column may be used once, more than once, or not at all.

Instructions for matching

Item numbers

Premises

Description of painter	Name of the painter
(e) 1 A society portraitist, who emphasized depicting a subject's social position rather than a clear-cut characterization of the subject.	a. Mary Cassatt b. Thomas Eakins c. John LaFarge d. Winslow Homer e. John Singer Sargent f. James A.M. Whistler
(d) 2 A realistic painter of nature; especially known for paintings of the sea.	
(b) 3 A realistic painter of people, who depicted strong characterizations and powerful, unposed form of the subject.	
(a) 4 An impressionist in the style of Degas, who often painted mother and child themes.	

Responses

create matching exercises with more responses than premises, more premises than responses, or an equal number of each. When there is an equal number of premise statements and response statements, this is called **perfect matching**. Most assessment specialists consider perfect matching to be undesirable because, if a student knows four of the five answers, the student automatically gets the fifth (last) choice correct, whether or not he knows the answer. This reduces the validity of the assessment results.

Use matching exercises only when you have several multiple-choice items that require repeating the identical set of alternatives. A matching exercise can be a space-saving and objective way to assess a number of important learning targets, such as a student's ability to identify associations or relationships between two sets of things. You can also develop matching exercises using pictorial materials to assess the students' abilities to match words and phrases with pictures of objects or with locations on maps and diagrams.

Critics often see matching exercises as limited to the assessment of memorized factual information, because they are often used that way. If you want to assess students on higher-level abilities, design exercises that present new examples or instances of the concept or principle to the students. Then require the students to match these examples with the names of appropriate concepts or principles. In this context, *new examples* are instances of concepts that students have not been previously taught or encountered. Similarly, a matching task can describe a situation novel to the student, and the student can decide which of several rules, principles, or classifications is likely to apply.

■ **Example of a matching exercise that measures application level thinking**

Directions: Each numbered statement below describes a testing situation in which ONE decision is represented. On the blank next to each statement, write the letter:

  A   if the decision is primarily concerned with *placement*

  B   if the decision is primarily concerned with *selection*

  C   if the decision is primarily concerned with *program improvement*

  D   if the decision is primarily concerned with *theory development*

  E   if the decision is primarily concerned with *motivating students*

 (A) 1.   After children are admitted to kindergarten, they are given a screening test to determine which children should be given special training in perceptual skills.

 (A) 2.   At the end of the third grade, all students are given an extensive battery of reading tests, and reading profiles are developed for each child. On the basis of these profiles, some children are given a special reading program, while others continue on with the regular program.

 (B) 3.   High school seniors take a national scholastic aptitude test and send their scores to colleges they wish to attend. On the basis of these scores, colleges admit some students and do not admit others.

 (E) 4.   Students are informed about the learning targets their examination will cover and about how many points each examination question will be worth.

Guideline 7.4 presents guidelines to evaluate your own matching exercises or those that you adapt from teachers' texts or other curricular materials.

Guideline 7.4 Guidelines for writing matching exercises

Guideline—Your matching exercise should	Negative Example—Poor Item	Good Example—Revised Item
Assess an important aspect of the unit's instructional targets. Match your assessment plan in terms of performance, emphasis, and number of points.	*We can't give examples without knowing your learning targets and your test blueprint. However, these are basic validity criteria. Evaluate every test item using these two criteria.*	
Have homogeneous premises and responses.	Select the letter of the best choice. (d) 1. Castle, seat of the Danish monarchy (b) 2. Young woman whom Hamlet loves (c) 3. Weapon Laertes uses to kill Hamlet (e) 4. former role of the deceased Yorick a. Hamlet b. Ophelia c. rapier d. Elsinore e. court jester	Match to identify the character. (c) 1. Friend of Hamlet (b) 2. Prince of Norway (a) 3. Current king of Denmark (e) 4. Chief councilor a. Claudius b. Fortinbras c. Horatio d. Laertes e. Polonius
Have responses that function as plausible alternatives for each premise.	(d) 1. Pennsylvania's official state flower (a) 2. Pennsylvania's official state bird (b) 3. Major steel producing city in the 1940s (c) 4. 2000 population of Philadelphia a. Ruffed grouse b. Pittsburgh c. 1,517,550 d. Mountain laurel e. Allegheny River	This exercise would be better as four multiple-choice or short-answer questions.
Have longer statements in the premise list and shorter ones in the response list.	Match the simple machine with its definition. (c) 1. Pulley (a) 2. Lever (b) 3. Wedge (d) 4. Inclined plane a. A stiff bar that rests on a support (fulcrum) and lifts or moves a load b. A machine with a slanted side and sharp edge that cuts or separates material c. A machine that uses grooved wheels and a rope to move a load d. A slanted surface that connects a lower level with a higher one e. A circular shaped machine with a rod through its center to lift or move loads	Match the simple machine with its definition. (b) 1. A stiff bar that rests on a support (fulcrum) and lifts or moves a load (e) 2. A machine with a slanted side and sharp edge that cuts or separates material (c) 3. A machine that uses grooved wheels and a rope to move a load (a) 4. A slanted surface that connects a lower level with a higher one a. Inclined plane b. Lever c. Pulley d. Screw e. Wedge

Guideline 7.4. (Continued)

Guideline—Your matching exercise should	Negative Example—Poor Item	Good Example—Revised Item
Have directions that clearly state the basis for matching.	Match Column A with Column B. Write your answer on the blank to the left.	Column A lists parts of a plant cell. For each cell part, choose from Column B the main purpose of that cell part. Write the letter of that purpose on the blank to the left of the cell part.
Arrange responses in a meaningful way, if possible.	*In the "good example" about the characters in Hamlet, the characters' names are arranged in alphabetical order. A student who knows the name can find it easily.*	
Avoid "perfect matching."	*Accomplish this by either having more responses than premises (as the examples above have 4 premises and 5 responses) or allowing students to use responses more than once.*	
Have fewer than 10 responses.		
Number the premises and letter the responses.	These are self-explanatory—but important!	

Source: Adapted from *Teacher's Guide to Better Classroom Testing: A Judgmental Approach* (p. 34), by A. J. Nitko & T-C Hsu, 1987, Pittsburgh, PA: Institute for Practice and Research in Education, School of Education, University of Pittsburgh. Adapted by permission of the copyright holders.

Conclusions

Short-answer, true-false, multiple-choice, and matching items are building blocks for objective tests. For each format, we identified the basic varieties and discussed their uses. We gave guidelines for writing each type and summarized them with checklists and examples. Many learning targets are well assessed with objective items. Other learning targets require students to construct, instead of select, their responses. We turn to those in the next chapter.

Exercises

1. Each of the following completion items contains one or more flaws. For each item, use the guidelines for short-answer items in Guideline 7.1 to identify the flaw(s), and rewrite the item so it remedies the flaw(s) you identified but creates no new flaws.
   a. _____ is the substance that helps plants turn light energy to food.
   b. The Johnstown Flood occurred during _____.
   c. The _____ is the major reason why _____ and _____ exhibit _____.
   d. San Francisco was named after _____.
   e. A kilogram is equivalent to _____.
   f. Was the population greater in 1941 or 1951? _____.

2. Each of the following true-false items contains one or more flaws. For each item, use the guidelines in Guideline 7.2 to identify the flaw(s), and rewrite the item so it remedies the flaw(s) you identified but creates no new flaws.
   a. The two categories, plants and animals, are all that biologists   T   F
      need to classify every living thing.
   b. In the United States, it is warm in the winter.   T   F
   c. Editing assessment tasks is an important step in the assessment   T   F
      development process.
   d. The major problem in the world today is that too many people   T   F
      want more than their "fair share" of the Earth's resources.
   e. There were more teachers on strike in 1982 than in 1942, even   T   F
      though the employment rate was lower in 1942 than in 1982.

3. Each of the following multiple-choice items contains one or more flaws. For each item, use the guidelines for multiple-choice items in Guideline 7.3 to identify the flaw(s), and rewrite the item so it remedies the flaw(s) you identified but creates no new flaws.
   a. What is the name of the temporary foot-like structure that amoebas use for locomotion?
      - A.   pseudopod
      - B.   sauropod
      - C.   iPod
      - D.   none of the above

    b. Which of the following are examples of a trope?
- A.   metaphor
- B.   metonymy
- C.   synecdoche
- D.   irony
- E.   all of the above

    c. What causes tides?
- A.   The moon's gravitational pull on the earth is stronger on the side toward the moon and weaker on the opposite side. This causes bulging. The rotation of the earth shifts the bulges such that most places on earth experience two high tides per day.
- B.   Earth's gravity
- C.   Moon's gravity
- D.   Earth's rotation

4. Evaluate the matching exercise below using the matching exercise guidelines in Guideline 7.4. Prepare a list of the flaws found. For each flaw listed, explain why it is a flaw in this exercise. After completing your analysis, revise the exercise so it has no flaws. Share your findings with your class.

Instructions: Match the two columns	
A	B
1. chlorophyll	A. Green plants contain this substance
2. igneous	B. Type of rock formed when melted rock hardens
3. photosynthesis	C. A substance made up of both hydrogen and oxygen
4. water	D. Process by which green plants produce their food

Companion
Website

Now go to our Companion Website at **www.prenhall.com/brookhart** to assess your understanding of chapter content with multiple-choice and essay questions. Broaden your knowledge of assessment with links to assessment related web sites.

Constructed Response Test Items

1. Constructed response test items ask students to compose their responses, and are scored with a judgment of the quality of those responses.
2. Restricted response essay items limit both the content of students' answers and the form of their written responses.
3. Extended response essay items require students to express their own ideas and to organize their own answers.
4. Good essay questions ask students to use the higher-order thinking skills specified in their learning targets.
5. Show-the-work problems on math and science tests are also constructed response items.

My best friend from college was something of a wit (and sometimes all the way to smart-aleck, if she thought the occasion warranted it). She has used her sense of humor well in a long career in early childhood education. Back when we were in college, we took some survey courses that ended with the conventional "blue book" final exam. Often the questions were too vague for us to write an answer, or too broad for us to do justice to an answer in the two hours allotted for the exam. Her description of those questions was: "Describe the universe briefly, and give three examples."

Constructed response test items ask students to compose their responses, and are scored with a judgment of the quality of those responses

Essays and **show-the-work problems** are common forms of **constructed response** test items. What is perhaps unique about the essay format is that it offers students the opportunity to display their abilities to write about, to organize, to express, and to explain interrelationships among ideas. Essay formats are usually classified into two groups: restricted response items and extended response items. You should align both the constructed response test question *and* its scoring with the learning target. Essay items and interpretive exercises (see Chapter 7) both can test complex learning targets. Example 8.1 provides a summary of these skills. The outcomes listed in the table are suggestive, but not exhaustive (Linn & Miller, 2005).

■ **EXAMPLE 8.1** Examples of varieties of learning outcomes that can be assessed using objective interpretive exercises and essay items

Type of test item	Examples of complex learning outcomes that can be measured
Objective interpretive exercises	Ability to— identify cause-effect relationships identify the application of principles identify the relevance of arguments identify tenable hypotheses identify valid conclusions identify unstated assumptions identify the limitations of data identify the adequacy of procedures (and similar outcomes based on the pupil's ability to *select* the answer)
Restricted response essay questions	Ability to— explain cause-effect relationships describe applications of principles present relevant arguments formulate tenable hypotheses formulate valid conclusions state necessary assumptions describe the limitations of data explain methods and procedures (and similar outcomes based on the pupil's ability to *supply* the answer)
Extended response essay questions	Ability to— produce, organize, and express ideas integrate learnings in different areas create original forms (e.g., designing an experiment) evaluate the worth of ideas

Source: Linn, Robert L. Miller & M. David, *Measurement and Assessment in Teaching*, 9th edition, © 2005, p. 232. Reprinted by permission of Pearson Education, Inc., Upper Saddle River, NJ.

Restricted response essay items limit both the content of students' answers and the form of their written responses

Restricted response items restrict or limit both the content of students' answers and the form of their responses. They should assess more than recall and comprehension. Restricted response items should ask students to apply their skills to solve new problems or to analyze novel situations. One way to do this is to include interpretive material with the assessment. Interpretive material could be, for example, a paragraph or two describing a particular problem or social situation, an extract from a literary work, or a description of a scientific experiment or finding. The following examples illustrate restricted response items and, by way of contrast, an extended response item that requires students to analyze a particular poem in various ways.

(We will discuss extended response items in the next section.) The items are intended for a high school literature course.

■ **Example of Restricted and Extended Response Essay Questions**

Interpretive material

On First Looking Into Chapman's Homer
1 Much have I travell'd in the realms of gold,
   And many goodly states and kingdoms seen;
   Round many western islands have I been
4 Which bards in fealty to Apollo hold.
   Oft of one wide expanse have I been told
   That deep-brow'd Homer ruled as his demesne;
   Yet did I never breathe its pure serene
8 Till I heard Chapman speak out loud and bold:
   Then felt I like some watcher of the skies
   When a new planet swims into his ken;
   Or like stout Cortez when with eagle eyes
12 He star'd at the Pacific—and all his men
   Look'd at each other with a wild surmise—
   Silent, upon a peak in Darien.

JOHN KEATS

Restricted response questions

1. What is the poet's attitude toward literature as is apparent in lines 1 to 8? What words in these lines make that attitude apparent?

2. Summarize the mood described in lines 9 to 14.

3. What is the relationship between the attitude described in lines 1 to 8 and the mood established in lines 9 to 14?

Extended response questions

4. Describe the way in which the structure of the poem reinforces the speaker's mood as it is presented in lines 9 to 14. In your essay show how the attitude in the first part of the poem is related to the mood at the end of the poem.

Source: From "Evaluation of Learning in Literature" by A. C. Purves, in *Handbook on Formative and Summative Evaluation of Student Learning* (pp. 736, 755, 756) by B. S. Bloom, J. T. Hastings, and G. F. Madaus (Eds.), New York: McGraw-Hill, 1971. Reprinted by permission.

The restricted response items above, written at the "analysis" level of the Bloom et al. *Taxonomy*, ask a few of the many (perhaps 15 or 20) questions that a teacher might write to assess students' ability to analyze the mood of a poem. The extended response item, by contrast, attempts to elicit from the student a rather complete and integrated analysis of the poem.

The restricted response format narrows the focus of assessment to a specific and well-defined performance. This makes it more likely that your students will interpret each question the way you intended. Thus, it is easier to judge the correctness of student answers. When you are clear about what makes up correct answers, scoring reliability, and hence the scores' validity, improves.

However, multiple-choice interpretive exercises assess many abilities more reliably than restricted response essays (see Example 8.1). Do not use restricted response essays to assess students' recall of factual information. You can assess a student's ability to recall factual information better through completion, true-false, multiple-choice, and matching items. Remember, restricted response items should be used to ask students to analyze content or apply skills to a new situation.

Extended response essay items require students to express their own ideas and to organize their own answers

Because of their open-ended nature, extended response essays usually have many possible correct answers. (Of course, there are many possible wrong answers, too.) Since a student is free to choose the way to respond, it takes a skilled teacher to judge the quality of a student's response. The two broad uses for the extended response essay format are to assess students' (a) general writing ability and (b) subject-matter knowledge.

If your intention is to assess only writing ability, your essay must present the students with a prompt. A **prompt** is a brief statement that suggests a topic to write about, provides general guidance to the student, motivates the student to write, and elicits the students' best performance. Evaluate students' performance by using scoring rubrics that define various characteristics or qualities of writing.

■ **Example of an extended response narrative writing prompt**

Pretend you are one of the characters in a fairy tale and have just been granted three wishes. What would your first wish be? Write the wish, and then write a story about what happens to you when the wish is granted.

If the primary purpose of your assessment is to evaluate students' knowledge, understanding, and reasoning in a subject, then a different kind of prompt and essay structure is needed. Here is an example in the subject of social studies. Students' responses are evaluated primarily using subject-matter criteria.

■ **Example of an extended response subject-matter essay prompt**

On June 28, 1914, a Serbian nationalist assassinated Archduke Francis Ferdinand, the heir to the Austro-Hungarian throne, in Sarajevo, Bosnia. Describe the political climate that caused this spark to escalate into a war between the Allied Powers and the Central Powers. Your description should explain how these political factors are related to at least two of the more general principles we have studied (e.g., power vacuum), and how those principles operated in what turned out to be the start of World War I.

The extended response essay format lends itself to assessing learning targets about a student's ability to organize ideas, develop a logical argument, discuss evaluations of certain positions or data, communicate thoughts and feelings, or demonstrate original thinking. The extended response essay is also suited to assessing learning targets that require students to use a combination of skills such as interpreting material, solving a problem, and explaining the problem and its solution coherently. The restricted response essay format does not lend itself to assessing these types of learning targets. Students need opportunities for more extended responses to demonstrate such skills and abilities.

One disadvantage of an extended response essay is poor **scoring reliability**. It is difficult to score an extended response objectively. A second disadvantage is that scoring essays is often time-consuming, especially if you want to give feedback to students so they can improve their learning. This time is well spent if essays are the best ways to assess important learning targets, if performing them is a meaningful student activity, and if the students benefit from your feedback on the quality of their responses.

A scoring rubric may improve the reliability (consistency), and thus the validity, of scoring essays. Using a scoring rubric also reduces scoring time. Scoring is discussed in more detail in Chapter 10. We separate scoring in order to devote a whole chapter to it, because it's that important. Good questions only yield good assessment information if the scoring system lets them do it. This chapter is about how to write good questions. However, your essay skills aren't complete without the skills in Chapter 10, as well.

Good essay questions ask students to use the higher-order thinking skills specified in their learning targets

You may find it helpful to study different ways of phrasing essay questions that encourage a student to use higher-level cognitive processes and skills. Example 8.2 provides some examples of ways to phrase essay questions so they assess different learning targets. If you construct essay items in a manner similar to those given in Example 8.2 you will help your students to be able to demonstrate those targets.

Guideline 8.1 presents guidelines for writing essay items. First, we will look at a poor essay item and apply the guidelines to it. This will give you an idea of how the item should be improved.

Suppose a teacher wanted to assess the following 10th-grade U.S. history learning target, and she wrote the essay question below.

■ **Example**

Tenth-grade learning target to be assessed

Analyze reasons for success of the Colonials during the American War of Independence and explain what alternative actions the British or the Colonials could have taken to alter the outcomes.

A poorly crafted essay item

Analyze the defeat of the British by the Colonials by listing the four factors discussed in class that led to the defeat.

■ **EXAMPLE 8.2 How to phrase essay questions to assess learning targets**

1. *Concept understanding:* Identifying examples, producing examples
   • Read the newspaper articles attached. Which events illustrate the concept of *political compromise?*
   • Explain in your own words the meaning of *prejudice.* Give an example of prejudice from your own experience.

2. *Concept understanding:* Classifying examples
   • Read the five mathematics word problems attached. Sort these problems into two groups. Explain why the problems in each group are similar and belong together. Explain how the two groups differ.
   • Study the pictures of the 10 paintings that are attached. Organize these paintings into two or more groups according to their style. Explain the reasons behind your grouping.

3. *Analysis*
   • Look at the family photo attached. Describe the mood or feeling in the photo as well as the body language of the people. Use metaphors or similes to make these descriptions.
   • Read the attached newspaper article. Which statements are opinions? Explain why.

4. *Comparison*
   • Compare Artist A's use of color in her paintings with Artist B's use of color in his mask. How are they similar and different? What moods do the colors convey in each piece?
   • Read the attached statements of Senator A and Senator B. In what ways are their points of view similar? Explain the reasons for your conclusions.

5. *Using principles and rules:* Inference, prediction
   • Read the situation above about the Basarwa, a cultural group we did not study. Based on what we did study about cultural groups, what would you predict would happen to the Basarwa in the next 20 years? Explain the principles you used to make your predictions.
   • Suppose the government of South Africa ordered all of the white citrus farmers to leave the country. Where would you expect them to go? Explain the principles you used to make these predictions.

6. *Inferences:* Deductions, predictions, generalizations
   • Compare the information in Table A with the information in Figure A. What conclusions do you draw about how successful rice farming will be in the region to which the data apply? Explain the reasons for your conclusions.
   • Read the attached statements from a scientist, senator, and newspaper editor about the consequences of continuing to use gasoline-powered automobile engines. What generalization can you make about the continued use of these engines in developed countries?
   • Study the data in the table above. What would you expect to happen to our exports of wheat over the next 5 years? Explain the assumptions you made for your predictions to be valid.

■ **EXAMPLE 8.2** Continued

7. *Evaluation*
   - Above are the criteria we use to judge how well an author has used "voice" in writing. Attached is a short piece of writing by a student in a nearby school. Use the criteria to evaluate the writer's use of voice. Explain why good voice is or is not used by this writer. Use examples from the piece to illustrate your evaluation.
   - Use your daily log and records of your plant's growth to explain the present state of your plant. Explain why your plant is better or worse than your classmate's plants. What could you have done differently? What effect would that have had on your plant's present state?

Using the principles in Guideline 8.1, this essay question does not fare very well.

1. Yes, the factors contributing to the success of the Colonials are important to the learning outcome of this unit. This item, in relation to other items (not shown), contributes to the breadth of coverage the teacher had in mind for the unit.

2. No, the learning target calls for students to analyze reasons for success and explain alternative possibilities. The item requires neither analysis nor explanation.

3. No, the item requires only listing (recalling) information presented during the class.

4. Yes, what the student is to do (i.e., list) is clearly stated.

5. No, the learning target implies that the students should be capable of more than the item requires. (The task set by the item, "listing from memory," is within the capability of the students, but it is below the level of complexity in the learning target.)

6. No, the item requires only recalling verbal information.

7. Questionable; some students may be confused by the word *analyze* but most will probably make a *list*.

8. a. Yes, the item says students should list four reasons.

   b. Perhaps the purpose is simply to repeat what was taught in class, but the purpose isn't stated.

   c. No, a time limit is not stated.

   d. No, but simply being right or wrong seems to be the implied basis for evaluation.

9. Not applicable; no opinion was asked.

After using the checklist, the teacher rethought the item in relation to the learning target and what he had taught. The teacher rewrote the item to make it more in line with the learning target. Here is the revised item.

Guideline 8.1 Guidelines for writing essay items assessing subject-matter learning

Guideline—Your essay item should	Negative Example—Poor Item	Good Example—Revised Item
1. Assess an important aspect of the unit's instructional targets.	*We can't give examples without knowing your learning targets and your test blueprint. However, these are basic validity criteria. Evaluate every test item using these two criteria.*	
2. Match your assessment plan in terms of performance, emphasis, and number of points.		
3. Require students to apply their knowledge to a new or novel situation.	Hamlet wrestles with a major question in his soliloquy, "To be or not to be: That is the question" in Act 3, scene 1, lines 64–98. What is the question in his mind, and how do you think he resolves it by the end of his soliloquy? State your interpretation of his major question and his resolution, and use evidence from the speech to support it. *This example assumes that the class had a full period of discussion on the "To be or not to be" soliloquy but did not do that for the other major soliloquies. Therefore, answering this essay question would be for students an exercise in repeating what they heard in class (recall).*	Hamlet wrestles with a major question in his soliloquy, "O, that this too, too solid flesh would melt" in Act 1, scene 2, lines 131–161. What is the question in his mind, and how do you think he resolves it by the end of his soliloquy? State your interpretation of his major question and his resolution, and use evidence from the speech to support it. *Answering this essay question would require students to recall the way in which they analyzed the "To be or not to be" soliloquy in class and then apply similar strategies to this soliloquy. The text itself is not "new" to them (assuming they did their assignments, which included reading the play); what is new is applying this kind of analysis to it.*
4. Define a task with specific directions (rather than leave the task so broad that virtually any response can satisfy it).	*[Regarding the poem, "On First Looking into Chapman's Homer"]* Analyze the poem.	*[Regarding the poem, "On First Looking into Chapman's Homer"]* What is the poet's attitude toward literature as is apparent in lines 1 to 8? What words in these lines make that attitude apparent?
5. Be within the level of complexity appropriate for students' level of maturity.	*Answering an essay requires students to read, think, and write. The item must be appropriate to your students' level of reading and writing development. If students do not have sufficient writing skill to express their knowledge on your essay question, consider using another means of assessment. Avoid complicated sentence structures and phrasings for elementary students. Avoid indirect or unnecessary phrases. Do not, however, oversimplify essays for more advanced students. Essays should challenge students to do their best thinking and use their best writing skills.*	

Rule	Poor	Better
6. Require the student to demonstrate more than recall of facts, definitions, generalizations or other ideas.	List the four stages in the life cycle of the butterfly. *Answering this question requires only recall. In fact, it could be done in four words, using no complete sentences, if the student takes the question literally.*	List the four stages in the life cycle of the butterfly. For each stage, explain how the physical feature of the butterfly is suited for the kind of development it has to do at that stage. *This is a question about physical form supporting life function, and it is clear that an explanation is required.*
7. Be worded in a way that leads all students to interpret the item in the way you intended.	Pretend you are a butterfly. Write the story of your life, beginning as a larva and progressing through all your stages until you burst forth as a beautiful, colorful, adult. *If the teacher meant to test knowledge of the life cycle of a butterfly, this is a poor item. Some students will interpret it that way, but others may see in this fanciful prompt ("pretend," "burst forth," "beautiful") an invitation to write a fantasy narrative.*	List the four stages in the life cycle of the butterfly. For each stage, explain how the physical feature of the butterfly is suited for the kind of development it has to do at that stage. *This is a question about physical form supporting life function, and it is clear than an explanation is required.*
8. Make clear to the students all of the following: (a) length of the required writing, (b) purpose for which they are writing, (c) amount of time to be devoted to answering this item, and (d) the basis on which their answers will be evaluated.	*[Regarding a newspaper article provided for the students to read]* Do you agree or disagree with the author's position? *The answer to this could be anything from a "yes" or "no" to a long-winded harangue.*	*[Regarding a newspaper article provided for the students to read]* Do you agree or disagree with the author's position? Use evidence from the newspaper article and information about recycling from the unit we have just finished. Your answer will be graded on the quality of your evidence and the logic of your argument, not on the position you take. Time limit: 20 minutes.
9. For essays requiring students to state and support their opinions on controversial matters, make clear to the students that their assessment will be based on the logic and evidence supporting their arguments, rather than the actual position taken or opinion stated.	*[Regarding a newspaper article provided for the students to read]* Do you agree or disagree with the author's position? Use evidence from the newspaper article and information about recycling from the unit we have just finished.	*[Regarding a newspaper article provided for the students to read]* Do you agree or disagree with the author's position? Use evidence from the newspaper article and information about recycling from the unit we have just finished. Your answer will be graded on the quality of your evidence and the logic of your argument, not on the position you take. Time limit: 20 minutes.

Source: Adapted from *Teachers' Guide to Better Classroom Testing: A Judgmental Approach* (p. 31), by A. J. Nitko and T-C Hsu, 1987, Pittsburgh, PA: Institute for Practice and Research in Education, School of Education, University of Pittsburgh. Adapted by permission of copyright holders.

■ **Example**

An improved essay task

A. List four of the factors that led to the Colonial victory over
   the British in the War of Independence   (4 points)

B. For every factor you list, write a short explanation of how
   that factor helped the Colonists defeat the British.   (4 points)

C. Choose one of these factors that in your opinion the British
   could have changed or overcome. Explain what actions the
   British could have taken to change or overcome this factor.   (4 points)

D. What probably would have happened in the war if the British
   had taken the actions you stated? Why do you think this
   would have happened?   (8 points)

Grading: Parts A and B will be marked on how correct your answers are. Parts C and D
will be marked on how well you support your opinion, but not on what position you take.

Time limit: 40 minutes

The revised item is more complex and more difficult than the original, but it comes closer to assessing the learning target. The revised item is expanded to include recalling information, explaining the recalled information, and using higher-level skills. These higher-level skills require students to explain the reasoning supporting their opinions and to describe probable consequences of actions. The teacher's basis for grading is specified, as is a time limit. Because the class period at this school is 50 minutes long, this essay will probably be the only assessment that the teacher could do that day. To cover other aspects of the unit the teacher would need additional assessments, including quizzes, homework, class discussions, and an objective test over the unit's content.

While your main consideration in writing essay questions is their match with your learning targets, some practical and logistical considerations are important, too.

Essay items, unlike short objective items, require significant student assessment time. Balance the available assessment time against the range of coverage you have planned. Viewed in conjunction with the other items on the test, your essay questions should contribute to covering the range of content and thinking skills specified in your assessment plan. You could focus your essay on higher-order thinking learning targets, for example, and use non-essay items for recall learning targets. If there is not enough time in one class period, you could do essay assessments one day and an objective format assessment on another day.

Focusing the question and specifying limits of the intended response do not mean providing information that gives away the answer. If you want the essay to assess the ability to organize a written argument or identify the central issue in a "fuzzy problem," for example, you should not provide students with a particular organization in the question. However, you should tell students that the way they choose to organize the answer is important, and that you will evaluate the essay on how well it is organized.

An important practical suggestion here is to have a colleague or friend review the questions and, if possible, to try the item with a few students. You can then revise the questions if necessary. Following such steps greatly improves the quality of essay questions.

Students need to learn how to express original ideas, compare and contrast, explain reasons, and the like. One strategy that will help students learn to do—and to express—higher-order thinking is to organize a small-group or class discussion about the upcoming essays. The students discuss the problem posed in the essay. The discussions familiarize students with the content covered and various ways to solve the problem stated in the essay. In the following class period, students respond to the essay individually. Another assessment strategy gives students some essay tasks to complete over several days or as take-home assignments. This gives students the opportunity to think, to use prewriting skills, to organize, and to revise their answers. This process is more like the ultimate situations in which your students will be writing.

Influence on studying strategies

You may use assessment to motivate students to study. It seems reasonable that the type of performances you expect from students on tests will influence their methods of study. Some classic research indicates that when students know that essay questions will be asked, they tend to focus on learning broad concepts and on articulating interrelationships, contrasting, comparing, and so on; those preparing for response-choice questions focus on recalling facts, details, and specific ideas (Douglas & Tallmadge, 1934; Terry, 1933). But despite reporting that they prepare differently for different types of assessments, students do not necessarily perform differently on the different forms. Studies have found little, if any, difference in *performance* on essay or response-choice assessments even though students reported using different study strategies (Hakstain, 1969; Vallance, 1947).

When a state department of education uses essay questions on its accountability tests, that motivates teachers to require students to write more, and they report that students' writing skills improve (Evaluation Center, 1995). Outside observers report, however, that although students write more, they do not necessarily write better (Viadero, 1995).

Because both essay and response-choice formats can call for knowledge of specific facts, and both can call for application of complex reasoning skills, the questions' format may not be the key issue in how students plan their study strategies (Ebel & Frisbie, 1991). The kinds of study strategies your students use in preparing for your assessments are more likely to reflect the type of the thinking skills your assessment tasks require rather than the format (essay or not essay) of the tasks. If two different assessment formats require students to use the same kind of thinking skills, the formats ought to require the same types of study strategies. If your "essays" are really a regurgitation of facts, students' study strategies will focus on remembering and recalling facts.

If you believe students must learn to write about ideas in a particular subject area, perhaps the best advice is to be sure you explain and teach writing about the subject to students in your class. Assign students a significant number of writing tasks so they can learn to write in this subject area. Do not limit writing tasks to examinations. Various written assignments such as short compositions and longer term papers can help your students achieve these writing-oriented goals. This often means relying less on the questions and homework assignments that are in the back of the students' textbook chapters and more on your own assignments. Keep in mind, however, that assessment results are more valid if you use multiple assessment formats. Your summative assessments should include both essay and response-choice items so they cover a proper range of learning targets.

Depth and breadth of content sampling

Answering essay questions takes a long time and limits the breadth of content about which the student can write. If your students can answer one or two response-choice items in one minute, then they can answer 30 to 60 response-choice items in a half-hour. Sixty items can cover a very broad area of content and at least parts of many instructional objectives. In the same 30 minutes, these same students can probably answer only one or two essay questions. Thus, you can assess in-depth learning of a narrower topic using one essay or broad, less in-depth, general coverage using many objective items. To improve the content coverage of their assessment, many teachers use both essay and objective test items.

To overcome the shortcoming of an essay's limited content sampling, use a series of compositions that students can write over a longer period. You can accumulate these in portfolios. Several out-of-class essays written over a marking period may better assess a particular learning target than a single essay written during a brief examination period. Out-of-class essays also remove the time pressure of an examination, which disadvantages some students.

Optional questions

When the purpose for assessment is summative evaluation, require all students to answer the same questions. It is extremely difficult, often impossible, to compare tests equitably when students have taken different items (Wang, Wainer, & Thissen, 1995). A student can write very well about some topics and very poorly about others. You might, for example, write a better essay on the frustrations of a teacher than on the frustrations of a professional golfer, simply because you know more about one area than the other. To mitigate this effect, use several essays instead of just one when you use essays to assess a student's understanding of a topic or unit of instruction.

If all the questions asked on an assessment represent important learning targets, then it seems logical and fair to hold all students accountable for answering all of them (Ebel & Frisbie, 1991). You can offer students choice on the essays and class assignments that they do for practice and feedback (formative assessment). For summative assessment, give all students except those with special accommodations the same essay questions.

Show-the-work problems on math and science tests are also constructed response items

Like essays, show-the-work problems should ask students to do more than recall information. You know these problems from your own math classes: your teacher asks you to do a proof or solve some other multi-step problem and show all your steps along the way. Students should use the information learned to solve a problem that is new to them. Just as for essays, the focus and complexity of a show-the-work problem should be appropriate, the task should be clear, and the set of problems should cover the range of thinking skills described in the learning targets. Scoring should also match the learning targets. In fact, all the principles for writing essay items in Guideline 8.1, except possibly the last one, apply to show-the-work problems, too.

Example 8.3 presents an example. It also presents the scoring guide and examples of student work. The student answers may look "short" if you think in terms of the length of an essay. The reason for this is that a lot of the reasoning is already encoded into the equation. Mathematical notation is a system of numbers and symbols, and rules for their use, designed to do just that—facilitate mathematical reasoning and present it in an efficient manner.

■ EXAMPLE 8.3 Example of a show-the-work math problem

Problem and Solution

Problem: This question requires you to show your work and explain your reasoning. You may use drawings, words, and numbers in your explanation. Your answer should be clear enough so that another person could read it and understand your thinking. It is important that you show all your work.

10.
$$15^2 = 225$$
$$25^2 = 625$$
$$35^2 = 1225$$

The examples above suggest the following statement.

When a positive integer that ends in the digit 5 is squared, the resulting integer ends in 25.

Explain why this statement is always true.

(Hint: $(10n + 5)^2 = ?$)

Solution:
$$(10n + 5)^2 = 100n^2 + 100n + 25$$
$$= 100(n^2 + n) + 25$$

Since n is an integer, n^2 is an integer; $n^2 + n$ is also an integer and $100(n^2 + n)$ is a multiple of 100 that ends in 00. When 25 is added to that integer, the sum ends in 25.

Note: If $(10n + 5)$ is squared incorrectly, the other work must be checked. The student can earn a Minimal or Partial depending on the correctness of the work.

Scoring Guide

Extended:
Student provides a complete, correct solution. (The student need not show 100 $(n^2 + n)$ if the explanation is clear and must demonstrate that $(10n + 5)$ has been squared correctly; e.g., "When 10n + 5 is squared, two of the terms will be multiples of 100 and the other will be 25."

Satisfactory:
States $(10n + 5)^2 = 100n^2 + 100n + 25$ and ties 25 to a multiple of 100. Explanation is incomplete or not clear.

Example of Student Work

$(10n+5)^2 = 100n^2 + 100n + 25$
$\quad = 100(n^2 + n) + 25$
two terms are multiples of 100,
third term is 25.

$(10n+5)^2 = 100n^2 + 100n + 25$
100 times any number of n leaves two empty spaces with only the 25 can fill

Partial:
States $(10n + 5)^2 = 100n^2 + 25$, and explains using multiples of 100; e.g., "An integer multiplied by 100 will always end in 2 zeros. Therefore, when you add 25, the number will always end in 25."

OR

Just ties 25 to a multiple of 100.

Minimal:
Student provides numerical examples other than $5 \times 5 = 25$ or the ones provided in the question, e.g., $45 \times 45 = 2025$.

OR

States $(10n + 5)^2 = 100n^2 + 25$ only.

OR

Student states $(10n + 5)^2 = 100n^2 + 100n + 25$, but does not mention zero(s).

Incorrect/Off Task:
The work is completely incorrect, irrelevant, or off task.

OR

Only repeats given information.

because $5^2 = 25$ and when you square something in the tens place, it equal an even hundreds number leaving '25' to always be in the last 2 digit.

Any Positive integer times itself will always have 25 at the end of the answer because if $15^2 =$ see $15 \times 15 = 225$ it ends on an 50 it will have 25 in the answer Example $\frac{1}{15} \times \boxed{15}$ see you got 25 at the $\boxed{2205}$ that's How you end up each answer

$5 \times 5 = 25$ versus answer

because 5 squared is always 25 just like all even numbers end in even Numbers

Source: U.S. Department of Education, *NAEP Questions Tool*, released item 1992-12M14, no. 10. Retrieved from http://nces.ed.gov/nationsreportcard/itmrls/ on July 25, 2006.

Conclusions

In many areas of the curriculum, the ability to reason in the content area, and to articulate that reasoning, are valued learning targets. Good essay questions embody those outcomes. Show-the-work problems are analogous; it's just that the reasoning and articulation are done in a different symbol system (with numbers, rather than with words).

When the learning targets go beyond reasoning and expression to more complex outcomes—for example, integrating planning, analysis, and original construction as in a term paper or project—we generally call that performance assessment. We turn to performance assessment in the next chapter.

Exercises

1. Each of these two essay items has one or more flaws. Using the guidelines for writing essay items in Guideline 8.1, identify the flaw(s), then rewrite each item to eliminate the flaw(s). Check your rewritten essay item to be sure you have not added another flaw.
   a. Item A: State the two examples of prejudices we discussed in class.
   b. Item B: Evaluate the effect of air pollution on the quality of life in the western part of this state.

2. Each of these two problems is intended to be a show-the-work problem. In both cases, the teacher would like to see an equation, properly written and solved (for Item A) or balanced (for Item B). However, the items as written suggest to students that all that is required is a correct answer. Rewrite each item to include brief directions that make clear what you want the student to show.
   a. Item A: What is the next term in the sequence {0, 3, 9, 18 . . . }?
   b. Item B: What happens when propane burns in oxygen?

Companion Website

Now go to our Companion Website at **www.prenhall.com/brookhart** to assess your understanding of chapter content with multiple-choice and essay questions. Broaden your knowledge of assessment with links to assessment related web sites.

Performance Assessment

1. Performance assessment involves observing a student process or evaluating a student product.
2. A performance assessment must have two components: the performance task itself and a clear rubric for scoring.
3. Performance assessment, alternative assessment, and authentic assessment are not the same things.
4. Write performance tasks to tap complex learning targets.
5. Tasks assessing the same content learning target can differ from one another.
6. Portfolios are purposeful collections of student work and student reflection on that work.

Picture this—a cartoon shows Ed, a rather lumpy little chameleon, standing in front of a mottled brown wall and looking glum. Three chameleon judges sit behind a table, in the style of "American Idol," clipboards and pencils poised. Unfortunately, Ed has chosen to turn his skin bright green. The caption reads, "Ed fails his chameleon aptitude test."

Performance assessment involves observing a student process or evaluating a student product

Performance assessment is useful when the learning target calls for student performance of a process or construction of a product; not every learning target does. Teachers may observe the process (e.g., watch a student measure and cut wood), assess the product (e.g., a bookshelf), or both. In academic subjects, helping students connect the intellectual work they do with something "useful"—even something as simple as contextualizing some math problems—can help them see the relevance of "school" learning to life (Resnick, 1987).

Well-designed performance tasks give students the opportunity to apply their learning to a new situation. Performance tasks can help students make connections between skills and abilities learned in separate subjects, or between "schoolhouse" learning and "real-world" activities. For example, planning a trip using a map, making a travel budget, and comparing politicians' points of view (from speeches, advertisements, and daily newspapers) all use sets of skills in "real" applications.

As with essay assignments, share your scoring rubrics with students at the same time you assign the performance assessment, to clarify the learning targets for them. The more students understand the skills and abilities they should use, the better they are able to identify where they should focus their practice and study efforts.

A performance assessment must have two components: the performance task itself and a clear rubric for scoring

A **performance task** is an assessment activity that requires a student to demonstrate achievement by producing an extended written or spoken answer, by engaging in group or individual activities, or by creating a specific product. A performance task requires students to demonstrate directly their achievement of a learning target. The performance task you administered may be used to assess the product the student produces and/or the process a student uses to complete the product. Short-answer or selection items require only indirect demonstration.

A **scoring rubric** is a coherent set of rules you use to assess the quality of a student's performance: The rules guide your judgments and ensure that you apply your judgments consistently. The rules may be in the form of a rating scale or a checklist. Complex performances require that you assess several learning targets or several parts of the performance. To do this, use several scoring rubrics, one for each learning target or part. See Chapter 10 for details on how to construct scoring rubrics and other scoring schemes.

It is critical to remember that the task *and* the scoring rubric together constitute a performance assessment. In this chapter, we are interested in the performance tasks. Many types of tasks fit the broad definition of performance assessment we adopted here. Example 9.1 lists most of these.

Advantages and criticisms of performance assessments

Performance assessments have several advantages (Hambleton & Murphy, 1992; Linn & Miller, 2005; Rudner & Boston, 1994; Shepard, 1991; Stiggins, 2005; Wiggins, 1990):

- Performance tasks clarify the meaning of complex learning targets.
- Performance tasks assess the ability "to do," rather than simply to answer questions about doing.
- Performance assessment is consistent with modern learning theory, which emphasizes that students should use their previous knowledge to build new knowledge structures, be actively involved in exploration and inquiry, and construct meaning for themselves from educational experiences.
- Performance tasks require integration of knowledge, skills, and abilities.
- Performance assessments may be linked more closely with teaching activities than are tests.

■ EXAMPLE 9.1 Common Types of Performance Assessment Techniques and Examples

Type of Performance Assessment		Example*
Structured, on-demand tasks for individual students, groups, or both The teacher decides what and when materials should be used, specifies the instructions for performance, describes the kinds of outcomes toward which students should work, tells the students they are being assessed, and gives students opportunities to prepare themselves for the assessment.	Paper-and-pencil tasks	• Solve this arithmetic story problem and explain how you solved it. • Study the following graph that shows how Sally uses her time. Then, write a story about a typical day in Sally's life using the information from the graph. • Draw a diagram to illustrate the mathematical ideas in the following word problem.
	Tasks requiring equipment and resources beyond paper and pencil	• Build as many geometric shapes as possible from this set of four triangles. • Talk on this telephone to ask about a job and to request a job application. • Show me how to mix acid and water.
	Demonstrations	• Demonstrate the proper way to knead dough for bread. • Demonstrate how to set up the microscope for viewing stained slides. • Demonstrate how to climb a rope. • Demonstrate how to look up information on the Internet.
Naturally occurring or typical performance tasks Observe students in natural settings: in typical classroom settings, on the playground, or at home. In natural settings you have to wait for the opportunity to arise for a particular activity you would like to assess. The activity may not occur while you are observing.		• Observe a student's way of dealing with conflicts on the playground. • Collect all pieces that each student wrote in every subject and analyze them for grammatical, spelling, and syntactic errors to determine a student's typical language usage (at least in school assignments). • Observe whether a student makes change correctly when running a refreshment stand at the school fair.
Long-term projects for individual students, groups, or both You can combine group and individual projects. Groups of students can work on a long-term project together; after the group activities are completed, individuals can prepare their own reports. The combination approach is useful when a project is complex and requires collaboration to complete in a reasonable time frame, yet the learning targets require individual abilities.	Long-term reports	• Collect and classify newspaper and magazine advertisements in the months before each holiday during the semester. • Using resources in the school library, write a research paper on why voter turnout is so low during primary elections. • Write a term paper on everyday life in Colonial America.
	Tasks requiring equipment and resources beyond paper and pencil	• Make a diorama depicting everyday life in Colonial America. • Build a model of the solar system. • Build a small piece of furniture using the hand tools you learned to use during the semester. • Build a working model of a camera using the optical principles taught in this unit.
	Experiments	• Plan, conduct, and report on a study to answer the question, "Do most students in this school support the death penalty laws in this state?" • Plan, conduct, and report on an experiment to investigate the hypothesis that a brightly colored advertisement will be remembered longer than a dull one.
	Oral presentations and dramatizations	• Write and present a skit depicting everyday life in Colonial America.
Portfolios	Best-work portfolios	• A portfolio organizing a student's best work around standards for graduation, with student explanations of why each piece was chosen and what it shows
	Growth and learning-progress portfolios	• A writing portfolio kept over a year, with drafts and finished papers for each type of writing studied that year. In a final reflection, the student describes his progress over the year.

*Examples are general descriptions for the purpose of illustration. Actual performance assessments for students would need clear directions, more specifics about the task, and scoring criteria.

■ Using performance assessment along with traditional objective formats broadens the types of learning targets you assess and offers students a variety of ways of expressing their learning. This increases the validity of your student evaluations.

■ Performance tasks let teachers assess the processes students use as well as the products they produce.

Although performance assessments offer several advantages over traditional objective assessment procedures, they have some distinct disadvantages (Hambleton & Murphy, 1992; Linn & Miller, 2005; Miller & Seraphine, 1993; Rudner & Boston, 1994):

■ High-quality performance *tasks* are difficult to craft.

■ High-quality scoring *rubrics* are difficult to craft.

■ Completing performance tasks takes students a lot of time.

■ Scoring performance task responses takes a lot of time.

■ Scores from performance tasks may have low scorer reliability.

■ Students' performance on one task provides little information about their performance on other tasks. A student's performance on a task very much depends on her prior knowledge, the particular wording and phrasing of the task, the context in which it is administered, and the specific subject-matter content embedded in the task (Shavelson & Baxter, 1991; Lane, Parke, & Moskal, 1992; Linn, 1993). This results in low reliability from the content-sampling point of view. You may have to use six or seven performance tasks to reliably evaluate a student in a unit of instruction.

■ Performance tasks do not assess all learning targets well.

■ Complex tasks that require students to sustain their interest and intensity over a long period may discourage less able students.

■ Performance assessments may underrepresent the learning of some cultural groups.

■ Performance assessments may be corruptible. As you use performance assessments, you will coach students on how to perform. If your coaching amounts to teaching all aspects of your state's standards and your school's curriculum framework's learning targets, you are doing the right thing. However, if you focus primarily on only one aspect of the learning targets (e.g., how to respond to one performance task), you will lower the validity of your results.

Performance assessment, alternative assessment, and authentic assessment are not the same things

Performance assessment is sometimes *called* alternative assessment or authentic assessment, but these terms are not interchangeable. The "alternative" in alternative assessment usually means in opposition to standardized achievement tests and to multiple-choice (or true-false, matching, completion) item formats. The "authentic" in authentic assessment usually means presenting students with tasks that are directly meaningful to their education instead of indirectly meaningful. For example, reading several long works and using them to compare and contrast different social viewpoints is directly meaningful because it is the kind of thoughtful reading educated citizens do. Reading short paragraphs and answering questions about the "main idea" or about what the characters in the passage did, on the other hand, is indirectly meaningful because it is only one fragment or component of the ultimate learning target of realistic reading. "Realistic" and "meaningful" are terms educators writing about authentic assessment often use. These terms beg further questions, such as, "Realistic in which context?" and "Meaningful for whom?"

Authentic tasks have the following characteristics (Wiggins, 1990):

■ They require students to use their knowledge to do a meaningful task.

■ They are complex and require students to use combinations of different knowledge, skills, and abilities.

■ They require high-quality polished, complete, and justifiable responses, performances, or products.

■ They clearly specify standards and criteria for assessing the possibly multiple correct answers, performances, or products.

■ They simulate the ways in which students should use combinations of knowledge, skills, and abilities in the real world.

■ They present to students ill-structured "challenges and roles" that are similar to those roles and tasks they are likely to encounter as adults at work and at home.

Not all performance tasks exhibit all of Wiggins's authenticity characteristics. Further, there are degrees of authenticity: Tasks will vary in the degree to which they meet any one of the characteristics just described.

To write authentic assessments, incorporate the following features into the assessments (Baron, 1991; Horvath, 1991; Jones, 1994):

■ Emphasize applications: Assess whether a student can use his knowledge in addition to assessing what the student knows. For example, you might use a construction paper task to see if students can apply the skill of measuring to the nearest inch.

■ Focus on direct assessment: Assess the stated learning target directly as contrasted with indirect assessment. For example, you might observe students in the science lab to see if they can use equipment properly.

■ Use realistic problems: Frame the tasks in a highly realistic way so that students can recognize them as a part of everyday life. For example, you might have students demonstrate map skills by planning a trip using a highway map of their own state.

■ Encourage open-ended thinking: Frame the tasks to encourage more than one correct answer, more than one way of expressing the answer, groups of students working together, and taking a relatively long time to complete (e.g., several days, weeks, months). For example, we know of a middle school teacher who had students make "CO_2 cars." They used math, design skills, and construction skills to build a balsa wood race car that ran on carbon dioxide, then raced them to find out whose was the fastest. Each car was a little different, but each student who built a car that ran was successful.

Write performance tasks to tap complex learning targets

Guideline 9.1 presents guidelines for writing performance tasks.

The tasks you craft should be meaningful *to the students*. This lets students become personally involved in solving a problem or doing well on the task. The following suggestions (Baron, 1991) will help you identify appropriate ideas you can use to build your tasks:

- Choose a situation or task that is likely to have personal meaning for most of your students.

- Carefully blend the familiar and the novel so students will be challenged by the task. Do not make the task so demanding or strange that it becomes frustrating for your students.

- Choose some situations or tasks that are grounded in the real-world experience of the students you are teaching.

- Choose some situations or tasks that require your students to apply the knowledge and skills they have acquired outside of your class.

- Choose situations or tasks that assess whether students can transfer their knowledge and skills from classroom activities and examples to similar, but new (for them) formats.

Guideline 9.1 Guidelines for writing performance tasks

Guideline—Your performance task should

1. Assess an important aspect of the unit's instructional targets.
2. Match your assessment plan in terms of performance, emphasis, and number of points.
3. Require a student to *do* something (i.e., a performance) rather than requiring only writing about how to do it, or simply to recall or copy information.
4. Allow enough time so all students can complete the task under your specified conditions.
5. If an open-response task, wording and directions make clear to students that they may use a variety of approaches and strategies, that you will accept more than one answer as correct, and that they need to fully elaborate their responses.
6. If the task is intended to be authentic or realistic, present a situation that your level of students will recognize as coming from the real world.

7. If the task requires locating and using resources outside the classroom, ensure all students fair and equal access to the expected resources.
8. In directions and other wording: (a) define a task appropriate to the educational maturity of students; (b) lead all students, including those from diverse backgrounds, to interpret the task requirements in the way you intend; (c) make clear the purpose or goal of the task; (d) make clear the length or degree of elaboration you expect in a response; (e) make clear the bases on which you will evaluate work.
9. Have drawings, graphs, diagrams, charts, manipulatives, and other task materials clearly drawn, properly constructed, appropriate to the intended performance, and in good working order.
10. If there are students with disabilities in your class, have appropriate accommodations to meet their needs.

Using tasks that are meaningful to students is well illustrated in the negative by a story that happened to me when I was first teaching. I was a substitute in a second-grade class in an inner-city school. The teacher was going to be out for two days, and had left a handwriting assignment on the board for the second day: the children were to copy the A. A. Milne poem "Daffodowndilly" in their best beginning cursive writing. The verse presents a wonderful metaphor describing a daffodil as if it were a lady in a yellow and green gown, coming out to say that winter is over. I could see the students' puzzled looks on the first day. They had no idea what the poem meant! Of course, copying it as a nonsense verse would have provided handwriting practice, but that seemed a waste of a wonderful poem and lots of kid time. The problem was they had never seen a daffodil.

Fortunately, I actually had daffodils blooming in the yard at my house at the time. I brought a vase full of them to school the next day. It was my intention simply to use the flowers to explain the poem, so that when they did their handwriting exercise they didn't feel like they were writing nonsense. But once the children saw they could figure out the poem by looking at the flowers, they got excited. One of them asked if he (yes—he!) could make a daffodil to decorate his handwriting paper. Another figured out that small paper cups and yellow construction paper would make three-dimensional daffodils. They were into it! That "lesson" produced the most beautiful handwriting—and also perhaps, the children's first lesson at interpreting poetic imagery (although I didn't call it that)—all from making the task meaningful to the students.

As an aside—this event happened during the period before my first full-time teaching position, when I was substituting because there were no full-time jobs available. It remains in my mind, however, as one of the most successful lessons I ever taught, and it gave me great motivation and hope for my own future (which at that time did not seem so clear!). It also taught me early in my career that the involvement of students in making sense of their own lessons is critical. To all the readers of this book—I wish that each of you has a "daffodil" experience early in your career, too.

Tasks may seem like they would be meaningful to students, but you wouldn't know for sure until you try them out. Trying out assessment tasks (whether performance or traditional paper-and-pencil) before using them is next to impossible for classroom teachers. You can, however, have your colleagues review and criticize your tasks before you use them. The next best thing to live student tryouts can and should be done: After you use an assessment task, use the information you obtain about flaws in the task or in the rubric to revise the task or rubric; then reuse the task and rubric next year with a new class of students.

Example 9.2 presents an example of a book report and rubrics for scoring it. Using the guidelines as a checklist to evaluate this assessment, we find:

1. Yes, this "Book Show and Tell" assesses several important instructional targets. These targets are from state standards.

2. Yes, the assessment matched the assessment plan in terms of performance, emphasis, and number of points. Of the five scales, four of them are about content related to reading and understanding the book, and one is about communication skills, a language arts target.

■ **EXAMPLE 9.2 Example of performance assessment assignment and rubrics**

Fourth-grade book report and presentation: "Book Show and Tell"

Learning targets assessed:

- Uses personal criteria to select reading materials
- Reads for meaning
- Conveys clear main points when speaking
- Uses oral communication skills

Select a book that you have enjoyed reading this year, one that you could recommend to others who have interests like yours.

1. Write a brief book report in two parts. Use as much space as you need, but aim for about four pages.
   - In the first part, briefly summarize the book. If your book is fiction, summarize the plot. If your book is nonfiction, summarize the main points of the book.
   - In the second part, tell why you chose this book. What in particular did you like about it? What are the reasons you want to share it?
2. Make something to share with the class in a presentation designed to interest others in reading your book. It could be a diorama of one of your favorite scenes, or a poster, or a figure of one of the characters, or a computer presentation, depending on the book and your interest.
   - Prepare a 3–5 minute talk for the class. Name your book, and tell why you selected it.
   - Tell enough about the book that others will know what it's about. Use the first part of your book report to help you.
   - End your presentation by showing what you made, telling what it is, and telling how it expresses something interesting from the book.

Rubrics (shared with students as part of the assignment)

Your "Book Show and Tell" will be assessed for your understanding of the book and for the way you present that to others. What you make will be assessed on how it relates to the book and to your presentation, not on its artistic value. (Of course, the better it looks, the more people will want to see it!)

Book Report

Summary

4—Summary is complete and accurate. Summary is clear to reader.

3—Summary is complete and accurate, although not too detailed. Summary is clear to reader.

2—Summary is incomplete but mostly accurate. Summary is somewhat clear to reader.

1—Summary is incomplete or inaccurate. Summary is not clear to reader.

Statement of Interest

4—Statement of personal interest is clear, and reasons are sensible and well explained.

3—Statement of personal interest is clear, and reasons are sensible and explained.

2—Statement of personal interest is somewhat unclear, and reasons are not explained.

1—No statement of personal interest, or statement doesn't make sense.

Presentation

Main Points

4—Summary and statement of personal interest are clear. Audience can understand the presentation.

3—Summary and statement of personal interest are somewhat clear. Audience can understand the presentation.

2—Summary and statement of personal interest are somewhat unclear. Audience can understand some of the presentation.

1—Summary and statement of personal interest are unclear. Audience can't understand the presentation.

Communication Skills (Audience Contact)

4—Audience contact is maintained with eye contact, body language, vocal expression, and word choice.

3—Audience contact is mostly maintained.

2—Audience contact "comes and goes."

1—No audience contact.

Artifact

4—Artifact relates to interest in the book, and explanation is clear.

3—Artifact relates to interest in the book, and explanation is fairly clear.

2—Artifact may relate to interest in the book, but explanation is unclear.

1—No artifact or unrelated artifact, and no explanation.

3. Yes, the assessment requires a student to *do* something. There is a written component, which serves to focus student understanding and also to provide content for the oral presentation.

4. The time allowed for the assignment is not specified. While this would differ in different classrooms with different students, it should be specified.

5. This is an open-response task. Wording and directions make clear to students that they may use a variety of approaches for their artifact, and that they will be evaluated on the substance of their responses.

6. This task is not "real world" per se, but is very participatory. It is active. It is "authentic" in the sense that students need to develop skills at communicating their thinking to others.

7. The task involves locating a book and using some art supplies. No mention is made of where to locate these. The teacher should remediate this shortcoming by making books and supplies available in the classroom (or in the school library).

8. Yes, the task (a) is defined appropriately for the maturity of students, (b) is clearly interpretable by all students, (c) has clear purposes, (d) specifies the length of both written and oral work, and (e) gives the rubric that will be used for evaluation.

9. The task does not present drawings or graphs to students.

10. No mention is made of accommodations for students with disabilities. These should be made on a case-by-case basis and based on student IEPs.

Tasks assessing the same content learning target can differ from one another

Table 9.1 shows five properties of a task that you can control to produce a task that is well aligned with your learning targets (and thus more valid for assessment).

Time needed

Some learning targets can be assessed in a relatively short period of 15 to 40 minutes. For example, the ability to work in groups, write an essay or an explanation, plot a graph, or carry out simple experiments can be assessed with short tasks. Many learning targets and dimensions, however, imply that students complete long tasks. For example, doing an opinion survey and writing it up, building a model town, and developing complex plans for community action require a week or more, and much of the work may need to be done outside of class. Task time limits must match the intent of the learning target and dimensions rather than your own convenience—if your goal is to use the results to make valid interpretations about how well a student has achieved that learning target.

Task structure

It may be misleading to talk about structured versus unstructured performance, because you can **structure a task** in various ways (Davey & Rindone, 1990), including the way you define the problem, scaffold the instructions, require alternate strategies, and require alternate solutions. At one extreme your task may *define a problem* for a student to solve (structured); at the other extreme you may require the student himself to identify what the problem is (unstructured or ill-defined). For example, some

Table 9.1 Properties of tasks that you can vary to better align students' performance with the requirements of the achievement dimensions and learning targets

Task property	Variations in the task requirements
Time to complete the task	*Short tasks* can be done in one class period or less. *Long tasks* require a month or more, and work may need to be done outside class.
Task structure provided	Structure may vary in: *Problem definition.* High structure means you carefully define the problem the student must solve. Low structure means the student is free to select and define the problem. *Scaffolding:* High structure means the student is given lots of guidance or directions in how to begin a solution and what materials to use. Low structure means a student has little or no guidance and must decide for him or herself. *Alternative strategies:* High structure means there are very few correct or appropriate pathways to get to the correct answer. Low structure means there are many correct or appropriate approaches to get an acceptable answer. *Alternative solutions:* High structure means there is a correct answer to the task. Low structure means there is no single correct answer to this task.
Participation of groups	The task may require: *Individual work* only throughout all phases of performance. *Mixed individual and group work* in which some of the performance occurs in groups and some is strictly individual effort. *Group work* only throughout all phases of performance.
Product and process focus	The task may require: *Process assessment* only in which the student's performance of the steps and procedures and not the outcome are observed and evaluated. *Both process and product assessment* in which both the steps and the concrete outcome (product) are evaluated. *Product assessment* only in which only the concrete product or outcome is evaluated.
Performance modality	The task may require: A *single modality* in which the performance is limited to one mode (e.g., oral, written, wood model, etc.). *Multiple modalities* in which the performance must be done in several modes (e.g., do both a written and an oral report).

Source: Based on ideas in Davey & Rindone (1990).

math performance assessments require students to explain their reasoning. You could structure the same math problem differently by telling students they had to illustrate their reasoning with diagrams, or that they had to illustrate their reasoning two different ways, or that they could explain their reasoning in any way they chose.

Scaffolding is the degree of support, guidance, and direction you provide the students when they set out to complete the task. You may suggest how to attack the problem, what books or material to use, and the general nature of the end product you require. These directions and guidance statements add structure to the task. Less scaffolding means less structure.

If your task can be performed or solved using only one or two procedures or strategies, it has fewer **alternate solution strategies** and is more structured in this respect. Unstructured alternatives mean that there are a great many equally correct pathways to the correct answer or to producing the correct product. A similar analysis applies to the solution or the product itself: A task is unstructured in this respect when it has many correct or *acceptable solutions or products.*

■ **Example showing how controlling properties can change a performance task**

Assume that students have been asked simply to build a scale model of the solar system. As far as problem definition goes, this task has fairly high structure—you have a specified goal to meet. However, there is very little scaffolding—students are not told what materials to use, or what proportions to use, or where to get information on the planetary distances and orbits. There are a lot of alternative pathways to the solution—consider the fact that no two models will look exactly alike, and will vary in terms of materials used, scale employed, special features included (such as neurons, orbital speeds, etc.), and in a way there's one best solution, a perfectly scaled model of the solar system. (Davey & Rindone, 1990, p. 5)

Participation of groups

Learning targets guide your task construction. If your learning targets call for cooperative or collaborative learning (or using other group-based skills), you should set a task using, at least in part, group activities. For assessment, it is important to specify whether the final product (e.g., a report on the American Revolution) will be a group output or a collection of individual work (e.g., different sections of the report done by different, identifiable group members). Follow the logic between what you ask students to do and the learning targets. A group report, for example, will not give you information about individual students' abilities to select and use information. For that you need individual reports or essays. A group project *will* give you information about how students work together around important subject matter.

Product and process

If you want to assess process, you need to do the assessing while a student is performing. You may take away a product, on the other hand, and evaluate it at your convenience. Further, you cannot assess cognitive processes (mental activities) directly, only indirectly through some intermediate or "partial" products. For example, you can ask students to tell you or to write what they were thinking about while they were doing the task. Or you may ask them to record the early drafts they made and ideas they used.

Your indirect assessments of a student's mental activities and thinking processes depend on the student having abilities other than those required to complete the task. They depend, for example, on the accuracy of the students' memories, their skills in understanding the thinking processes they used, and their abilities to describe these thinking processes orally or in writing. Because you assess cognitive processes only indirectly, your inferences and judgments about how well a student uses them—that is, the validity of your evaluation of a student's use of cognitive processes—might be weak. Other processes, such as group processes and behavior that occurs in a sequence of steps, are more directly assessed because you can observe them directly.

Response mode

Some learning targets specify that students should be able to communicate their knowledge in several ways, solve a problem using several methods, or express themselves in a variety of modalities. You should not use multiple response modes on a whim, however. Align the modalities with the learning targets, state standards, and curriculum framework. Use alternate modes to accommodate students with disabilities or cultural differences if the mainstream, single mode is not appropriate for them. For example, a student with a verbal learning disability may be allowed to explain his or her reasoning for a math problem using diagrams.

Number of tasks

As a general rule, the fewer the number of tasks, the fewer learning targets you can assess, the lower the score reliability, and the lower the validity of your interpretations. The number of performance tasks to include in your assessment depends on several factors, some of which you cannot control. The following issues will help you decide on the appropriate number of tasks:

- *Crucial decisions.* Assessments for high-stakes decisions (e.g., promotion or graduation), in which the consequences of failing are severe, require more tasks and longer assessment times to gather sufficiently reliable information. Letter-grade assignments are also crucial decisions, especially if you are unwilling or unable to change the grade once it's entered. Grades for a term or a marking period should not be based on a single assessment, either.

- *Scope of your assessment.* How much instruction are you covering with this assessment—a unit or only one lesson? How much content is covered in a unit? The broader the scope of your assessment, the more tasks you will need.

- *Mixture of assessment formats.* If you mix objective formats with performance tasks, you will be able to cover more aspects of the learning targets, balance your assessment, and broaden your assessment scope. In this case, you may need fewer performance tasks because your assessment scope will be broader than if you used performance tasks alone.

- *Complexity of the learning target.* A complex learning target requires integration of many skills and abilities and may need to be performed over a long time.

- *Time needed to complete each task.* As a practical matter, you can administer only a few tasks during a typical class period. Decide how much time one task will take a student to complete, and divide this into the length of the class period to determine the maximum number of tasks possible. Students usually take longer to complete a task than you think, so allow for that.

- *Time available for the total assessment.* You may be willing to devote more or less than one period to assessment. The number of tasks may shrink or expand depending on the available time.

- *Diagnostic detail needed.* If you need a lot of detail to diagnose a student's learning or conceptual problems, you need to create tasks that provide this rich detail. This usually means fewer tasks, more detailed performance, and more detailed scoring of the responses. If you assess many students for diagnostic purposes, practicalities of time for performance and scoring will usually limit you to only a few tasks per student.

■ *Available human resources.* If you have an aide or a parent to help you administer or score the assessments, this may free up some time so that you can use a few more tasks.

Project management

Because projects usually span several weeks, you must plan to manage them. Of course, you "manage" tests and quizzes, too, but that amounts to passing them out, monitoring and maintaining a period of quiet, collecting, and grading them. Project management is more complicated, although the reasons for doing it are similar. If you don't manage tests well (e.g., if you allow cheating), then you don't get useful information from the test results. Similarly, if you don't manage projects well, you don't get useful information about what students know and can do from the results. Guideline 9.2 presents classroom and assessment management strategies. Note that all of them present opportunities for formative assessment as the project develops.

Portfolios are purposeful collections of student work and student reflection on that work

For purposes of assessment, a **portfolio** is a limited collection of a student's work used either to present the student's best work(s) or to demonstrate the student's educational growth over a given time, on one or a set of learning targets. Items included in a portfolio are carefully selected so the collection as a whole accomplishes its purpose. Although there are other purposes for creating a portfolio, this chapter discusses only two assessment purposes: presenting one's best work and demonstrating educational growth.

A best-works portfolio contains a student's best final products. Use best-works portfolios primarily for summative purposes. For example, a best-works portfolio serving the purpose of giving evidence of subject-matter mastery and learning would include a student's best works on specific learning targets and could be part of the basis for a report card grade.

Very often the contents of the best-works portfolio are prescribed. For example, to certify a student's accomplishment in art, educational authorities may require a drawing, a painting, a sculpture, a craft product, and one work in a medium of the student's choosing. In mathematics, an educational authority may require that a student's portfolio contain a table of contents, a letter telling the portfolio evaluator about the entries included, and five to seven best works involving a variety of types of activities, tools, and topics (Kentucky Department of Education, 1993).

Guideline 9.2 Strategies for Managing Group and Individual Projects

Strategy	Example
Monitor individual students to be sure they are making regular progress and keep them focused on completing the project.	A student gets "sidetracked" or procrastinates. Your reminders or questions help him get back on track.
Mentor students to help them overcome operational problems that may be beyond their control.	A key person students were to interview for the project has become ill and cannot see them. You help them find another acceptable source of information.
Monitor the procedures and processes the students are using to ensure they will be able to address the learning targets set for the project.	A project intended to help students learn to interpret stock reports in the newspaper. The father of one of your students works in a brokerage firm, and the student has been asking her dad about how the market is doing rather than learning to read the stock pages herself. You help her to redirect her efforts.
Clarify the outcome(s) you expect. Each student should understand both the purpose(s) of the project (the learning target being assessed) and what you expect the project to look like.	Show and discuss examples of high-quality projects you saved from former students.
Put your expectations in writing.	Distribute to and discuss with students a written description of what you expect in the way of a project, processes, and the major purpose of the project.
Clarify the standards you will use to evaluate the project.	Explain and give students copies of the scoring rubrics you will be using to evaluate the project.
Let students participate in setting standards. Each student should internalize the quality standards and have a sense of ownership of them.	Use past projects to help students induce achievement dimensions. Help students to describe the quality levels within each dimension.
Clarify deadlines.	Set deadlines that are • long enough so students can develop and complete authentic projects and • short enough to be practical and so that students must keep on task, have no time to waste, and finish on time.
Require progress reports.	For longer projects, specify weekly or biweekly dates for students to report their progress (e.g., every Friday) • to keep the students on task, • to assess the processes and progress toward completing the project, and • to alert you to any problems beyond student control that may require your intervention.
Minimize plagiarism opportunities. Each student should do his or her work to the best of his or her ability.	• Explain to students what constitutes plagiarism. • Explain the seriousness of doing one's own work even though it is not perfect. • Avoid projects that may inadvertently encourage students to plagiarize material. Projects that help to reduce the students' temptation to copy include interviews, comparing opinions, making models, designing ideal projects, locating contrasting views on an issue, producing an object, and creating a dramatization for another group or class (Harmin, 1994).

Students need to learn how to create a best-works portfolio to present themselves in the best possible way. Among the portfolio-making skills students need to learn are deciding exactly what they want to communicate or accomplish through the portfolio, choosing the pieces to include in the portfolio, presenting the pieces chosen, and evaluating the qualities of the pieces selected using the scoring rubrics that will be applied to their portfolios.

As with other forms of performance assessment, assess best-works portfolios only after you have developed a scoring rubric based on the learning target(s). Scoring rubrics for portfolios usually apply to the entire portfolio rather than to each piece separately, although there are exceptions. As we've stated before, we devote a whole chapter (10) to scoring because it's just as important as creating the tasks for assessment.

A **growth and learning-progress portfolio** contains examples of a student's work, along with comments, that demonstrate how well the student's learning has progressed over a given period. It does not focus on the final products a student produces. Instead, you and the student use the portfolio for formative purposes to monitor the student's learning and thinking progress, to diagnose learning and thinking difficulties, and to guide new learning and thinking. The student plays a significant role in deciding what should be included in this portfolio and learns to use the portfolio to understand and evaluate her own progress.

■ **EXAMPLE 9.3 Example of how the Bellevue, Washington, teachers organized their students' reading and writing portfolios to assess growth**

Learning target	What is put into the portfolio	Frequency of entry and assessment
1. Develop a meaningful ownership of one's own learning and work to be evaluated	1. (a) Student-selected pieces of work (b) Entry slip explaining why each piece was included	1. Three or more times per year
2. Evaluate one's own progress over time	2. (a) Student reviews his or her own portfolio (b) Student answers questions about his or her development as a reader and writer	2. Two or more times per year
3. Interact with the text to create meaning	3. Entry slip retelling the piece read or explaining its meaning	3. Two or three times per year
4. Choose to read a variety of material	4. Log of books/articles read during a two-week period	4. Two or three times per year
5. Communicate effectively through writing	5. Samples of longer pieces of writing	5. Two or three times per year
6. Student develops as a reader and writer	6. (a) Student drafts, notes, and other work selected by the teacher (b) Teacher's notes and comments about the student's progress	6. Left to the teacher's discretion

Source: Adapted from "Literacy Portfolios for Teaching, Learning, and Accountability: The Bellevue Literacy Assessment Project," by S. W. Valencia and N. A. Place, in *Authentic Reading Assessment: Practices and Possibilities* (pp. 139–141), by Sheila W. Valencia, E. H. Hiebert, and Peter P. Afferbach (Eds.). Copyright © 1994 by the International Reading Association. Adapted by permission.

Step	Questions to Answer
Step 1. Identify Portfolio's Purpose and Focus	• Why do I want a portfolio? • What learning targets and curriculum goals will it serve? • Will other methods of assessment serve these learning targets better? • Should the portfolio focus on best work, growth and learning progress, or both? • Will the portfolio be used for students' summative evaluation, formative evaluation, or both? • Who should be involved in defining the purpose, focus, and organization of the portfolio (e.g., students, teachers, parents)?
Step 2. Identify the General Achievement Dimensions to Be Assessed	• What kinds of knowledge, skills, and abilities will be the major focus of the portfolio? • Do I need to use the same content and thinking processes framework (blueprint) as I do for individual performance tasks? • Should I focus primarily on how well the student uses the portfolio to reflect on his or her progress or growth? • For a growth-and-learning-progress portfolio, what do I want to learn about students' self-reflections?

Step 3. Identify Appropriate Organization	• What types of entries (student products and activity records) will provide assessment information about the content and process dimensions identified in Step 2?
	• What should the outline or table of contents for each portfolio contain?
	• Define each category or type of entry:
	  • Which content and process dimension does it assess?
	  • What will the teacher or the student "get out of" each entry?
	  • What is the time frame for each entry being put into the portfolio?
	• When will the entries be evaluated?
	• What are the minimum and maximum numbers of entries per category?
	• How will the entries within a student's portfolio be organized?
	• Will this set of entries fully represent the student's attainment or growth and learning progress?
	• What type of container will I need to hold all of the students' entries, and where will I keep them?

Step 4. Use Portfolio in Practice	• When will the students work on or use their portfolios (e.g., 15 minutes of every class period)? • How will the portfolio fit into the classroom routine? • Will the teacher, student, or both decide what to include in the portfolio? • How do I create a climate in the classroom that promotes good use of portfolios? • When will the student and/or the teacher review and evaluate the portfolio? • How will the portfolio be weighted, if at all, when the time comes to assign letter grades for the marking period? • Will I schedule a conference to go over the portfolio with the student? • Will the portfolio be shared with parents? Other teachers? Other students?
Step 5. Evaluate Portfolios and Entries	• Are scoring rubrics already available for each type of entry? • Does an evaluation framework or scoring rubric exist for each type of entry? • Are the rubrics aligned with the state standards and school district's curriculum framework? • Will students, teachers, or both evaluate entries? Which ones? • Will evaluations of every entry count toward a marking-period grade? • Given its purpose, is it necessary to have an overall score for the portfolio? • What type of rubric should I use (see Chapter 10)? • Who will score the portfolio (e.g., student, teacher, outsider)? • How often will the whole portfolio need to be scored (e.g., each week or each marking period)? • Does an evaluation framework or scoring rubric exist for evaluating the portfolio as a whole?
Step 6. Evaluate Rubrics	• Are scoring rubrics available that are consistent with the purpose of the portfolio? With the way each individual entry was evaluated? With the overall curriculum framework? • Has the scoring rubric been tried on portfolios from different students? From students with different teachers? With what results? • Does the scoring rubric give the same results for the same students when applied by different teachers?

For example, a growth and learning-progress portfolio to monitor progress and show change in achievement would help the student look over his or her work to see the "long view" or "whole picture" of what has been accomplished. The portfolio would contain student works that appear at intermediate stages in the course of the student's learning. These may include early drafts, records of thinking, and rewrites. The final product is placed into the portfolio, too.

To use a growth and learning-progress portfolio to full advantage, you will need to know the typical learning progressions in the discipline for which you are assessing progress (Shepard, Hammerness, Darling-Hammond, & Rust, 2005). You will need that to help you recognize progress, or lack of it, when you see it and to help you provide feedback to the student at the right point in his or her learning. Example 9.3 shows an example of how teachers in one school district organized growth portfolios to show progress. Organization was based on six learning targets in reading and writing.

The clearer you are about your portfolio's learning targets and purpose(s), the better. If the portfolio must serve more than one purpose, consider carefully the focus of each portfolio entry, so that each entry serves at least one of your intended purposes. Media for portfolios can vary. Some portfolios are in folders, others in crates or boxes, some in electronic format. Practical considerations about what kinds of entries are allowed and how they will be stored are important for planning classroom portfolio use.

Guideline 9.3 presents six steps for developing a portfolio system. Because portfolios are used for such a wide range of formative and summative purposes, a single set of design guidelines is difficult to devise. The six steps are general enough, however, to give you overall guidance in the portfolio development process. Adapt the steps to suit your particular purposes. Notice that after answering the questions in Step 1, you may decide *not* to develop a portfolio system. Steps 2 through 5 assume that you have completed Step 1, have decided to use a portfolio system, and are using the answers from Step 1 to guide you in the last five steps.

Conclusions

This chapter must end by repeating our caution: You aren't finished yet! We have talked about selecting appropriate learning targets for performance assessment and creating the tasks or assignments for students. A performance assessment is not complete without a scoring scheme. Therefore, Chapter 9 is not complete without Chapter 10.

Exercises

1. Each of the scenarios below describes a science project assignment. Compare and contrast the properties of these tasks. Use Table 9.1 to help you. What can you conclude about the two different assignments?

a. Mrs. MacRae assigned a science project to her students. They had a month to work on it, and they were allowed to choose any topic they wished, as long as there were materials and resources available in the school library on that topic. The project had to include some sort of experiment or demonstration, and a write-up of it that included at least one chart or graph. Once students had an idea, they were to write one page describing what they wanted to do, and why, and have a conference with Mrs. MacRae. [In this paper they needed to show what they had found in the school library.] She either approved the project or gave feedback on how to change it. Each student did his or her own project. At the end of the month, Mrs. MacRae had a class "science fair" at which each student displayed his project. Students voted on the best five projects, which were entered into the school science fair.

b. Mr. Ritchie assigned a science project to his students as the final project for a weather unit. He put them into learning groups of four students each. They were to do four things: (a) select a location in the United States, follow the weather for that location for a week (using a log); (b) use their research to predict the weather for that location for the following week; (c) follow the weather for that location over the next week (using a log); and (d) create a display that included their logs, weather charts, and a report explaining what they did, including how they applied the concepts they had learned in the first part of the weather unit and how accurate their predictions were. They had a total of three weeks to do the project (two to collect the weather data and a final week to work on the display and report).

2. Pretend you are working in a seventh-grade classroom where students have been reading chapter books or novels of their choice (limited choice, depending on their reading level). Below are four different "performances" that a teacher might ask students to do as part of classroom assessment. For each, describe how "authentic" you think the task would seem to students. Also, describe what the students would probably deduce was their learning target (what they were "supposed to learn") if this was the assignment the teacher gave.

a. Write a standard book report (summarize the plot, then describe what was your favorite part and why).

b. Participate in a student-led literature circle with three other students who had read the same book.

c. Participate in a teacher-led class discussion where the teacher asked general questions and called on students to answer with examples from their particular book (e.g., "How important is it for you to like the main character in a book?")

Now go to our Companion Website at **www.prenhall.com/brookhart** to assess your understanding of chapter content with multiple-choice and essay questions. Broaden your knowledge of assessment with links to assessment related web sites.

Companion
Website

10

Scoring: Points, Rubrics, and Other Scales

1. The purpose of a scoring scheme is to communicate the intended meaning of the assessment results.
2. Score objective items as right or wrong (usually 1 or 0 points, respectively).
3. Score essays, show-the-work problems, and performance assessments with partial credit scoring (rubrics, checklists, rating scales, or point-based scoring schemes).
4. Create rubrics that clarify standards of achievement.
5. Score partial credit items with strategies that maximize scoring reliability.
6. Checklists mark attributes as present or absent.
7. Ratings scales assess the degree to which students have demonstrated various attributes.
8. Some scoring schemes assign points to various aspects of a response.

Recently I attended a fund-raising dinner for a scholarship program for minority students. It was held in a downtown hotel ballroom. About forty African American high school seniors sat at tables on a raised platform. Their parents were there, as were members of the sponsoring organization and others like me, who had come with colleagues from my university.

I was looking forward to the evening. All of the honorees had won at least a small scholarship. Some of the scholarships, however, were larger amounts, and some were for four years. Announcing the recipients of those bigger awards was part of the program for the evening. There was also an inspirational speaker.

It did turn out to be fun, but there was one surprise—at least for me. When the time came to introduce the honorees, the master of ceremonies read—in addition to their name, high school, and where they planned to go to college—their grade point average and SAT score. Wow! I was surprised enough that those scores were read out loud, and was even more surprised that the students didn't seem to mind at all.

I was bothered at first, because I study such things and know, for example, that two grade point averages from two different high schools aren't comparable. Upon reflection, I think I missed the bigger point. The meaning of those scores, both grades and SAT scores, in that context was "This student is a success." What was the moral of the story for me should turn into your theme song as you read the chapter. It's all about **score meaning**.

The purpose of a scoring scheme is to communicate the intended meaning of the assessment results

Suppose that you took a spelling test and your score was 45, found by giving one point for each correctly spelled word. How well have you performed? Knowing only that your task was "a spelling test" and that your score was 45 leaves you unable to interpret your performance.

Raw scores are the number of points (marks) you assign to a student's performance on an assessment. You may obtain these marks by adding the number of correct answers, the ratings for each task, or the number of points awarded to separate parts of the assessment. As in the spelling score example, a raw score tells a student what he or she "got," but tells very little about the meaning of the score.

Almost all educational and psychological assessments require you to use some type of referencing framework to interpret students' performance. A *referencing framework* is a structure you use to compare a student's performance to something external to the assessment itself. An external framework enhances your interpretation of a student's assessment results. We discuss four referencing frameworks in this chapter.

A **norm-referencing** framework interprets a student's assessment performance by comparing it to the performance of a well-defined group of other students who have taken the same assessment. The well-defined group of other students is called the **norm group**. To make valid norm-referenced interpretations, all persons in the norm group must have been given the same assessment as your students and under the same conditions (same time limits, directions, equipment and materials, etc.). This is why you must follow administration instructions exactly when administering a standardized achievement test.

To understand a norm-referenced interpretation, let's return to your score on the spelling test. Suppose your raw score of 45 means that your percentile rank (PR) is 99—that is, 99% of the persons who took the spelling test have scored lower than 45. Before you congratulate yourself, find out who is in the norm group to which your raw score is being referenced. You would interpret your performance differently if you knew the norm group was comprised of third graders than if the norm group was comprised of adults.

A **criterion-referencing** framework interprets results in terms of the kinds of performances a student can do in an academic domain, rather than the student's relative standing in a norm group. This domain of performance to which you reference a student's assessment results is called the *criterion*. When you teach, the criterion that is of most interest is the domain of performance implied by your state's standards, your curriculum framework, and your lessons' learning targets. Your spelling score of 45, for example, might mean you could spell correctly 90% of the words in a particular spelling unit.

A **self-referencing** framework interprets a student's results in terms of improvement from his or her own starting point or in terms of achievement compared with expectations for that student. This is the best kind of interpretation for formative assessment, but it falls short as a method for summative assessment. It puts each student's work on his or her own "scale," and the score has little meaning to others who don't know the child and his work. A spelling score of 45, for example, can only mean "5 points better than last week" if you know that last week's score was 40.

Standards-referencing combines aspects of criterion- and norm-referencing to address states' needs for No Child Left Behind reporting (Young & Zucker, 2004). Ranges of test scores are identified to be interpreted as "basic," "proficient," or "advanced." Cut scores—the borderline scores that define these categories—for these criterion-referenced judgments are typically suggested by panels of teachers and other educators in standard-setting sessions. The results of standard-setting sessions are reviewed by the state, which makes the ultimate decisions.

Score objective items as right or wrong (usually 1 or 0 points, respectively)

You're probably familiar with this method. How many classroom tests did you take that scored items as either right or wrong? Spelling tests, math facts tests, multiple-choice tests: You name it, we've all done it. What we want to stress here is that the right/wrong decision and its 1/0 point designation should add up to a score that means something. So each item needs to make a solid, and relatively equivalent, contribution to the sum total.

That means no silly or fluff items. If you do use a silly item to add humor to a test, then don't add its score into the total. It also means that the number of items for any given learning target should be proportional to its importance and instructional emphasis. For example, if half of the unit was about an important concept, and you only have a few points (questions) about it on the test, the total score will not indicate students' achievement in the unit as you taught it.

Consider how many total points there are before you transform number correct into percent correct. If there are only 5 items, for example, and a student gets 4 out of 5, that's 80%. Eighty percent (a B or C on many grading scales) implies there's room for improvement—and short of perfection, there isn't in this case. If you're going to use percent correct, have enough items. We like to say at least 20, but that's just arbitrary. Twenty items will result in scores of 100%, 95%, 90%, and so on. Thirty would be better.

Now think about what gets those points—they're based on questions you wrote or selected. That means *you* control how "hard" it is to earn a point. For which level of difficulty should an item be written? There is no general rule, but keep in mind these main points: the type of students, the level of instruction, the purpose for which you will use the assessment results, and the level of knowledge your students need to attain at this point in their educational development. Consider the levels of thinking skills your test will assess. Decide, at least roughly, what level of proficiency is sufficient for each important learning target. Then construct test items that will allow you to distinguish students who lack sufficient proficiency from those who have acquired it.

If you are trying to map students along a range of proficiencies (A, B, C, D, F, for example; or Basic, Proficient, Advanced; etc.), you should include items along the range of the continuum, so that each category of student will have some items that indicate their level of proficiency. A "C" student, for example, should be appropriately measured as a "C" by getting questions at that level correct, not just by missing some number of questions intended for "A" students.

Item analysis

If your school has a scanner and students use answer sheets to bubble in their answer choices, right/wrong selected response items can be scored by machine. Of course, the machine will easily mark each student's answers right or wrong and give each student's number right and percent correct.

Your scanning software may also be able to give you information about the test items themselves from an **item analysis**. Item analysis is the process of collecting, summarizing, and using information from each student's item responses to make decisions about how each item is functioning. If you are interested in the way item statistics are calculated, see Nitko and Brookhart (2007). Here, we focus on how to interpret item analysis output from common scanning software. You can use this information to revise and improve multiple-choice items.

The **item difficulty index** (p) tells you what proportion of students got the item right. It ranges from .00 (none) to 1.00 (all). If an item is too hard or too easy, you may want to consider revising it. For classroom assessment, however, there may be many items that look statistically "easy"—simply indicating learning targets that were met. For a multiple-choice test, the average of all the item difficulties is the class average proportion correct. A test with all "hard" (low item difficulty values) items will have a low class average score; a test with all "easy" (high item difficulty values) items will have a high class average score. You may read recommendations for ideal difficulty levels, but most of those are for standardized tests. For classroom tests, our advice is decide how difficult your test should be based on the learning targets it measures.

There are two commonly used **item discrimination indices**. Most item analysis software will produce one or the other, but not both. They are interpreted similarly. The statistic D compares the proportion of high-scoring students who got an item right with the proportion of low-scoring students who did so. The **point-biserial correlation** (r_{pbis}) relates item performance (right/wrong) to total test performance (total score). Items that discriminate negatively (that have a negative value for D or r_{pbis}) are not working well. Students with a poor grasp of the learning targets do better on these than students with a good grasp. Eliminate or revise any negatively discriminating items or nondiscriminating items (zero D or r_{pbis}). Higher discrimination is better (say +.20 or above—for standardized tests +.30 or above is usually the goal), although for very easy items not much discrimination is possible.

Most item analysis programs will provide a table for each multiple-choice item that shows how many students selected each answer choice. Of course, you hope most picked the correct answer (the key). The wrong answers should be spread out among the others (thus, representing random guessing), especially for low-scoring students. If no one picked a particular answer choice, it's not functioning as a distractor. If one particular wrong answer choice gets as many, or almost as many, choices as the key, it may be ambiguous. If either of these is the case, go back to the item and read the choices; they may need editing in order to function properly to measure student learning.

Item analysis programs also provide a reliability coefficient that measures the extent to which students' responses were consistent from one item to the next. We discussed reliability in Chapter 2, and listed kinds of reliability coefficients in Table 2.3. Most often the reliability coefficient on your printout will be KR20 (Kuder-Richardson Formula 20 from Table 2.3). KR20 ranges from .00 (no reliability) to 1.00 (perfect reliability). For norm-referenced standardized tests, KR20 values should be +.90 or above, but for the limited sample and criterion-referenced framework used in most classroom tests, the reliability coefficient may not be that high (+.70 or above is nothing to worry about, and values may occasionally be even lower, especially for easy tests). For classroom tests, the reliability strategies in Guideline 2.2 are more important than a high KR20 value.

Score essays, show-the-work problems, and performance assessments with partial credit scoring (rubrics, checklists, rating scales, or points-based scoring schemes)

As an example to have in mind as you read the practical suggestions for scoring rubrics (below), Example 10.1 presents two sets of task-specific scoring rubrics for the Keats poem on page 153.

Essay questions should be scored with scoring scales that fit the point values planned in the test blueprint. If your planned weight for a given topic/thinking cell in your test blueprint is 10 points, that could be two five-point essays, one ten-point essay, or any other combination that makes ten points. Similarly, the number of points for one essay's score should represent a reasonable weighting given the learning targets to be measured.

Guideline 10.1 provides guidance for writing or selecting a scoring rubric. The guidelines can be used to evaluate classroom rating scales, too.

Rubrics have many positive features. Probably the most important is that the descriptions of the qualities of work in general rubrics define what "good work" is and help students conceptualize the kind of performance they are aiming for. Thus, rubrics are a powerful instructional tool as well as an assessment tool.

Create rubrics that clarify standards of achievement

Rubrics not only improve scoring consistency, they also improve validity by clarifying the standards of achievement you will use to evaluate your students. Rubrics can be categorized in two ways: according to how many scales are used (*analytic* rubrics

■ **EXAMPLE 10.1 Example of Scoring Rubrics for an Essay Question**

Example—Essay #2 on the Keats poem (page 153)

The second essay question about the Keats poem on page 153 read, "Summarize the mood described in lines 9 to 14." First, you must know what a good answer would say. That means you have to understand the poem very well yourself. Chapman did the first good English translations of Homer's *Iliad* and *Odyssey* (which, of course, were written in Greek). At that time (early 1600's), therefore, a whole body of classic literature became available to English-speaking people. This poem is about a reader who reads these works for the first time. He likens literature to a wonderful land ("realms of gold"; lines 1 to 8) and explains that coming across these works of Homer was like discovering a new land. He uses two images: the image of an astronomer discovering a new planet (lines 9–10) and the image of the explorer Cortez discovering the Pacific Ocean (lines 11–14).

Suppose you decided, then, that good student essays would identify these images and conclude that the mood was one of discovery, with its attendant feelings of surprise and delight. And you also wanted good essays to be well organized for readers and written according to standard English grammar and usage conventions. These three dimensions (content, organization, and grammar/usage) are your criteria. You might use the following set of rubrics. Note that the content rubric ("description of mood") is task-specific. You could not share this rubric with the students before they wrote their essays because that would analyze the poem for them. Also note that the weights for the content rubric are doubled, making the ideas worth half (6 points) and the writing worth half (6 points).

Example of Analytic Scoring Rubrics for Essay #2 on the Keats poem (page 153)

3 criteria, 12 points possible

Description of Mood (Discovery)

6   Identifies both astronomer and explorer images as discovery images and gives clear explanation

4   Identifies mood but explanation absent or unclear

2   Mood not identified or incorrectly identified

Organization

3   Thesis is clearly stated in topic sentence; how details support thesis is explicitly stated

2   Topic sentence includes thesis; supporting details are present

1   No topic/thesis sentence and/or no supporting details

■ **EXAMPLE 10.1** (Continued)

Grammar/Usage

3   No errors or minor ones that do not impede reading

2   Some errors in grammar or usage, but meaning is clear

1   So many errors that meaning is unclear

Use analytic scoring (above) if feedback on different aspects of performance is required (for example, so a student knows what to work on to improve). Use holistic scoring (below) if one overall judgment is required (for example, on a final exam whose results a student might not see). Notice, however, that the holistic rubrics use the same criteria: content, organization, and grammar/usage. Assign the grade or score whose description most closely matches the student's essay.

**Example of Holistic Scoring Rubrics for Essay #2
on the Keats poem (page 153)**

A   Mood of discovery is clearly identified; support for this is derived from images of astronomer and explorer; writing is clear and well organized.

B   Mood of discovery is identified; support is implied but not made explicit in discussion of images of astronomer and explorer; writing is clear and organized.

C   Mood of discovery is identified; one of the images is described; organization is minimal; writing needs editing.

D   Mood is not clearly identified or incorrectly identified; writing is not clear or well organized.

F   Essay is not about mood and/or so many errors in grammar and usage make meaning impossible to interpret.

Notice that your standards of achievement are embodied in these scoring levels. It would be possible to have "harder" or "easier" rubrics, for example, where the D in this scale might be an F in another.

use several scales; *holistic* rubrics use one) and according to whether the rubrics are *task-specific* or *generic* (or *general*) rubrics.

An **analytic scoring rubric** (also called scoring key, point scale, or trait scale) requires you to evaluate specific dimensions, traits, or elements of a student's response. A **holistic scoring rubric** (also called global, sorting, or rating) requires you to make a judgment about the overall quality of each student's response. **Generic rubrics** (also called general rubrics) describe performance quality in

Guideline 10.1 Guidelines for Writing Scoring Rubrics and Rating Scales

Guideline—Your rubric or rating scale should
1. Emphasize the most important content and processes of the learning targets.
2. For each achievement dimension's score, match the emphasis for that achievement dimension in your assessment plan.
3. For the maximum possible total points, match the emphasis for that learning target(s) in your assessment plan.
4. Be clear to students.
5. Be useful for giving students the guidance they need to improve their performance on the learning targets.
6. Be a faithful application of a general rubric, conceptual framework, or learning progression appropriate to the learning target.
7. Have clear, observable levels of performance.
8. Allow for assessment of all knowledge, skills, and use of processes that are important to the learning targets.
9. Clearly describe how alternative correct answers or strategies are to be rated, if applicable.
10. Allow for distinctions between achievement levels.

general terms so the scoring can be applied to many different tasks. **Task-specific rubrics** describe performance quality in terms that include reference to the specific assignment. Whether a rubric is analytic or holistic is independent of whether it is generic or task-specific. Rubrics can be described on both factors.

Analytic rubrics

To create analytic scoring rubrics, list the major criteria of good work (sometimes called *dimensions* or *traits*) and prepare a rubric for each of these criteria. Use the following questions to identify a conceptual framework and the important achievement dimensions or criteria to assess (Herman, Aschbacher, & Winters, 1992):

- What are the characteristics of high-quality achievement (e.g., good writing, good problem solving, good collaboration, good scientific thinking, etc.)? What evidence should I look for to decide if a student has produced an excellent response?

- What are the important characteristics of the learning target that I should assess?

- What is it about the students' responses that distinguish the poor, acceptable, and excellent student?

- Are there samples of student work (excellent and poor) that I can contrast to identify the characteristics that differentiate them?

- Does my school district, state assessment program, a national curriculum panel, or a professional society have examples of rubrics or curriculum frameworks that show standards and criteria?

- Are there any suggestions in teacher's magazines, state teachers' newsletters, professional journals, or textbooks?

Decide the number of points to award to students for each criterion. The scales may all be of equal weight, or you may decide that one or more of the aspects of performance is worth more points. An example of analytic, task-specific scoring rubrics for a restricted response essay on the Keats poem was presented in Example 10.1. An example of analytic, generic rubrics was presented in Example 9.2.

Describe the characteristics of a student's performance that distinguish one achievement level from another. These descriptions anchor the scale at each level.

The *top-down approach* to writing rubrics begins with a conceptual framework that you can use to evaluate students' performance to develop scoring rubrics. Follow these steps:

Step 1.   Adapt or create a conceptual framework of achievement dimensions that describes the content and performance that you should assess.

Step 2.   Develop a detailed outline that arranges the content and performance from Step 1 in a way that identifies what you should include in the general rubric.

Step 3.   Write a general scoring rubric that conforms to this detailed outline and focuses on the important aspects of content and process to be assessed across different tasks. The general rubric can be shared with students. It can be used as is to score student work, or it can be used to write specific rubrics.

Step 4.   Write a specific scoring rubric for the specific performance task you are going to use.

Step 5.   Use the specific scoring rubric to assess the performances of several students; use this experience to revise the rubric as necessary.

In the top-down approach you need a framework-based organization to develop a rubric. Thus, Steps 1, 2, and 3 may be difficult to achieve on your own and may require you to work with groups of teachers.

The *bottom-up approach* to writing rubrics begins with samples of students' work, using actual responses to create your own framework. Use examples of different quality levels to help you identify the dimensions along which students can be assessed. The following steps may be helpful:

Step 1.   Obtain copies of about 10 to 12 students' actual responses to a performance item. Be sure the responses you select illustrate various levels of quality of the general achievement you are assessing (e.g., science understanding, letter writing, critical reasoning, etc.).

Step 2.   Read the responses and sort all of them into three groups: high-quality responses, medium-quality responses, and low-quality responses. Alternatively, you can ask students to do this. For tasks with which they have some experience (e.g., writing), and for which they therefore have some basis to begin to judge quality, this is a particularly powerful learning experience. The resulting bottom-up rubrics that students have helped to create can be used for student self-evaluation and teacher-provided formative feedback.

Step 3.   After sorting, carefully study each student's responses within the groups, and write (or have students write) very specific reasons why you put that response into that particular group. How are the students' responses in one group (e.g., high-quality group) different from the responses in each of the other groups? Be as specific as you can. For example, don't say they write better or have better ideas. Rather, say the student's sentences are more complex, or the student expresses unusual ideas in a very clear way. Write a specific and complete explanation on every student's response as to why it is placed into the group.

Step 4.   Look at your comments across all categories and identify (or have students identify) the emerging dimensions. In essence, you are creating your own conceptual framework in this step of the process. For example, if the responses are for a mathematics task, you may see computation, complete explanations, logical approach, and good mathematical reasoning as the dimensions.

Step 5.   Separately for each of the quality levels of each achievement dimension you identified in Step 4, write (or have students write) a specific student-centered description of what the responses at that level are typically like. You may have one to six achievement dimensions. The descriptions become the scoring rubric for marking new responses.

The two methods for creating rubrics are not equivalent procedures. You can verify that the rubrics and framework you created are on the right track by comparing them to externally created frameworks and rubrics. We have given some examples of these in this book. Your school district and state department of education may have others. You can search the Internet for still others. The Northwest Regional Educational Laboratory (1998) has used the bottom-up approach extensively to train teachers to develop scoring rubrics.

Usually students' responses will match the scoring rubric to various degrees. Assigning a rubric level to particular student work is like a "choose the best answer" type of multiple-choice question. The score is the one whose description most closely matches a student's work. The top and bottom of a rubric scale are usually easier categories to decide than the middle. When you match student work to rubric levels in an inconsistent way, you lower the reliability of the scoring process.

Holistic rubrics

Holistic scoring is appropriate for extended response subject-matter essays or papers involving a student's abilities to synthesize and create when no single description of good work can be prespecified. It is also appropriate for final exams or projects where giving feedback to students is not a consideration. States that do large-scale assessment of either writing or subject-matter essay responses often prefer holistic scoring. The large numbers of papers to be marked often precludes the detailed scoring required by analytic rubrics. An example of an holistic, task-specific scoring rubric for the Keats essay was presented in Example 10.1.

To create holistic rubrics, you still need to identify the criteria for good work on which your scoring will be based. The difference is that for analytic rubrics, descriptions of levels of performance on each criterion are considered separately. For holistic rubrics, levels of performance on all criteria are considered simultaneously. The description that best fits the student work identifies the score to be given.

One way to implement the holistic method is to decide beforehand on the number of categories of the overall quality of the work into which you will sort the students' responses to each question. Usually, you can use between three and five categories, such as A, B, C, D, and F; distinguished, proficient, apprentice, and novice; or 4, 3, 2, and 1. Categories that correspond to your school's grading system are easiest to use. If your school uses grades A through F, for example, then use five categories. Using a different number of quality levels in a scoring rubric will complicate grading.

After deciding on the number of categories, define the *quality* of the papers that belong in each category. What is an A performance? a B performance? and so on. Try out the draft version on several performances (papers, assignments, projects) and revise it. Reexamine all the performances within a category to be sure they are enough alike in quality to receive the same grade or quality rating.

A refinement that will help you use the rubrics more reliably, and make them even easier to use the next time, is to select specimens or **exemplars** that are good examples of each scoring category. You can then compare the current students' answers to the exemplars that define each quality level. You then decide into which category to place them.

Some educators have successfully used a third type of scoring rubric, the **annotated holistic rubric**, which is a hybrid approach. Use holistic scoring. After reaching a holistic judgment, write on the student's paper very brief comments, based on the prespecified traits, that point out one or two strengths and one or two weaknesses. Write only about what led you to reach your holistic judgment of the paper.

Generic rubrics

Generic (general) rubrics use descriptions of work that apply to a whole family or set of assignments. Generic rubrics for writing, math problem solving, science laboratory work, analyzing literature, and so on, are important instructional as well as assessment tools. As students practice and perform many different learning targets in a subject throughout the school year, their learning improves if they apply the same general evaluation framework to all of the same type of work in that subject. Some research evidence supports the idea that when students routinely use generic, analytic rubrics in the classroom, their achievement improves (Khattri, Reeve, & Adamson, 1997).

A generic scoring rubric contains guidelines for scoring that apply across many different tasks of a similar type (e.g., writing, or math problem solving), not just to one specific instance of that kind of task. The generic rubric can serve as a general framework for developing more specific rubrics, or it can be used as is. Example 10.2 presents an example of a holistic general scoring rubric for math problem-solving tasks.

■ **EXAMPLE 10.2 Example of a holistic general scoring rubric for mathematics problem-solving tasks**

Score level = 4

Mathematical knowledge
- Shows understanding of the problem's mathematical concepts and principles;
- Uses appropriate mathematical terminology and notations;
- Executes algorithms completely and correctly.

Strategic knowledge
- May use relevant outside information of a formal or informal nature;
- Identifies all the important elements of the problem and shows understanding of the relationships between them;
- Reflects an appropriate and systematic strategy for solving the problem;
- Gives clear evidence of a solution process, and solution process is complete and systematic.

Communication
- Gives a complete response with a clear, unambiguous explanation and/or description;
- May include an appropriate and complete diagram;
- Communicates effectively to the identified audience;
- Presents strong supporting arguments, which are logically sound and complete;
- May include examples and counter-examples.

Score level = 3

Mathematical knowledge
- Shows nearly complete understanding of the problem's mathematical concepts and principles;
- Uses nearly correct mathematical terminology and notations;
- Executes algorithms completely. Computations are generally correct but contain minor errors.

Strategic knowledge
- May use relevant outside information of a formal or informal nature;
- Identifies the most important elements of the problems and shows general understanding of the relationships between them;
- Gives clear evidence of a solution process. Solution process is complete or nearly complete, and systematic.

Communication
- Gives a fairly complete response with reasonably clear explanations or descriptions;
- May include a nearly complete, appropriate diagram;
- Generally communicates effectively to the identified audience;
- Presents supporting arguments which are logically sound but may contain some minor gaps.

■ **EXAMPLE 10.2** (Continued)

Score level = 2

Mathematical knowledge
- Shows understanding of the problem's mathematical concepts and principles;
- May contain serious computational errors.

Strategic knowledge
- Identifies some important elements of the problems but shows only limited understanding of the relationships between them;
- Gives some evidence of a solution process, but solution process may be incomplete or somewhat unsystematic.

Communication
- Makes significant progress towards completion of the problem, but the explanation or description may be somewhat ambiguous or unclear;
- May include a diagram which is flawed or unclear;
- Communication may be somewhat vague or difficult to interpret;
- Argumentation may be incomplete or may be based on a logically unsound premise.

Score level = 1

Mathematical knowledge
- Shows very limited understanding of the problem's mathematical concepts and principles;
- May misuse or fail to use mathematical terms;
- May make major computational errors.

Strategic knowledge
- May attempt to use irrelevant outside information;
- Fails to identify important elements or places too much emphasis on unimportant elements;
- May reflect an inappropriate strategy for solving the problem;
- Gives incomplete evidence of a solution process; solution process may be missing, difficult to identify, or completely unsystematic.

Communication
- Has some satisfactory elements but may fail to complete or may omit significant parts of the problem; explanation or description may be missing or difficult to follow;
- May include a diagram which incorrectly represents the problem situation, or diagram may be unclear and difficult to interpret.

Score level = 0

Mathematical knowledge
- Shows no understanding of the problem's mathematical concepts and principles.

(Continued)

■ **EXAMPLE 10.2** (Continued)

Strategic knowledge
- May attempt to use irrelevant outside information;
- Fails to indicate which elements of the problem are appropriate;
- Copies part of the problem, but without attempting a solution.

Communication
- Communicates ineffectively; words do not reflect the problem;
- May include drawings which completely misrepresent the problem situation.

Source: From "The Conceptual Framework for the Development of a Mathematics Performance Assessment Instrument," by S. Lane, 1993. *Educational Measurement: Issues and Practice, 12*(2), p. 23: Copyright 1992 by the National Council on Measurement in Education. Reprinted by permission of Blackwell Publishing.

Task-specific rubrics

Sometimes you write rubrics just for one task and make a task-specific scoring rubric that includes specific things that need to be in the answer. Or, you can adapt general scoring rubrics to specific tasks. (Either way, you can't share them with students, which is a significant disadvantage.) The reliability and validity of your scores improve when you use a general scoring framework as a guideline to craft specific scoring rubrics. For example, you may use the state's generic rubric to develop a specific rubric for your classroom because it helps you to align your class assessments with the state standards.

Different scoring approaches are not interchangeable. They serve different purposes for scoring your students' performance. Table 10.1 gives advantages and disadvantages for each type of rubrics.

Score partial credit items with strategies that maximize scoring reliability

Principles for scoring essays are summarized in Guideline 10.2. These principles apply to any partial credit scoring scheme: rubrics, rating scales, or point-based scoring schemes.

Use scoring rubrics and model answers to improve the consistency of your scoring so that you apply the same standards from paper to paper. Some states have adopted general rubrics that you should use. Check your state's requirements on its web site. If rubrics reflect state standards directly—as, for example, some writing rubrics do—then all teachers can use the same rubrics.

If there is more than one essay question, score all students on the first question before moving on. Then grade all answers to the next question. This method improves the uniformity with which you apply scoring standards to each student.

Table 10.1 Advantages and disadvantages of different types of rubrics

Type of rubric	Definition	Advantages	Disadvantages
Holistic or Analytic: One or Several Judgments?			
Analytic	• Each criterion (dimension, trait) is evaluated separately.	• Gives diagnostic information to teacher • Gives formative feedback to students • Easier to link to instruction than holistic rubrics • Good for formative assessment; adaptable for summative assessment; if you need an overall score for grading, you can combine the scores	• Takes more time to score than holistic rubrics • Takes more time to achieve inter-rater reliability than with holistic rubrics
Holistic	• All criteria (dimensions, traits) are evaluated simultaneously.	• Scoring is faster than with analytic rubrics • Requires less time to achieve inter-rater reliability • Good for summative assessment	• Single overall score does not communicate information about what to do to improve • Not good for formative assessment
Description of Performance: Generic or Task-Specific?			
Generic	• Description of work gives characteristics that apply to a whole family of tasks (e.g., writing, problem solving).	• Can share with students, explicitly linking assessment and instruction • Reuse same rubrics with several tasks or assignments • Supports learning by helping students see "good work" as bigger than one task • Support student self-evaluation • Students can help construct generic rubrics	• Lower reliability at first than with task-specific rubrics • Requires practice to apply well
Task-specific	• Description of work refers to the specific content of a particular task (e.g., gives an answer, specifies a conclusion).	• Teachers sometimes say using these makes scoring "easier" • Requires less time to achieve inter-rater reliability	• Cannot share with students (would give away answers) • Need to write new rubrics for each task • For open-ended tasks, good answers not listed in rubrics may be evaluated poorly

It also makes you more familiar with the scoring guide for a given question, and you are less likely to be distracted by responses to other questions. Finally, using this method helps to reduce carryover errors. You can reduce carryover errors further by reshuffling the papers after scoring each question.

A **carryover effect** error occurs when your judgment of a student's response to Question 1 affects your judgment of the student's response to Question 2. For example, a student may have a brilliant answer to Question 1 but a mediocre answer to Question 2. The carryover effect occurs when you mark Question 2 correct after

Guideline 10.2 Summary of principles for scoring responses to subject-matter essay items

1. Prepare some type of scoring guide (e.g., an outline, a rubric, an "ideal" answer, or "specimen" responses from past administrations).
2. Grade all responses to one question before moving on to the next question.
3. Periodically rescore previously scored papers.
4. Score penmanship, general neatness, spelling, use of prescribed format, and English mechanics separately from subject-matter correctness.
5. Score papers without knowing the name of the pupil writing the response.
6. Provide pupils with feedback on the strengths and weakness of their responses.
7. When the grading decision is crucial, have two or more readers score the essays independently.

marking Question 1: You mark Question 2 more favorably because you "carried over" your favorable impression from Question 1. Unless you score all answers to each question before moving to the next, the scores you assign to adjacent questions will likely be more similar regardless of the quality of the students' answers than scores on nonadjacent questions.

When marking subject-matter essays, factors other than an answer's content often affect your evaluation. Among such factors are spelling, penmanship, neatness, and language usage. To avoid blending your judgment of the quality of the ideas or substantive content of a student's answer with these other factors, score the other factors separately. Scoring separately for quality of ideas, correctness of content, and other factors also gives you the freedom to weight each factor appropriately in calculating the grade.

Even if scoring criteria are well defined, raters tend either to not pay attention to criteria over time or to interpret them differently as time passes. This tendency to change the way scoring criteria are applied over time occurs slowly and is called rater drift. Periodically stop and determine whether you are applying the scoring standards the same way to later-scored papers as you did to earlier-scored papers.

We also recommend you score essays anonymously. Scoring is more valid when you do not know the name of the student who wrote the response. Anonymous scoring of essays prevents the halo effect. Further, if students know that you score papers anonymously, they are likely to perceive the grading process as fair (Mehrens & Lehmann, 1991).

The halo effect error occurs when your judgments of one characteristic of a person reflect your judgments of other characteristics or your general impression of that person. Thus, you may tend to grade a particular essay more leniently for a student you admire because you know in your heart that the student has command of the objective or topic. The halo effect can work in the negative direction, too.

An important reason for using essays is the opportunity they give you to assess students' expressive abilities and thought processes. You can note strengths, weaknesses, and suggestions for improvement. Explain how you arrived at the grade you assigned. This provides an opportunity for further student learning. The following list offers suggestions for commenting on students' written work (Hirsch, 1977, pp. 160–161).

- Comment on just two or three points in any paper.
- Select those matters for comment that are most important for an individual student at a particular time.
- Summarize the commentary in usable form.
- Begin writing comments only after a rapid analysis of the paper as a whole.
- Choose those comments that will be likely to induce the greatest assessment improvement in the intrinsic effectiveness of the student's next paper.
- State the comments in an encouraging manner.
- Do not hesitate to repeat a comment over several papers.
- Keep track of the comments, so that nothing of great importance for a particular student is omitted during the course.
- Make clear from the tone of the comments that they deal with a craft to be learned and not with the teacher's personal taste.

Another suggestion for giving feedback is to hold individual student conferences. A brief conference with each student is more personal and can provide clearer guidance to the student than written comments in the paper's margin. A short, direct conference with each student may also save you hours of writing copious notes and commentary to clarify a point for the student.

The quirks of individual teachers do affect essay scores. The suggestions in Guideline 10.2 help reduce the impact of your quirks, but they do not entirely eliminate them. A second opinion—a second scorer—would help improve reliability. Realistically, you can't carry out independent scoring of essays very often. At the least, talk with colleagues to develop shared understanding of criteria, and consider asking a colleague to do a second read on the occasional papers where you find scoring a particularly difficult call to make.

Another factor that causes your assessment results to be inconsistent is the topic (subject) of the essay. A student's scores may vary widely, even when marked by the same reader, because of the topic, prompt, or questions (Breland, Camp, Jones, Morris, & Rock, 1987; Dunbar, Koretz, & Hoover, 1991). This is a serious problem: If you base your evaluation of a student on one essay question, you will not be able to make general statements about this student's performance on different topics. If your statements about a student are limited to only the one essay a student wrote, the validity of your overall evaluation (e.g., grades) is lowered.

So far we have been talking about rubrics. There are other partial credit scoring methods, most notably checklists and rating scales. Some people use the terminology loosely and call all these partial-credit scoring schemes "rubrics." We discuss checklists and rating scales separately, below, because they have distinct formats.

Checklists mark attributes as present or absent

Table 10.2 presents several useful ways to record your assessments of student performance. Checklists (this section) and rating scales (next section) are frequently used for performance tasks. A **checklist** consists of a list of specific behaviors, characteristics, or activities and a place for marking whether each is present or absent.

A **behavior checklist** consists of a list of discrete behaviors related to a specific area of a student's performance. For example, you may wish to identify the particular difficulties a student is having in the phonological, semantic, and syntactic aspects of spoken language. The behavior checklist might have items such as "uses only simple sentence structure" or "responds without delay to questions." Example 10.3 illustrates such a checklist.

Table 10.2 Some useful methods of recording students' responses to performance tasks

Recording method	Description	Recommended use	Example of uses
Anecdotal records	You observe the performance and write a description of what the student did	These are primarily useful for keeping records of unanticipated or naturally occurring performances. Usually you can record only one student at a time.	A student shows unusual insights into current events and you want to keep a record of these to put into his portfolio or to recommend the student for a summer program for leadership.
Behavior tallies	You create a list of specific behaviors of which you want to keep a record for a student. As you observe the performance you tally how many times each behavior occurs. The list is usually limited to only a few behaviors.	These are primarily useful for well-defined lists of behaviors that you can expect to occur frequently. They may be useful to keep track of undesirable behaviors, too.	As a communications teacher, you keep track of how often a student uses "uh-h-h" when speaking in front of the class.
Checklists	You create a list of specific steps in a procedure or specific behaviors. You check each behavior that occurs. The list may be long.	These are primarily useful if the behaviors are in a sequence or if all the subtasks that make up the complete performance can be listed.	You are a science teacher and want to be sure that each student performs the steps in setting up a microscope properly. You are an automotive shop teacher and want to be sure that each student properly completes all the tasks necessary to change the oil in a car.
Rating scales	You create standards or criteria for evaluating a performance. Each standard has levels of competence, and you rate students according to how well they performed each standard as they complete the task.	These are especially useful if each standard can be judged according to the level or the degree of quality rather than as simply being present or absent.	You are an art teacher and rate each student's painting on its composition, texture, theme, and technique. You are a mathematics teacher and rate a student's problem solution according to how well the student demonstrates mathematical knowledge, uses a good strategy to solve the problem, and communicates her explanation of the solution in writing.

■ **EXAMPLE 10.3 Example of a portion of a checklist used to report a high school student's speaking behavior**

Speaking Behavior DATES ▶				
Speaks clearly and audibly				
Speaks fluently in home language				
Expresses thoughts in complete sentences				
Uses appropriate phrasing and sentence patterns				
Choose appropriate topic for presentation				
Organizes material				
▲ Presents both introductory and concluding statements				
▲ Uses notes or note cards				
▲ Uses appropriate visual aids or other support material				
▲				
▲				
Establishes and maintains eye contact to ensure listener attention				
Varies tone, stress, and volume to convey meaning				
Displays good posture while speaking				
Demonstrates poise and confidence				
Uses appropriate gestures and body language to convey meaning				
Uses appropriate language for the form of communication				
Emphasizes main idea(s)				
Uses persuasive devices (e.g., glad names, bad names, bandwagon, testimonial)				
Conveys intended purpose when speaking				

Source: From *Listening and Speaking Checklist,* grades 9–12 (p.4), *California Achievement Tests,* 5th Edition, by permission of the publisher, CTB/McGraw-Hill LLC, a subsidiary of the McGraw-Hill Companies, Inc. Copyright © 1992 by CTB/McGraw-Hill LLC. All rights reserved.

A **product checklist** focuses on the quality of the thing a student makes. Products include drawings, constructed models, essays, and term papers. These checklists identify the parts or other properties a product is supposed to have. Inspect each product, checking whether those properties are present. To create a product checklist, examine several students' products, especially those products that differ greatly in quality. Careful study of these products will help you identify the characteristics and flaws you want to include in your checklist.

A **procedure checklist** assesses whether a student follows the appropriate steps in a process or procedure. For example, a checklist may assess whether a student is able to use a microscope properly. The form represents both the presence or absence of each step and the sequence that a particular student used to perform the task. A procedure checklist is only appropriate when there is one accepted procedure; if there are several good ways to do a task, a procedure checklist isn't appropriate. To create a procedure checklist, first observe and study students performing so you can identify all the steps. You may find the following steps (Linn & Miller, 2005) helpful when crafting procedure checklists:

Step 1. List and describe clearly each specific subperformance or step in the procedure you want the student to follow.

Step 2. Add to the list specific errors that students commonly make (avoid unwieldy lists, however).

Step 3. Order the correct steps and the errors in the approximate sequence in which they should occur.

Step 4. Make sure you include a way either to check the steps as the student performs them or to number the sequence in which the student performs them.

Ratings scales assess the degree to which students have demonstrated various attributes

A **rating scale** assesses the *degree to which* students have attained the achievement dimensions in the performance task. As an example, consider assessing the quality of a student's oral presentation to the class. You would probably identify several dimensions of a "good oral presentation" and then judge the degree to which a student demonstrates each of them. A good oral presentation might include such characteristics as the degree to which a student presents material relevant to the topic; speaks in a smooth, unhesitating manner; uses correct grammar and language patterns; and makes visual contact with the audience. The degree to which a student demonstrates each dimension, rather than the present-or-absent decision for a checklist, is what you need to know. Example 10.4 presents a simple rating scale for doing this. Also see the rating scale example in Example 4.3.

Rating scales can be used for teaching purposes as well as assessment. Like rubrics, rating scales help students understand the learning target and focus their attention on the important aspects of the performance. You can give them to students as they prepare for the performance task. The completed rating scale gives specific feedback to a student concerning the strengths and weaknesses of the performance. Students not only achieve the learning targets but also may internalize the criteria used to evaluate their achievement. If you use comparable rating scales over time, students can use them to chart their own progress.

■ **EXAMPLE 10.4 Example of a simple rating scale for assessing the quality of a student's oral presentation**

Rating Scale for Classroom Speech

Pupil's name _____ Date _____

Speech topic _____

1. Did the speech contain content meaningful to the topic?

1	2	3	4
Most of speech content not truly meaningful	Only about 50 percent of speech relevant	Most content relevant; occasional irrelevant idea	All content obviously and clearly related

2. Was the delivery smooth and unhesitating?

1	2	3	4
Long pauses and groping for words in almost every sentence	Pauses and groping for words in about 50 percent of sentences	Occasional pauses and groping for words	Delivery smooth; no pauses or groping for words

3. Did the speaker use correct grammar?

1	2	3	4
Errors in most sentences	Errors in about 50 percent of sentences	From 1 to 3 errors	No errors

4. Did the speaker look at his audience?

1	2	3	4
Looked away most of the time	Looked at audience only 50 percent of the time	Looked at audience most of the time	Looked continually at audience

Source: From *Measuring Pupil Achievement and Aptitude* (2nd ed., p. 200), by C. M. Lindvall and A. J. Nitko, 1975, New York: Harcourt Brace Jovanovich.

Some scoring schemes assign points to various aspects of a response

Point-based scoring schemes are most useful for scoring essay or show-the-work test questions. This is where you find them used most often, and they are usually task-specific. They are most appropriate for comprehension-level questions when the student response to the question should contain certain facts or concepts that can be counted.

■ **Example of a point-based scoring scheme**

Essay question: The Great Depression began in the United States with the stock market crash of October 1929. List three effects of the Great Depression in the United States, and explain how each developed from this economic disaster.

Scoring scheme: Up to 9 points, 3 each for any 3 of the following effects, [1 point for naming the effect, up to 2 points for its explanation (0 = no explanation or incorrect explanation, 1 = partial explanation, 2 = solid explanation)]:

- Many U.S. citizens went bankrupt.
- Millions became unemployed.
- Industrial production dropped.
- Franklin D. Roosevelt defeated Herbert Hoover in the 1932 presidential election.

Conclusions

Scores are supposed to convey meaning. If they don't, they might as well be random numbers drawn from a hat. This chapter described different kinds of scoring, and ways to maximize scoring accuracy, that are especially suited for classroom assessment. So far, we've been talking about scoring individual assessments. In the next chapter we'll look at how to put individual scores together to assign report card grades.

Exercises

1. Following are four questions that together constitute a 12-point science quiz. After each question is the keyed answer provided by the teacher and Jane Smith's answer.
   a. Evaluate Jane Smith's answers against the answer key and award her points according to her answers' degree of correctness.

   Question 1: What is the shape of a quartz crystal?

       Answer key: Hexagonal

       Maximum marks: 1

       Jane's answer: "Six-sided hectogon."

       Jane's score: _____

   Question 2: What is a saturated solution?

       Answer key: A solution that contains as much dissolved substance as it can for a particular temperature.

       Maximum marks: 3

Jane's answer: "Large crystals contain a great deal of substance that has been formed. This process of forming crystals is called crystallization. It occurs both in the laboratory and in nature."

Jane's score: _____

Question 3: Write a paragraph describing how you can grow very large crystals.

Answer key: Any answer that says size of crystal is directly related to the rate of crystallization.

Maximum marks: 5

Jane's answer: "Large crystals contain a great deal of substance that has been formed. This process of forming crystals is called crystallization. It occurs both in the laboratory and in nature."

Jane's score: _____

Question 4: Name three major categories of rocks.

Answer key: Igneous, sedimentary, and metamorphic

Maximum marks: 3

Jane's answer: "The three kinds are fire-formed, settled, and those that have changed their form."

Jane's score: _____

b. Compare the scores you gave Jane on each question with the scores given by others in this course. On which items is there more agreement? On which is there less agreement?

c. Discuss during class the reasons for an agreement and disagreement in marking. Make a list of the factors that seem to affect the scores assigned to Jane for each question.

2. A fifth-grade teacher assigned her class to work in groups of four to make a coat-of-arms that described the main character in a story they had read. The coat-of-arms was to be shield-shaped, have four divisions, and in each division picture something important about the character or his family. Each group was to draw its coat-of-arms on poster board and make a brief presentation to the class about why they selected the particular designs they used (referring to the story). The learning targets were: (a) reads appropriate grade-level text for meaning and (b) uses oral communication skills. She devised the following rubric:

Excellent—Nice pictures in all four spots, good eye contact

Good—Good pictures in all four spots

Fair—At least some pictures

Poor—Sloppy work, mumbling

Failing

Using the guidelines for writing rubrics in Example 10.2, you will find that this rubric falls short on all of them. Evaluate these rubrics on each of the guidelines in turn, explaining the specific problem for each one.

Now go to our Companion Website at **www.prenhall.com/brookhart** to assess your understanding of chapter content with multiple-choice and essay questions. Broaden your knowledge of assessment with links to assessment related web sites.

Grading

1. The main purpose of grading is to communicate information about student achievement.
2. Report cards are an official means of reporting student progress.
3. A criterion-referenced grading method matches the typical standards-based or objectives-based approach to teaching.
4. Use criterion-referenced methods for combining scores into one summary achievement grade.
5. Grading creates a measurement scale that—like any scale—should be valid and reliable.
6. Gradebook computer programs can help with the record keeping, calculating, and reporting needed for grading.

In a school district I once worked with, eighth-grade teachers were using a portfolio system. The portfolios contained records of grades from conventional language arts tests (scored as percent correct and then given a letter grade) and writing samples, scored on a 4-point rubric. They needed five levels for report card grades (their system used A, B, C, D, F). They were left with no choice but to use a complicated method to combine the grades, and that brought its own problems. Some students and parents didn't quite understand the algorithm used to put the scores together. Even though it was a pretty fair system, the "unknown" is always suspect. It had not occurred to any one of the several teachers who adopted the 4-point writing rubric that it would not be very helpful for assigning five levels of grades. This was a more complicated problem to solve after the fact than it would have been to solve at the design stage (for example, by adopting a 5-level writing rubric).

Chapter 10 dealt with scoring individual assignments. This chapter is about combining individual pieces of evidence to assign report card grades.

The main purpose of grading is to communicate information about student achievement

Example 11.1 gives examples of information frequently found on formal student progress reports and various kinds of decisions that may be based on such information. Grades have serious meaning beyond your classroom. Different people—students, parents, counselors, future teachers and employers, colleges—will use

■ EXAMPLE 11.1 Examples of the types of information found on report cards and the types of decisions made from that information

Information in report	Decisions that can be made			
	Selection	Placement remediation	Guidance, counseling	Course improvement
1. Content or objectives learned	Promotion, probation, graduation, admissions	Selecting courses to take, remedial help needed	Selecting next courses to take, additional schooling needed, career-related choices	Deciding where instruction can be improved
2. Comparison of performance in different subjects	Admission	Selecting advanced and/or remedial courses	Determining pattern of a pupil's strengths and weaknesses	Identifying areas that are strong points of school
3. Performance relative to other people	Scholarships prizes, admission	Estimating likely success, eligibility for special programs	Estimating likely success in certain areas	
4. Social behavior		Matching personal characteristics to course and teacher placement	Determining need for adjustment, likes, dislikes, ability to get along with others	Identifying problems with a course or with a teacher

grades in different ways. The meaning of the grades you assign must be clear in order to judge whether any of these uses are valid.

Assessment specialists generally recommend that you keep the meaning of grades clear by basing them only on a student's achievement of your course's learning targets. Many teachers do not follow this advice (Brookhart, 1991; Stiggins, Frisbie, & Griswold, 1989; Waltman & Frisbie, 1994), because they want to send messages about effort and behavior, too.

If obedience to your classroom rules is rewarded by an A or "performing satisfactorily" in *reading*, but "fooling around" during class means the *reading grade* is lowered, in spite of successful reading performance, you have communicated that obedience is valued more than reading well. If you give an unsatisfactory grade to a student whose academic performance is satisfactory and then say, "I warned you about passing notes during class!" you communicate vindictiveness. If the grade you report intertwines social behavior and achievement, you encourage confusion.

By all means, do evaluate effort and behavior, but separate your evaluations of achievement from your evaluations of other student characteristics (Guskey, 2006; Winger, 2005). Many districts' report cards rate citizenship, behavior, and so on separately from achievement, especially at the elementary level (Kunder & Porwoll, 1977). Communicate with students and parents about effort and behavior regularly, whether or not there is space on the report card for all this information. Tardiness, failure to complete work, and other problems—reported separately from achievement—may be used to explain a student's lack of school accomplishment and to help decide what to do about it.

Communicating to parents is especially challenging. Some research shows that parents' and teachers' understanding of what report card grades mean are often far apart (Waltman & Frisbie, 1994). For example, parents may see grades as reflecting pure achievement. Or, they may see grades as predictive of future success on the job or in postsecondary school.

Report cards are an official means of reporting student progress

Schools use many methods to communicate with students and parents and to keep records of students' achievement. Table 11.1 summarizes the advantages and disadvantages of different methods.

Your school district may use more than one method of reporting student progress, because different methods may serve different purposes and different audiences. For example, letter grades may report a student's subject-matter achievement; rating scales may report the student's attitudes and deportment. A parent-teacher conference may convey information on achievement, effort, attitudes, and behavior.

Some methods of reporting student progress are used more frequently at certain grade levels. Letter grades, for example, are used with high frequency in the upper elementary, junior high, and senior high school levels. Parent-teacher conferences do not occur often in junior and senior high schools.

Narrative reports are detailed, written accounts of what each student has learned in relation to the school's curriculum framework and the student's effort in class. The hope is that narrative reports will replace the shortcomings of letter grades, which tend to condense too much information into a single symbol. Narratives also allow teachers to include unique information about students' learning or something unique the teacher has done for that student—things that would not appear on a standardized form (Power & Chandler, 1998). When done well, narrative descriptions can mean much more to parents and students than the simple summaries that grades provide.

Because meaningful long narrative reports are time-consuming and difficult to write well, some schools have modified the reporting process to include some shorter narrative description. One way to do this is by combining checklist or rating-scale procedure with short written comments about each student. Example 11.2 shows one section of a primary-school pupil narrative report. The full report is four pages and includes a few pages showing the school's educational developmental continuum (Egawa & Azwell, 1995).

Along the same lines is the *standards-based report card*, developed in the Tucson Unified School System (Clarridge & Whitaker, 1997). Example 11.3 shows an example. For each curriculum area, standards were written for grades 1–2 and 3–6. Each standard was adopted from the state's standards and written to match the district's core curriculum. In that way, standards were linked to specific learning targets. If a student achieves a state's standard, the teacher gives the student a quality score of 4. Teachers also prepared verbal descriptions of levels 3, 2, and 1 for each standard to

Table 11.1 Advantages and disadvantages of some commonly used methods of reporting student progress

Name	Type of code used	Advantages	Disadvantages
Letter grades	A, B, C, etc., also "+" and "−" may be added.	a. Administratively easy to use b. Believed to be easy to interpret c. Concisely summarize overall performance	a. Meaning of a grade varies widely with subject, teacher, school b. Do not describe strengths and weaknesses c. Kindergarten and primary school children may feel defeated by them
Number or percentage grade	Integers (5, 4, 3, . . .) or percentages (99, 98, . . .)	a. Same as points a, b, and c above b. More continuous than letter grades c. May be used along with letter grades	a. Same as points a, b, and c above b. Meaning not immediately apparent unless explanation accompanies them
Two-category grade	Pass-fail, satisfactory-unsatisfactory, credit-entry	a. Less devastating to younger students b. Can encourage older students to take courses normally neglected because of fear of lowered GPA	a. Less reliable than more continuous system b. Does not communicate enough information about pupil's performance for others to judge progress
Checklist and rating scales	Checks (✓) next to objectives mastered or numerical ratings of degree of mastery	a. Give the details of what the pupil achieved b. May be combined with letter grades or with group-referenced data	a. May become too detailed for parents to comprehend b. Administratively cumbersome for record keeping
Narrative report	None, but may refer to one or more of the above: however, usually does not refer to grades	a. Allows teacher the opportunity to describe a student's educational development b. Shows a student's progress in terms of standards, indicators of achievement, learning targets, or a continuum of educational growth c. Provides opportunity to open dialogue and other types of communication with parents and students	a. Very time consuming b. Requires excellent writing skill and effective communication skills on the teacher's part c. May require translation into language read by parents, with possible loss of meaning in the translation d. Parents who are not skilled readers may misunderstand it or may be put off e. Parents may be overwhelmed and not respond f. Often modified to include checklist-like list of indicators with short teacher comments
Pupil-teacher conference	Usually none, but any of the above may be discussed	a. Offers opportunity to discuss progress personally b. Can be an ongoing process that is integrated into instruction	a. Teacher needs skill in offering positive as well as negative comments b. Can be time consuming c. Can be threatening to some pupils d. Doesn't offer the institution the kind of summary record desired
Parent-teacher conference	None, but often one or more of the above may be discussed	a. Allows parents and teachers to discuss concerns and clarify misunderstandings b. Teachers can show samples of students' work and explain basis for judgments made c. May lead to improved home-school relations	a. Time consuming b. Requires teachers to prepare ahead of time c. May provoke too much anxiety for some teachers and parents d. Inadequate means of reporting large amounts of information e. May be inconvenient for parent to attend
Letter to parents	None, but may refer to one or more of the above	a. Useful supplement to other progress-reporting methods	a. Short letters inadequately communicate pupil progress b. Requires exceptional writing skill and much teacher time

■ **EXAMPLE 11.2 Example of a section of a primary-level narrative student progress report using indicators and teacher comments**

Primary Progress Report

Name _____   Class _____

Parents _____   Teacher _____

Reporting Period _____   Phone _____

Days Present _____ Absent _____ Tardies _____

> **Note to parents:** *Under each area of curriculum I have listed indicators which I look for when assessing and evaluating students. Student should be demonstrating or working toward these goals. These indicators are on the left hand side of the report. Specific comments about your child are to right of the indicators. ** These items will be emphasized in the spring.*

Learning & Social Skills
The members of our school community focus on the following:
- doing their personal best
- being trustworthy
- being truthful
- actively listening to others
- not "putting down" others

- contributes to the learning of other class members
- settles down quickly in appropriate area
- works cooperatively with others
- actively participates in discussions and projects
- takes responsibility for learning
- cleans up before starting the next activity
- respects classroom materials and the property of others
- pays attention when others are speaking

Personal comments are added here for each child:

Reading and the Language Arts
Activities of the curriculum included in this category include: classroom newspaper, dialogue journals, personal notebook and sketchpad, author's folders, literature study, literacy strategies and the arts (drama, music, art)

Classroom Newspaper
- volunteers stories to the weekly news
- contributes conventions (punctuation, spelling, calendar information, temperature, etc.) at teacher request
- joins in the re-reading or shared reading of the dictated news of classmates
- contributes his or her own writing to the second page*
- actively participates and pays attention while others share
- stays in place/seat
- illustrates his/her own news
Parent Comments:

The newspaper is created daily on a plastic overlay that is projected on a large screen. The students contribute information as the teacher writes. *Personal comments are added here for each child:*

■ **EXAMPLE 11.3 Example of a section of a computer-assisted narrative student progress report using standards- and rubric-based procedure along with teacher comments**

| | Semester | | | |
	1st	2nd	3rd	4th
Self-Directed Learner	3			
Student often sets achievable goals, considers risks, and makes some choices about what to do and in what order to do them, usually reviews progress, and often takes responsibility for own actions.	Comments:			
Collaborative Worker	2			
Student is developing the ability to work in groups, has positive relationships with other students, and is learning to work toward group goals.	Comments:			
Problem Solver	4			
Students reasons, makes decisions, and solves complex problems in many situations, and uses these skills regularly, independently, and efficiently.	Comments:			

Note: The report is for the first marking period (4 = the highest rating).

Source: Reprinted with permission from *Rolling the Elephant Over: How to Effect Large-Scale Change in the Reporting Process* by P. B. Clarridge and E. M. Whittaker. Copyright © 1997 by P. B. Clarridge and E. M. Whittaker. Published by Heinemann, a division of Reed Elsevier, Inc., Portsmouth, NH. All rights reserved.

explain the meaning of lesser levels of achievement, much in the same way one would develop general scoring rubrics. All of these verbal descriptions were computerized using a database program.

Parent-teacher conferences are one of the best ways to build strong connections with parents, to provide them with an understanding of their children's learning strengths and needs, and to help them to be involved in their children's learning. Guideline 11.1 lists some of the things you can do to organize and conduct a successful conference.

Parent-teacher conferences have their drawbacks, however. They are time-consuming for the teacher, both in preparation time and in actual contact time. Attendance may also be a problem. Not all parents will come to conferences. Finally, teachers and/or parents may have too much information, too many issues, or too many concerns to discuss in the brief time allotted to the conference. Parent conferences should be private and between one teacher and the parent(s) or guardian(s) of one student. Avoid holding a conference where other teachers,

| **Guideline 11.1** Suggestions for organizing and conducting a parent conference |

Set Purpose
- Set goals for the conference.
- Decide what information you need to communicate with parents.
- Decide how, if at all, students will be involved, and what their role and tasks will be at the conference.

Plan Logistics
- If possible, send home report cards or other information about a week before, so parents have time to prepare questions and talk with their child.
- Schedule times and locations for each appointment. Include breaks for yourself at regular intervals.
- Keep to the schedule to respect everyone's time.
- Arrange for a waiting area where waiting parents cannot overhear year conference with other parents.
- Arrange a comfortable setting (chairs, tables, etc.) where you can converse easily

Collect Evidence
- Have grades, portfolios, student work samples, checklists, anecdotal records, etc., as appropriate, organized to share with parents. Work samples should illustrate the general level of student work and help parents understand their student's grades, current achievement level, and next steps.
- Involve students in the collection of evidence whenever possible.

Interpret Evidence
- Prepare your main points ahead of time. Don't rely on spur-of-the moment thinking to convey important information about students. Clear oral communication requires just as much preparation as written comments do.
- Prepare questions you may have for parents about their child's work, interests, activities, etc.
- If you are well prepared, you can communicate clearly and remain confident.

Communicate
- Aim for clarity of expression, make your points clearly and briefly and support them with evidence.
- Listen carefully to what parents say. Respond to their concerns. Be open to learning more about the student than you know from the school setting.
- Use interpersonal skills: communicate genuine care for the student, develop rapport, and reflect parents' feelings.
- If the child is present, include him or her in the communication; if the child is not present, plan with parents how to share what went on so the child does not experience the conference as "people talking behind my back."
- Plan the next steps for the student jointly with parents.
- Do not allow antagonistic parents to derail communication. Your job is to understand the child's work and behavior as best you can, not to become the family's counselor or to become afraid or anxious. Listen and try to understand.

Source: Based on ideas from Brookhart (2004); Newman (1997–1998); Perl (1995); Swiderek (1997).

other students, or other parents can overhear what is being said. This protects the rights of all involved.

When a school uses more than one method to report students' progress, such as a report card with several kinds of marks or symbols, this is called a **multiple marking system**. A report card, especially for the elementary schools, usually uses a multiple marking system. Example 11.4 is an example of a **report card** employing a multiple marking system for grades 4 through 6 in one school district. In this example report card, the nonacademic areas are defined by specific, observable student performances, instead of asking teachers to rate general traits such as "personality" or "deportment."

A **permanent record** is the official record of a student's school performance. Not all information needs to appear on a student's permanent record. Putting elementary students' letter grades in a permanent record is controversial. Many educators (and some professional associations) argue that reporting or recording grades at the elementary level is inappropriate. However, students and parents may become upset if, for the first time in junior high, a student receives a C (or lower) in a subject, when previously the student has received only "performing satisfactorily" checks on the elementary report card or a narrative report.

EXAMPLE 11.4 Example of a multiple marking system report card for grades 4, 5, 6

KEY

A dash(—) indicates that performance was not measured during the report period.
(i) indicates improved performance.

The evaluations in this section refer to personal interaction and task-related skill development as viewed by your child's regular subject teacher(s). Special subject teachers may use these numerals to explain improvement needed in their respective areas.

YOUR CHILD IN SCHOOL

Personal Interaction Skills

1 Is courteous in speech and actions
2 Shows respect for others
3 Responds positively to help and correction
4 Respects property of the school and others
5 Takes care of personal belongings
6 Demonstrates self-control
7 Observes rules and regulations

Task-related skills

8 Follows directions
9 Utilizes time effectively
10 Listens attentively
11 Works independently when necessary
12 Starts and finishes work on time
13 Completes assigned work
14 Contributes to class discussion
15 Observes standards of neatness
16 Works quietly
17 Brings necessary material to class

ESTHETIC DEVELOPMENT

Vocal Music

Develops basic performing skills
Comprehends and interprets musical elements
Participates appropriately in activities
Performs commendably

Art

Manipulates a variety of materials
Applies principles of design in projects
Participates appropriately in activities
Uses constructive imagination in art projects
Performs commendably

PHYSICAL DEVELOPMENT

Physical Education

Displays good sportsmanship
Participates in activities
Maintains minimal fitness level
Behaves appropriately
Performs commendably

Health

Demonstrates knowledge of health concepts
Behaves appropriately

Days Absent
Times Tardy
Times Excused Early
Absences affecting progress

EXPLANATION OF MARKING

Experiencing Difficulty — Basic skills have not been acquired, the student has not reached the performance level set for his or her group or set for the child individually.

Performing Successfully — The student has attained the performance level set for his or her group or set for the child individually. Knowledge and skills have developed satisfactorily.

Commendable — Knowledge and skills are well developed. The student has exceeded the expectations set for him or her individually or for the group. Performance is praiseworthy.

THE LANGUAGE ARTS

Reading

Reads with understanding
Recognizes and applies vocabulary
Uses study and reference skills
Understands elements of literature

Spelling

Spells assigned words accurately
Spells accurately in written communication

Language

Recognizes parts of speech
Applies correct sentence structure
Uses conventional punctuation
Expresses ideas clearly

Handwriting

Writes legibly

MATHEMATICS

Understands concepts
Recalls basic facts (+, −, ×, −)
Works accurately
Uses reasoning in solving word problems
Applies principles of measurement and geometry

SOCIAL STUDIES

Understands basic concepts
Uses research skills

SCIENCE

Understands basic concepts
Uses process skills

Lower Int.	Middle Int.	Upper Int.	Grade 7
Book 4	Book 5	Book 6	Book 7

Intermediate basal reading materials used to date

*A check mark indicates the performance level in the basal reading program which has been covered.

Source: Courtesy of the Mt. Lebanon, Pennsylvania, Public Schools.

Some intermediate policy may help a student with this transition from the elementary school marking code to a new marking code at the junior high. For example, a school may decide to have teachers prepare letter grades for fifth and sixth graders and their parents, but not to report them on permanent record cards. Thus, a "performing satisfactorily" can mean a C for some students and a B for others. At the end of the year, the letter-grades records are destroyed.

If report cards are an official means of reporting student progress, the next logical question is: What sort of progress should you report? For most K-12 purposes, it's progress on classroom learning targets, which in turn are based on curriculum goals, which in turn are based on state standards. Therefore, the answer to the question "what kind of progress" is "progress referenced to learning targets." That means criterion-referenced grading.

A criterion-referenced grading method matches the typical standards-based or objectives-based approach to teaching

Basic grading frameworks include norm-referencing (relative standards), criterion-referencing (absolute standards), and self-referencing (growth standards), similar to any scoring method (see Chapter 10). Each way of referencing provides a different perspective on a student. You must be able to explain your *grading framework* to students, parents, and school officials (AFT, NCME, & NEA, 1990). Example 11.5 illustrates the three different referencing frameworks.

Criterion-referenced grading

Most teachers focus on having students achieve worthwhile learning targets. Almost all teacher education programs recommend this approach. This approach has several names: standards-based (or standards-driven) instruction, performance-based instruction, or learning-objectives-based instruction. Teaching and instruction provide the conditions for students to achieve the standards. Criterion-referenced grading frameworks (also called *absolute standards grading* or *task-referenced grading*) are consistent with this teaching approach. You base your grades on the same learning targets as your instruction. The next section shows you four ways to do this.

Criterion-referenced grading is most meaningful when you have a well-defined domain of performance for students to learn. You assign grades by comparing a student's performance to a defined set of standards to be achieved, targets to be learned, or knowledge to be acquired. Thus, it is possible that you may give all students As and Bs if they all meet the absolute standards specified by the learning targets. Similarly, when you use this framework, you must be prepared to assign all students Fs and Ds if none of them meet the standards set by the learning targets. In the latter case, you might also try to figure out why and what to do about it!

■ **EXAMPLE 11.5** Examples of definitions of grades under three different referencing frameworks

Absolute scale: task-referenced, criterion-referenced	Relative scale: group-referenced, norm-referenced	Growth scale: self-referenced, change scale
Grade *Relative to the learning targets specified in the curriculum, the student has:*	*Relative to the other students in the class, the student is:*	*Relative to the ability and knowledge this student brought to the learning situation, the student:*
A • Excellent command of concepts, principles, strategies implied by the learning targets • High level of performance of the learning targets and skills • Excellent preparation for more advanced learning	• Far above the class average	• Made significant gains • Performed significantly above what the teacher expected
B • Solid, beyond the minimum, but not an excellent, command of the concepts, principles, strategies implied by the learning targets • Advanced level of performance of the learning targets and of most skills • Prepared well for more advanced learning	• Above the class average	• Made very good gains • Performed somewhat higher than what the teacher expected
C • Minimum command of concepts, principles, strategies implied by the learning targets • Demonstrated minimum ability to perform the learning targets and to use basic skills • Deficiencies in a few prerequisites needed by later learning	• At or very near the class average	• Made good gains • Met the performance level the teacher expected
D • Not learned some of the *essential* concepts, principles, and strategies implied by the learning targets • Not demonstrated ability to perform some *very essential* learning targets and basic skills • Deficiencies in many, but not all, of the prerequisites needed for later learning	• Below the class average	• Made some good gains • Did not quite meet the level of performance the teacher expected
F • Not learned *most* of the basic concepts, principles, and strategies implied by the learning targets • Not learned most of the *very essential* learning targets and basic skills • Not acquired most of the prerequisites needed for later learning	• Far below the class average	• Made insignificant or no gains • Performed far below what the teacher expected

Note: This figure is an adaptation of some of the ideas in Frisble & Waltman (1992).

Norm-referenced grading

Some educational approaches emphasize having students attain high achievement by outperforming their peers. Advocates of norm-referenced grading base their arguments on the necessity of competition in life (the "cream rises to the top"), the value of knowing one's standing in relation to peers, and the belief that not all students are capable of achieving high standards. Arguments against this approach center on the ill effects of competition and that standing in a peer group does not describe what a student has learned. Bellanca and Kirschenbaum (1976) offer a more detailed summary of these arguments.

Norm-referenced grading frameworks (also called *grading with relative standards* or *group-referenced grading*) are consistent with this teaching approach. You assign grades based on how a student's performance compared with others in the class: Students performing better than most classmates receive the higher grades. With norm-referenced grading, you must define the reference group against which you compare a student (e.g., the other students in this one class, or in all sections of the class this year, or all students in the same class during the past five years). Two common norm-referenced grading methods are **grading on the curve** (ranking students and assigning a predetermined proportion to each grade) and the **standard deviation method** (using the standard deviation to calculate grade boundaries).

To act consistently within a norm-referenced framework, you should give good grades to the "top" students, whether or not they have met the level of competence specified by the learning targets. Similarly, you should give poor grades to the low-ranking students even if they have met the minimum level of competence that the learning targets specify. Therefore, we do not recommend norm-referenced grading, and we don't give detailed directions for how to use these methods. Interested readers can find out how to do norm-referenced grading in Chapter 15 of Nitko and Brookhart (2007).

Self-referenced grading

Self-referenced grading is also called *growth-based grading* or *change-based grading*. You assign grades by comparing students' performance with your perceptions of their capability: Students performing at or above the level at which you believe them capable of performing receive the better grades, regardless of their absolute levels of attainment or their relative standing in the group. A student who came to the class with very little previous knowledge but who has made great strides may be given the same grade as a student who has learned more but who initially came to the class with a great deal more previous learning.

Arguments in favor of self-referenced grading center on the possibility of reducing competition among students and the concept that grades can be adjusted to motivate, to encourage, and to meet the students' needs. Arguments against the system center on the unreliable nature of teachers' judgments of capability, the need for parents and students to know standing relative to peers, the fact that this procedure tends to be applied mostly to lower ability students, and the possibility that this system may eventually lead to grading based solely on effort (Dunbar, Float, & Lyman, 1980). Additionally, students may not achieve the state's standards set for the grade.

Your school district's grading policy is an important factor in selecting a grading framework. If your school district has a grading policy, you will be required to work within its guidelines. If it is a poor or inconsistent policy, you may wish to suggest ways to improve it.

Use criterion-referenced methods for combining scores into one summary achievement grade

In this section we will discuss four criterion-referenced methods for combining scores into one summary achievement grade. One criterion-referenced method is known as the **fixed-percentage method**. First, convert the scores on each component (individual assignment grade) entering into the composite (final grade) to percentage correct (or percent of total points). Then, multiply each component percentage by its corresponding weight, add these products together, and divide the sum of products by the sum of the weights. This procedure may be summarized by the following formula:

$$\text{composite percentage score} = \frac{\Sigma(\text{weight} \times \text{percentage score})}{\Sigma(\text{weight})}$$

where

$$\Sigma = \text{sum of}$$

weight = weight you give to a component

percentage score = the percentage you gave the student on the component

Example 11.6 illustrates this method. If you give letter grades for individual assessments (components), use the same grade boundaries as for the final (composite) grade.

A second method is called the **total points method**: Each component included in the final composite grade is assigned a maximum point value (e.g., quizzes may count 10 points, exams may count a maximum of 50 points each, and projects may count a maximum of 40 points each); the letter grades are assigned based on the number of total points a student accumulated over the marking period. The points you assign for each component should reflect the weight you want each component to contribute to the total composite. For example, if the weights you want for the components are quizzes 20%, homework 10%, term paper 20%, and exam 50%, then points for each component should reflect these percentages of the total maximum points. Thus, if the maximum total points is 200, then all of the quizzes are worth a maximum of 40 points (= 20% of 200), all of the homework a maximum of 20 points, term paper 40 points, and exam 100 points.

Neither the fixed-percentage method nor the total points method work well if your individual assignments are mostly graded with rubrics. For example, a score of "3" on a 4-point rubric usually means work is of better quality than a "75%" would imply. The following methods work better if the components are mostly rubrics.

A third method is the **quality level method** or the **rubric method**. It is sometimes called the *content-based method* (Frisbie & Waltman, 1992) or the *logic rule method* (Arter & McTighe, 2001). In this method, you describe the quality level of performance a student must demonstrate for each letter grade—what types of

■ **EXAMPLE 11.6 Example of how to calculate the composite score using the fixed-percentage method**

Suppose your had four components (quizzes, homework, term paper, and exam) that you want to combine into a composite score for the end of a marking period. Suppose, further, that each component was originally marked as a percentage correct. Suppose, too, you did not want to weigh each component the same. Finally, suppose that the students marks and weights for each-component were as follows:

Student	Quizzes (wt. = 20%)	Homework (wt. = 10%)	Term paper (wt. = 20%)	Exam (wt. = 50%)	Weighted composite percentage
Bob	87	85	70	80	80
Chad	85	80	80	70	75
Susan	75	82	85	60	65
Theresa	70	78	75	65	69

You calculate the weighted composite score (last column) and compare that score to the boundaries you set for the letter grades. Use the equation 15.2 to calculate the weighted composite score. The calculations are as follows:

weighted composite score for Bob =

$$[20 \times 87 + 10 \times 85 + 20 \times 70 + 50 \times 80] \div [100] = 80$$

weighted composite score for Chad =

$$[20 \times 85 + 10 \times 80 + 20 \times 80 + 50 \times 70] \div [100] = 75$$

weighted composite score for Susan =

$$[20 \times 75 + 10 \times 82 + 20 \times 85 + 50 \times 60] \div [100] = 70$$

weighted composite score for Theresa =

$$[20 \times 70 + 10 \times 78 + 20 \times 75 + 50 \times 65] \div [100] = 69$$

Suppose your grade boundaries were:

A = 90 − 100; B = 80 − 89; C = 70 − 79; D = 60 − 69; and F = 0 − 59

Then using the weighted composite percentages as calculated, the grades for these students are:

Bob = B; Chad = C; Susan = C; and Theresa = D

performance will constitute an A, B, C, and so on. (An example of these definitions of quality is shown in Example 11.5 in column one.) Given these definitions, you evaluate the student's work on each component, decide the quality level of work, and then assign the corresponding grade. This method is very similar to using scoring rubrics for performance tasks, treating the set of work for a marking period as the "performance" to be rated.

The **minimum attainment method** is a variation of the quality level method. You base the composite grades on whether students meet minimum standards on the most important assessments that comprise the final grade, while at the same time allowing somewhat lower performance on a few of the less important components. Although this method could be used in a variety of circumstances, it is suitable when you have marked the components using quality level scores such as letter grades, rubric scores, or quality level labels (e.g., basic, proficient, advanced) but you do not want to convert these quality level marks to percentages.

The minimum attainment rules method is a *noncompensatory approach to grading*.[1] Example 11.7 gives an example of the minimum attainment method. This

---

■ **EXAMPLE 11.7 Example of the Minimum Attainment Method for Grading**

Assume an English class with one test (graded in percentages that are then converted to letter grades), four small writing assignments (graded with rubrics as A, B, C, D, F), and one longer paper (also graded with rubrics as A, B, C, D, F). That is, six components go into the final grade. Assume, also, you wanted the combined test and paper marks to be worth twice as much as the four smaller assignments.

If a student scores	Then the grade is
A's on at least three of the writing assignments; *and* A's on the paper and test, or an A on one and a B on the other	A
A's or B's on at least three of the writing assignments; *and* at least B's on the paper and test or an A on one and a C on the other	B
C or better on at least three of the writing assignments; *and* at least C's on the paper and test, or a B or better on one and a D or better on the other	C
D or better on at least three of the writing assignments; *and* at least D's on the paper and test, or a C or better on one and an F on the other	D
A combination lower than the above	F

Here is an example of how these rules would be applied for eight students:

	Writing 1	Writing 2	Writing 3	Writing 4	Long paper	Test	Final grade
Aiden	A	A	C	A	A	A	**A**
Anthony	A	B	A	A	A	B	**A**
Ashley	A	B	B	C	B	B	**B**
Billy	A	B	B	C	B	B	**B**
Blake	C	C	C	A	C	C	**C**
Chad	D	D	D	A	D	D	**D**
Jesse	D	D	D	A	F	C	**D**
Sophia	D	D	F	F	D	D	**F**

---

[1]The methods whereby you add together scores from the components are called *compensatory* methods because a student's low score on one component may be compensated by a high grade on another.

method is only one such noncompensatory approach to grading. Of course, you may use other decision rules beside the ones we used in the example.

A fourth method, the **median score method**, uses the student's median mark to calculate the grade instead of using the sum of marks or the average mark. Before taking the median, convert all scores (rubrics, percents, and so on) to the same scale (for example, A, B, C, D, F). Using the median score works well for components that include a mixture of rubrics and percent-correct scores, for statistical as well as practical reasons. See Brookhart (2004) for a more complete explanation of this method.

Grading creates a measurement scale that—like any scale—should be valid and reliable

Grades should be valid and reliable. To achieve this, select and combine evidence to arrive at a grade in such a way that the final grade means what you intend it to mean—and you can say what that is—and is an accurate, dependable measure of that meaning.

- Consider what types of student performance you should grade. We will discuss three categories of student performances: those assessed, those reported, and those graded.
- Consider how to make your marking scales consistent across all assignments throughout the marking period.
- Decide the components making up the grade and their weighting in relation to the final grade.
- Consider the standards or boundaries for each letter grade: How are they set and are they meaningful?
- What do you do with students who are just at the border between two letter grades?
- What does failure (F) mean?
- Understand the impact of assigning zero for a mark on one or more components of a grade. Decide when, if at all, you will give a zero.

Your assessment plan (see Chapter 5) describes what component assessments will make up the summative assessment for each instructional unit and for the marking period. Specify the weights the components will carry in the grade for each unit as well as the units' weights in calculating the final grade for the marking period.

What to assess, report, and grade

The complete set of those characteristics for which you gather information are called *assessment variables* (or sometimes *evaluation variables* [Frisbie & Waltman, 1992]). You don't need to report everything you assess. Information that is primarily formative should not make its way into a grade.

Your school district will expect you to report a subset of the assessment variables to parents and for official purposes. These are called **reporting variables** (Frisbie & Waltman, 1992). They often include the students' achievement in the subject, study skills, social behavior and interpersonal skills, motivation and study efforts in class, leadership skills, and aesthetic talents. This is illustrated by the multiple marking system's report card example shown earlier in this chapter.

Reporting variables represent important school outcomes and therefore should be appropriately recorded and reported to parents and others. From among all the reporting variables, there is a more limited subset on which you may base your grades. The variables in this limited subset are called **grading variables** (Frisbie & Waltman, 1992). Use the grading variables to describe a student's accomplishments in the subject. Assess these achievements with more formal procedures such as performance tasks, portfolios, projects, tests, and quizzes. They are the most valid and reasonable bases for assigning grades. Figure 11.1 shows the relationships among these variables.

Figure 11.1 Relationships among different types of assessment variables and grading variables.

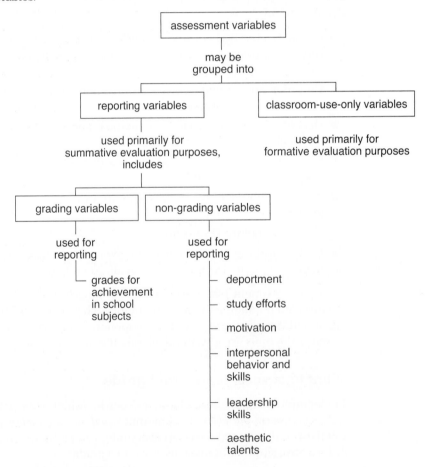

Scales

Make marking scales consistent across different assessments. Think ahead to make your assessment scales compatible across all the components that go into the summative grade. The assessment plan for the weather unit in Example 5.1, for example, shows five components entering into the summative grade for the unit: homework, quizzes, independent investigation, map drawing, and the end-of-unit test. Suppose each of these is marked on a different scale as follows:

Component	Scale
Homework	0–10
Quizzes	0–5
Independent investigation	1–20
Map drawing	1–4
End-of-unit test	0–100

If you simply add students' marks from each of these components using these scales, you will have difficulty because they are incompatible. The map-drawing scale, for example, may be based on a rubric with four levels of quality while the end-of-unit test is based on a percentage scale from 0% to 100%. Such incompatibilities make a simple sum of the marks an invalid basis for a grade. Even a perfect map (score 4) would not make much difference when added to a test percentage score. Mark each assessment in a way that makes scales compatible.

Further complicating the issue of compatibility of scale length is the issue of precision. "Precision" in measurement means pretty much what you would think it means. For example, I can't say I'm 62.384756237 inches tall—my yardstick doesn't measure that precisely. Figure 11.2 describes the issue of measurement precision in grading.

Weighting

Decide how much weight to assign to the components of a grade—home assignments, tests, quizzes, term papers, and other elements—after you decide their importance to the description of a student's achievement of the learning targets. List all the components you want to use for evaluating achievement of the grade. Next, decide how these components relate to the learning objectives and determine how important each is (and thus how heavily each will weigh) in relation to the overall summative grade. Consider at least six factors when deciding how much to weight each component:

- Importance of the learning target for the assessment.
- Amount of time you spent teaching the learning target for the assessment.
- Cognitive level of the learning target for the assessment (give more weight to higher-order thinking).
- When two components assess some of the same learning targets, each should be given less weight individually than other components that assess an equal number of unique learning targets (i.e., nonoverlapping components) (Frisbie & Waltman, 1992).

Figure 11.2 Precision of Measurement Is an Issue in Grading.

Design your scoring scales as carefully as you design your assessment instruments, with the amount of precision you need to convey the meaning you intend. Rubrics with four or five levels convey meaning accurately if you can only distinguish four or five quality levels in the work. Percents convey meaning accurately when you can reliably distinguish achievement along a continuum with many points.

The most reliable scores are those that can distinguish small differences in the quality of students' learning. A scale that shows Sally at 89 and Johnny at 82 measures their learning more precisely than a scale that shows them both receiving the same rating of B. Percents are not reliable in this way unless the difference between 89 and 82 means a real difference in achievement (and don't kid yourself, that is not always the case!). If Sally and Johnny both are more or less equivalent achievers, the same rating of B is the more reliable indicator.

You lose precision when you transform scores from a fine-grained scale (e.g., percentage correct scale) to a coarse-grained one (e.g., letter grades). If a B were defined to be a score from 80–89, then both Sally and Johnny would receive the same grade, B. Because they both receive the same grade, their true difference cannot be distinguished with the letter-grade scale. By transforming the 89 and 82 both to a B, you have lost reliability.

Not all percentage scales are fine-grained. For example, if you have five test questions, each worth one point, then the only possible percentages are 0, 20, 40, 60, 80, and 100. Thus, only six possible percentage values are used, not the 100 values you usually associate with a percentage scale. Similarly, a test of 10 questions, each worth one point, is not very fine-grained. If you use only a few of the many possible values of a scale, then you lose precision.

Although you lose precision when you move from a fine-grained scale to a coarse-grained scale, you do not gain precision by moving from a coarse-grained to a fine one. If you have only the coarse scores initially, no transformation will make them more precise.

Suppose, for example, you had the following writing scale: 4 = advanced, 3 = proficient, 2 = basic, 1 = unacceptable. You could transform the 3 to a percentage—3 out of 4 points means 75%. You have not gained any precision, however, in distinguishing among students since all students who received 3s now receive 75%. From the precision standpoint, the scale has only 4 points after the transformation (25%, 50%, 75%, and 100%), the same as before the transformation. Only the labels have changed. In addition, because the 100-percent scale implies there are other possible percentages between those reported (especially between 75% and 100%), you have changed the meaning of the scale from advanced, proficient, basic, unacceptable (if those were the rubric levels) to an implied (from the percents) scale of A = 100%, C = 75%, F = 50%, and F = 25%. You can see that these so-called "grades" have a corrupted meaning—they are not aligned the original meaning intended by the verbal labels of the writing scale.

- Fairness of the assessment to all groups of students.
- Reliability of the assessment information.

Boundaries between grades

An important practical consideration is how to establish boundaries between the grades. What constitutes an A, B, and so on? The answer will depend on (a) which framework you are using and (b) your school district's policy. Your grade boundaries should have the same meaning across all assessments that will make up the grade. This doesn't mean that you need to use the same number of marks (points) for each assessment. It does mean, however, that an A on one assessment should be of approximately the same standard of quality across all assessments.

You will always have **borderline cases**—students whose composite marks are very near or right on the boundary between two grades. Many teachers are comfortable reviewing students' work and raising grades for those who are just under the borderline, but do not consider lowering the grades of those just above the borderline (Brookhart, 1993). Nevertheless, lowering borderline grades is just as valid as raising them when additional achievement evidence justifies it.

All assessments contain measurement error, and the "true" grade may be above or below the observed one. Using additional *achievement* information to help make boundary decisions is more valid than using information about how much effort a student put forth in studying (Brookhart, 1999). If you are still in doubt, it is better pedagogy to give the next higher grade than to give the lower grade.

The meaning of failure

In a criterion-referenced grading framework, a failing grade (F) should mean failure to achieve a set of learning targets. The least confusing way to assign a failing grade is to set reasonable minimum standards regarding performance on the curriculum learning targets. Students who *consistently* perform below these minimum performance standards receive an F.

Consider this common situation. Billy does not turn in an important assignment, even though he knew the deadline and you made several announcements in class. You decide to give Billy a zero. James, on the other hand, turns in the assignment on time, but the work is so poor you must give it a 55, which is in the F range. Both James and Billy receive Fs, but these Fs do not mean the same thing.

This distinction is sometimes called scoring *failure* vs. scoring *failure to try*. In "failure-to-try" cases, giving a failing grade (or lowering a grade) is always invalid because the resulting grade does not accurately describe achievement. This does not mean that you should not report failure to try; it does mean that describing these two types of student responses with the same grade (F) is not valid.

A closely related issue is the question of lowering a student's grade when the assignment is turned in late. Again, such a practice lowers the validity of the marks and the resulting grades because it mixes up their meaning. Do not use the same grade to describe for some students only achievement, but for other students a mixture of achievement, attitudes, and personality evaluations.

The issue of what to do with missing and late assignments is a real one with which you and your colleagues must struggle, but it is not a measurement problem per se. It is a result of the conditions of teaching, school policies, and assumptions people make about the way one should educate (Brookhart, 1999). For example, from strictly a measurement point of view, assigning an "Incomplete" when assignments are missing seems reasonable. However, many schools do not allow Incomplete grades.

A school district's policy needs to address how to handle students who do not turn in assignments or who turn them in late. A policy should be legal, fair, and valid; reflect sound educational philosophy; and avoid punishing, threatening, or manipulating students. A policy should address the concerns of teachers. For example, is it fair to students who habitually complete their work on time to allow other students not to complete theirs on time? Are there circumstances under which late work is allowed (without penalty or commentary) or appropriate (e.g., illness, personal tragedy)? Will a flexible policy on when to turn in work result in classroom chaos?

The deadly zero

One zero can greatly affect a composite score. Suppose Ashley is a good student, capable of B work. What happens to her average marks if she fails to turn in one assignment and you give her a zero for it? The impact of a zero, of course, depends on the component marks a student receives, how many marks enter into the composite grade, the weights assigned to the component, and the mark the student would have received had she turned in the assignment. Example 11.8 illustrates the impact of zero on a student's grade.

From a measurement perspective, Strategy 3 (basing the grade only on assignments turned in) would be the best of the three when (a) assignments are of approximately equal difficulty for the students, (b) assignments are weighted equally (or are worth the same number of points), and (c) there are several assignments and only one or two are missing. This recommendation does not consider other factors, such as whether (a) the "missing assignment" is the most important one to complete (e.g., a project or a final examination), (b) a student didn't turn in an assignment because of illness or personal tragedy, (c) a student didn't complete the assignment because she didn't understand how to do the work, and (d) a student has made a habit of not turning in work on time. As we stated previously, these are not measurement issues per se but matters of educational practice, classroom management, and school policy.

■ **EXAMPLE 11.8 Hypothetical example of the impact of substituting zero or 59 for one assignment a student did not turn in.**

		1	2	3	4	5	Avg	Grade
A. True Performance		80	70	85	75	90	80	B
B. Strategy 1—Substitute zero for the missing assessment								
	Case 1	(0)	70	85	75	90	64	D
	Case 2	80	(0)	85	75	90	66	D
	Case 3	80	70	(0)	75	90	63	D
	Case 4	80	70	85	(0)	90	65	D
	Case 5	80	70	85	75	(0)	62	D
C. Strategy 2—Substitute the highest possible failing mark (i.e., 59) for the missing assessment								
	Case 1	(59)	70	85	75	90	76	C
	Case 2	80	(59)	85	75	90	76	C
	Case 3	80	70	(59)	75	90	75	C
	Case 4	80	70	85	(59)	90	75	C
	Case 5	80	70	85	75	(59)	74	C
D. Strategy 3—Base the grade on only those assignments that were turned in								
	Case 1	—	70	85	75	90	80	B
	Case 2	80	—	85	75	90	83	B
	Case 3	80	70	—	75	90	79	C
	Case 4	80	70	85	—	90	81	B
	Case 5	80	70	85	75	—	76	C

Note: Substituted values are shown in parentheses: (Assume A = 90–100; B = 80–89; C = 70–79; D = 60–69; F = 0–59.)

All of these grading methods require record-keeping and calculations. When I was a new teacher, that meant black, spiral-bound "grade-books" issued by the school district. The grade-book was the only thing we were instructed to take outside during fire drills, so we had a complete class roster. Those days are long gone. Now, record-keeping usually means computers.

Gradebook computer programs can help with the record keeping, calculating, and reporting needed for grading

If you have a personal computer, you may want to use a simple spreadsheet program to make the calculations. Several **gradebook programs** in the marketplace can also help you. The advantage is that a gradebook program provides you with a spreadsheet already set up for recording and reporting grades. The better programs combine spreadsheets and database functions. These will allow you to choose from a variety of grading frameworks, keep a class roster, keep attendance, record comments about students' assignments, obtain class summaries, and print reports for the total class or for one student to take home.

Try to find a program that will allow you to choose and use one or more of the grading methods you learned in this chapter—and that will tell you what method it's using! The program should allow you to keep grades and records for multiple classes or multiple subjects.

School districts sometimes provide—and require—teachers to use a particular gradebook program. These programs are sometimes linked to the district's administrative software so that report cards can be printed without the extra step of "turning in grades." Some of these programs are linked to a web site where parents, with password and identification, can log in and check their students' grades at any time, and sometimes even compare their student's grade with the rest of the class. This opens up new opportunities for home-school communication. It also requires even clearer grading plans and policies, so that students and parents who check interim records for a marking period correctly interpret the information in front of them.

One disadvantage of some gradebook programs is that they may limit the type of grading you may employ, or they may not permit you to use your own grading method to override the method(s) built into the program. We have seen a gradebook program advertised that claims to "think like an elementary school teacher" and includes ways to encode "effort" into students' grades! Be careful to be a critical consumer of any program you choose. If your district chooses a gradebook program for you, you should still investigate what kind of framework it uses for its calculations and adjust default settings to what you intend for your grades whenever possible.

Software for delivering online courses also includes gradebook capability. If you are teaching online, use the same approach to these gradebooks as you would for a gradebook program you use for a face-to-face class. Find out what its capabilities are, what kinds of data it will accommodate, and how it will display summaries or print reports. Most importantly, find out what framework it uses for combining individual grades or scores into composite marks and check that the method is what you intend. If not, adjust the program's settings.

Conclusions

The first key concept—the main purpose of grading is to communicate information about student achievement—is the basic principle from which the rest of the chapter flows. Scaling and weighting issues are important because those things encode the meaning into the grade. Report cards or other communication methods also affect the meaning that grades convey.

Exercises

Table 11.2 contains information about the performance of a class of five students. Use it to complete these exercises.

1. Determine an overall report card grade for each student using the following methods. For any methods that require using percent cut-off scores, use A = 90–100, B = 80–89, C = 70–79, D = 60–69, F = 59 or below.
   a. Criterion-referencing, fixed percentage
   b. Criterion-referencing, total points
   c. Criterion-referencing, minimum attainment method
   d. Self-referencing

2. Prepare a table with the students' names as the row headings and the four different methods as the column headings. Enter the students' grades under each method and compare the results. Where do you see the most agreement and most disagreement? Explain the reasons for agreements and disagreements for each method.

3. For each of the students below, write brief narrative comments to accompany the report card grade.
   a. Pupil B
   b. Pupil C

Table 11.2 List of Students and the Marks They Received on Each Component during One Marking Period. (Use this table for exercises.)

Pupil	Last year's grade average	Teacher's judgment of ability	Deportment	Homework 1	Homework 2	Homework 3	Project	Quizzes 1	Quizzes 2	Test score
A	B	Average	Very good	10	3	8	12	8	4	25
B	C	Average	Very good	9	2	7	15	7	4	20
C	A	Very high	Poor	10	0	9	15	10	5	29
D	A	Above average	Excellent	10	4	10	15	6	5	28
E	D	Average	Poor	0	2	5	0	5	3	10
Maximum possible score:				10	10	10	15	10	5	30

Companion Website

Now go to our Companion Website at **www.prenhall.com/brookhart** to assess your understanding of chapter content with multiple-choice and essay questions. Broaden your knowledge of assessment with links to assessment related web sites.

12

Interpreting Standardized Test Scores

1. Standardized tests are tests for which the procedures, administration, materials, and scoring rules are fixed so that as far as possible the assessment is the same at different times and places.
2. Standardized test results can be used both within and outside the classroom.
3. Prepare your students for standardized testing.
4. Follow prescribed administrative procedures when you give standardized tests.
5. Use normative information to describe student strengths, weaknesses, and progress.
6. Status measures are norm-referenced scores specific to a particular grade or age.
7. Growth measures are norm-referenced scores that can be used to chart educational development or progress.
8. Criterion- or standards-referenced interpretations of standardized test results require looking at the kinds of questions students can answer.
9. Five guidelines for score interpretation will serve you well.

One of our former students was a school district administrator enrolled in a graduate program for aspiring school superintendents. While he was in our class on educational measurement, catastrophe struck in his district. The administrators in his district were concerned that "a third of our students are below the 40th percentile in reading." They were about to institute a special reading program, and he wanted our advice about how likely it was to have an effect on standardized test scores.

"Whoa!" we said. "If your district matches the norm group, you would expect—you guessed it—40 percent of students to be below the 40th percentile. The fact that you only have 33% below that mark means your kids, on average, are reading *better* than the norm group." Apparently none of the administrators in that district knew that. It was scary to think that a program (and people's time and money that could have been more effectively spent elsewhere) were almost committed on the basis of lack of understanding of the meaning of a score.

Standardized tests are tests for which the procedures, administration, materials, and scoring rules are fixed so that as far as possible the assessment is the same at different times and places

Standardizing is necessary if you want test results to be comparable from time to time, place to place, and person to person. Most group tests provide reports of district, school building, and classroom test results. Examples 12.1 and 12.2 show reports that you would be expected to be able to read and interpret for your students. In Example 12.1, the test publisher has included an explanation of what the scores mean.

Published achievement tests vary in their purpose, usefulness, and quality. To appreciate their variety, you may find it helpful to classify them. Table 12.1 shows one classifying scheme. You may be used to thinking of standardized tests as multiple-choice tests. However, not all standardized test questions are multiple-choice. In recent years, publishers have added constructed-response items or performance tasks to some tests.

Multilevel survey batteries

The workhorse of standardized achievement testing is the multilevel survey battery. Each battery is group administered and contains several subtests. A subtest assesses one area, such as reading, mathematics, listening skills, and so on, and has its own separate score.

Different publishers may have different subtest names for the same curriculum area. Even when different publishers' survey batteries look similar, they are not interchangeable. The specific content emphasized, the cognitive skills required, and the way the norms and scales are developed differ from publisher to publisher. For example, a study of the mathematics subtests of four standardized survey batteries for the fourth-grade level indicated that the percentage of items covering a topic such as fractions varied widely among tests—from 5.4% to 14.4% (Freeman, Kuhs, Knappen, & Porter, 1982). Inspect the test items before you adopt a battery to make sure the test's content and skills emphasis matches your local curriculum.

Publishers think of each subtest (e.g., reading comprehension) as assessing a continuous dimension that grows or develops over a range of grades. The publisher links the levels together to place the scores of students from every grade on one numerical scale that spans all the grades. This allows you to use a multilevel subtest to measure a student's year-to-year educational development and growth in a curricular area.

Each publisher norms and standardizes its tests on different samples of students, so you can't compare norm-referenced scores from different publishers. However, all the subtests in one publisher's survey battery are administered to the same national sample of students. Therefore, you can compare a student's relative strengths and weaknesses across the different curricular areas. Compare a student's percentile rank (not grade-equivalent) in one curricular area to that student's

■ **EXAMPLE 12.1 Example of a computer-prepared narrative report on an individual student's standardized test performance. The report is meant to be sent home to parents**

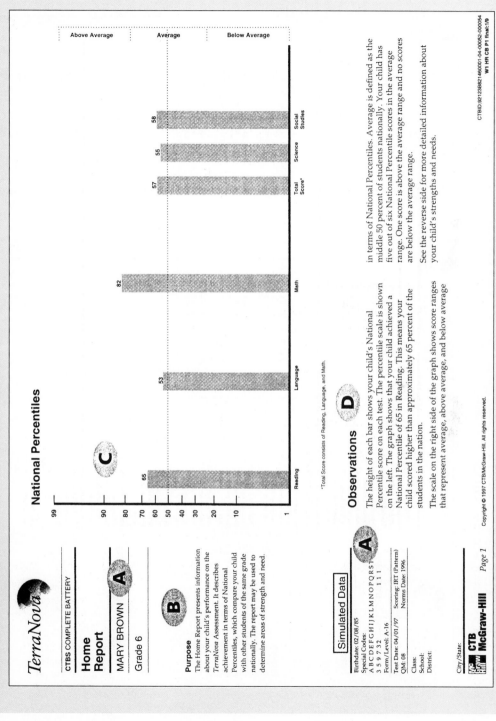

■ EXAMPLE 12.2 Example of a building report showing the performance of a school's grade 4 students on each subtest. This report shows (a) how the local 90th, 75th, 50th, 25th, and 10th percentile students performed relative to the national norm group; (b) how the local quarters of the fourth graders performed relative to the national norm group; (c) how many local students were in each quarter of the national norm group; and (d) what percentage of the local students were in each quarter of the national norm group

TerraNova

Evaluation Summary Report

School: WINFIELD

Grade 4

Purpose

This page gives administrators numeric information to evaluate the overall effectiveness of the educational program. This page displays a comprehensive numeric description of your students' achievement. This page is for those who prefer to analyze the data in tabular form.

| Simulated Data |

No. of Students: 89

Form/Level: A-14
Test Date: 11/01/99   Scoring: PATTERN (IRT)
QM: 08   Norms Date: 1996

District Winfield USD

City/State: Metropolis, CA

Page 4

		Reading		Lang.		Math		Total Score*		Science		Social Studies
Number of Students		86		87		89		86		88		88
Mean Scores & Standard Deviations												
Grade Mean Equivalent	—	4.6	—	5.0	—	4.5	—	4.8	—	4.6	—	4.3
Standard Deviation	—	1.5	—	2.0	—	1.9	—	1.3	—	1.7	—	1.8
Mean Normal Curve Equiv.	—	48.0	—	52.0	—	49.5	—	51.4	—	49.9	—	47.0
Standard Deviation	—	13.9	—	14.9	—	19.3	—	15.7	—	18.2	—	18.1
NP of the Mean NCE	—	46	—	54	—	49	—	53	—	50	—	44
Mean Scale Scores	—	696.7	—	715.3	—	694.4	—	696.7	—	700.5	—	696.1
Standard Deviation	—	35.2	—	33.2	—	45.4	—	31.0	—	40.5	—	48.3
Local Percentiles/Quartiles												
90th Local Percentile												
National Percentile	—	84.3	—	91.2	—	89.0	—	88.3	—	88.9	—	86.1
Grade Equivalent	—	8.5	—	9.9	—	7.8	—	7.4	—	8.2	—	9.0
Normal Curve Equiv.	—	71.2	—	78.3	—	76.4	—	75.4	—	76.2	—	73.0
Scale Score	—	748.1	—	765.3	—	754.4	—	744.2	—	756.6	—	758.5
75th Local Percentile Q3												
National Percentile	—	62.8	—	75.4	—	72.3	—	70.2	—	74.3	—	65.6
Grade Equivalent	—	5.4	—	6.8	—	5.8	—	5.5	—	5.8	—	5.4
Normal Curve Equiv.	—	56.9	—	64.4	—	62.7	—	61.0	—	63.9	—	58.7
Scale Score	—	719.8	—	741.5	—	725.3	—	719.7	—	731.3	—	726.6
50th Percentile (median) Q2												
National Percentile	—	41.8	—	53.3	—	54.0	—	52.7	—	56.7	—	49.8
Grade Equivalent	—	4.3	—	4.8	—	4.8	—	4.6	—	4.9	—	4.6
Normal Curve Equiv.	—	45.9	—	52.0	—	52.0	—	50.2	—	53.3	—	50.6
Scale Score	—	695.3	—	719.3	—	704.0	—	699.7	—	711.3	—	707.8
25th Local Percentile Q1												
National Percentile	—	30.0	—	36.1	—	24.8	—	30.1	—	26.0	—	29.0
Grade Equivalent	—	3.6	—	3.5	—	3.3	—	3.7	—	3.4	—	3.5
Normal Curve Equiv.	—	39.0	—	42.4	—	35.5	—	38.9	—	36.5	—	38.5
Scale Score	—	678.0	—	698.2	—	665.5	—	678.0	—	647.0	—	679.0
10th Local Percentile												
National Percentile	—	12.1	—	15.5	—	10.9	—	13.2	—	11.0	—	12.3
Grade Equivalent	—	2.6	—	2.7	—	2.9	—	2.9	—	2.6	—	2.7
Normal Curve Equiv.	—	25.2	—	29.0	—	24.3	—	26.1	—	24.1	—	25.6
Scale Score	—	635.3	—	661.0	—	639.7	—	646.9	—	647.0	—	644.3
National Quarters												
Local/Number 76-99	—	10	—	22	—	19	—	16	—	20	—	13
Per Quarter 51-75	—	24	—	25	—	26	—	30	—	27	—	30
26-50	—	38	—	26	—	21	—	25	—	20	—	26
01-25	—	14	—	14	—	23	—	15	—	21	—	19
Local/Percent 76-99	—	11.6	—	25.3	—	21.3	—	18.6	—	22.7	—	14.8
Per Quarter 51-75	—	27.9	—	28.7	—	29.2	—	34.9	—	30.7	—	34.1
26-50	—	44.2	—	29.9	—	23.6	—	29.1	—	22.7	—	29.5
01-25	—	16.3	—	16.1	—	25.8	—	17.4	—	23.9	—	21.6

*Total Score consists of Reading, Language, and Mathematics.

CTBID/921238B21490001-04-00052-00054
W1 ES GR4 P4 final:11/05

Source: From *Score Reports for TerraNova,* 2nd Edition, by permission of the publisher, CTB/McGraw-Hill LLC, a subsidiary of The McGraw-Hill Companies, Inc. Copyright © 2000 by CTB/McGraw-Hill LLC. All rights reserved.

Table 12.1 Common Types of Standardized Tests

Test type	Description
Standardized, empirically documented tests	*Multilevel survey batteries* are the familiar, annually administered tests that survey students' general educational growth or basic skill development in each of several curricular areas. *Multilevel* means that the test content spans several grade levels; *battery* means that several curricular areas are assessed by different subtests.
	Multilevel criterion-referenced tests for a single curricular area provide detailed information about students' status for a well-defined domain of performance in a single subject area (e.g., mathematics). The test spans several grade levels.
	Other multilevel tests for a single curricular area are noncriterion-referenced tests that assess students in a broader way than do subtests in a survey battery.
	Single-level standardized tests for one course or subject are developed for assessing achievement at only one educational level or for one course (e.g., Algebra I). Usually, they are stand-alone tests, not coordinated with tests from other courses, and not normed on the same students as other tests.
State-mandated customized tests	Tests developed by publishers of standardized multilevel survey batteries for use only in a particular state. The tests are said to be *customized* because a publisher contracts with a state to prepare standardized tests that are aligned with the state's standards and is secure so that it can be used for accountability purposes. Since the NCLB Act, the grades typically covered are 3 through 12 and the subjects tested are reading, language arts, mathematics, and, perhaps, science.

percentile rank in another to assess strengths and weaknesses. You might say something like this: "Shanna is better in mathematics than she is in social studies because her score in mathematics is higher than 98% of the students at her grade level, whereas her score in social studies is higher than only 60% of students at her grade level."

Most publishers of standardized, empirically documented tests provide auxiliary materials to help you interpret and use the assessment results. Teacher's manuals describe in considerable detail the intended purpose and uses of the results, often suggesting ways to improve students' skills by using assessment results for instructional planning. Some publishers provide separate manuals for curriculum coordinators and school administrators to help them use assessment results in curriculum evaluation and reports to the school board. Most publishers provide score reports that the school district may use both within the school and with students and parents.

If your state mandates its own assessment, take its coverage into account before choosing a published standardized test. Most state assessments have accountability as their main purpose. This is not the case for a published standardized test, which is used primarily to measure individual students' educational growth.

Choose a standardized test that requires students to demonstrate learning that is consistent with your state's standards or curriculum framework. Plan to use the chosen test over a period of at least 5 years, so that you can track changes in your school district. Test at grade levels not tested by the state-mandated assessment to avoid overburdening students and teachers.

The results of survey tests can be used to help you plan for a year or a term. Survey tests measure broad, long-term educational goals rather than immediate learning outcomes. It may take all year for a student to learn to read well enough, for example, to show some sign of improvement on a survey test. Meanwhile, however, the student may learn many specific skills and reading strategies. Your classroom assessments provide better measures of these immediate learning targets.

Another kind of standardized test is the National Assessment of Educational Progress (NAEP) (Mullis, 1991; Tyler, 1966). NAEP is an assessment program designed to survey the U.S. educational *system* rather than individual students. NAEP assesses the impact of the nation's educational efforts by describing what students are able to do.[1] Assessment tasks are assigned to students on a random sampling basis, so that not every student has the same or even comparable tasks. Thus, it is not meaningful to use the scores with individual students. The assessment is intended to pool the results from all students in the sample to show the progress of education in the entire country.

Multilevel criterion-referenced tests

Multilevel criterion-referenced tests provide information about a student's status on specific learning targets in a domain. Although some survey batteries also provide this information, most surveys assess very broadly or globally defined educational development. Multilevel criterion-referenced tests tend to focus on a more narrowly defined set of learning targets.

Other multilevel tests

Other types of multilevel tests are stand-alone products that cover one curricular area, such as reading or mathematics, across several grades. These assessments provide a deeper and broader sampling of content than a corresponding subtest of a survey battery. However, if the same sample of students was not used to norm a stand-alone multilevel test concurrently with tests from other curricular areas, you cannot use the stand-alone tests to compare a student's relative strengths and weaknesses across curricular areas. For example, you could not say a student is better in reading than in mathematics.

Single-level standardized tests

If you do not want to measure growth or development, a **single-level** test may be useful. Rather than cover several grade or age levels, such tests are directed toward one level or a particular course. Usually these assessments are built for high school and college courses. There are, for example, tests for Algebra 1, first-year college chemistry, and first-year college French. Each test is a stand-alone product and is not coordinated with other tests. Thus, these test results cannot be used to compare a student's relative standing in several subjects. Scores from this group of achievement tests are most often interpreted using norm-referencing schemes such as percentile ranks and standard scores.

---

[1] Details are found at http://nces.ed.gov/nationsreportcard.

State-mandated customized tests

State-mandated tests vary greatly in their focus, makeup, and quality. The NCLB Act requires accountability at the school level in an attempt to assure all students in the school receive quality instruction. Some states require individual student accountability in addition to school accountability. This usually takes the form of a graduation test.

State assessments are based on a state's curriculum framework and standards. The trend had been to make standards that are challenging to students rather than to limit them to minimum competencies or basic skills. Customized state assessments are usually built and marked by a proprietary agency under a state contract. Test publishers tender bids in response to a state's request for proposals.

Usually, the publisher winning the bid uses a secure form of their own survey battery and then adds additional test items that match state standards not covered by the original battery. Alignment studies use panels of educators to judge the match of test items to state standards. Panels are also used to set cut scores between achievement levels (e.g., between "basic" and "proficient," "proficient" and "advanced," and so on). These are often called standard-setting studies—"standard" here means performance standard, not content standard. You can usually find out about your state's assessment program through its education department's web site.

Standardized test results can be used both within and outside the classroom

When I taught school, I knew teachers who prided themselves on never looking at students' standardized test results. They felt it prejudiced them against some students, and they preferred to "get to know" students on their own. These were noble—but misguided—intentions. What a waste of information to give a standardized test and then not use the results! The key is to use standardized tests results for appropriate purposes only, and try not to prejudge students for any reason (test scores or otherwise!). Here are some suggestions for within-classroom use of test results. First suggested by Hieronymus (1976), they are still applicable today:

- Describe the educational developmental levels of each student. Use this information about the differences among your students to modify or adapt teaching to accommodate individual students' needs.

- Describe specific strengths and weaknesses in students. Use this information to remediate deficiencies and capitalize on strengths.

- Describe the extent to which a student has achieved the prerequisites needed to go on to new or advanced learning. Combine these results with a student's classroom performance to make recommendations for placement.

- Describe commonalties among students. Use this information to group students for instruction.

- Describe students' achievement of specific learning targets. Use students' performance on clusters of items to make immediate teaching changes.

- Provide students with illustrations of the kinds and levels of performances expected of them. Discuss these expectations with students and how you can work with them to fulfill them.

- Provide students and parents with feedback about students' progress toward learning goals. Use this information to establish a plan for home and school to work together.

- Confirm or corroborate your judgment about a student's general educational development. Standardized tests can provide information in addition to your own observations that may alert you to the need to consider a particular student further.

Guideline 12.1 outlines suggestions for using survey battery information in planning classroom instruction.

Guideline 12.1 A systematic procedure for using the results of a state or other standardized achievement test to plan instruction for a class

Step 1. Review the class report to determine weaknesses
Use a report that summarizes performance on clusters of items for all students in your class. Within each curriculum area, identify on which clusters your students need improvement most. Match the clusters to your state's standards and determine the class's weakness and strengths with respect to the standards. Use your knowledge of the subject and of your students to verify the areas of greatest need. Don't be afraid to contradict the picture given by the test if you have good evidence that supports the fact that the students know more than they have shown on the test.

Step 2. Establish instructional priorities
Review your list of instructional needs. Put them into an order for instruction. Be sure to teach prerequisite needs first. Concentrate on the most important areas—those that will help students in their further understanding of concepts and principles in the subject.

Step 3. Organize the class for instruction
The test information may help you form small groups of students who have similar instructional needs. Alternately, you could form small groups that have students at different levels of learning so that these who already know the material can help instruct those who have not yet mastered it. You will need to use your own resources to organize your class, as the test cannot do that directly.

Step 4. Plan your instruction before you begin
Be clear about your instructional targets. Look at the test items to get an idea of the types of tasks you want students to learn to do, but remember that you are trying to teach generalizable skills and

abilities. The tasks on the test are only a small sample of the domain of tasks implied by the curriculum.

Look to the curriculum to see where the areas of need fit into the larger scheme. Teach within this larger framework, rather than narrowing your teaching to the test items. Create your own assessment instrument for each of the areas of need so you can clarify what you will expect students to do at the end of the lessons. Organize your teaching activities to accomplish these ends.

Step 5. Assess students' progress toward your instructional targets and state's standards
Monitor students' progress through both informal and formal assessments. Observe students as they complete the assignments you give them to see if they are making progress toward your learning targets and state standards. Use performance and paper-and-pencil assessments to monitor their progress in more formal ways. Adjust your teaching for those students who are not making appropriate progress. Give feedback to students by showing them what they are expected to do (i.e., the learning target or state standard), explaining to them what their performance is like now, how it is different from the target performance, and what they have yet to learn to accomplish the target performance.

Step 6. Carry out summative assessment
Use a variety of assessment techniques to assess each student so that you are certain that the student has learned the target and can apply the concepts and principles to appropriate realistic situations. Use performance assessments, extended responses, and objective items in appropriate combinations. Do not limit your assessment to only one format.

Standardized survey tests are also useful for extraclassroom purposes. Among these external uses of test results are the following.

■ School officials use the average scores of a group (class, building, or school system) as one piece of information to make decisions about needed curriculum or instructional changes.

■ Educational evaluators compare the relative effectiveness of alternate methods of instruction.

■ Educational researchers describe the relative effectiveness of innovations or experiments in education.

■ School superintendents describe to school boards and other stakeholders the relative effectiveness of the local district. School board members should realize that no single instrument could account for all the factors that affect the learning of students in a particular community.

All of these purposes relate in some way to accountability. But accountability is poorly determined if the test does not correspond to what is happening in the classroom. Further, when school officials overemphasize standardized tests, some teachers may believe that having the students "pass the test" is more important than teaching them the important abilities defined in the broader curriculum framework. This ultimately leads to a narrowing of the curriculum in undesirable ways, such as teaching only what will appear on the test and not teaching anything that will not appear on the test (Amrein & Berliner, 2002).

Criticisms of standardized tests

Critics often describe perceived misuses of tests. For example, they may say that tests (a) measure only a small portion of what is taught in the classroom, (b) do not measure the real goals of an educational program, and (c) foster undesirable changes in school curricula or teacher emphasis. Some criticisms are contradictory. The same test may be criticized by some persons because its focus is too narrow and by others because its scores are influenced by too broad a range of human characteristics. Many of the criticisms can be overcome, either by using the test in the way the publisher intended it to be used or by choosing another, more appropriate test. And by all means, do not use standardized test results *alone* for any major decision.

Do not use standardized test results alone for decisions about student placement into special programs or retention in grade. Use many pieces of information for decisions about students, including students' daily classroom performance, teachers' assessments, and results from other assessments in addition to the survey achievement battery.

Do not use standardized test results alone for evaluation of teachers or programs. Assessment results have many causes, including match of test content to what was taught in the classroom, the general aptitude of students in this year's class, this year's teachers, previous teachers, home factors, school leadership, and others.

Prepare your students for standardized testing

The goal of a standardized test is to generalize from the student's performance to the larger domain of abilities and knowledge that the curriculum framework is supposed to foster. Responses on a particular test or assessment are only signs or pointers to the student's possible performance in the larger domain implied by the learning targets of the curriculum framework. If you give specific practice only on the questions or tasks on the assessment, you focus a student's learning only on these few tasks. Such narrowly focused instruction and learning does not generalize to the broader learning targets that are the real goals of education.

A variety of practice activities may help students improve their performance on an assessment. The following is an ordered list of assessment preparation activities, arranged in order from the most to least legitimate (Mehrens & Kaminski, 1989):

1. Teaching the learning targets in the curriculum without narrowing your teaching to those targets that appear on a standardized assessment.

2. Teaching general test-taking strategies.

3. Teaching only those learning targets that specifically match the targets that will appear on the standardized assessment your students will take.

4. Teaching only those learning targets that specifically match the targets that will appear on the standardized assessment your students will take and giving practice using the same types of task formats that will appear on the assessment.

5. Giving your students practice on a published parallel form of the assessment they will take.

6. Giving your students practice on the same questions and tasks that they will take later.

Most educators would agree that the first activity is always ethical, because it is the teacher's job to teach the official curriculum. Most educators would also agree that the second activity, teaching students how to take tests and do their best on them, is ethical. The fifth and sixth activities would always be considered unethical, because they narrow instruction to only the specific assessment procedures that your students will be administered and practically eliminate your ability to generalize from the assessment results to the performance domain specified by the curriculum.

Thus, the boundary between ethical and unethical test preparation practices is somewhere between Activities 2 and 5. The deciding factor lies in the degree to which a school wishes to generalize the test results. The closer the activity is to the fifth one, the less able are school officials to generalize students' assessment results to the official curriculum—unless, of course, the official curriculum is identical to the assessment instrument.

We know teachers whose school districts expect them to do Activities 1 through 4 with respect to their state accountability test. Our best advice to you—if you find yourself in one of these districts—is to do what is expected of you but emphasize Activity 1. Teach the learning targets. Use a full range of instructional and formative assessment strategies to do so, not just drill and practice. There is some research evidence that this strategy actually will have a better effect on standardized test results in the long run than drill (Meisels, Atkins-Burnett, Xue, & Bickel, 2003; Newman, Bryk, & Nagaoka, 2001; William, Lee, Harrison, & Black, 2004). And it's certainly better for teachers' and students' motivation than classes that are really just "test prep."

Follow prescribed administrative procedures when you give standardized tests

You will be required to administer a standardized assessment to your students, most likely one or more per year. These assessments may be standardized achievement tests, performance assessments, or assessments mandated by your state department of education.

Students should be aware of (a) the fact that they will be assessed, (b) what they will be assessed on, (c) the reasons for the assessment, and (d) how their results will be used. Help students be prepared to do their best. Familiarize yourself with the assessment procedures and materials. Prepare the assessment environment so that a valid assessment can be done. Learn how to administer the assessment, including what you are permitted to say to the students.

Validity of assessment results will depend on how well you follow standardized procedures during the administration phase. If you don't follow the procedures stated in the manual, the assessment results will not be comparable across students and the norms will not be usable. Monitor students to be sure they are following directions, marking their answers in the proper manner, and otherwise attending to the tasks.

Use normative information to describe student strengths, weaknesses, and progress

Norm-referencing indicates how one student's performance compares to the performances of others. Here are four major reasons for standardized assessment. The first two purposes are best served by a criterion-referencing framework. The second two purposes are best served by a norm-referencing framework.

- Criterion-referenced purposes
  - To describe the performances a student has achieved within each subject area.
  - To describe student deficiencies that need further improvement within each subject area.

■ Norm-referenced purposes

- To describe which subjects are the student's strengths and weaknesses across the curriculum.
- To describe the amount of educational development (progress) a student has made over the course of one or more years within each subject area.

Criterion-referenced results describe what a student can do in reading and math, for example, but you need norms to conclude whether these are relative strengths or weaknesses. A teacher may say that a student is able to solve routine linear and quadratic equations in mathematics and is able to read with comprehension age-appropriate stories. Normative information can determine which is the stronger area. If ninth-grader Blake ranks at the top of the norm group in mathematics but in the middle of the same norm group in reading, we know that of the two subjects, Blake is stronger in mathematics.

Measuring educational growth and development also requires norm-referencing. Norm groups provide the basis for defining an educational development scale (such as the grade-equivalent scale) across different grade levels. We assess a student once every year or two, each time referencing the results to this developmental scale. We measure growth by the student's progress along this scale.

A **norm group** is the large representative sample of students for which test manuals report performance. The performance of a norm group on a particular assessment represents the present, average status of that group of students on that particular assessment. A group's current average does not represent a standard, however, nor does it establish what your school or your students should attain. Your state's content and performance standards and your curriculum's learning targets tell you what students should achieve.

Most norm-referenced, standardized achievement, and aptitude batteries have **national norms**. In principle, the national norm groups are supposed to be representative of the students in the country. But each publisher samples differently. Norms from different publishers are not comparable, and no publisher's norming sample exactly mirrors the nation's schools. For many of your norm-referenced interpretations, the most appropriate group with which you should compare a student is the **local norm group**: the group of students in the same grade in the same school district.

A publisher may provide separate male/female norms or may provide other **special norm groups**. Examples include norms for students with deafness or blindness, students with mental retardation, students enrolled in a certain course of study or curriculum, and students attending urban, rural, low-SES, or parochial schools. A student may belong to more than one special group.

School averages norms consist of a tabulation of the average (mean) score from each school building in a national sample of schools and provide information on the relative ordering of these averages (means). This distribution of averages is much less variable than the distribution of individual student scores. If your school wants to know how the school's third-grade average score compares with that of other school buildings, use school averages norms.

Published norms data should satisfy three Rs: relevance, representativeness, and recency (APA, AERA, & NCME, 1999). *Relevance* means that the norm group(s) a publisher provides should be the group(s) to which you will want to compare your students. *Representativeness* means that the norm sample must be based on a carefully planned sample. The test publisher should provide you with information about the factors (sex, age, socioeconomic level, etc.) used to ensure representativeness. *Recency* means that the norms are based on current data. As the curriculum, schooling, and social and economic factors change, so will students' performance on tests. Further, if your school uses the same form of a test year after year, scores will generally increase, because the students become familiar with the format and teachers tend to prepare students specifically for that test (Linn, Graue, & Sanders, 1990; Shepard, 1990; Wiser & Lenke, 1987). If the norms are not recent, they will mislead, conveying the impression that your students are learning better than they really are.

You obtain the most accurate estimate of a student's standing in a norm group when the student is tested on a date nearest the time of year the publisher established the norms. Publishers commonly interpolate and extrapolate (i.e., project numbers forward or back) to develop norm tables. They may provide spring norm tables, for example, even though no tests were actually administered to the norm group in the spring. The publisher should state the empirical norming dates in the test manual or technical report. To be accurate, your school should administer a standardized test within two or three weeks before or after the midpoint date of the publisher's empirical norming period.

Norm-referenced scores are derived from the raw scores of an assessment. In this book, we discuss only the norm-referenced scores you will most often encounter, which are represented in the concept map shown in Figure 12.1.

Figure 12.1 Organization of major score-referencing schemes.

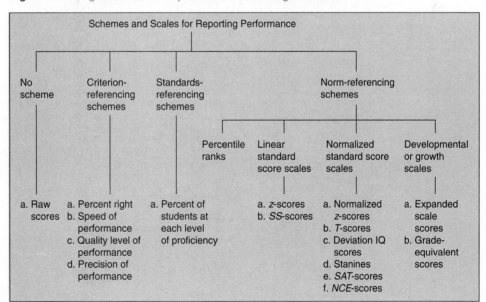

Status measures are norm-referenced scores specific to a particular grade or age.

First, we will show you the scores designed for use at one point in time. Use these scores to describe *what is* at any given point, not to describe change or growth. (So, for example, you would not subtract percentile ranks to describe change from one year to the next.) We begin at the left-most branch of norm-referencing schemes in Figure 12.1. The **percentile rank** tells the percentage of the students in a norm group that have scored *lower* than the raw score in question. The percentile rank is perhaps the most useful and easily understood norm-referenced score.

All scores contain measurement error. Some publishers report **percentile bands** (also called *uncertainty intervals* or *confidence intervals*) instead of a single percentile rank. These percentile bands are based on the assessment's standard error of measurement (*SEM*). When you add the *SEM* to, and subtract it from, the value of each student's obtained score, the resulting interval has a 68% chance of containing the student's true score. Use percentile bands to interpret a student's score on one test, a student's score on two tests, or two different students' scores on one test. If the bands overlap, there is no reliable difference. Example 12.3 gives some examples of how to do this.

■ **EXAMPLE 12.3 Examples of How to Interpret Standardized Test Score Intervals**

These examples use grade-equivalent scores from a hypothetical standardized achievement test that has a standard error of measurement of 0.4. It would be quite likely that, upon retesting, a student's score would shift up or down the scale 4 grade-equivalent months (0.4).

Confidence Interval for One Student's Score

To show the interval for a student, you would add +0.4 to the student's obtained score to compute the upper limit of the interval and subtract 0.4 from the student's obtained score to find the lower limit of the band. Any number between the upper and the lower limits of the interval could be the student's true score. Suppose Harry's obtained grade-equivalent score in science is 7.8. After making the interval, our interpretation is that Harry's true grade-equivalent score is probably between 7.4 and 8.2.

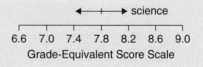

■ **EXAMPLE 12.3** (Continued)

Using SEM to Interpret the Difference Between Two Scores for One Student

When a student takes a battery of achievement tests, the student usually has two or more scores, one for each subject. These scores may not be identical. We can set an interval around each of these scores. If the intervals for two scores overlap, it is likely that the student's true scores are not meaningfully different. If the intervals overlap, the observed-score differences for the student could have come about 68% of the time simply by measurement error. Harry's obtained grade-equivalent score in science is 7.8, while in mathematics it is 7.4. The confidence band for science is 7.4 to 8.2; for math it is 7.0 to 7.8. Since the intervals overlap, it is likely that his true scores on the two tests are not meaningfully different.

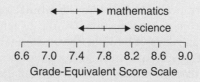

Using the SEM to Interpret the Difference Between Two Students' Scores

Sometimes you want to see if one student is stronger than another student in a subject by comparing their scores on the same achievement test. Form an interval around each student's score. Then, see if the intervals overlap. No overlap means that the students' true scores are probably meaningfully different. If the intervals do overlap, there may be no meaningful differences in the two students' true scores because differences of the size observed could arise simply by errors of measurement 68% of the time. In reading, Sally's obtained grade-equivalent score was 8.2 while Jane's was 7.0. The interval for Sally is 7.8 to 8.6; for Jane it is 6.6 to 7.4. Since the intervals do not overlap, Sally is a stronger reader than Jane.

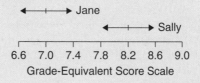

A **linear standard score** tells how far a raw score is from the mean of the norm group, the distance being expressed using standard deviation units. Linear standard scores can be used to make two sets of scores more comparable by placing them on the same numerical scale. The fundamental linear standard score is the *z*-**score**, which tells the number of standard deviation units a raw score is above (or below) the mean of a given distribution. For example, if a student's raw score falls below the mean a distance equal to one and one-half times the standard deviation of the group, the student's z-score equals -1.50. A z-score is negative when the raw score is below the mean, positive when the raw score is above the mean, and equal to zero when the raw score is exactly equal to the mean. Other linear standard scores are computed from z-scores. An **SS-score** tells the location of a raw score in a distribution having a mean of 50 and a standard deviation of 10.

Before we discuss the normalized standard score branch of Figure 12.1, we need to discuss normal distributions of scores. A **normal distribution**, sometimes called a *normal curve*, is a mathematical model invented in 1733 by Abraham deMoivre (Pearson, 1924). It is defined by a particular equation that depends on two specific numbers: the mean and the standard deviation. Many normal distributions exist and each has a different mean and/or standard deviation. Every normal curve is smooth and continuous; each has a symmetrical, bell-shaped form. In theory, a normal curve never touches the baseline (horizontal axis) but is asymptotic to it, extending out to infinity in either direction. Graphs of actual raw-score distributions are nonsymmetrical, jagged, and bounded by the lowest and highest possible raw scores.

If we cut up a normal distribution into sections one standard deviation wide, each section will have a fixed percentage of cases or area under the normal curve (see Figure 12.2). For example, a section that is one standard deviation wide and located just above the mean contains approximately 34% of the area. The comparable section just below the mean contains 34% as well. Together those two sections

Figure 12.2 Relationships among percentile ranks, z-scores, and T-scores in a normal distribution.

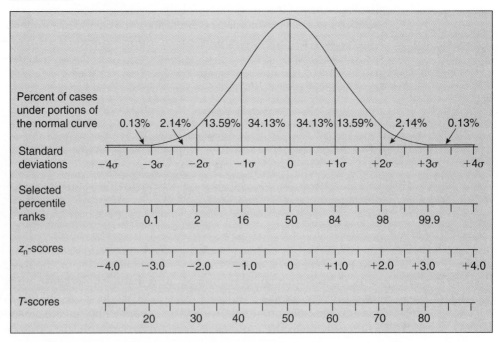

contain 68% of the area. Thus, 68% of the area in a normal distribution will be within one standard deviation of the mean; 95% will be within two standard deviations; and 99.7% of the area will fall within three standard deviations. So if a distribution is normal, nearly all of the scores will span a range equivalent to six standard deviations.

Now that you have a little background on the meaning of a normal curve, let's return to the third branch of Figure 12.1: normalized standard scores. Test publishers may transform raw scores to a new set of scores that is distributed normally (or nearly so). Such transformation changes the shape of the original distribution, squeezing and stretching the scale to make it conform to a normal distribution. Once this is accomplished, various types of standard scores can be derived, and each can have an appropriate normal curve interpretation. The general name for these derived scores is **normalized standard scores**.

When the z-scores have percentile ranks corresponding to what we would expect in a normal distribution, they are called **normalized z-scores** (z_n). "Normalized" z_n-values are the z-scores that would have been attained if the distribution had been normal in form.

Other normalized standard scores also may be interpreted according to the normal curve. A **normalized T-score** tells the location of a raw score in a normal distribution having a mean of 50 and a standard deviation of 10. The normalized *T*-score is the counterpart to the linear *SS*-score. A **deviation IQ (DIQ)** score tells the location of a raw score in a normal distribution having a mean of 100 and a standard deviation of 15 or 16. The norm group is usually made up of all those students with the same chronological age, regardless of grade placement. The *SAT*-score is a normalized standard score from a distribution that has a mean of 500 and a standard deviation of 100.

A **stanine** score tells the location of a raw score in a specific segment of a normal distribution. Publishers frequently recommend using **national stanines** for norm-referenced interpretation of achievement and aptitude assessments. Figure 12.3 illustrates the meaning of a stanine score. A normal distribution is divided into nine segments, numbered from a low of 1 through a high of 9. Scores falling within the boundaries of these segments are assigned one of these nine numbers (hence, the term *stanine*, from "standard nine"). Each segment is one-half a standard deviation wide, except for stanines 1 and 9. The percentage of cases in a normal curve falling within each segment is shown in Figure 12.3, along with the range of percentile ranks associated with each. All scores falling within an interval are assigned the stanine of that interval. For example, all students with percentile ranks from 11 through 22 are assigned a stanine of 3; all from 23 through 29 a stanine of 4; and so on.

The **normal curve equivalent (NCE)** is a normalized standard score with a mean of 50 and a standard deviation of 21.06. A standard deviation of 21.06 was chosen so the *NCE*-scores would span the range 1 to 99. *NCE*s were developed primarily for use with federal program evaluation efforts (Tallmadge & Wood, 1976). Their primary value is evaluating gains from various educational programs that use different publishers' tests. Although some publishers present norm tables for *NCE*s in their assessment manuals, using these scores for reporting individual student results is not recommended.

Figure 12.3 Illustration of a normal distribution showing stanines, percentile ranks, and percentage of cases having each stanine.

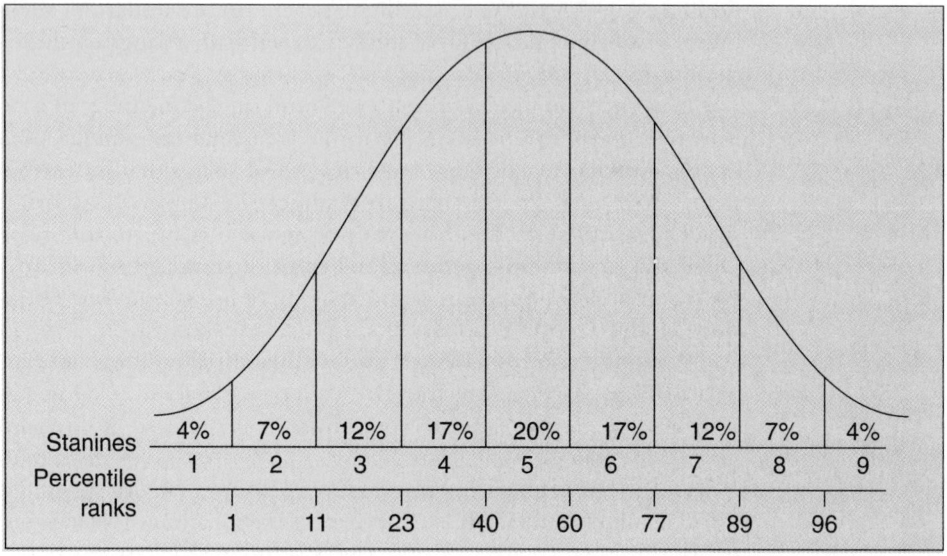

Stanines	4%	7%	12%	17%	20%	17%	12%	7%	4%
	1	2	3	4	5	6	7	8	9
Percentile ranks	1	11	23	40	60	77	89	96	

Growth measures are norm-referenced scores that can be used to chart educational development or progress

One use of a standardized test is to measure students' growth on a continuous scale. If a growth scale is constructed properly, it is possible to track students' educational growth over the various grade levels. Status measures (scales specific to a particular grade) like those we described in the previous section cannot measure growth as a student moves from one grade to the next. For example, suppose Billy tested at the 84th percentile in grades 5, 6, and 7. Although Billy would be growing in skills and knowledge, his percentile rank (84) has stayed the same. The number, 84, by reflecting only location in each grade's norm group, does not communicate Billy's growth.

Figure 12.1 shows two developmental or growth scales: expanded scale scores (extended normalized standard scores) and grade-equivalent scores. These scales were designed to measure growth (comparing current performance to previous performance), not status. Neither grade-equivalent scores nor extended standard scores can be used to compare a student's strengths and weaknesses across different subject matters. Nor can they be used to determine a student's rank among his or her peers.

An **extended normalized standard score** tells the location of a raw score on a scale of numbers that is anchored to a lower grade reference group. Program evaluators and school researchers find that a "ruler" or achievement continuum on which a student's progress can be measured over a wide range of grades is very useful. On this continuum, low scores represent the lowest levels of educational development and high scores the highest level of educational development. Publishers refer to this type of scale with a variety of names: obtained scale score, scale score, extended standard score, developmental standard score, or growth-scale values.

Extended standard scores tend to show that on the average students show less achievement growth in the upper elementary grades than in the lower grades. Extended standard scores show different standard deviations between subjects and progressively increasing standard deviations as grade levels increase.

A **grade-equivalent score** (*GE*) tells the grade placement at which a particular raw score is average. *GE*s are the development scores most often used with achievement tests at the elementary school level. A grade-equivalent score is reported as a decimal fraction, such as 3.4 or 7.9. The whole number part of the score refers to a grade level, and the decimal part refers to a month of the school year within that grade level. For example, you read a grade-equivalent score of 3.4 as "third grade, fourth month"; similarly, you read 7.9 as "seventh grade, ninth month." These scores assume that the time between June and September (i.e., the summer months) represents an increment of one-tenth (or one month) on the grade-equivalent scale. Use grade-equivalent scores as coarse indicators of educational development or growth and report them with their corresponding percentile ranks.

Grade-equivalents are norm-referenced growth indicators. It is not true that students ought to have the same placement as their grade-equivalent scores. For one thing, such an interpretation would depend on how well the test content matches what was taught to the students up to the point at which the test was administered. Second, grade-equivalents are based on the median (expected) performance of students in that grade.month. By definition, half the students in the norm groups at a particular grade placement will have scores above the median. Thus, half the students in the norm group have grade-equivalent scores higher than their actual grade placement. Third, you can't interpret a third grader's grade-equivalent score of, say, 5.7 on a mathematics test covering third-grade content to mean that this student ought to be placed in fifth-grade mathematics. The test shows that the student did very well on third-grade content, but the student was not assessed on fifth-grade mathematics.

Two views of growth

There are different views on what constitutes "normal" growth. Sometimes teachers and school administrators use grade-equivalents to answer questions of what educational growth they should expect of a student. This is not a good practice and the results of doing it are not satisfactory. One view of **normal growth** is this: "A student ought to exhibit a growth of 1.0 grade-equivalent units from one grade to the next." Under this view, a student taking the test in second grade and scoring 1.3, for example, would need to score 2.3 in third grade, 4.3 in fifth, and so on to show "normal" or expected growth.

This *grade-equivalent view of normal growth* cannot be supported at all percentile ranks. Example 12.4 shows examples of what will happen to three hypothetical students on the mathematics subtest of two published tests if this view is adopted.

■ **EXAMPLE 12.4 Examples of changes in the percentile ranks for three hypothetical students as each "gains" one year in grade-equivalent units from second through eighth grade**

Grade placement at the time of testing	Metropolitan Achievement Tests, Total Mathematics						Iowa Tests of Basic Skills, Total Mathematics					
	Student A: "Below grade level"		Student B: "On grade level"		Student C: "Above grade level"		Student A: "Below grade level"		Student B: "On grade level"		Student C: "Above grade level"	
	GE	PR	GE	PR	GE	PR	GE	PR	GE	PR	GE	PR
2.3	1.3	16	2.3	63	3.3	86	1.3	18	2.3	54	3.3	92
3.3	2.3	29	3.3	64	4.3	85	2.3	18	3.3	55	4.3	85
4.3	3.3	34	4.3	63	5.3	80	3.3	28	4.3	56	5.3	77
5.3	4.3	37	5.3	61	6.3	77	4.3	34	5.3	54	6.3	71
6.3	5.3	36	6.3	57	7.3	73	5.3	34	6.3	52	7.3	66
7.3	6.3	39	7.3	60	8.3	70	6.3	38	7.3	52	8.3	65
8.3	7.3	42	8.3	55	9.3	60	7.3	41	8.3	53	9.3	64

Source: Data reproduced from *The Metropolitan Achievement Test®: Seventh Edition, Fall Norms Table.* Copyright © 1993 by Harcourt Assessment, Inc. Reproduced with permission. All rights reserved; Copyright © 1993 by The University of Iowa. "Grade Equivalent Data" from the *Iowa Tests of Basic Skills®* (ITBS®) reproduced with permission of The Riverside Publishing Company. All rights reserved. Reproduced with permission of the Riverside Publishing Company.

In Example 12.4, Student A is one year behind in terms of grade-equivalents, Student B is at grade level, and Student C is one year ahead. Each year, the students' grade-equivalents show a one-year "growth" over the preceding year. But look at the percentile ranks corresponding to their scores. Student A, who starts out one year behind, has to *exceed more people* in the norm group to maintain a one-year-behind grade-equivalent. Being one year behind in second grade means being at the 16th or 17th percentile. However, one year behind in grade 8 means being around the *41st or 42nd percentile.* One has to move from the bottom of the group toward the middle. An opposite phenomenon occurs for Student C, who begins one grade ahead at around the *86th or 92nd percentile.* In this case, the student can fall behind more and more students and still be "one year ahead." Only students who are exactly at the average each year (like Student B) will maintain their percentile rank from year to year.

An alternate norm-referenced definition is the *percentile view of normal growth:* A student shows normal growth if that student maintains the same position (i.e., percentile rank) in the norm from year to year. Example 12.5 shows examples of what happens to a student's grade-equivalent score if that student's percentile rank stays the same each year.

Lower-scoring students (such as Students A and C)—even though they do not change their position in the norm group—have grade-equivalents indicating they are further and further behind. An opposite trend occurs for initially high-scoring students. The exact magnitude of this falling-behind phenomenon will vary from

■ **EXAMPLE 12.5 Examples of changes in the grade-equivalent score for four hypothetical students as each student's percentile rank remains the same from second through eighth grade**

Grade placement at the time of testing	Metropolitan Achievement Tests, Total Mathematics				Iowa Tests of Basic Skills, Total Mathematics			
	Student A: "Below grade level" (*PR* = 16 each year)		Student B: "Above grade level" (*PR* = 84 each year)		Student C: "Below grade level" (*PR* = 16 each year)		Student D: "Above grade level" (*PR* = 84 each year)	
	GE	"Grades behind"	GE	"Grades ahead"	GE	"Grades behind"	GE	"Grades ahead"
3.3	2.1	1.2	4.8	1.5	2.1	1.2	4.7	1.4
4.3	2.6	1.7	6.3	2.0	2.8	1.5	5.9	1.6
5.3	3.1	2.2	7.7	2.4	3.3	2.0	7.3	2.0
6.3	3.9	2.4	9.0	2.7	4.0	2.3	8.8	2.5
7.3	4.5	2.8	10.1	2.8	4.7	2.6	10.3	3.0
8.3	5.1	3.2	10.6	2.3	5.1	3.2	11.9	3.6

Source: Data reproduced from *The Metropolitan Achievement Test®: Seventh Edition, Fall Norms Table.* Copyright © 1993 by Harcourt Assessment, Inc. Reproduced with permission. All rights reserved; Copyright © 1993 by the University of Iowa. "Grade Equivalent Data" from the *Iowa Tests of Basic Skills®* (ITBS®) reproduced with permission of The Riverside Publishing Company. All rights reserved.

one publisher's test to another's and depends on the student's percentile rank. The grade-equivalent scales of some tests are created to minimize the falling-behind effect. Students close to the 50th percentile will exhibit less of the falling-behind effect than will those further from the center of the distribution.

Criterion- or standards-referenced interpretations of standardized test results require looking at the kinds of questions students can answer

If you want information about the content of a student's learning, you need to look carefully at the kinds of performances the student can do. To do that, you need to review for each student the kinds of test items the student answered correctly. When you do this, of course, you are making criterion-referenced interpretations.

Some standardized tests report a percentage of items on each objective, strand, or subtest to allow for limited criterion-referenced interpretations of student scores. These are sometimes based on very short scales (3 to 5 items) and are thus not very reliable. Some state tests report scores on standards by setting cutoff scores for proficiency levels (e.g., Below Basic, Basic, Proficient, Advanced). The judgments of educators about where to place the cut scores are a kind of proxy for looking at student performance or what students can do.

Five guidelines for score interpretation will serve you well

Consider the following points when interpreting student scores on norm-referenced standardized tests (Prescott, Balow, Hogan, & Farr, 1978; Nitko & Brookhart, 2007):

- Look for unexpected patterns of scores. An assessment should confirm what a teacher knows from daily interactions with a student; unusually high or low scores for a student should be a signal for exploring instructional implications.

- Seek an explanation for patterns. Ask why a student is higher in one subject than another. Check for motivation, special interests, special difficulties, etc.

- Don't expect surprises for every student. Most students' assessment results should be as you expect from their performance in class. A valid assessment should confirm your observations.

- Small differences in subtest scores should be viewed as chance fluctuations. Use the standard error of measurement (in a confidence interval) to help decide whether differences are large enough to have instructional significance.

Guideline 12.2 How to answer parents' questions about standardized test results

Category	Examples of questions	Suggestions for answering
Standing	• How is my child doing compared to others? • Is my child's progress normal for his or her grade?	Use percentile ranks to describe standing. Explain that a standardized test gives partial information only. Use information from classroom performance to explain progress.
Growth	• Has my child's growth been as much as it should be?	Use grade-equivalent scores to show progress from previous years. Use composite scores (i.e., all subjects combined) to show general growth; use scores from each subject to explain growth in particular curricular areas. Obtain past performance information from the child's cumulative folder. Use information from classroom performance to explain growth.
Improvement needed	• Does my child have any learning weaknesses? • How can I help improve my child's learning?	Use percentile ranks to identify relative weaknesses. Use information about a student's performance to clusters of similar questions to pinpoint weaknesses. Use information from class performance to explain specific weaknesses. Don't overemphasize weaknesses. Explain a student's relative strengths, too; give specific suggestions as to how parents can help.
Strengths	• What does my child do well?	Use percentile ranks to pick out areas of relative strengths. Use class information to illustrate the point. Make suggestions for how parents can help improve these areas even more.
Intelligence	• How smart is my child? Is my child gifted?	Explain that an achievement test is not an intelligence test. Explain that an achievement test is very sensitive to what was taught in class and that high scores may only reflect specific opportunities to learn. Use class information to illustrate your points.

Source: This figure is based on suggestions in Hoover et al., 1993.

- Use information from various assessments and observation to explain performance on other assessments. Students low in reading comprehension may perform poorly on the social studies subtest, for example.

Guideline 12.2 contains examples of many of the questions parents ask when they receive standardized test results from a school. The questions are organized into five categories: standing, growth, improvement needed, strengths, and intelligence. The table contains suggestions for answering each category of questions, including which type of norm-referenced score to use. Although other scores might be used, we believe the ones suggested will be most helpful to your explanation.

We suggest always using a student's classroom performance to complement and explain the student's standardized test results. Because in the majority of cases students' standardized test performance will be very consistent with their classroom performance, using students' classroom performance to illustrate their standardized test performance will help you reinforce to the parents your assessment of the students.

Conclusions

Classroom teachers will need to use the information in this chapter for two important reasons. One, teachers get calls to interpret standardized test scores to parents because teachers are the first person parents call when they have questions about school. And two, teachers are more and more being required to use standardized test scores in planning instruction. This chapter discussed standardized tests and the different kinds of scores first, and then presented more general principles of interpretation.

Exercises

1. Table 12.2 shows part of a norms table that might appear in a manual of a standardized achievement test. The table shows selected raw scores, grade-equivalent scores, and percentile ranks for the publisher's standardization sample (i.e., norm group). Assume that (a) the local school system has judged the test's

Table 12.2 Use with Exercise 1

Raw score	Vocabulary (*V*) GE	PR	Reading (*R*) GE	PR	Language (*L*) GE	PR	Work-study (*W*) GE	PR	Arithmetic (*A*) GE	PR
5	1.8	1	1.6	1	1.9	1	2.3	1	2.5	1
20	4.1	34	3.3	17	4.4	41	5.6	74	5.5	65
30	5.1	61	4.2	36	5.6	75	7.0	96	6.2	74
40	6.2	74	4.8	52	6.4	86	7.6	99	6.9	97
50	7.0	96	5.6	74	7.9	99	8.0	99	7.7	99
70			8.1	99						

content to be a good match to its curriculum, (b) the norm data were collected during the seventh month of the fourth grade, (c) the norms are appropriate for use with the local school system, (d) the publisher has computed grade equivalents and percentile ranks in the usual way and with no errors, and (e) the school tested the students in April.

Use the table and your knowledge of norm-referenced frameworks to judge each of the following statements as true or false. Explain and justify your judgment in each case.

a. James is a fourth-grade student with a grade-equivalent profile of $V = 6.2$, $R = 5.6$, $L = 5.6$, $W = 5.6$, $A = 6.2$. Decide whether each of the following conclusions is true or false, and explain the basis for your judgment.

   i. James should be in fifth grade.

   ii. James is strongest in vocabulary and arithmetic.

   iii. James's scores are above average for his grade.

b. Fourth-grader Sue's raw score on Reading is 50, and on Language it is 30. Decide whether each of the following conclusions is true or false, and explain your decision.

   i. Sue is more able in reading because her raw score in reading is higher.

   ii. Because Sue's grade-equivalent scores are equal, she is equally able in reading and vocabulary (relative to the norm group).

   iii. Sue is more able in language than reading (relative to the norm group) because her percentile rank in language is higher.

2. Judge each of the following statements true or false. Explain the basis for your judgment in each case.

a. A person's percentile rank is 45. This means that the person's raw score was the same as 45% of the group assessed.

b. Sally's arithmetic assessment score is 40. The class's mean score is 45, and its standard deviation is 10. Therefore, Sally is located one standard deviation below the mean.

c. The norm tables show that the distribution of deviation IQ scores on a school ability test is approximately normal in form. This means that for the people in the norm groups, the intellectual ability that naturally underlies the scores is normally distributed.

Now go to our Companion Website at **www.prenhall.com/brookhart** to assess your understanding of chapter content with multiple-choice and essay questions. Broaden your knowledge of assessment with links to assessment related web sites.

Standards for Teacher Competence in Educational Assessment of Students

Developed by the American Federation of Teachers
National Council on Measurement in Education
National Education Association

The standards are intended for use as:

- a guide for teacher educators as they design and approve programs for teacher preparation

- a self-assessment guide for teachers in identifying their needs for professional development in student assessment

- a guide for workshop instructors as they design professional development experiences for in-service teachers

- an impetus for educational measurement specialists and teacher trainers to conceptualize student assessment and teacher training in student assessment more broadly than has been the case in the past

1. Teachers Should be Skilled in Choosing Assessment Methods Appropriate for Instructional Decisions

Skills in choosing appropriate, useful, administratively convenient, technically adequate, and fair assessment methods are pre-requisite to good use of information to support instructional decisions. Teachers need to be well-acquainted with the kinds of information provided by a broad range of assessment alternatives and their strengths and weaknesses. In particular, they should be familiar with criteria for evaluating and selecting assessment methods in light of instructional plans.

Teachers who meet this standard will have the conceptual and application skills that follow. They will be able to use the concepts of assessment error and validity when developing or selecting their approaches to classroom assessment of students. They will understand how valid assessment data can support instructional activities such as providing appropriate feedback to students, diagnosing group and individual learning needs, planning for individualized educational programs, motivating students, and evaluating instructional procedures. They will understand how invalid information can affect instructional decisions about students. They will also be able to use and evaluate assessment options available to them, considering among other things the cultural, social, economic, and language backgrounds of students. They will be aware that different assessment approaches can be incompatible with certain instructional goals and may impact quite differently on their teaching.

Teachers will know, for each assessment approach they use, its appropriateness for making decisions about their pupils. Moreover, teachers will know where to find information about and/or reviews of various assessment methods. Assessment options are diverse and include text- and curriculum-embedded questions and tests, standardized criterion-referenced and norm-referenced tests, oral questioning, spontaneous and structured performance assessments, portfolios, exhibitions, demonstrations, rating scales, writing samples, paper-and-pencil tests, seatwork and homework, peer- and self-assessments, student records, observations, questionnaires, interviews, projects, products, and others' opinions.

2. Teachers Should be Skilled in Developing Assessment Methods Appropriate for Instructional Decisions

While teachers often use published or other external assessment tools, the bulk of the assessment information they use for decision-making comes from approaches they create and implement. Indeed, the assessment demands of the classroom go well beyond readily available instruments.

Teachers who meet this standard will have the conceptual and application skills that follow. Teachers will be skilled in planning the collection of information that facilitates the decisions they will make. They will know and follow appropriate principles for developing and using assessment methods in their teaching, avoiding common pitfalls in student assessment. Such techniques may include several of the options listed at the end of the first standard. The teacher will select the techniques which are appropriate to the intent of the teacher's instruction.

Teachers meeting this standard will also be skilled in using student data to analyze the quality of each assessment technique they use. Since most teachers do not have access to assessment specialists, they must be prepared to do these analyses themselves.

3. Teachers Should be Skilled in Administering, Scoring and Interpreting the Results of Both Externally Produced and Teacher-Produced Assessment Methods

It is not enough that teachers are able to select and develop good assessment methods; they must also be able to apply them properly. Teachers should be skilled in administering, scoring, and interpreting results from diverse assessment methods.

Teachers who meet this standard will have the conceptual and application skills that follow. They will be skilled in interpreting informal and formal teacher-produced assessment results, including pupils' performances in class and on homework assignments. Teachers will be able to use guides for scoring essay questions and projects, stencils for scoring response-choice questions, and scales for rating performance assessments. They will be able to use these in ways that produce consistent results.

Teachers will be able to administer standardized achievement tests and be able to interpret the commonly reported scores: percentile ranks, percentile band scores, standard scores, and grade equivalents. They will have a conceptual understanding of the summary indexes commonly reported with assessment results: measures of central tendency, dispersion, relationships, reliability, and errors of measurement.

Teachers will be able to apply these concepts of score and summary indices in ways that enhance their use of the assessments that they develop. They will be able to analyze assessment results to identify pupils' strengths and errors. If they get inconsistent results, they will seek other explanations for the discrepancy or other data to attempt to resolve the uncertainty before arriving at a decision. They will be able to use assessment methods in ways that encourage students' educational development and that do not inappropriately increase students' anxiety levels.

4. Teachers Should be Skilled in Using Assessment Results When Making Decisions about Individual Students, Planning Teaching, Developing Curriculum, and School Improvement

Assessment results are used to make educational decisions at several levels: in the classroom about students, in the community about a school and a school district, and in society, generally, about the purposes and outcomes of the educational enterprise. Teachers play a vital role when participating in decision-making at each of these levels and must be able to use assessment results effectively.

Teachers who meet this standard will have the conceptual and application skills that follow. They will be able to use accumulated assessment information to organize a sound instructional plan for facilitating students' educational development. When using assessment results to plan and/or evaluate instruction and curriculum, teachers will interpret the results correctly and avoid common misinterpretations, such as basing decisions on scores that lack curriculum validity. They will be informed about the results of local, regional, state, and national assessments and about their appropriate use for pupil, classroom, school, district, state, and national educational improvement.

5. Teachers Should be Skilled in Developing Valid Pupil Grading Procedures Which Use Pupil Assessments

Grading students is an important part of professional practice for teachers. Grading is defined as indicating both a student's level of performance and a teacher's valuing of that performance. The principles for using assessments to obtain valid grades are known and teachers should employ them.

Teachers who meet this standard will have the conceptual and application skills that follow. They will be able to devise, implement, and explain a procedure for developing grades composed of marks from various assignments, projects, in-class activities, quizzes, tests, and/or other assessments that they may use. Teachers will understand and be able to articulate why the grades they assign are rational, justified, and fair, acknowledging that such grades reflect their preferences and judgments. Teachers will be able to recognize and to avoid faulty grading procedures such as using grades as punishment. They will be able to evaluate and to modify their grading procedures in order to improve the validity of the interpretations made from them about students' attainments.

6. Teachers Should be Skilled in Communicating Assessment Results to Students, Parents, Other Lay Audiences, and Other Educators

Teachers must routinely report assessment results to students and to parents or guardians. In addition, they are frequently asked to report or to discuss assessment results with other educators and with diverse lay audiences. If the results are not communicated effectively, they may be misused or not used. To communicate effectively with others on matters of student assessment, teachers must be able to use assessment terminology appropriately and must be able to articulate the meaning, limitations, and implications of assessment results. Furthermore, teachers will sometimes be in a position that will require them to defend their own assessment procedures and their interpretations of them. At other times, teachers may need to help the public to interpret assessment results appropriately.

Teachers who meet this standard will have the conceptual and application skills that follow. Teachers will understand and be able to give appropriate explanations of how the interpretation of student assessments must be moderated by the student's socio-economic, cultural, language, and other background factors. Teachers will be able to explain that assessment results do not imply that such background factors limit a student's ultimate educational development. They will be able to communicate to students and to their parents or guardians how they may assess the student's educational progress. Teachers will understand and be able to explain the importance of taking measurement errors into account when using assessments to make decisions about individual students. Teachers will be able to explain the limitations of different informal and formal assessment methods. They will be able to explain printed reports of the results of pupil assessments at the classroom, school district, state, and national levels.

7. Teachers Should be Skilled in Recognizing Unethical, Illegal, and Otherwise Inappropriate Assessment Methods and Uses of Assessment Information

Fairness, the rights of all concerned, and professional ethical behavior must undergird all student assessment activities, from the initial planning for and gathering of information to the interpretation, use, and communication of the results. Teachers must be well-versed in their own ethical and legal responsibilities in assessment. In addition, they should also attempt to have the inappropriate assessment practices of others discontinued whenever they are encountered. Teachers should also participate with the wider educational community in defining the limits of appropriate professional behavior in assessment.

Teachers who meet this standard will have the conceptual and application skills that follow. They will know those laws and case decisions which affect their classroom, school district, and state assessment practices. Teachers will be aware that various assessment procedures can be misused or overused resulting in harmful consequences such as embarrassing students, violating a student's right to confidentiality, and inappropriately using students' standardized achievement test scores to measure teaching effectiveness.

Source: From *Standards for Teacher Competence in Educational Assessment of Students* (pp. 1–4) by American Federation of Teachers, National Council on Measurement in Education, and National Education Association, 1990, Washington, DC: National Council on Measurement in Education. Copyright 1990 by the National Council on Measurement in Education. Reprinted by permission of the publisher.

Code of Fair Testing Practices in Education

Prepared by the Joint Committee on Testing Practices

The Code of Fair Testing Practices in Education (**Code**) is a guide for professionals in fulfilling their obligation to provide and use tests that are fair to all test takers regardless of age, gender, disability, race, ethnicity, national origin, religion, sexual orientation, linguistic background, or other personal characteristics. Fairness is a primary consideration in all aspects of testing. Careful standardization of tests and administration conditions helps to ensure that all test takers are given a comparable opportunity to demonstrate what they know and how they can perform in the area being tested. Fairness implies that every test taker has the opportunity to prepare for the test and is informed about the general nature and content of the test, as appropriate to the purpose of the test. Fairness also extends to the accurate reporting of individual and group test results. Fairness is not an isolated concept, but must be considered in all aspects of the testing process.

The **Code** applies broadly to testing in education (admissions, educational assessment, educational diagnosis, and student placement) regardless of the mode of presentation, so it is relevant to conventional paper-and-pencil tests, computer based tests, and performance tests. It is not designed to cover employment testing, licensure or certification testing, or other types of testing outside the field of education. The Code is directed primarily at professionally developed tests used in formally administered testing programs. Although the Code is not intended to cover tests made by teachers for use in their own classrooms, teachers are encouraged to use the guidelines to help improve their testing practices.

The **Code** addresses the roles of test developers and test users separately. Test developers are people and organizations that construct tests, as well as those that set policies for testing programs. Test users are people and agencies that select tests, administer tests, commission test development services, or make decisions on the basis of test scores. Test developer and test user roles may overlap, for example, when a state or local education agency commissions test development services, sets policies that control the test development process, and makes decisions on the basis of the test scores.

Many of the statements in the **Code** refer to the selection and use of existing tests. When a new test is developed, when an existing test is modified, or when the administration of a test is modified, the Code is intended to provide guidance for this process.

The **Code** is not intended to be mandatory, exhaustive, or definitive, and may not be applicable to every situation. Instead, the Code is intended to be aspirational, and is not intended to take precedence over the judgment of those who have competence in the subjects addressed.

The **Code** provides guidance separately for test developers and test users in four critical areas:

A. Developing and Selecting Appropriate Tests

B. Administering and Scoring Tests

C. Reporting and Interpreting Test Results

D. Informing Test Takers

The **Code** is intended to be consistent with the relevant parts of the Standards for Educational and Psychological Testing (American Educational Research Association [AERA], American Psychological Association [APA], and National Council on Measurement in Education [NCME], 1999). The Code is not meant to add new principles over and above those in the Standards or to change their meaning. Rather, the Code is intended to represent the spirit of selected portions of the Standards in a way that is relevant and meaningful to developers and users of tests, as well as to test takers and/or their parents or guardians. States, districts, schools, organizations and individual professionals are encouraged to commit themselves to fairness in testing and safeguarding the rights of test takers. The Code is intended to assist in carrying out such commitments.

The **Code** has been prepared by the Joint Committee on Testing Practices, a cooperative effort among several professional organizations. The aim of the Joint Committee is to act, in the public interest, to advance the quality of testing practices. Members of the Joint Committee include the American Counseling Association (ACA), the American Educational Research Association (AERA), the American Psychological Association (APA), the American Speech-Language-Hearing Association (ASHA), the National Association of School Psychologists (NASP), the National Association of Test Directors (NATD), and the National Council on Measurement in Education (NCME).

Copyright 2004 by the Joint Committee on Testing Practices. This material may be reproduced in whole or in part without fees or permission, provided that acknowledgment is made to the Joint Committee on Testing Practices. Reproduction and dissemination of this document are encouraged. This edition replaces the first edition of the **Code**, which was published in 1988. Please cite this document as follows: Code of Fair Testing Practices in Education. (2004). Washington, DC: Joint Committee on Testing Practices. (Mailing Address: Joint Committee on Testing Practices, Science Directorate, American Psychological Association, 750 First Street, NE, Washington, DC 20002-4242; http://www.apa.org/science/jctpweb. html.) Contact APA for additional copies.

A. Developing and Selecting Appropriate Tests*

Test developers should provide the information and supporting evidence that test users need to select appropriate tests.

Test Developers Should:

A-1. Provide evidence of what the test measures, the recommended uses, the intended test takers, and the strengths and limitations of the test, including the level of precision of the test scores.

A-2. Describe how the content and skills to be tested were selected and how the tests were developed.

A-3. Communicate information about a test's characteristics at a level of detail appropriate to the intended test users.

A-4. Provide guidance on the levels of skills, knowledge, and training necessary for appropriate review, selection, and administration of tests.

---

* Many of the statements in the Code refer to the selection of existing tests. However, in customized testing programs test developers are engaged to construct new tests. In those situations, the test development process should be designed to help ensure that the completed tests will be in compliance with the Code.

A-5. Provide evidence that the technical quality, including reliability and validity, of the test meets its intended purposes.

A-6. Provide to qualified test users representative samples of test questions or practice tests, directions, answer sheets, manuals, and score reports.

A-7. Avoid potentially offensive content or language when developing test questions and related materials.

A-8. Make appropriately modified forms of tests or administration procedures available for test takers with disabilities who need special accommodations.

A-9. Obtain and provide evidence on the performance of test takers of diverse subgroups, making significant efforts to obtain sample sizes that are adequate for subgroup analyses. Evaluate the evidence to ensure that differences in performance are related to the skills being assessed.

Test users should select tests that meet the intended purpose and that are appropriate for the intended test takers.

Test Users Should:

A-1. Define the purpose for testing, the content and skills to be tested, and the intended test takers. Select and use the most appropriate test based on a thorough review of available information.

A-2. Review and select tests based on the appropriateness of test content, skills tested, and content coverage for the intended purpose of testing.

A-3. Review materials provided by test developers and select tests for which clear, accurate, and complete information is provided.

A-4. Select tests through a process that includes persons with appropriate knowledge, skills, and training.

A-5. Evaluate evidence of the technical quality of the test provided by the test developer and any independent reviewers.

A-6. Evaluate representative samples of test questions or practice tests, directions, answer sheets, manuals, and score reports before selecting a test.

A-7. Evaluate procedures and materials used by test developers, as well as the resulting test, to ensure that potentially offensive content or language is avoided.

A-8. Select tests with appropriately modified forms or administration procedures for test takers with disabilities who need special accommodations.

A-9. Evaluate the available evidence on the performance of test takers of diverse subgroups. Determine to the extent feasible which performance differences may have been caused by factors unrelated to the skills being assessed.

B. Administering and Scoring Tests

Test developers should explain how to administer and score tests correctly and fairly.

Test Developers Should:

B-1. Provide clear descriptions of detailed procedures for administering tests in a standardized manner.

B-2. Provide guidelines on reasonable procedures for assessing persons with disabilities who need special accommodations or those with diverse linguistic backgrounds.

B-3. Provide information to test takers or test users on test question formats and procedures for answering test questions, including information on the use of any needed materials and equipment.

B-4. Establish and implement procedures to ensure the security of testing materials during all phases of test development, administration, scoring, and reporting.

B-5. Provide procedures, materials and guidelines for scoring the tests, and for monitoring the accuracy of the scoring process. If scoring the test is the responsibility of the test developer, provide adequate training for scorers.

B-6. Correct errors that affect the interpretation of the scores and communicate the corrected results promptly.

B-7. Develop and implement procedures for ensuring the confidentiality of scores.
Test users should interpret scores correctly.

Test users should administer and score tests correctly and fairly.

Test Users Should:

B-1. Follow established procedures for administering tests in a standardized manner.

B-2. Provide and document appropriate procedures for test takers with disabilities who need special accommodations or those with diverse linguistic backgrounds. Some accommodations may be required by law or regulation.

B-3. Provide test takers with an opportunity to become familiar with test question formats and any materials or equipment that may be used during testing.

B-4. Protect the security of test materials, including respecting copyrights and eliminating opportunities for test takers to obtain scores by fraudulent means.

B-5. If test scoring is the responsibility of the test user, provide adequate training to scorers and ensure and monitor the accuracy of the scoring process.

B-6. Correct errors that affect the interpretation of the scores and communicate the corrected results promptly.

B-7. Develop and implement procedures for ensuring the confidentiality of scores.

C. Reporting and Interpreting Test Results

Test developers should report test results accurately and provide information to help test users interpret test results correctly.

Test Developers Should:

C-1. Provide information to support recommended interpretations of the results, including the nature of the content, norms or comparison groups, and other technical evidence. Advise test users of the benefits and limitations of test results and their interpretation. Warn against assigning greater precision than is warranted.

C-2. Provide guidance regarding the interpretations of results for tests administered with modifications. Inform test users of potential problems in interpreting test results when tests or test administration procedures are modified.

C-3. Specify appropriate uses of test results and warn test users of potential misuses.

C-4. When test developers set standards, provide the rationale, procedures, and evidence for setting performance standards or passing scores. Avoid using stigmatizing labels.

C-5. Encourage test users to base decisions about test takers on multiple sources of appropriate information, not on a single test score.

C-6. Provide information to enable test users to accurately interpret and report test results for groups of test takers, including information about who were and who were not included in the different groups being compared, and information about factors that might influence the interpretation of results.

C-7. Provide test results in a timely fashion and in a manner that is understood by the test taker.

C-8. Provide guidance to test users about how to monitor the extent to which the test is fulfilling its intended purposes.

Test users should report and interpret test results accurately and clearly.

Test Users Should:

C-1. Interpret the meaning of the test results, taking into account the nature of the content, norms or comparison groups, other technical evidence, and benefits and limitations of test results.

C-2. Interpret test results from modified test or test administration procedures in view of the impact those modifications may have had on test results.

C-3. Avoid using tests for purposes other than those recommended by the test developer unless there is evidence to support the intended use or interpretation.

C-4. Review the procedures for setting performance standards or passing scores. Avoid using stigmatizing labels.

C-5. Avoid using a single test score as the sole determinant of decisions about test takers. Interpret test scores in conjunction with other information about individuals.

C-6. State the intended interpretation and use of test results for groups of test takers. Avoid grouping test results for purposes not specifically recommended by the test developer unless evidence is obtained to support the intended use. Report procedures that were followed in determining who were and who were not included in the groups being compared and describe factors that might influence the interpretation of results.

C-7. Communicate test results in a timely fashion and in a manner that is understood by the test taker.

C-8. Develop and implement procedures for monitoring test use, including consistency with the intended purposes of the test.

D. Informing Test Takers

Under some circumstances, test developers have direct communication with the test takers and/or control of the tests, testing process, and test results. In other circumstances the test users have these responsibilities.

Test developers or test users should inform test takers about the nature of the test, test taker rights and responsibilities, the appropriate use of scores, and procedures for resolving challenges to scores.

Test Developers or Test Users Should:

D-1. Inform test takers in advance of the test administration about the coverage of the test, the types of question formats, the directions, and appropriate test-taking strategies. Make such information available to all test takers.

D-2. When a test is optional, provide test takers or their parents/guardians with information to help them judge whether a test should be taken—including indications of any consequences that may result from not taking the test (e.g., not being eligible to compete for a particular scholarship)—and whether there is an available alternative to the test.

D-3. Provide test takers or their parents/guardians with information about rights test takers may have to obtain copies of tests and completed answer sheets, to retake tests, to have tests rescored, or to have scores declared invalid.

D-4. Provide test takers or their parents/guardians with information about responsibilities test takers have, such as being aware of the intended purpose and uses of the test, performing at capacity, following directions, and not disclosing test items or interfering with other test takers.

D-5. Inform test takers or their parents/guardians how long scores will be kept on file and indicate to whom, under what circumstances, and in what manner test scores and related information will or will not be released. Protect test scores from unauthorized release and access.

D-6. Describe procedures for investigating and resolving circumstances that might result in canceling or withholding scores, such as failure to adhere to specified testing procedures.

D-7. Describe procedures that test takers, parents/guardians, and other interested parties may use to obtain more information about the test, register complaints, and have problems resolved.

Note: The membership of the Working Group that developed the Code of Fair Testing Practices in Education and of the Joint Committee on Testing Practices that guided the Working Group is as follows:

Peter Behuniak, PhD
Stephanie H. McConaughy, PhD
Lloyd Bond, PhD
Julie P. Noble, PhD
Gwyneth M. Boodoo, PhD
Wayne M. Patience, PhD
Wayne Camara, PhD
Carole L. Perlman, PhD
Ray Fenton, PhD
Douglas K. Smith, PhD (deceased)
John J. Fremer, PhD (Co-Chair)
Janet E. Wall, EdD (Co-Chair)
Sharon M. Goldsmith, PhD
Pat Nellor Wickwire, PhD
Bert F. Green, PhD
Mary Yakimowski, PhD
William G. Harris, PhD
Janet E. Helms, PhD
Lara Frumkin, PhD, of the APA served as staff liaison.

The Joint Committee intends that the Code be consistent with and supportive of existing codes of conduct and standards of other professional groups who use tests in educational contexts. Of particular note are the Responsibilities of Users of Standardized Tests (Association for Assessment in Counseling, 1989), APA Test User Qualifications (2000), ASHA Code of Ethics (2001), Ethical Principles of Psychologists and Code of Conduct (1992), NASP Professional Conduct Manual (2000), NCME Code of Professional Responsibility (1995), and Rights and Responsibilities of Test Takers: Guidelines and Expectations (Joint Committee on Testing Practices, 2000).

Code of Professional Responsibilities in Educational Measurement

Prepared by the NCME Ad Hoc Committee on the Development of a Code of Ethics: Cynthia B. Schmeiser, ACT—Chair; Kurt F. Geisinger, State University of New York; Sharon Johnson-Lewis, Detroit Public Schools; Edward D. Roeber, Council of Chief State School Officers; William D. Schafer, University of Maryland

Preamble and General Responsibilities

As an organization dedicated to the improvement of measurement and evaluation practice in education, the National Council on Measurement in Education (NCME) has adopted this Code to promote professionally responsible practice in educational measurement. Professionally responsible practice is conduct that arises from either the professional standards of the field, general ethical principles, or both.

The purpose of the Code of Professional Responsibilities in Educational Measurement, hereinafter referred to as the Code, is to guide the conduct of NCME members who are involved in any type of assessment activity in education. NCME is also providing this Code as a public service for all individuals who are engaged in educational assessment activities in the hope that these activities will be conducted in a professionally responsible manner. Persons who engage in these activities include local educators such as classroom teachers, principals, and superintendents; professionals such as school psychologists and counselors; state and national technical, legislative, and policy staff in education; staff of research, evaluation, and testing organizations; providers of test preparation services; college and university faculty and administrators; and professionals in business and industry who design and implement educational and training programs.

This Code applies to any type of assessment that occurs as part of the educational process, including formal and informal, traditional and alternative techniques for gathering information used in making educational decisions at all levels. These techniques include, but are not limited to, large-scale assessments at the school, district, state, national, and international levels; standardized tests; observational measures; teacher-conducted assessments; assessment support materials; and other achievement, aptitude, interest, and personality measures used in and for education.

Although NCME is promulgating this Code for its members, it strongly encourages other organizations and individuals who engage in educational assessment activities to endorse and abide by the responsibilities relevant to their professions. Because the Code pertains only to uses of assessment in education, it is recognized that uses of assessments outside of educational contexts, such as for employment, certification, or licensure, may involve additional professional responsibilities beyond those detailed in this Code.

The Code is intended to serve an educational function: to inform and remind those involved in educational assessment of their obligations to uphold the integrity of the manner in which assessments are developed, used, evaluated, and marketed. Moreover, it is expected that the Code will stimulate thoughtful discussion of what constitutes professionally responsible assessment practice at all levels in education.

Section 1: Responsibilities of Those Who Develop Assessment Products and Services

Those who develop assessment products and services, such as classroom teachers and other assessment specialists, have a professional responsibility to strive to produce assessments that are of the highest quality. Persons who develop assessments have a professional responsibility to:

1.1 ensure that assessment products and services are developed to meet applicable professional, technical, and legal standards.

1.2 develop assessment products and services that are as free as possible from bias due to characteristics irrelevant to the construct being measured, such as gender, ethnicity, race, socioeconomic status, disability, religion, age, or national origin.

1.3 plan accommodations for groups of test takers with disabilities and other special needs when developing assessments.

1.4 disclose to appropriate parties any actual or potential conflicts of interest that might influence the developers' judgment or performance.

1.5 use copyrighted materials in assessment products and services in accordance with state and federal law.

1.6 make information available to appropriate persons about the steps taken to develop and score the assessment, including up-to-date information used to support the reliability, validity, scoring and reporting processes, and other relevant characteristics of the assessment.

1.7 protect the rights to privacy of those who are assessed as part of the assessment development process.

1.8 caution users, in clear and prominent language, against the most likely misinterpretations and misuses of data that arise out of the assessment development process.

1.9 avoid false or unsubstantiated claims in test preparation and program support materials and services about an assessment or its use and interpretation.

1.10 correct any substantive inaccuracies in assessments or their support materials as soon as feasible.

1.11 develop score reports and support materials that promote the understanding of assessment results.

Section 2: Responsibilities of Those Who Market and Sell Assessment Products and Services

The marketing of assessment products and services, such as tests and other instruments, scoring services, test preparation services, consulting, and test interpretive services, should be based on information that is accurate, complete, and relevant to those considering their use. Persons who market and sell assessment products and services have a professional responsibility to:

2.1 provide accurate information to potential purchasers about assessment products and services and their recommended uses and limitations.

2.2 not knowingly withhold relevant information about assessment products and services that might affect an appropriate selection decision.

2.3   base all claims about assessment products and services on valid interpretations of publicly available information.

2.4   allow qualified users equal opportunity to purchase assessment products and services.

2.5   establish reasonable fees for assessment products and services.

2.6   communicate to potential users, in advance of any purchase or use, all applicable fees associated with assessment products and services.

2.7   strive to ensure that no individuals are denied access to opportunities because of their inability to pay the fees for assessment products and services.

2.8   establish criteria for the sale of assessment products and services, such as limiting the sale of assessment products and services to those individuals who are qualified for recommended uses and from whom proper uses and interpretations are anticipated.

2.9   inform potential users of known inappropriate uses of assessment products and services and provide recommendations about how to avoid such misuses.

2.10   maintain a current understanding about assessment products and services and their appropriate uses in education.

2.11   release information implying endorsement by users of assessment products and services only with the users' permission.

2.12   avoid making claims that assessment products and services have been endorsed by another organization unless an official endorsement has been obtained.

2.13   avoid marketing test preparation products and services that may cause individuals to receive scores that misrepresent their actual levels of attainment.

Section 3: Responsibilities of Those Who Select Assessment Products and Services

Those who select assessment products and services for use in educational settings, or help others do so, have important professional responsibilities to make sure that the assessments are appropriate for their intended use. Persons who select assessment products and services have a professional responsibility to:

3.1   conduct a thorough review and evaluation of available assessment strategies and instruments that might be valid for the intended uses.

3.2   recommend and/or select assessments based on publicly available documented evidence of their technical quality and utility rather than on unsubstantiated claims or statements.

3.3   disclose any associations or affiliations that they have with the authors, test publishers, or others involved with the assessments under consideration for purchase and refrain from participation if such associations might affect the objectivity of the selection process.

3.4   inform decision makers and prospective users of the appropriateness of the assessment for the intended uses, likely consequences of use, protection of examinee rights, relative costs, materials and services needed to conduct or use the assessment, and known limitations of the assessment, including potential misuses and misinterpretations of assessment information.

3.5   recommend against the use of any prospective assessment that is likely to be administered, scored, and used in an invalid manner for members of various groups in our society for reasons of race, ethnicity, gender, age, disability, language background, socioeconomic status, religion, or national origin.

3.6   comply with all security precautions that may accompany assessments being reviewed.

3.7 immediately disclose any attempts by others to exert undue influence on the assessment selection process.

3.8 avoid recommending, purchasing, or using test preparation products and services that may cause individuals to receive scores that misrepresent their actual levels of attainment.

Section 4: Responsibilities of Those Who Administer Assessments

Those who prepare individuals to take assessments and those who are directly or indirectly involved in the administration of assessments as part of the educational process, including teachers, administrators, and assessment personnel, have an important role in making sure that the assessments are administered in a fair and accurate manner. Persons who prepare others for, and those who administer, assessments have a professional responsibility to:

4.1 inform the examinees about the assessment prior to its administration, including its purposes, uses, and consequences; how the assessment information will be judged or scored; how the results will be kept on file; who will have access to the results; how the results will be distributed; and examinees' rights before, during, and after the assessment.

4.2 administer only those assessments for which they are qualified by education, training, licensure, or certification.

4.3 take appropriate security precautions before, during, and after the administration of the assessment.

4.4 understand the procedures needed to administer the assessment prior to administration.

4.5 administer standardized assessments according to prescribed procedures and conditions and notify appropriate persons if any nonstandard or delimiting conditions occur.

4.6 not exclude any eligible student from the assessment.

4.7 avoid any conditions in the conduct of the assessment that might invalidate the results.

4.8 provide for and document all reasonable and allowable accommodations for the administration of the assessment to persons with disabilities or special needs.

4.9 provide reasonable opportunities for individuals to ask questions about the assessment procedures or directions prior to and at prescribed times during the administration of the assessment.

4.10 protect the rights to privacy and due process of those who are assessed.

4.11 avoid actions or conditions that would permit or encourage individuals or groups to receive scores that misrepresent their actual levels of attainment.

Section 5: Responsibilities of Those Who Score Assessments

The scoring of educational assessments should be conducted properly and efficiently so that the results are reported accurately and in a timely manner. Persons who score and prepare reports of assessments have a professional responsibility to:

5.1 provide complete and accurate information to users about how the assessment is scored, such as the reporting schedule, scoring process to be used, rationale for the scoring approach, technical characteristics, quality control procedures, reporting formats, and the fees, if any, for these services.

5.2 ensure the accuracy of the assessment results by conducting reasonable quality control procedures before, during, and after scoring.

5.3 minimize the effect on scoring of factors irrelevant to the purposes of the assessment.

5.4   inform users promptly of any deviation in the planned scoring and reporting service or schedule and negotiate a solution with users.

5.5   provide corrected score results to the examinee or the client as quickly as practicable should errors be found that may affect the inferences made on the basis of the scores.

5.6   protect the confidentiality of information that identifies individuals as prescribed by state and federal law.

5.7   release summary results of the assessment only to those persons entitled to such information by state or federal law or those who are designated by the party contracting for the scoring services.

5.8   establish, where feasible, a fair and reasonable process for appeal and rescoring the assessment.

Section 6: Responsibilities of Those Who Interpret, Use, and Communicate Assessment Results

The interpretation, use, and communication of assessment results should promote valid inferences and minimize invalid ones. Persons who interpret, use, and communicate assessment results have a professional responsibility to:

6.1   conduct these activities in an informed, objective, and fair manner within the context of the assessment's limitations and with an understanding of the potential consequences of use.

6.2   provide to those who receive assessment results information about the assessment, its purposes, its limitations, and its uses necessary for the proper interpretation of the results.

6.3   provide to those who receive score reports an understandable written description of all reported scores, including proper interpretations and likely misinterpretations.

6.4   communicate to appropriate audiences the results of the assessment in an understandable and timely manner, including proper interpretations and likely misinterpretations.

6.5   evaluate and communicate the adequacy and appropriateness of any norms or standards used in the interpretation of assessment results.

6.6   inform parties involved in the assessment process how assessment results may affect them.

6.7   use multiple sources and types of relevant information about persons or programs whenever possible in making educational decisions.

6.8   avoid making, and actively discourage others from making, inaccurate reports, unsubstantiated claims, inappropriate interpretations, or otherwise false and misleading statements about assessment results.

6.9   disclose to examinees and others whether and how long the results of the assessment will be kept on file, procedures for appeal and rescoring, rights examinees and others have to the assessment information, and how those rights may be exercised.

6.10 report any apparent misuses of assessment information to those responsible for the assessment process.

6.11 protect the rights to privacy of individuals and institutions involved in the assessment process.

Section 7: Responsibilities of Those Who Educate Others About Assessment

The process of educating others about educational assessment, whether as part of higher education, professional development, public policy discussions, or job training, should prepare individuals to understand and engage in sound measurement practice and to become discerning users of tests and test results. Persons who educate or inform others about assessment have a professional responsibility to:

7.1   remain competent and current in the areas in which they teach and reflect that in their instruction.

7.2   provide fair and balanced perspectives when teaching about assessment.

7.3   differentiate clearly between expressions of opinion and substantiated knowledge when educating others about any specific assessment method, product, or service.

7.4   disclose any financial interests that might be perceived to influence the evaluation of a particular assessment product or service that is the subject of instruction.

7.5   avoid administering any assessment that is not part of the evaluation of student performance in a course if the administration of that assessment is likely to harm any student.

7.6   avoid using or reporting the results of any assessment that is not part of the evaluation of student performance in a course if the use or reporting of results is likely to harm any student.

7.7   protect all secure assessments and materials used in the instructional process.

7.8   model responsible assessment practice and help those receiving instruction to learn about their professional responsibilities in educational measurement.

7.9   provide fair and balanced perspectives on assessment issues being discussed by policymakers, parents, and other citizens.

Section 8: Responsibilities of Those Who Evaluate Educational Programs and Conduct Research on Assessments

Conducting research on or about assessments or educational programs is a key activity in helping to improve the understanding and use of assessments and educational programs. Persons who engage in the evaluation of educational programs or conduct research on assessments have a professional responsibility to:

8.1   conduct evaluation and research activities in an informed, objective, and fair manner.

8.2   disclose any associations that they have with authors, test publishers, or others involved with the assessment and refrain from participation if such associations might affect the objectivity of the research or evaluation.

8.3   preserve the security of all assessments throughout the research process as appropriate.

8.4   take appropriate steps to minimize potential sources of invalidity in the research and disclose known factors that may bias the results of the study.

8.5   present the results of research, both intended and unintended, in a fair, complete, and objective manner.

8.6   attribute completely and appropriately the work and ideas of others.

8.7   qualify the conclusions of the research within the limitations of the study.

8.8   use multiple sources of relevant information in conducting evaluation and research activities whenever possible.

8.9   comply with applicable standards for protecting the rights of participants in an evaluation or research study, including the rights to privacy and informed consent.

Afterword

As stated at the outset, the purpose of the Code of Professional Responsibilities in Educational Measurement is to serve as a guide to the conduct of NCME members who are engaged in any type of assessment activity in education. Given the broad scope of the field of educational assessment as well as the variety of activities in which professionals may engage, it is unlikely that any code will cover the professional responsibilities involved in every situation or activity in which assessment is used in education. Ultimately, it is hoped that this Code will serve as the basis for ongoing discussions about what constitutes professionally responsible practice. Moreover, these discussions will undoubtedly identify areas of practice that need further analysis and clarification in subsequent editions of the Code. To the extent that these discussions occur, the Code will have served its purpose.

To assist in the ongoing refinement of the Code, comments on this document are most welcome. Please send your comments and inquiries to:

Executive Officer
National Council on Measurement in Education
1230 Seventeenth Street, NW
Washington, DC 20036-3078

Summaries of Taxonomies of Educational Objectives: Cognitive, Affective, and Psychomotor Domains

Table D.1 Categories and subcategories of the Bloom et al. taxonomy of cognitive objectives

1.00 Knowledge

    1.10 Knowledge of Specifics

    1.11 Knowledge of Terminology Knowledge of the referents for specific symbols (verbal and nonverbal). …

    1.12 Knowledge of Specific Facts Knowledge of dates, events, persons, places, etc.

    1.20 Knowledge of Ways and Means of Dealing with Specifics

    1.21 Knowledge of Conventions Knowledge of characteristic ways of treating and presenting ideas and phenomena.

    1.22 Knowledge of Trends and Sequences Knowledge of the processes, directions, and movements of phenomena with respect to time.

    1.23 Knowledge of Classifications and Categories Knowledge of the classes, sets, divisions, and arrangements that are regarded as fundamental for a given subject field, purpose, argument, or problem.

    1.24 Knowledge of Criteria Knowledge of the criteria by which facts, principles, and conduct are tested or judged.

    1.25 Knowledge of Methodology Knowledge of the methods of inquiry, techniques, and procedures employed in a particular subject field as well as those employed in investigating particular problems and phenomena.

2.00 Comprehension

    2.10 Translation Comprehension as evidenced by the care and accuracy with which the communication is paraphrased or rendered from one language or form of communication to another.

    2.20 Interpretation The explanation or summarization of a communication.

    2.30 Extrapolation The extension of trends or tendencies beyond the given data to determine implications, consequences, corollaries, effects, etc., that are in accordance with the conditions described in the original communication.

3.00 Application The use of abstractions in particular and concrete situations. The abstractions may be in the form of general ideas, rules of procedures, or generalized methods.

4.00 Analysis

    4.10 Analysis of Elements Identification of the elements included in a communication.

    4.20 Analysis of Relationships The connections and interactions between elements and parts of a communication.

    4.30 Analysis of Organized Principles The organization, systematic arrangement, and structure that hold the communication together.

5.00 Synthesis

    5.10 Production of a Unique Communication The development of a communication in which the writer or speaker attempts to convey ideas, feelings, and/or experiences to others.

    5.20 Production of a Plan or Proposed Set of Operations The development of a plan of work or the proposal of a plan of operations.

    5.30 Derivation of a Set of Abstract Relations The development of a set of abstract relations either to classify or to explain particular data or phenomena, or the deduction of propositions and relations from a set of basic propositions or symbolic representations.

6.00 Evaluation

    6.10 Judgments in Terms of Internal Evidence Evaluation of the accuracy of a communication from such evidence as logical accuracy, consistency, and other internal criteria.

    6.20 Judgments in Terms of External Criteria Evaluation of material with reference to selected or remembered criteria.

Source: Adapted from Benjamin S. Bloom et al., *Taxonomy of Educational Objectives Book 1, Cognitive Domain* (pp. 201–207). Published by Allyn & Bacon, Boston, MA. Copyright © 1984 by Pearson Education. Reprinted with permission of the publisher.

Table D.2 Gagné's levels of complexity in human skills, characteristics of responses to tasks assessing these capacities, and examples of specific objectives written for each capacity

Type of ability or capacity	Characteristics of responses to assessment tasks	Example of a specific learning target
1. **Discrimination:** ability to respond appropriately to stimuli that differ. The stimuli can differ in one or more physical attributes such as size, shape, or tone. (capacity verb: *discriminates*)	The leader's response must indicate that the learner has distinguished between the different stimuli. The leader may do this by indicating "same" or "different."	Given two cardboard cutouts, one a triangle shape and the other a square shape, the leader can point to the one that is a "square."
2. **Concrete concept:** ability to identify a stimulus as belonging to a particular class or category. The members of the class have one or more physical properties in common. (capacity verb: *identifies*)	The learner's response must indicate that two or more members of the class have been identified.	Given several differently shaped figures of various colors and shapes, half of which have triangular shapes, the learner can point to all the "triangles."
3. **Defined concept:** ability to demonstrate what is meant by a defined class of objects, events, or relations—that is, demonstrate an understanding of a concept. (capacity verb: *classifies*)	The learner's response must go beyond memorization to identify specific instances of the defined concept and to show how these instances are related to each other (and are thereby members of the same concept or category).	Given descriptions and brief biographies of each of several different persons not born in this country, the learner is able to identify all the persons who are immigrants and state their relationship to each other.
4. **Rule:** ability to make responses that indicate a rule is being applied in a variety of different situations. (capacity verb: *demonstrates*)	The learner's response must indicate that a particular rule is being applied in one or more concrete instances, but the learner need not be able to state the rule.	Given a "story" problem of the type presented in class involving two single-digit addends, the pupil is able to add the digits correctly.
5. **Higher-order rule:** (problem solving): ability to form a new (for the learner) rule to solve a problem, by combining two or more previously learned rules. (capacity verb: *generates*)	The learner's response must indicate that a new complex rule has been "invented" and applied to solve a problem that is new or novel for the learner. Once the rule is invented, the learner should be able to apply it to other situations (transfer of learning).	Given an announcement about a specific job opening for which the learner is qualified, the learner is able to generate and write an appropriate letter of application for that job.
6. **Cognitive strategies:** ability to use internal processes to choose and change ways to focus attention, learn, remember, and/or think. (capacity verb: *adopts*)	The learner's responses provide only a way of inferring that internal cognitive strategies were used. Among the cognitive strategies a learner may use are rehearsing (practicing), elaborating, organizing information, and metacognition. It is sometimes necessary to ask a learner to "think aloud" while performing a task in order to discover the cognitive processes the learner is using.	Given the task of learning a list of new Spanish vocabulary words, the learner is able to associate an English word with an "acoustical link" to help memorize the Spanish words' definitions.

Source: Table and excerpts adapted from *Principles of Instructional Design* (3rd ed., pp. 12, 57–68), by Robert M. Gagné, Leslie J. Briggs, & Walter W. Wager. Copyright © 1988. Reprinted by permission of Wadsworth, a division of Thomson Learning: www. thomsonrights. com. Fax 800-730-2215.

Table D.3 Summary of the Quellmalz taxonomy

Classification	Definition	Illustration
Recall	Most tasks require that students recognize or remember key facts, definitions, concepts, rules, and principles. Recall questions require students to repeat verbalim or to paraphrase given information. To recall information, students need most often to rehearse or practice it, and then to associate it with other, related concepts.	Identify the main characters in a novel.
Analysis	In this operation, students divide a whole into component elements. Generally, the different part/whole relationships and the parts of cause/effect relationships that characterize knowledge within subject domains are essential components of more complex tasks. The components can be the distinctive characteristics of objects or ideas, or the basic actors of procedures or events.	Describe the authors use of imagery in her characterization.
Comparison	These tasks require students to recognize or explain similarities and differences. Simple comparisons require attention to one or a few very obvious attributes or component processes, while complex comparisons require identification of the differentiation among many attributes or component actions. The comparison category emphasizes the distinct information processing required when students go beyond breaking the whole into parts in order to compare similarities and differences.	Describe how the protagonist and antagonist are alike and how they are different.
Inference	Both deductive and inductive reasoning fall into this category. In deductive tasks, students are given a generalization and are required to recognize or explain the evidence that relates to it. Applications of rules and "if then" relationships require inference. In inductive tasks, students are given the evidence or details and are required to come up with the generalization. Hypothesizing, predicting, concluding, and synthesizing all require students to relate and integrate information.	What might have happened if a key event early in the plot had had a different outcome?
Evaluation	These tasks require students to judge quality, credibility, worth, or practicality. Generally, we expect students to use established criteria and explain how these criteria are or are not met. The criteria might be established rules of evidence, logic, or shared values. To evaluate, students must *assemble* and *explain* the interrelationship of evidence and reasons in support of their conclusion. Explanation of criteria for reaching a conclusion is unique to evaluative reasoning.	Does the use of imagery enhance readers' understanding of the characters and their motivations? Why or why not?

Source: Adapted from E. J. Quellmalz, "Developing Reasoning Skills," p. 91, in J. B. Baron & R. J. Sternberg, *Teaching Thinking Skills*, 1987. Adapted by permission of the author.

Table D.4 Categories and subcategories of the Krathwohl et al. taxonomy of affective objectives with illustrative statements of objectives

Category	Definition	Learning targets
1.0 Receiving (attending)		
1.1 Awareness	Be conscious of something ... take into account a situation, phenomenon, object, or state of affairs. ...	Develops awareness of aesthetic factors in dress, furnishings, architecture, city design, good art, and the like.
1.2 Willingness to Receive	Being willing to tolerate a given stimulus, not to avoid it. ... Willing to take notice of the phenomenon and give it ... attention. ...	Appreciation (tolerance) of cultural patterns exhibited by individuals from other groups—religious, social, economic, national, etc.
1.3 Controlled or Selected Attention	The control of attention, so that when certain stimuli are presented they will be attended to. ... The favored stimulus is selected and attended to despite competing and detracting stimuli. ...	Alertness toward human values and judgments on life as they are recorded in literature.
2.0 Responding		
2.1 Acquiescence in Responding	"Obedience" or "compliance." ... There is a passiveness so far as the initiation of behavior is concerned. ...	Follows school rules on the playground.
2.2 Willingness to Respond	The learner is sufficiently committed to exhibiting the behavior that he does so not just because of fear ... but "on his own" or voluntarily. ...	Volunteers to help classmates who are having difficulty with the science project.
2.3 Satisfaction in Response	The behavior is accompanied by a feeling of satisfaction, an emotional response, generally of pleasure, zest, or enjoyment.	Finds pleasure in reading for recreation.
3.0 Valuing		
3.1 Acceptance of a Value	The emotional acceptance of a proposition or doctrine upon what one considers adequate ground. ...	Continuing desire to develop the ability to speak and write effectively.
3.2 Preference for a Value	The individual is sufficiently committed to a value to pursue it, to seek it out, to want it. ...	Assumes responsibility for drawing reticent members of a group into conversation.
3.3 Commitment	"Conviction" and "certainty beyond a doubt." ... Acts to further the thing valued ... to extend the possibility of ... developing it, to deepen ... involvement with it. ...	Devotion to those ideas and ideals that are the foundation of democracy.
4.0 Organization		
4.1 Conceptualization of a Value	The quality of abstraction or conceptualization is added (to the value or belief which permits seeing) ... how the value relates to those he already holds or to new ones. ...	Forms judgments as to the responsibility of society for conserving human and material resources.
4.2 Organization of a Value System	To bring together a complex of values ... into an ordered relationship with one another. ...	Weighs alternative social policies and practices against the standards of the public welfare rather than the advantage of ... narrow interest groups.
5.0 Characterization by a Value or Value Complex		
5.1 Generalized Set	Gives an internal consistency to the system of attitudes and values. ... Enables the individual to reduce and order the complex world ... and to act consistency and effectively in it.	Judges problems and issues in terms of situations, issues, purposes, and consequences involved rather than in terms of fixed, dogmatic precepts or emotional wishful thinking.
5.2 Characterization	One's view of the universe, one's philosophy of life, one's *Weltanschauug*. ...	Develops for regulation of one's personal and civic life a code of behavior based on ethical principles consistent with democratic ideals.

Source: Adapted from David R. Krathwohl, Benjamin S. Bloom, & Bertram B. Masia, *Taxonomy of Educational Objectives: Book 2: Affective Domain* (pp. 176–185). Published by Allyn & Bacon, Boston, MA. Copyright © 1964 by Pearson Education. Reprinted by permission of the publisher.

Table D.5 Psychomotor Domain Taxonomy

This domain is characterized by progressive levels of behaviors from observation to mastery of a physical skill.

Level	Definition	Example
1. Observing	Active mental attending of a physical event.	Observes a more experienced person perform the skill. Observes sequences, relationships, and finished products. Direct observation may supplement reading or watching a video. Thus, the learner may read about the topic and then watch a performance.
2. Imitating	Attempted copying of a physical behavior.	Begins to acquire the rudiments of the skill. Follows directions and sequences with supervision. The total act is not important, nor is timing or coordination emphasized. The learner is aware of deliberate effort to imitate the model.
3. Practicing	Trying a specific physical activity over and over.	Performs the entire sequence repeatedly. All aspects of the act are performed in sequence. Performance becomes more or less habitual. Timing and coordination are emphasized. The person has acquired the skill but is not an expert.
4. Adapting	Fine tuning. Making minor adjustments in the physical activity in order to perfect it.	Perfects the skill. Makes minor adjustments that influence the total performance. Coaching often very valuable here. This is how a good player becomes a better player.

Source: From Penn State Teaching and Learning with Technology Center. Psychomotor Domain Taxonomy (http://tlt.psu.edu/suggestions/research/Psychomotor_Taxonomy.shtml). Adapted by permission.

Table D.6.a The Knowledge Dimension

Major Types and Subtypes	Examples
A. Factual Knowledge—The basic elements students must know to be acquainted with a discipline or solve problems in it	
Aᴀ. Knowledge of terminology	Technical vocabulary, musical symbols
Aʙ. Knowledge of specific details and elements	Major national resources, reliable sources of information
B. Conceptual Knowledge—The interrelationships among the basic elements within a larger structure that enable them to function together	
Bᴀ. Knowledge of classifications and categories	Periods of geological time, forms of business ownership
Bʙ. Knowledge of principles and generalizations	Pythagorean theorem, law of supply and demand
Bᴄ. Knowledge of theories, models, and structures	Theory of evolution, structure of Congress
C. Procedural Knowledge—How to do something, methods of inquiry, and criteria for using skills, algorithms, techniques, and methods	
Cᴀ. Knowledge of subject-specific skills and algorithms	Skills used in painting with watercolors, whole-number division algorithm
Cʙ. Knowledge of subject-specific techniques and methods	Interviewing techniques, scientific method
Cᴄ. Knowledge of criteria for determining when to use appropriate procedures	Criteria used to determine when to apply a procedure involving Newton's second law, criteria used to judge the feasibility of using a particular method to estimate business costs
D. Metacognitive Knowledge—Knowledge of cognition in general as well as awareness and knowledge of one's own cognition	
Dᴀ. Strategic knowledge	Knowledge of outlining as a means of capturing the structre of a unit of subject matter in a textbook, knowledge of the use of heuristics
Dʙ. Knowledge about cognitive tasks, including appropriate contextual and conditional knowledge.	Knowledge of the types of tests particular teachers administer, knowledge of the cognitive demands of different tasks
Dᴄ. Self-knowledge	Knowledge that critiquing essays is a personal strength, whereas writing essays is a personal weakness, awareness of one's own knowledge level of business costs

Table D.6.b The Cognitive Process Dimension

Categories & Cognitive Processes	Alternative Names	Definitions and Examples
1. Remember—Retrieve relevant knowledge from long-term memory		
1.1 Recognizing	Identifying	Locating knowledge in long-term memory that is consistent with presented material (e.g., Recognize the dates of important events in U.S. history)
1.2 Recalling	Retrieving	Retrieiving relevant knowledge from long-term memory (e.g., Recall the dates of important events in U.S. history)
2. Understand—Construct meaning from instructional messages, including oral, written, and graphic communication		
2.1 Interpreting	Clarifying, paraphrasing, representing, translating	Changing from one form of representation (e.g., numerical) to another (e.g., verbal) (e.g., Paraphrase important speeches and documents)
2.2 Exemplifying	Illustrating, instantiating	Finding a specific example or illustration of a concept or principle (e.g., Give examples of various artistic painting styles)
2.3 Classifying	Categorizing, subsuming	Determining that something belongs to a category (e.g., concept or principle) (e.g., Classify observed or described cases of mental disorders)
2.4 Summarizing	Abstracting, generalizing	Abstracting a general theme or major point(s) (e.g., Write a short summary of the events portrayed on a videotape)
2.5 Inferring	Concluding, extrapolating, interpolating, predicting	Drawing a logical conclusion from presented information (e.g., In learning a foreign language, infer grammatical principles from examples)
2.6 Comparing	Contrasing, mapping, matching	Detecting correspondences between two ideas, objects, and the like (e.g., Compare historical events to contemporary situations)
2.7 Explaining	Constructing models	Constructing a cause-and-effect model of a system (e.g., Explain the causes of important 18th-century events in France)
3. Apply—Carry out or use a procedure in a given situation		
3.1 Executing	Carrying out	Applying a procedure to a familiar task (e.g., Divide one whole number by another whole number, both with multiple digits)
3.2 Implementing	Using	Applying a procedure to an unfamiliar task (e.g., Use Newton's Second Law in situations in which it is appropriate)
4. Analyze—Break material into its constituent parts and determine how the parts relate to one another and to an overall structure or purpose		
4.1 Differentiating	Discriminating, distinguishing, focusing, selecting	Distinguishing relevant from irrelevant parts or important from unimportant parts of presented material (e.g., Distinguish between relevant and irrelevant numbers in a mathematical word problem)
4.2 Organizing	Finding coherence, integrating, outlining, parsing, structuring	Determining how elements fit or function within a structure (e.g., Structure evidence in a historical description into evidence for and against a particular historical explanation)
4.3 Attributing	Deconstructing	Determine a point of view, bias, values, or intent underlying presented maiterial (e.g., Determine the point of view of the author of an essay in terms of his or her political perspective)
5. Evaluate—Make judgments based on criteria and standards		
5.1 Checking	Coordinating, detecting, monitoring, testing	Detecting inconsistencies or fallacies within a process or product; determining whether a process or product has internal consistency; detecting the effectiveness of a procedure as it is being implemented (e.g., Determine if a scientist's conclusions follow from observed data)

Table D.6.b *Continued*

Categories & Cognitive Processes	Alternative Names	Definitions and Examples
5.2 Critiquing	Judging	Detecting inconsistencies between a product and external criteria, determining whether a product has external consistency; detecting the appropriateness of a procedure for a given problem (e.g., Judge which of two methods is the best way to solve a given problem)
6. Create—Put elements together to form a coherent or functional whole; reorganize elements into a new pattern or structure		
6.1 Generating	Hypothesizing	Coming up with alternative hypotheses based on criteria (e.g., Generate hypotheses to account for an observed phenomenon)
6.2 Planning	Designing	Devising a procedure for accomplishing some task (e.g., Plan a research paper on a given historical topic)
6.3 Producing	Constructing	Inventing a product (e.g., Build habitats for a specific purpose)

Source: Adapted from Lorin W. Anderson & David R. Krathwohl, *A Taxonomy for Learning, Teaching, and Assessing: A Revision of Bloom's Taxonomy of Educational Objectives* (pp. 46, 67–68). Published by Allyn & Bacon, Boston, MA. Copyright © 2001 by Pearson Education. Reprinted with permission of the publisher.

Categories of Learning Targets Derived from the Dimensions of Learning Model

Declarative Knowledge
Procedural Knowledge
Complex Thinking

A. Effectively translates issues and situations into meaningful tasks that have a clear purpose.

B. Effectively uses a variety of complex reasoning strategies.

REASONING STRATEGY 1: COMPARISON Comparison involves describing the similarities and differences between two or more items. The process includes three components that can be assessed:

a. Selects appropriate items to compare.
b. Selects appropriate characteristics on which to base the comparison.
c. Accurately identifies the similarities and differences among the items, using the identified characteristics.

REASONING STRATEGY 2: CLASSIFICATION Classification involves organizing items into categories based on specific characteristics. The process includes four components that can be assessed:

a. Selects significant items to classify.
b. Specifies useful categories for the items.
c. Specifies accurate and comprehensive rules for category membership.
d. Accurately sorts the identified items into the categories.

REASONING STRATEGY 3: INDUCTION Induction involves creating a generalization from implicit or explicit information and then describing the reasoning behind the generalization. The process includes three components that can be assessed:

a. Identifies elements (specific pieces of information or observations) from which to make inductions.
b. Interprets the information from which inductions are made.
c. Makes and articulates accurate conclusions (inductions) from the selected information or observations.

REASONING STRATEGY 4: DEDUCTION Deduction involves identifying implicit or explicit generalizations or principles (premises) and then describing their logical consequences. The process includes three components that can be assessed:

a. Identifies and articulates a deduction based on important and useful generalizations or principles implicit or explicit in the information.
b. Accurately interprets the generalizations or principles.
c. Identifies and articulates logical consequences implied by the identified generalizations or principles.

REASONING STRATEGY 5: ERROR ANALYSIS Error analysis involves identifying and describing specific types of errors in information or processes. It includes three components that can be assessed:

a. Identifies and articulates significant errors in information or in process.
b. Accurately describes the effects of the errors on the information or process.
c. Accurately describes how to correct the errors.

REASONING STRATEGY 6: CONSTRUCTING SUPPORT Constructing Support involves developing a well-articulated argument for or against a claim. The process includes three components that can be assessed:

a. Accurately identifies a claim that requires support rather than a fact that does not require support.
b. Provides sufficient or appropriate evidence for the claim.
c. Adequately qualifies or restricts the claim.

REASONING STRATEGY 7: ABSTRACTING Abstracting involves identifying and explaining how the abstract pattern in one situation or set of information is similar to or different from the abstract pattern in another situation or set of information. The process includes three components that can be assessed:

a. Identifies a significant situation or meaningful information that is a useful subject for the abstracting process.
b. Identifies a representative general or abstract pattern for the situation or information.
c. Accurately articulates the relationship between the general or abstract pattern and another situation or set of information.

REASONING STRATEGY 8: ANALYZING PERSPECTIVES Analyzing perspectives involves considering one perspective on an issue and the reasoning behind it as well as an opposing perspective and the reasoning behind it. The process includes three components that can be assessed:

a. Identifies an issue on which there is disagreement.
b. Identifies one position on the issue and the reasoning behind it.
c. Identifies an opposing position and the reasoning behind it.

REASONING STRATEGY 9: DECISION MAKING Decision making involves selecting among apparently equal alternatives. It includes four components that can be assessed:

a. Identifies important and appropriate alternatives to be considered.
b. Identifies important and appropriate criteria for assessing the alternatives.
c. Accurately identifies the extent to which each alternative possesses each criteria.
d. Makes a selection that adequately meets the decision criteria and answers the initial decision question.

REASONING STRATEGY 10: INVESTIGATION Investigation is a process involving close examination and systematic inquiry. There are basic types of investigation:

• Definitional Investigation: Constructing a definition or detailed description concept for which such a definition or description is not readily available or accepted.

• Historical Investigation: Constructing an explanation for some past event for which an explanation is not readily available or accepted.

• Projective Investigation: Constructing a scenario for some future event or hypothetical past event for which a scenario is not readily available or accepted.

Each type of investigation includes three components that can be assessed:

a. Accurately identifies what is already known or agreed upon about the concept (definitional investigation), the past event (historical investigation), or the future event (projective investigation).
b. Identifies and explains the confusions, uncertainties, or contradictions about the concept (definitional investigation), the past event (historical investigation), or the future event (projective investigation).

c. Develops and defends a logical and plausible resolution to the confusions, uncertainties, or contradictions about the concept (definitional investigation), the past event (historical investigation), or the future event (projective investigation).

REASONING STRATEGY 11: PROBLEM SOLVING Problem solving involves developing and testing a method or product for overcoming obstacles or constraints to reach a desired outcome. It includes four components that can be assessed:

a. Accurately identifies constraints or obstacles.
b. Identifies viable and important alternatives for overcoming the constraints or obstacles.
c. Selects and adequately tries out alternatives.
d. If other alternatives were tried, accurately articulates and supports the reasoning behind the order of their selection, and the extent to which each overcame the obstacles or constraints.

REASONING STRATEGY 12: EXPERIMENTAL INQUIRY Experimental inquiry involves testing hypotheses that have been generated to explain phenomenon. It includes four components that can be assessed:

a. Accurately explains the phenomenon initially observed using appropriate and accepted facts, concepts, or principles.
b. Makes a logical prediction based on the facts, concepts, or principles underlying the explanation.
c. Sets up and carries out an activity or experiment that effectively tests the prediction.
d. Effectively evaluates the outcome of the activity or experiment in terms of the original explanation.

REASONING STRATEGY 13: INVENTION Invention involves developing something unique or making unique improvements to a process to satisfy an unmet need. It includes four components that can be assessed:

a. Identifies a process or product to develop or improve to satisfy an unmet need.
b. Identifies rigorous and important standards or criteria the invention will meet.
c. Makes detailed and important revisions in the initial process or product.
d. Continually revises and polishes the process or product until it reaches a level of completeness consistent with the criteria or standards identified earlier.

Information Processing

A. Effectively interprets and synthesizes information.
B. Effectively uses a variety of information-gathering techniques and resources.
C. Accurately assesses the value of information.
D. Recognizes where and how projects would benefit from additional information.

Effective Communication

A. Expresses ideas clearly.
B. Effectively communicates with diverse audiences.
C. Effectively communicates in a variety of ways.
D. Effectively communicates for a variety of purposes.
E. Creates quality products.

Collaboration/Cooperation

    A. Works toward the achievement of group goals.

    B. Demonstrates effective interpersonal skills.

    C. Contributes to group maintenance.

    D. Effectively performs a variety of roles within a group.

Habits of Mind

    A. Is aware of own thinking.

    B. Makes effective plans.

    C. Is aware of and uses necessary resources.

    D. Evaluates the effectiveness of own actions.

    E. Is sensitive to feedback.

    F. Is accurate and seeks accuracy.

    G. Is clear and seeks clarity.

    H. Is open-minded.

    I. Restrains impulsivity.

    J. Takes a position when the situation warrants it.

    K. Is sensitive to the feelings and level of knowledge of others.

    L. Engages intensively in tasks even when answers or solutions are not immediately apparent.

    M. Pushes the limits of own knowledge and ability.

    N. Generates, trusts, and maintains own standards of evaluation.

    O. Generates new ways of viewing a situation outside the boundaries of standard convention.

Source: Adapted from *Assessing Student Outcomes: Performance Assessment Using the Dimensions of Learning Model* (pp. 65–93) by R. J. Marzano, D. Pickering, and J. McTighe, 1993, Alexandria, VA: Association for Supervision and Curriculum Development. (Copyright by McREL, 4601 DTC Blvd. #500, Denver, CO 80237.) Adapted by permission.

Examples of Alternative Blueprints for a Summative Unit Assessment

Example F.1 Complete specifications with modified taxonomy headings

Content outline	Recalling information taught or read	Applying knowledge in situation very similar to those taught	Applying knowledge in a new or novel context
I. *Basic Parts of Cell* 　A. *Nucleus* 　B. *Cytoplasm* 　C. *Cell membrane*	1. *Names and tells functions of each part of cell*	8. *Labels parts of cell shown on a line drawing*	11. *Given photographs of actual plant and animal cells, labels the parts*
<u>40</u>% of Total = <u>8</u> pts	<u>37</u>% of Row = <u>3</u> pts	37% of Row = <u>3</u> pts	<u>26</u>% of Row = 2 pts
II. *Plant vs. Animal cells* 　A. *Similarities* 　B. *Differences* 　　1. *cell wall vs. membrane* 　　2. *food manufacture*	2. *Explains differences between plant and animal cells* 3. *Describes the cell wall and cell membrane*		
<u>10</u>% of Total = <u>2</u> pts	<u>100</u>% of Row = <u>2</u> pts	__% of Row = _ pts	__% of Row = _ pts
III. *Cell Membrane* 　A. *Living nature of* 　B. *Diffusion* 　C. *Substances diffused by cells*	4. *Lists substances diffused and not diffused by cell membranes* 5. *Gives definition of diffusion*	9. *Distinguishes between diffusion and oxidation*	
<u>20</u>% of Total = <u>4</u> pts	<u>75</u>% of Row = <u>3</u> pts	25% of Row = <u>1</u> pts	__% of Row = _ pts
IV. *Division of Cells* 　A. *Phases in division* 　B. *Chromosomes and DNA* 　C. *Plant vs. Animal cell division*	6. *Gives definitions of division, chromosomes, and DNA* 7. *States differences between plant and animal cell division*	10. *Given the numbers of chromosomes in a cell before division, states the number in each cell after division*	
<u>30</u>% of Total = <u>6</u> pts	<u>67</u>% of Row = <u>4</u> pts	<u>33</u>% of Row = <u>2</u> pts	__% of Row = _ pts

Source: Adapted from *Teacher's Guide to Better Classroom Testing: A Judgmental Approach* (p. 4) by A. J. Nitko and T-C Hsu, 1987, Pittsburgh, PA: Institute for Practice and Research in Education, School of Education, University of Pittsburgh. Adapted by permission of the authors.

Example F.2 Blueprint without objectives stated.

Content outline	Recalling information taught or read	Applying knowledge in situations very similar to those taught	Applying knowledge in a new or novel context
I. *Basic Parts of Cell* A. *Nucleus* B. *Cytoplasm* C. *Cell membrane*	*1 item, scored 0–3 (short-answer)*	*1 item, scored 0–3 (label parts of cell drawing)*	*2 items, each scored 0–1 (label parts of cell photographs)*
<u>40</u>% of Total = <u>8</u> pts	<u>37</u>% of Row = <u>3</u> pts	<u>37</u>% of Row = <u>3</u> pts	<u>26</u>% of Row = <u>2</u> pts

II. *Plant vs. Animal cells*
 A. *Similarities*
 B. *Differences*
   1. *Cell wall vs. membrane*
   2. *food manufacture*
	2 items, each scored 0–1 (short-answer)		

<u>10</u>% of Total = <u>2</u> pts	<u>100</u>% of Row = <u>2</u> pts	_% of Row = _ pts	_% of Row = _ pts
III. *Cell Membrane* A. *Similarities* B. *Diffusion* C. *Substances diffused by cells*	*2 items, one scored 0–2, the other scored 0–1 (short-answer)*	*2 items, each scored 0–1 (multiple-choice)*	
<u>20</u>% of Total = <u>4</u> pts	<u>75</u>% of Row = <u>3</u> pts	<u>25</u>% of Row = <u>1</u> pts	_% of Row = _ pts
IV. *Division of Cells* A. *Phases in division* A. *Phases in division* B. *Chromosomes and DNA* C. *Plant vs. Animal cell division*	*4 items, each scored 0–1 (definitions, short-answer)*	*1 item, scored 0–1 (short-answer)*	
<u>30</u>% of Total = <u>6</u> pts	<u>67</u>% of Row = <u>4</u> pts	<u>33</u>% of Row = <u>2</u> pts	_% of Row = _ pts

Source: Adapted from *Teacher's Guide to Better Classroom Testing: A Judgmental Approach* (p. 4) by A. J. Nitko and T-C Hsu, 1987, Pittsburgh, PA: Institute for Practice and Research in Education, School of Education, University of Pittsburgh. Adapted by permission of the authors.

Example F.3 Blueprint using only a list of learning targets

Objectives of the unit	Number of items	Number of points
1. Names and tells functions of each cell part.	1	3
2. Explains differences between plant and animal cells.	1	1
3. Describes the cell wall and cell membrane.	1	1
4. Lists substances, diffused and not diffused through cell membrane.	1	2
5. Gives definition of diffusion.	1	1
6. Gives definition of division, chromosomes, and DNA.	3	3
7. States differences between plant and animal cell division.	1	1
8. Labels parts of a cell when shown a line drawing.	3	3
9. Distinguishes between diffusion, oxidation, and fission.	2	2
10. Given the number of chromosomes in a cell before division, states the number in each cell after division.	1	1
11. Given photographs of plant and animal cells, identities parts of cells without using prompts.	2	2
	Total points = 17	Total points = 20

Source: From *Teacher's Guide to Better Classroom Testing: A Judgmental Approach* (p. 39), by A. J. Nitko and T-C. Hsu, 1993. Pittsburgh, PA. Institute for Practice and Research in Education, School of Education, University of Pittsburgh. Reprinted by permission.

Example F.4 Blueprint using only a content listing

Major topics of unit	Number of items	Number of points per item	Total number of points
I. Basic Parts of a Cell			
A. Nucleus	2	2	4
B. Cytoplasm	3	1	3
C. Cell membrane	1	1	1
	subtotal = 6		subtotal = 8
II. Plant vs. Animal Cells			
A. Similarities	1	1	1
B. Differences			
1. cell wall vs. cell membrane	1	1	1
2. food manufacture	0		0
	subtotal = 2		subtotal = 2
III. Cell Membrane			
A. Living nature of	0		0
B. Diffusion	2	1	2
C. Examples of different substances	1	2	2
	subtotal = 3		subtotal = 4
IV. Division of Cells			
A. Phases of division	2	1	2
B. Role in chromosomes and DNA	2	1	2
C. Plant vs. animal cell division	2	1	2
	subtotal = 6		subtotal = 6
	Total test items = 17		Total test points = 20

Source: From *Teacher's Guide to Better Classroom Testing, A Judgmental Approach* (p. 38), by A. J. Nitko and T-C. Hsu, 1993. Pittsburgh, PA. Institute for Practice and Research in Education, School of Education, University of Pittsburgh. Reprinted by permission of the authors.

Scoring Guide for Nebraska's Writing Assessment

Grade 8, Descriptive Writing

Source: From *STARS School-based Teacher-led Assessment and Reporting System: Summary 2004* (p. 20), by Nebraska Department of Education. Available: http://www.nde.state.ne.us/stars/documents/STARSbooklet.04.pdf. Reprinted by permission.

GRADE 8 NEBRASKA DEPT OF EDUCATION SCORING GUIDE FOR DESCRIPTIVE WRITING

	1 1+	2− 2 2+	3− 3 3+	4− 4
IDEAS/CONTENT	• creates no picture of what is being described • severe digressions from the prompt • lacks supporting details • description is missing	• creates a limited picture of what is being described • some digressions from the prompt • contains some supporting, relevant details • description is limited	• creates a general picture of what is being described • is generally focused on the prompt • contains adequate, supporting, relevant details • description is acceptable	• creates a clear picture of what is being described • is well-focused on prompt • contains numerous, supporting relevant details • description is distinctive
ORGANIZATION	• structural development does not include a beginning/introduction, middle/body, and end/conclusion • sequencing is random • pacing is awkward • transitions are missing; connections are unclear	• structural development of a beginning/introduction, middle/body, and end/conclusion is incomplete • sequencing is somewhat logical • pacing is sometimes inconsistent • transitions may be repetitious, predictable or weak	• structural development includes a functional beginning/introduction, middle/body, and end/conclusion • sequencing is functional and logical • pacing is generally controlled • transitions are generally effective	• structural development includes an effective beginning/introduction, middle/body, and end/conclusion • sequencing is thoughtful, logical and effective • pacing is well-controlled • transitions clearly show how ideas connect
VOICE	• conveys no sense of the person behind the words • tone is not appropriate for purpose and audience • is lifeless and/or mechanical	• conveys a limited sense of the person behind the words • tone is sometimes not appropriate for purpose and audience • is occasionally expressive	• conveys a general sense of the person behind the words • tone is generally appropriate for purpose and audience • is generally individualistic or expressive	• conveys a strong sense of the person behind the words • tone is well-suited to the purpose and audience • is individualistic, expressive, and engaging throughout
WORD CHOICE	• uses language that is neither specific nor precise • contains numerous misused or repetitious words and phrases • overuse of clichés and jargon • lacks vivid words or phrases	• uses language that is occasionally specific and precise • uses language that may seem forced or contrived • occasionally uses vivid words and phrases • some overuse of clichés and jargon	• uses language that is usually specific and precise • uses language that is generally appropriate for the purpose and audience • uses some vivid words and phrases • generally avoids clichés and jargon	• uses language that is consistently specific and precise • uses language that seems natural and appropriate for the purpose and audience • effectively uses vivid words and phrases • avoids clichés and jargon
SENTENCE FLUENCY	• uses sentences that almost never vary in length or structure • uses phrasing that is choppy, incomplete, rambling, or awkward • fragments or run-ons confuse the reader • dialogue, if present, sounds unnatural	• uses sentences that sometimes vary in length or structure • uses phrasing that occasionally sounds natural • fragments, if present, may confuse the reader • dialogue, if present, may occasionally sound unnatural	• uses sentences that generally vary in length and structure • uses phrasing that usually sounds natural and conveys meaning • fragments, if present, may add style • dialogue, if present, generally sounds natural	• uses sentences of varying length and structure throughout • uses phrasing that consistently sounds natural and conveys meaning • fragments, if present, add style • dialogue, if present, sounds natural
CONVENTIONS	• paragraphing is missing • errors in grammar, usage, punctuation, and spelling throughout distract the reader	• paragraphing, if attempted, is irregular • errors in grammar, usage, punctuation, and spelling may distract the reader	• attempts at paragraphing are generally successful • a few errors in grammar, usage, punctuation, and spelling—especially with more sophisticated words and concepts do not distract the reader	• paragraphing is sound • grammar, usage, spelling and punctuation are mostly correct • conventions—especially grammar and spelling—may be manipulated for stylistic effect

Appendix **H**

Key Elements of Good Answers to Exercises

Chapter 1—Classroom Decision Making

1a. Mrs. Jones scenario

Sound—giving quizzes regularly; notifying students

Unsound—not planning assessment questions until the last minute; not engaging in professional development in assessment

b. Mr. Mohan scenario

Sound—making accommodations for a special needs student (in this case, changes in presentation and setting); working with the student's sign language interpreter

c. Mrs. Taibbi scenario

Sound—testing at the end of a unit of instruction

Unsound—not planning assessment to match classroom learning targets; "cramming" in additional learning; counting in official assessment points for material not related to learning targets for which the students were responsible

d. Mr. Williams scenario

Sound—testing at the end of a unit of instruction

Unsound—not reviewing the test or key for quality; unquestioning reliance on the "authority" of a publisher; unwillingness to discuss assessment with student and parent

2a. Mr. Gordon scenario

Unsound—not notifying students about the timing or nature of assessments; using quizzes for behavior control instead of for evaluating achievement of learning targets

b. Mrs. Stravinski scenario

Unsound—failing to follow prescribed directions when administering a standardized test (which invalidates using the norms); not telling anyone about the breach of administrative protocol

c. Mrs. Appleton scenario

Sound—using appropriate accommodations

Unsound—changing students' answers

    d. Mr. Pennel scenario

       Sound—using essays and performance assessment (assuming they are used for assessing appropriate learning targets)

       Unsound—not matching scoring schemes (whether rubrics, checklists, rating scales, or point schemes) to the learning targets means student performance on the essays or performance assessments may not be interpreted appropriately as indicators of achievement

    e. Mrs. Dingle scenario

       Sound—being willing to adjust borderline grades

       Unsound—not using additional *achievement* information to make the adjustment; using her perceptions/opinions to make the adjustment (causing a "halo effect"); not having a sound rationale to give the students about their grades; making comments about the students that could be perceived as personal rather than as about their achievement; and, if the scenario is read to imply that the students indeed are at the same achievement level, giving two different grades for the same achievement level

Chapter 2—Validity and Reliability

    1a. content representativeness and relevance (content evidence)

    b. relationships of assessment results to the results of other variables (external structure evidence)

    c. reliability over assessors (reliability evidence)

    d. content representativeness and relevance (content evidence) and types of thinking skills required (substantive evidence)

    e. content representativeness and relevance (content evidence); secondarily substantive evidence and internal structure evidence

    2a. accuracy of rater (teacher) judgment; consistency across questions

    b. accuracy of rater (teacher) judgment; consistency across assignments (projects)

    c. consistency across assignments (projects); decision consistency (do similar performances get the same grade?)

    d. consistent performance from item to item

    e. accuracy of rater (teacher) judgment; consistency across assignments (entries)

    f. consistency across problems; dependability of interpretation (does performance indicate what student can do with help, with book, with calculator, without these things?)

    g. dependability of interpretation; accuracy of teacher judgment

    h. consistent performance from item to item

Chapter 3—Learning Goals

    1a. mastery

    b. developmental

    c. mastery

    2a. psychomotor, because it requires perception and judgment of color (some cognitive—need to know how to use the remote, the on-screen programming, and so on)

b. cognitive, because the main requirement is understanding of parliamentary procedures (some affective—need to use some interpersonal skills to conduct the meeting successfully)

c. affective, because group maintenance requires interpersonal skills (some cognitive—operating without working on the science would not contribute to group maintenance)

d. psychomotor, because eye-hand coordination and skill at throwing is the primary target (some cognitive—need to understand what a foul line is)

Chapter 4—Higher Order Thinking

1a. Identify the problem (and solve it).

b. Identify the problem (and solve it). Model the problem.

c. Identify the problem (and solve it). Describe multiple strategies. Model the problem.

These strategies require progressively more explicit problem-solving thinking. Students who solve version (a) might use various methods, but all they need to do is write "3 cookies each." Students who solve version (b) would need to draw a dozen cookies and circle four (equal) groups of 3 cookies each, as well as write "3 cookies each." Therefore, you would be sure that those who did this correctly could use drawing to solve the problem. Students who solve version (c) would need to illustrate two different solution strategies (perhaps drawing and also using the equation $12 \div 4 = 3$), as well as write "3 cookies each." Therefore, you would be sure that those who did this correctly could use two different methods to solve the problem. You would also know that they could select methods to solve the problem. In version (b), the teacher specified "drawing" as a solution strategy. In version (c), the teacher left the identification and selection of strategies to the student.

2a. Make judgments about values.

b. Judge inductions.

c. Judge deductions.

These three questions all require basic comprehension of the fable. Beyond that, however, they each exercise different critical thinking skills. Item (a) requires that students identify the value bases on which the Cat decided to lie to the others. (The Cat thought she and her kittens were more important than the Eagle family or the Wild Sow family. She had no problem with actions that led her family to prosper and the others to die.) Item (b) requires that students make inferences from the Cat's actions about these values, conclude that these actions were not good for the others, and use those patterns to come up with a moral. The successful student would have written a moral that had something to do with gossiping or lying being a bad thing to do. Item (c) requires that students compare two different conclusions (that the teacher has already put into the question), and recognize that the broader principle is a better moral for the story. Which of these would be the better question to ask would depend on the learning target for that lesson. They are not interchangeable.

Chapter 5—Planning Assessment and Instruction

1a. Questioning students in class; questionnaires

b. In-depth interview of individual student

c. Project or task focusing on a product (an assignment based on watching the Weather Channel)

d. Growth and learning-progress portfolio

2. The assessment plan would have to include some performance assessment for at least the first learning goal. Specifically, they would have to read and respond to various poems. The second learning goal could be assessed with tests (knowledge of literary devices), but the tests would have to include some essay questions (for identifying and explaining literary devices in particular poems). There should be some formative assessments along the way, in the form of classwork and/or homework, for students to practice these skills.

Chapter 6—Formative Assessment

1a. Individual assistance in a "just in time" fashion, focused on the student-perceived source of difficulty

b. Revising; Future writing; Reflecting on why the revision is better than the first draft

c. Students adjust own study strategies; Students see exactly what they know and don't, and have control over moving their own knowledge

d. Identifying and correcting misconceptions; Adjust pacing of future instruction; Adjust content of future instruction

2a. Evaluative, negative, disapproving

b. Descriptive, specifying improvement

c. Descriptive, constructing achievement

d. Evaluative, positive, rewarding

Chapter 7—Completion and Selected Response Test Items

1a. Have the blank toward the end of the sentence.

b. Be written as a question (with only one answer).

c. Have only one or two blanks. Have the blank toward the end of the sentence.

d. Be written as a question (with only one answer).

e. Be written as a question (with only one answer). Have directions for amount of precision required.

f. Population of what? Without that, it is impossible to know whether the question assesses an important aspect of the learning targets.

2a. Avoid verbal clues.

b. Assess important ideas (not trivia or common sense). Be definitely true or definitely false.

c. Assess important ideas (not trivia or common sense).

d. State the source of the opinion, if your item presents an opinion.

e. Focus on only one important idea or on one relationship between ideas.

3a. Put the word in the stem and definition in alternatives, if testing definitions. Have plausible distractors; have homogeneous alternatives. Use "none of the above" sparingly.

b. Avoid "all of the above." [Secondarily, arrange alternatives in a logical order.]

c. Avoid textbook wording. Avoid "cluing." Avoid textbook wording. Have homogeneous alternatives. Have one correct or best answer.

4. Premises and responses are not homogeneous. All responses are not plausible for each premise. Longer statements go in premises, not responses. Directions should clearly state the basis for matching. Avoid "perfect matching."

Chapter 8—Constructed Response Test Items

1a. Match the assessment plan (which probably required higher-order thinking regarding students' understanding of prejudice). Require students to apply knowledge to a new situation. Require the students to demonstrate more than recall. Make clear length, purpose, amount of time, and evaluation criteria.

b. Define a task with specific directions (this is too broad—one appropriate answer might be, "It's horrible!"). Word the question in a way that leads all students to interpret the item as intended. Make clear length, purpose, amount of time, and evaluation criteria.

2a. Item A: Write an equation to describe the sequence {0, 3, 9, 18 ...}, and then use it to find the next term in the sequence.

b. Item B: Write the chemical equation that shows what happens when propane burns in oxygen. Make sure it is balanced.

Chapter 9—Performance Assessment

1.

Task Property (from Table 9.1)	Project (a)	Project (b)
Time	One month	Three weeks
Task structure provided	Low structure (student is free to select and define the problem, within broad limits)	High structure (teacher defined the problem)
Participation of groups	Individual work	Groups of four
Product and process focus	Both process and product assessed (experimental procedures would be reported); Emphasis on product (the display and report)	Both process and product assessed (logs and charts of weather from day to day show process, report shows final learning); Emphasis on process (what was learned is more important than whether the weather was predicted correctly)
Performance modality	Multiple modalities (written report, chart, display)	Multiple modalities (written report, logs, weather charts, display)

These two science projects are most alike in time and performance modality. They are most different in task structure and participation. Project (a) is much more defined by the student than project (b). Project (a) requires individual work, and project (b) is a group assignment. While the projects are similar in requiring multiple modalities, the individual nature of project (a) would require that each student use all the modalities. The group nature of project (b) might allow for students to participate more heavily in the modality of their choice. For example, students in the group who were good at (or enjoyed) writing might do more of the report, and students who were good at (or enjoyed) graphics might do more of the charts and display work.

2a. Not terribly authentic to real life, but perhaps authentic to future "school" assignments. Students may perceive they need to learn how to report on things they've read because it is important in school. The learning targets seems to be comprehension (understanding the story) and deriving personal enjoyment from reading (one is supposed to have a favorite part).

b. A relatively authentic assignment, although seventh graders may not know that yet! Discussing books with others who have read the same thing is a common enough activity among educated adults. The learning target seems to be being able to discuss what one has read (which would assume comprehension). Because the literature circle is to be student-led, another learning target would seem to be knowing how to ask questions about what one has read.

   c. A relatively inauthentic assignment. The learning target would be variable (and differ with each teacher questions). Therefore, to students the learning target might seem to be "having something to say" rather than focusing on any particular reading achievement goal.

Chapter 10—Scoring

1a. Because there are no rubrics or point schemes associated with the maximum marks, there should be disagreement on how to score Jane's responses.

   b. Most likely, there will be more disagreement on the items that have more points.

   c. Discussion may point to the fact that there are no descriptions of performance required for each point level. Discussion may also highlight the difference between points for varying degrees of correctness of short answer questions (#1, #2, #4) and the points for varying degrees of quality on the paragraph (#3). Discussion may also note that the essay question (#3) does not follow the guidelines for good essay writing (Guideline 8.3); lack of definition of the task contributes to its being difficult to score.

2.

Guideline	These rubrics fall short because
Emphasize the most important content and processes of the learning targets.	The learning targets were: (a) reads appropriate grade-level text for meaning and (b) uses oral communication skills. The rubrics say nothing about the pictures demonstrating understanding of meaning. The "excellent" level mentions eye contact and the "poor" level mentions mumbling, two different aspects of oral communication. Both learning targets need to be referenced consistently at all performance levels.
For each achievement dimension's score, match the emphasis for that achievement dimension in your assessment plan.	These rubrics have only one dimension (one scale). With two such different learning targets, it would be clearer and easier to have two (one for the understanding of meaning demonstrated by the pictures selected, and one for oral communication skills).
For the maximum possible total points, match the emphasis for that learning target(s) in your assessment plan.	We have no information about the assessment plan, or even if there was one.
Be clear to students.	The words themselves are understandable to students, but they don't add up to a clear picture of what students should do.
Be useful for giving students the guidance they need to improve their performance on the learning targets.	The descriptions are not very helpful for improvement. What would a student do, for example, if he or she was rated "good"? What would be needed to become "excellent"? Terms should be more descriptive and less evaluative—including the category names themselves.

(Continued)

Be a faithful application of a general rubric, conceptual framework, or learning progression appropriate to the learning target.	"Excellent, good, fair, poor, failing" does not count as a general rubric!
Have clear, observable levels of performance	The performance levels are written as judgments (nice, good, etc.), not in observable terms.
Allow for assessment of all knowledge, skills, and use of processes that are important to the learning targets.	No mention is made in the rubrics of having to explain the reasons for choosing the pictures, which was the part of the assignment intended to indicate comprehension and understanding of the character in the story.
Clearly describe how alternative correct answers or strategies are to be rated, if applicable.	No mention is made in the rubrics of this. The question about "alternatives" that would most likely be of interest in this case is how to judge students whose coats of arms depicted interesting, but less important, aspects of the character.
Allow for distinctions between achievement levels.	Differences between levels are not clear, especially between "excellent" and "good" and between "fair" and "poor."

Chapter 11—Grading

1.

Pupil	(a) C-R grade, fixed percentage	(b) C-R grade, total points	(c) C-R grade, minimum attainment	(d) self-ref. grade
A	B	B	B	B
B	C	C	B	C
C	A	A	A	B
D	B or A*	B or A*	A	B
E	F	F	F	D

Note—The fixed percentage (column a) and total points (column b) methods give the same results, once total points are recalculated to reflect teacher's weights. Pupil D's "average" is 89.66667, an A if rounded to the nearest percent and a B if "less than 90" is the rule used. Typically one would round, and the grade would be an A. There will be disagreement about minimum attainment grades and self-referenced grades (columns c and d), depending on the decision rules adopted.

2. The main point of the exercise is not "agreeing" with the answers suggested above (except for the fixed percent and total points methods); rather, it is in the explanation about how grades were assigned, and in the understanding that such decisions can lead to very different grades for the same performance. Ultimately, the most important thing is reflecting on how these decisions should be put in service of communicating student achievement in a meaningful way.

3a. [Answers will vary.] Pupil B did well on his project (you would describe it), but not so well on his test (describe). Based on his quiz scores, I thought he would do better on his test than he did. I have talked with him about it, and he says he "clutched" on the test. We are going to work on study strategies so he can approach tests feeling more prepared.

b. [Answers will vary.] Pupil C did very well on both his test (describe) and his project (describe), as well as homework and quizzes. He seems to have an excellent grasp of the material.

However, he failed to turn in one of the homework assignments, and his behavior is [describe the "poor deportment" here]. I have talked with him about it, and he says he is bored in class. He has agreed to work on some special assignments with me in place of some of the homework.

Chapter 12—Interpreting Standardized Test Scores

1a. James scenario
   i. False. The fifth- and sixth-grade equivalent scores represent that James performed like typical fifth- or sixth- graders would on fourth-grade level tests. They don't say how he would perform on fifth- or sixth-grade level tests.
   ii. False. Don't use GE scores to compare strengths and weaknesses across subjects; use percentile bands to do that. In fact, all these scores are at the 74th or 75th percentile, which means James is relatively equal in all subjects tested.
   iii. True. James' scores are "average" for fifth- or sixth-graders, respectively, on the various tests.

 b. Sue scenario
   i. False. A raw score of 50 in Reading is at the 74th percentile, and raw score of 30 in Language is at the 75th percentile.
   ii. False. Don't use GE scores to compare strengths and weaknesses across subjects; use percentile bands to do that.
   iii. False. The percentile rank in Language is 75, and in Reading it is 74. It is likely that when using confidence bands to interpret this difference, the bands would overlap. Of course, we don't know that for sure because the standard errors are not given here.

2a. False. A percentile rank of 45 means that the person's raw score was higher than 45% of the group assessed.

 b. False. Sally's score of 40 is 5 points below the mean of 45, which means it is one-half a standard deviation (10) below the mean.

 c. False. *DIQ* scores are normalized standard scores. That means the normal distribution was imposed mathematically on an underlying distribution that may or may not have been normal.

Glossary

accountability testing: Testing done for the purpose of holding schools (and/or students) responsible for achievement of state standards.

achievement target: The specific learning objective on which lessons and assessments are based.

affective domain: Learning targets that focus on feelings, interests, attitudes, and dispositions.

alternate solution strategies: Different, but equally correct, procedures or methods for obtaining a correct solution to a problem or for producing the correct product.

alternative assessment: Usually refers to performance assessment. The "alternative" in alternative assessment usually means in opposition to standardized achievement tests and to multiple-choice (true-false, matching, completion) item formats.

alternatives: The list of choices from which an examinee answering a multiple-choice item must select the correct or best answer. Also known as *choices, options,* and *response choices.*

analytic rubrics, analytic scoring rubrics: A rule that you use to rate or score the separate parts or traits (dimensions) of a student's product or process first, then sum these part scores to obtain a total score.

annotated holistic rubrics: Rules you use to conduct holistic rating of a student's product or process, then rate or describe a few characteristics that are strengths and weaknesses to support your holistic rating.

assessment: The process for obtaining information that is used for making decisions about students, curricula and programs, and educational policy.

assessment accommodations, assessment modifications: Changes in either the conditions or materials of assessment that allow students with disabilities to be assessed in the same areas as students who are assessed with unmodified assessments. Some add the distinction that *accommodations* do not alter the construct being measured, while *modifications* may alter the construct.

assessment variables: Characteristics about which you gather information needed for teaching, including sizing up the class and diagnosing students' needs, prerequisite achievements, attitudes, work habits, study skills, and motivation.

association variety (of short answer item): A list of terms or a picture for which students have to recall numbers, labels, symbols, or other terms and write them in the spaces provided.

authentic assessment: A type of performance assessment in which students are presented with tasks that are directly educationally meaningful instead of indirectly meaningful.

behavior checklist: A list of discrete behaviors related to a specific area of a student's performance that is used by observing a student and marking the behaviors observed.

best-works portfolio: A portfolio containing only a student's best final products or work in a subject.

bias (assessment or test): A general term to describe a test or an assessment used unfairly against a particular group of persons for a particular purpose or decision.

blueprint: See **table of specifications**.

borderline cases: Students whose marks place them at or very near the border between two letter grades.

carryover effect: A type of scoring error that occurs when your judgment of a student's response to Question 1 affects your judgment of the student's response to Question 2.

checklist: A list of specific behaviors, characteristics of a product, or activities, and a place for marking whether each is present or absent.

classification decision: A decision that results in a person being assigned to one of several different but unordered categories, jobs, or programs.

closed-response task: An assessment task allowing only a single correct answer.

cognitive domain: Learning targets that focus on memory, thinking, and reasoning.

cognitive feedback: Feedback that describes connections between the student's performance or achievement and the processes that led to it.

completion variety (of short-answer item): A format of achievement assessment that presents a student with incomplete sentences and asks the student to "fill in the blanks" to complete them correctly.

constructed response item: A test question in which the examinee is expected to respond to an item using his or her own ideas and words rather than choosing an answer.

content standards: Statements about the subject-matter facts, concepts, principles, and so on that students are expected to learn.

context-dependent item sets: See **interpretive exercises**.

correction variety (of true-false item): An item format that requires students to judge a proposition, as does the true-false variety, but students are also required to correct any false statement to make it true.

correlation coefficient: A statistical index that quantifies, on a scale of -1 to $+1$, the degree of relationship between the scores from one assessment and the scores from another.

criterion-referenced grading: Assigning grades by comparing a student's performance to a defined set of standards to be achieved, targets to be learned, or knowledge to be acquired.

criterion-referencing: A score-interpreting framework that compares a student's test performance against the domain of performances that the assessment samples to answer the question, "How much of the targeted learning did this student achieve?"

critical thinking: "Reasonable, reflective thinking that is focused on deciding what to believe or do" (Ennis, 1985, p. 54). Critical thinking educational goals focus on developing students who are fair-minded, are objective, reach sound conclusions, and are disposed toward seeking clarity and accuracy.

decision consistency index: A statistical index used to describe the consistency of decisions made from scores rather than the consistency of the scores themselves.

descriptive feedback: Feedback that characterizes aspects of the performance, usually in terms of learning target(s).

developmental learning target: Skills and abilities that are continuously developed throughout life. Learning targets such as these are more aptly stated at a somewhat higher level of abstraction than **mastery learning targets**.

deviation IQ (*DIQ***):** A type of normalized standard score with a mean of 100 and a standard deviation of 15 (or 16 in some tests).

diagnostic assessment: Assessment done to describe specific content (often specific weaknesses) and particular instructional strategies required to help a student attain a particular learning target.

disaggregate: To separate the test results for the total population of students and to report separately for subgroups of students such as the poor, minorities, students with limited English proficiency, and students with disabilities.

distractors: Alternatives in a multiple-choice item that are not the correct or best answer to the question or problem posed by the stem, but that appear to be correct or plausible answers to less knowledgeable examinees.

equivalence: In the context of classroom assessment, the degree to which past and present students are required to know and perform tasks of similar (but not identical) complexity and difficulty to get the same grade on the same content of the units.

essay item: Test item requiring students to compose a written answer.

evaluation: The process of making value judgments about the worth of a student's product or performance.

evaluative feedback: Feedback that passes judgment on student work.

exemplar: Examples of student work that illustrate or exemplify different levels on a scoring rubric.

extended normalized standard score: A type of normalized standard score that spans multiple grades and is anchored to a lower grade reference group.

extended response essay item: An essay prompt that requires students to express their own ideas and organize their answers.

feedback: Information about how a student can improve his or her work, usually given by a teacher to a student on the basis of observation and diagnosis of performance on *formative assessments* or *classroom activities*.

fixed-percentage method: Assigning grades by using percentages as bases for marking and grading papers. The relationship between percentage correct and letter grade is arbitrary.

foils: See **distractors**.

formative assessment: Assessment used to improve teaching and to improve students' learning.

formative evaluation: Judgment about the worth of curricula, materials, and programs made while they are under development, leading to suggestions for ways to redesign, refine, or improve them.

general learning target: Statements of expected learning outcomes derived from educational goals; they are more specific than the goals but not specific enough to be useful as classroom learning targets.

generic rubrics: Rubrics that use descriptions applying to a whole family or set of tasks (e.g., math problem solving, writing). These can be shared with students and used in instruction.

gradebook program: A computer program combining a spreadsheet and database that allows you to enter students' names and grades and automatically calculates averages and letter grades.

grade-equivalent score (GE): A norm-referenced growth scale score that tells the grade placement at which a raw score is average. A grade-equivalent score is reported as a decimal fraction, such as 3.4. The whole number part of the score refers to a grade level, and the decimal part refers to a month of the school year within that grade level.

grading on the curve: A method for assigning grades that ranks students' marks from highest to lowest, and assigns grades (A, B, C, etc.) on the basis of this ranking.

grading variables: A subset of variables, selected from among all the reporting variables, on which you may base your grades for a marking period.

growth and learning-progress portfolio: A portfolio containing a selection of a sequence of a student's work that demonstrates progress or development toward achieving the learning target(s).

halo effect: A type of error that occurs when a teacher's general impression of the student affects how the teacher rates the student on specific dimensions.

high-stakes tests: Assessments (or tests) the results of which are used for decisions that result in serious consequences for school administrators, teachers, or students.

holistic scoring rubrics: Rubrics that require a teacher to rate or score a student's product or process as a whole without first scoring parts or components separately.

ill-structured problems: A type of problem in which the problem-solver must (a) organize the information to understand it; (b) clarify the problem itself; (c) obtain all the information needed, which may not be immediately available; and (d) recognize that there may be several equally correct answers.

individual education plan (IEP): An educational plan designed by a child study team (including a teacher) and agreed to by the student's parents or guardians describing what learning targets the student should attain, the time frame for attaining them, the proposed methods for attaining them, and the methods of evaluating the student's progress in achieving the learning targets.

instructional decision: Choices about what and how to teach, choices about planning for teaching.

interpretive exercises: A set of items or assessment tasks that require the student to use reading material, graphs, tables, pictures, or other material to answer the items.

item analysis: Summarizing and using information from students' item responses to make decisions about how each test item is functioning.

item difficulty index (p): Proportion of the total group that answered an item correctly.

item discrimination index (D): A measure of the extent to which an item can discriminate higher scoring from lower scoring students

kappa coefficient: A statistical index that reports percent of agreement corrected for the percent of agreement expected by chance.

key: The correct answer to any type of item or assessment task.

learning objective or target: See **specific learning target**.

linear standard score (z, SS): Norm-referenced scores that tell the location of the raw scores in relation to the mean and standard deviation of the distribution of all scores.

local norms group: The local sample of students who took the test (usually the school district).

marking period: The period over which a teacher's summative evaluation of each student's achievement in each subject area is reported to the student, parents, and school officials.

mastery learning target: Statement of what students can do at the end of instruction. Sometimes these are called "can do" statements, specific learning outcomes, or behavioral objectives.

matching exercise: This format presents a student with three things: (a) directions for matching, (b) a list of premises, and (c) a list of responses. The student's task is to match each premise with one of the responses, using the criteria described in the directions as a basis for matching.

measurement: A procedure for assigning numbers (usually called *scores*) to a specified attribute or characteristic of a person in such a way that the numbers describe the degree to which the person possesses the attribute.

median score method (of grading): A procedure for combining several component grades into a composite report card grade. All scores are converted to the same scale, usually a rubric or grade (A,B,C,D,F) scale, and the median mark is used as the composite grade.

minimum attainment method (of grading): A procedure for combining several component grades into a composite report card grade by the following process: determine which components of students' final grades are more important to demonstrating the students' achievement of the learning targets; specify, for each of these "more important" components, the minimum level of performance you will accept for each of the final grade levels; establish rules for what levels of performance you will accept, at each final grade level, on each of the "less important" components. These rules form a set of decision rules for how to assign grades.

multilevel survey battery: A survey battery of standardized tests that spans a wide range of grades in each school subject.

multiple-assessment strategy: Combining the results from several different types of assessments (such as homework, class performance, quizzes, projects, and tests) to improve the validity of your decisions about a student's attainments.

multiple-choice item: A stem that poses a question or sets a problem and a set of two or more responses choices for answering the question or solving the problem. Only one of the response choices is the correct or best answer.

multiple-marking system: A system of reporting summative evaluation of educational progress to students and parents using several kinds of symbols and marks. Multiple-marking systems usually take the form of a report card and report on academic achievement, attendance, deportment, and nonacademic achievement.

mutliple true-false item: This format looks similar to a multiple-choice item. However, instead of selecting one option as correct, the student treats every option as a separate true-false statement.

narrative report: A detailed, written report describing what each student has learned in relation to the school's curriculum framework and the student's effort in class.

national norms: The distribution of scores in the national sample of students who took the test.

national stanine: A stanine score based on the distribution of scores in the national sample of students who took the test.

normal curve equivalent (*NCE*): A normalized standard score with a mean of 50 and a standard deviation of 21.06, developed primarily for use with federal program evaluation efforts.

normal distribution (normal curve): A mathematical model defined by an equation with two variables: mean and standard deviation. All normal distributions are smooth, bell-shaped curves that approach but never touch (are *asymptotic* to) the horizontal axis.

normal growth: The *grade-equivalent view* of normal growth is that a student ought to exhibit a growth of 1.0 grade-equivalent unit from one grade to the next. Under this view, a student taking the test in second grade and scoring 1.3, for example, would need to score 2.3 in third grade, 4.3 in fifth, and so on to show "normal" or expected growth. The *percentile rank view* of normal growth is that a student shows normal growth if that student maintains the same position (i.e., percentile rank) in the norm from year to year.

normalized standard score *(z_n, T, DIQ, NCE, SAT)*: A category of scores in which the raw scores have been changed or transformed into other scores that are distributed more like a normal distribution.

normalized *z*-score: The z score that would have been obtained if a set of scores had been normally distributed.

norm group: A well-defined group of students who have been given the same assessment under the same conditions (same time limits, directions, equipment and materials, etc.).

norm-referenced grading: A framework for assigning grades on the basis of how a student's performance (achievement) compares with other students in the class: Students performing better than most classmates receive the higher grades.

norm-referencing: A framework for interpreting a student's score by comparing her test performance with the performance of other students in a well-defined group who took the same test.

open-response task: An assessment task allowing multiple correct answers.

options: See **alternatives**.

outcome feedback: Feedback in the form of knowledge of results.

paper-and-pencil assessments: Assessment techniques for which students write their responses to the questions. Written homework, seatwork, and tests are typical paper-and-pencil assessment techniques.

parent-teacher conferences: A personal meeting between the parent(s) and the teacher that involves a summative report of a student's achievement.

partial credit: Giving the student some portion of an item's maximum possible points because the student's response is partially correct.

participation: Students with disabilities have the right, and sometimes the obligation, to be assessed, including taking part in accountability assessment programs.

percentage of agreement: An index of the consistency of decisions made by two independent judges. It is the percentage of students for whom the two judges reached the same decision.

percentile band: An interval formed around a percentile rank by adding and subtracting the standard error of measurement. There is a 68% chance that the true score is within the range defined by the band.

percentile rank: A norm-referenced score that tells the percentage of persons in a norm group scoring lower than a particular raw score.

perfect matching: When a matching exercise has an equal number of premise statements and response statements.

performance assessment: Any assessment technique that require students physically to carry out a complex, extended *process* (e.g., present an argument orally, play a musical piece, or climb a knotted rope) or produce an important *product* (e.g., write a poem, report on an experiment, or create a painting).

performance standards: Statements about the things students can perform or do once the content standards are learned.

performance task: One activity or item in a performance assessment.

permanent record: The official summative record by grade level of a student's achievement in each subject and his attendance in a particular school.

placement decision: A decision in which persons are assigned to different levels of the same general type of instruction, education, or work; no one is rejected, but all remain within the institution to be assigned to some level.

point-based scoring scheme: A scheme for scoring essay or show-the-work test items that assigns points to various aspects of the answer.

point-biserial correlation (r_{pbis}): Correlation of item performance with total test score, used as a measure of item discrimination

portfolio : A limited collection of a student's work, and student reflection on that work, used either to present the student's best work(s) or demonstrate the student's educational growth over a given time span.

preinstruction unit assessment framework: A plan to help assess cognitive and affective learning targets of an upcoming unit.

premise: The left-most list of statements or elements in a matching exercise.

principle: A rule that describes what to do or the relationships between two concepts.

principle-governed thinking: Thinking that is manifested when a person consistently uses appropriate rules to identify how two or more concepts are related.

problem solving: Attaining a desired outcome by using higher-order thinking.

procedure checklist: A checklist of the steps necessary to complete a process correctly.

product checklist: A checklist of the necessary and important characteristics of a student product, used to evaluate the quality of the work.

professional responsibility: Acting toward students in a way that is ethical and consistent with one's role as a professional person.

prompt: Material, often in the form or a question or a scenario, presented to a student to stimulate a written response in order to assess writing ability.

proposition: Any sentence that can be said to be true or false.

psychomotor domain: Learning targets that focus on motor skills and perceptual processes.

quality level method (of grading): A method for assigning letter grades in which the type of student performance required for each letter grade is specified beforehand.

question variety (of short-answer item): A short-answer item that asks a direct question.

rater drift: A type of rating error that occurs when the raters, whose ratings originally agreed, begin to redefine the rubrics for themselves. As a result, the raters no longer produce ratings that agree.

rating scale: A scoring rubric that helps a teacher assess the degree to which students have attained the achievement dimensions in the performance task.

raw scores: The number of points assigned to a student's performance on an assessment.

reliability: The amount of consistency of assessment results (scores). Reliability is a limiting factor for validity.

reliability coefficient: Any of several statistical indices that quantifies the amount of consistency in assessment scores.

report card: The document that reports the summative achievement grades to students and parents.

reporting variables: A subset, from among all the assessment variables, that a school district will expect a teacher to report to parents and for official purposes.

response-choice items: Test items that provide students with alternatives from which to choose to answer the question or solve the problem.

response list: The list of plausible response alternatives in a matching exercise. This list is placed to the right of the premise list.

restricted response essay item: An essay prompt that restricts or limits both the substantive content and the form of the written response.

right-wrong variety (of true-false item): This item format presents a computation, equation, or language sentence that the student judges as correct or incorrect (right or wrong).

rubric(s): A coherent set of rules to evaluate the quality of a student's performance (either trait-by-trait or as a whole), usually with descriptions of performance at each level.

rubric method (of grading): See **quality level method for grading**.

SAT-**score:** A normalized standard score from a distribution that has a mean of 500 and a standard deviation of 100.

scaffolding: The degree of support, guidance, and direction provided to students when they set out to complete a task.

school averages norms: A tabulation of the average (mean) score from each school building in a national sample of schools that provides information on the relative ordering of these averages (means).

scoring key: A rubric or list of rules that shows the correct answer and the kinds of partially correct answers that are to receive various amounts of credit.

scoring reliability: See **decision consistency**.

scoring rubric: See **rubrics**.

selection decision: A decision in which an institution or organization decides that some persons are acceptable while others are not; those not acceptable are rejected and no longer are the concern of the institution or organization.

self-assessment: Students' evaluation of their own performance.

self-referenced grading: The assignment of grades by comparing a student's performance with your perceptions of his capability.

self-referencing: A score-interpreting framework that compares a student's test performance against his past work or expectations for his work.

short-answer item: An item format that requires a student to respond with a word, short phrase, number, or symbol.

show-the-work problems: Problems or exercises, usually in mathematics or science, where students are asked to show the intermediate steps to a solution.

single-level standardized test: A standardized survey battery that is used only at one grade level or a one narrow range of grade levels.

special norm groups: Specific subpopulations of students such as deaf students, Catholic schools, and so on.

specific learning target: A clear statement about what students are to achieve by the end of a unit of instruction.

SS-**score:** A linear standard score telling the location of the raw score in a distribution with a mean of 50 and a standard deviation of 10.

standard deviation method (of grading): A norm-referenced grading method that uses the standard deviation of the class' scores as a unit of measure on the grading scale.

standard error of measurement: An estimate of the standard deviation or the spread of a hypothetical obtained-score distribution resulting from repeated testing of the same person with the same assessment.

standardized test: A test for which the procedures, administration, materials, and scoring rules are fixed so that as far as possible the assessment is the same at different times and places.

standards: Statements about what students are expected to learn. Some states call these statements *essential skills, learning expectations, learning outcomes, achievement expectations,* or other names. Often there are two sets of standards: **content standards** and **performance standards**.

standards-referencing: A score-interpreting framework that compares a student's test performance against a particular state standard; typically, the results are reported as categories like "basic," "proficient," and "advanced."

stanine: A type of normalized standard score that tells the location of a raw score in one of nine specific segments of a normal distribution.

stem: The part of a multiple-choice item that asks a question or poses a problem to be solved.

summative assessment: Judgments about the quality or worth of a student's achievement after the instructional process is completed.

summative evaluation: Judgments about the worth of programs, curricula, or materials after they are completed with the idea of suggesting whether they should be adopted or used.

table of specifications: A table of the major content categories and skills that a test assesses, describing the percentage of tasks (items or points) for each content-skills combination included on the test.

task-specific rubrics: Scoring rubrics in which the description of quality levels refers to the specific task and expected responses.

task structure: The elements of a task that can vary (e.g., time, amount of support, modality).

taxonomy: Any of several methods of classifying the cognitive level of learning targets, instructional activities, and assessment questions or tasks.

test: An instrument or systematic procedure for observing and describing one or more characteristics of a student using either a numerical scale or a classification scheme.

total points method (of grading): A criterion-referenced method of assigning grades in which each component included in the final composite grade is given maximum point value; letter grades are assigned on the basis of the number of total points a student accumulated over the marking period.

true-false item: An item format consisting of a statement or proposition that the student must judge as true or false.

unit of instruction: A teaching sequence covering from one to seven weeks of lessons, depending on the students and topics.

validity: The soundness of interpretations and uses of students' assessment results.

well-structured problems: Problems are presented as assessment tasks that are clearly laid out. All the information students need is given, the situations are very much the same as students were taught in class, and there is usually one correct answer that students can attain by applying a procedure that was taught.

yes-no variety (of true-false item): An item format that asks a direct question, to which a student's answers are limited to yes or no.

z-score: A type of linear standard score that expresses a raw score's distance from the mean in standard deviation units.

z_n-score: A type of normalized standard score: z_n-scores have percentile ranks corresponding to what would be expected in a normal distribution.

References

Airasian, P. W. (2005). *Classroom assessment*(5th ed.). New York: McGraw-Hill.

Alexander, P. A. (1992). Domain knowledge: Evaluating themes and emerging concerns. *Educational Psychologist, 27*, 33–51.

American Federation of Teachers, National Council on Measurement in Education, & National Education Association. (1990). *Standards for teacher competence in educational assessment of students*. Washington, DC: National Council on Measurement in Education. (Download from http://www.unl.edu/buros/bimm/html/subarts. html)

American Psychological Association, American Educational Research Association, & National Council on Measurement in Education. (1999). *Standards for educational and psychological testing*. Washington, DC: American Psychological Association.

Amrein, A. L., & Berliner, D. C. (2002, March). High-stakes testing, uncertainty, and student learning. *Education Policy Analysis Archives, 10*(18). Available: http://epaa.asu.edu/epaa/v10n18/

Anderson, L. W. (Ed.), Krathwohl, D. R. (Ed.), Airasian, P. W., Cruikshank, K. A., Mayer, R. E., Pintrich, P. R., Raths, J., & Wittrock, M. C. (2001). *A taxonomy for learning, teaching, and assessing: A revision of Bloom's Taxonomy of Educational Objectives* (Complete edition). New York: Longman.

Arter, J., & McTighe, J. (2001). *Scoring rubrics in the classroom*. Thousand Oaks, CA: Corwin Press.

Baker, E. L. (1992). Issues in policy, assessment, and equity. In *Proceedings of the National Research Symposium on Limited English Proficiency Student Issues: Vol. 1 and 2: Focus on Evaluation and Measurement*. Washington, DC.

Baron, J. B. (1991). Strategies for the development of effective performance exercises. *Applied Measurement in Education, 4*, 305–318.

Bellanca, J. A., & Kirschenbaum, H. (1976). An overview of grading alternatives. In S. B. Simon & J. A. Bellanca (Eds.), *Degrading the grading myths: A primer of alternatives to grades and marks*. Washington, DC: Association for Supervision and Curriculum Development.

Black, P. & Wiliam, D. (1998). Assessment and classroom learning. *Assessment in Education, 5*, 7–74.

Bloom, B. S., Englehart, M. D., Furst, E. J., Hill, W. H., & Krathwohl, D. R. (1956). *Taxonomy of educational objectives: The classification of educational goals. Handbook I: Cognitive domain*. White Plains, NY: Longman.

Bransford, J. D., & Stein, B. S. (1984). *The IDEAL problem solver*. New York: W. H. Freeman.

Brelend, H. M., Camp, R., Jones, R. J., Morris, M. M., & Rock, D. A. (1987). *Assessing writing skill*. (Research Monograph No. 11.). New York: College Entrance Examination Board.

Brookhart, S. M. (1991). Letter: Grading practices and validity. *Educational Measurement: Issues and Practice, 10*(1), 35–36.

Brookhart, S. M. (1993). Teachers' grading practices: Meaning and values. *Journal of Educational Measurement, 30*, 123–142.

Brookhart, S. M. (1999). Teaching about communicating assessment results and grading. *Educational Measurement: Issues and Practice, 18*(1), 5–13.

Brookhart, S. M. (2001). Successful students' formative and summative uses of assessment information. *Assessment in Education, 8*, 153–169.

Brookhart, S. M. (2004). *Grading*. Upper Saddle River, NJ: Merrill/Prentice Hall.

Butler, D. L., & Winne, P. H. (1995). Feedback and self-regulated learning: A theoretical synthesis. *Review of Educational Research, 65*, 245–281.

Clarridge, P. B., & Whitaker, E. M. (1997). *Rolling the elephant over: How to effect large-scale change in the reporting process*. Portsmouth, NH: Heinemann.

Cohen, J. (1960). A coefficient of agreement for nominal scales. *Educational and Psychological Measurement, 20*, 37–46.

Collis, K. F. (1991). *Assessment of the learned structure in elementary mathematics and science*. Paper presented at the Assessment in the Mathematical Sciences Conference, Victoria, Australia.

Covington, M. V. (1992). *Making the grade: A self-worth perspective on motivation and school reform*. Cambridge: Cambridge University Press.

CTB/McGraw-Hill (1992). *Listening and speaking checklist, Grades 9–12: California Achievement Tests* (5th ed.). Monterey, CA: Author.

Davey, B., & Rindone, D. A. (1990, April). *Anatomy of a performance task*. Paper presented at the annual meeting of the American Educational Research Association, Boston.

DeLandsheere, V. (1988). Taxonomies of educational objectives. In J. P. Keeves (Ed.), *Educational research, methodology, and measurement: An international handbook* (pp. 345–354). Oxford: Pergamon Press.

Douglas, H. R., & Tallmadge, M. (1934). How university students prepare for new types of examinations. *School and Society, 39,* 318–320.

Dunbar, D. A., Float, B., & Lyman, F. J. (1980, November). *Report card revision steering committee final report.* Mount Lebanon, PA: Mt. Lebanon School District.

Dunbar, S. B., Koretz, D., & Hoover, H. D. (1991). Quality control in the development and use of performance assessments. *Applied Measurement in Education, 4*(4), 289–303.

Ebel, R. L., & Frisbie, D. A. (1991). *Essentials of educational measurement* (4th rev. ed.). Englewood Cliffs, NJ: Prentice Hall.

Egawa, K., & Azwell, T. (1995). Telling the story: Narrative reports. In T. Azwell and E. Schmar (Eds.), *Report on report cards: Alternatives to consider.* Portsmouth, NH: Heinemann.

Ennis, R. H. (1985). Goals for a critical thinking curriculum. In A. Costa (Ed.), *Developing minds: A resource book for teaching thinking.* Alexandria, VA: Association for Supervision and Curriculum Development.

Evaluation Center. (1995). *An independent evaluation of the Kentucky Instructional Results Information System (KIRIS).* Frankfort, KY: Kentucky Institute for Education Research.

Flaugher, R. L. (1978). The many definitions of test bias. *American Psychologist, 33,* 671–679.

Forsyth, R. A. (1976, March). *Describing what Johnny can do.* (Iowa Testing Program, Occasional Paper, No. 17). Iowa City: University of Iowa.

Frederiksen, N. (1984). Implications of cognitive theory for instruction in problem-solving. *Review of Educational Research, 54,* 363–407.

Freeman, D. J., Kuhs, T. M., Knappen, L. B., & Porter, A. C. (1982). A closer look at standardized tests. *Arithmetic Teacher, 29*(7), 50–54.

Frisbie, D. A., & Becker, D. F. (1990). An analysis of textbook advice about true-false tests. *Applied Measurement in Education, 4,* 67–83.

Frisbie, D. A., & Waltman, K. K. (1992). Developing a personal grading plan. *Educational Measurement: Issues and Practice, 11*(3), 35–42.

Gagné, R. M., Wager, W. W., Golas, K. C., & Keller, J. M. (2005). *Principles of instructional design* (5th ed.). New York: Holt, Rinehart & Winston.

Good, T. L., & Brophy, J. E. (2003). *Looking in classrooms* (9th ed). Glenview, IL: Addison Wesley Longman.

Gow, D. T. (Ed.). (1976). *Design and development of curricular materials: Instructional design articles* (Vol. 2). Pittsburgh: University Center for International Studies, University of Pittsburgh.

Green, K. (1984). Effects of item characteristics on multiple-choice item difficulty. *Educational and Psychological Measurement, 44,* 551–561.

Gronlund, N. E. (1973). *Preparing criterion-referenced tests for classroom instruction.* New York: Macmillan.

Guskey, T. R. (2006). Making high school grades meaningful. *Phi Delta Kappan, 87,* 670–675.

Hakstain, A. R. (1969, February). *The effects of type of examination anticipated on student test preparation and performance.* Paper presented at the annual meeting of the American Educational Research Association, Washington, DC.

Haladyna, T. M., Downing, S. M., & Rodriguez, M. C. (2002). A review of multiple-choice item-writing guidelines for classroom assessment. *Applied Measurement in Education, 15,* 309–334.

Hambleton, R. K., & Murphy, E. (1992). A psychometric perspective on authentic measurement. *Applied Measurement in Education, 5,* 1–16.

Harmin, M. (1994). *Inspiring active learning: A handbook for teachers.* Alexandria, VA: Association for Supervision and Curriculum Development.

Herman, J. L., Aschbacher, P. R., & Winters, L. (1992). *A practical guide to alternative assessment.* Alexandria, VA: Association for Supervision and Curriculum Development.

Hieronymus, A. N. (1976, December). *Uses of Iowa Tests of Basic Skills in evaluation.* Paper presented at the 61st Annual Education Conferences, Iowa City, IA.

Higgins, K. M., Harris, N. A., & Kuehn, L. L. (1994). Placing assessment into the hands of young children: A study of self-generated criteria and self-assessment. *Educational Assessment, 2,* 309–324.

Hirsch, E. D., Jr. (1997). *The philosophy of composition.* Chicago: University of Chicago Press.

Hoover, H. D., Hieronymus, A. N., Frisbie, D. A., & Dunbar, S. (1993). *Interpretive guide for teachers and counselors: Iowa Tests of Basic Skills, Levels 9–14, Forms K and L.* Chicago: Riverside Publishing.

Horvath, F. G. (1991). *Assessment in Alberta: Dimensions of authenticity.* Paper presented at the annual meeting of the National Association of Test Directors and the National Council on Measurement in Education, Chicago.

Jennings, J., & Rentner, D. S. (2006). Ten big effects of the No Child Left Behind Act on Public Schools. *Phi Delta Kappan, 88,* 110–113.

Jones, R. W. (1994). *Performance and alternative assessment techniques: Meeting the challenges of alternative evaluation strategies.* Paper presented at the Second International Conference on Educational Evaluation and Assessment, Pretoria, Republic of South Africa.

Kane, M. T. (1992). An argument-based approach to validity. *Psychological Bulletin, 112,* 527–535.

Kane, M. T. (2002). Validating high-stakes testing programs. *Educational Measurement: Issues and Practice, 21*(1), 31–41.

Kentucky Department of Education. (1993). *KIRIS assessment Portfolio: Mathematics, Grade 4, 1993–1994.* Frankfort, KY: Office of Assessment and Accountability.

Khattri, N., Reeve, A. L., & Adamson, R. J. (1997). *Studies of education reform: Assessment of student performance.* Washington, DC: Office of Educational Research and Improvement.

Klopfer, L. E. (1969). *An operational definition of "understand."* Unpublished manuscript, Learning Research and Development Center, University of Pittsburgh.

Kuhn, D. (1999). A developmental model of critical thinking. *Educational Researcher, 28*(2), 16–25, 46.

Kunder, L. H., & Porwoll, P. J. (1977). *Reporting student progress: Policies, procedures, and systems.* Arlington, VA: Educational Research Service.

Lane, S. (1993). The conceptual framework for the development of a mathematics performance assessment instrument. *Educational Measurement: Issues and Practice, 12* (2), 16–23.

Lane, S., Parke, C., & Moskal, B. (1992). *Principles for developing performance assessments.* Paper presented at the annual meeting of the American Educational Research Association, San Francisco.

Lindvall, C. M., & Nitko, A. J. (1975). *Measuring pupil achievement and aptitude* (2nd ed.). New York: Harcourt Brace Jovanovich.

Linn, R. L. (1993). Educational assessment: Expanded expectations and challenges. *Educational Evaluation and Policy Analysis, 15,* 1–16.

Linn, R. L. (1994). Performance assessment: Policy, promises, and technical measurement standards. *Educational Researcher, 23*(4), 4–14.

Linn, R. L., Baker, E. L., & Dunbar, S. B. (1991). Complex, performance-based assessment: Expectations and validation criteria. *Educational Researcher, 20*(8), 5–21.

Linn, R. L., Graue, M. E., & Sanders, N. M. (1990). Comparing state and district test results to national norms: The validity of claims that 'everyone is above average'. *Educational Measurement: Issues and Practice, 9*(3), 5–14.

Linn, R. L., & Miller, M. D. (2005). *Measurement and evaluation in teaching* (9th ed.). Upper Saddle River, NJ: Merrill/Prentice Hall.

Marzano, R. J., Brandt, R. S., Hughes, C. S., Jones, B. F., Presseisan, B. Z., Rankin, S. C., & Suhor, C. (1998). *Dimensions of thinking: A framework for curriculum and instruction.* Alexandria, VA: Association for Supervision and Curriculum Development.

Marzano, R. J., Pickering, D., & McTighe, J. (1993). *Assessing student outcomes: Performance assessment using the Dimensions of Learning Model.* Alexandria, VA: Association for Supervision and Curriculum Development.

McClymer, J. F., & Knowles, L. Z. (1992). Ersatz learning, inauthentic teaching. *Journal on Excellence in College Teaching, 3,* 33–50.

Mehrens, W. A., & Kaminski, J. (1989). Methods for improving standardized test scores: Fruitful, fruitless, or fraudulent? *Educational Measurement: Issues and Practice, 8*(1), 14–22.

Mehrens, W. A., & Lehmann, I. J. (1991). *Measurement and evaluation in education and psychology* (4th ed.). Chicago: Holt, Rinehart, & Winston.

Meisels, S., Atkins-Burnett, S., Xue, Y., & Bickel, D. D. (2003). Creating a system of accountability: The impact of instructional assessment on elementary children's achievement scores. *Educational Policy Analysis Archives, 11*(9), 19 pp. Retrieved from http://epaa.asu.edu/eapp/v11n9/

Messick, S. (1989). Validity. In R. L. Linn (Ed.), *Educational measurement* (3rd ed., pp. 13–103). Englewood Cliffs, NJ: Prentice Hall.

Messick, S. (1994). The interplay of evidence and consequences in the validation of performance assessments. *Educational Researcher, 23*(2), 13–23.

Miller, M. D., & Seraphine, A. E. (1993). Can test scores remain authentic when teaching to the test? *Educational Assessment, 1,* 119–129.

Mullis, I. V. S. (1991). *The NAEP guide.* Princeton, NJ: National Assessment of Educational Progress, Educational Testing Service.

National Center on Educational Outcomes. (2005). *Accommodations for students with disabilities.* (Downloaded from http://education.umn.edu/ NCEO).

Newman, R. (1997–98). Parent conferences: A conversation between you and your child's teacher. *Childhood Education, 74,* 100–101.

Newmann, F. M., Bryk, A. S., & Nagaoka, J. K. (2001, January). *Authentic intellectual work and standardized tests: Conflict or coexistence?* Chicago: Consortium on Chicago School Research.

Nitko, A. J. (1989). Designing tests that are integrated with instruction. In R. L. Linn (Ed.), *Educational measurement* (3rd ed., pp. 447–474). New York: Macmillan.

Nitko, A. J., & Brookhart, S. M. (2007). *Educational assessment of students* (5th ed.). Upper Saddle River, NJ: Merrill/Prentice Hall.

Nitko, A. J., & Hsu, T-C. (1987). *Teacher's guide to better classroom testing: A judgmental approach.* Pittsburgh: Institute for Practice and Research in Education, School of Education, University of Pittsburgh.

Norris, S. P., & Ennis, R. H. (1989). *Evaluating critical thinking.* Pacific Grove, CA: Midwest Publications, Critical Thinking Press.

Northwest Regional Educational Laboratory. (1998). *Improving classroom assessment: A toolkit for professional developers*(2nd ed.). Portland, OR: Author.

Odell, C. W. (1928). *Traditional examinations and new-type tests.* New York: Century Co.

Parkes, J., & Giron, T. (2006). *Making reliability arguments in classrooms.* Paper presented at the annual meeting of the National Council on Measurement in Education, San Francisco.

Pearson, K. (1924). Historical note on the origin of the normal curve of errors. *Biometrika, 16,* 402–404.

Perkins, D. N., & Salomon, G. (1989). Are cognitive skills context-bound? *Educational Researcher, 18,* 16–25.

Perl, J. (1995). Improving relationship skills for parent conferences. *Teaching Exceptional Children, 28*(1), 29–31.

Phillips, S. E. (2005). Legal corner: Reconciling IDEA and NCLB. *NCME Newsletter, 13* (2), June, 2. (Downloaded from www.ncme.org/pubs/ vol13_2_June2005.pdf)

Pogrow, S. (2005). HOTS revisited: A thinking development approach to reducing the learning gap after grade 3. *Phi Delta Kappan, 87,* 64–74.

Popham, W. J. (2005). Wyoming's instructionally supportive NCLB Tests. *NCME Newsletter, 13*(1), March, 3. (Downloaded from www.ncme.org/pubs/ vol13_1_Mar2005.pdf)

Power, B. M., & Chandler, K. (1998). *Well-chosen words.* York, ME: Stenhouse Publishers.

Prescott, G. A., Balow, I. H., Hogan, T. P., & Farr, R. C. (1978). *Metropolitan achievement tests* (Complete Survey Battery, Intermediate, Form JS). New York: Harcourt Brace Jovanovich.

Quellmalz, E. S. (1987). Developing reasoning skills. In J. B. Baron & R. J. Sternberg (Eds.), *Teaching thinking skills: Theory and practice.* New York: W. H. Freeman and Co.

Resnick, L. B. (1987). Learning in school and out. *Educational Researcher, 16*(9), 13–20.

Rodriguez, M. C. (2005). Three options are optimal for multiple-choice items: A meta-analysis of 80 years of research. *Educational Measurement: Issues and Practice, 24*(2), 3–13.

Ross, J. A., Rolheiser, C., & Hogaboam-Gray, A. (2002). Influences on student cognitions about evaluation. *Assessment in Education, 9,* 81–95.

Rudner, L. M., & Boston, C. (1994). Performance assessment. *The ERIC Review, 3*(1), 2–12.

Ryan, R. M., Connell, J. P., & Deci, E. L. (1985). A motivational analysis of self-determination and self-regulation in the classroom. In C. Ames and R. Ames (Eds.), *Research on motivation in education: Vol. 2. The classroom milieu* (pp.13–51). Orlando, FL: Academic.

Sadler, D. R. (1983). Evaluation and the improvement of academic learning. *Journal of Higher Education, 54,* 60–79.

Sadler, D. R. (1989). Formative assessment and the design of instructional systems. *Instructional Science, 18,* 119–144.

Sadler, P. M., & Good, E. (2006). The impact of self- and peer-grading on student learning. *Educational Assessment, 11,* 1–31.

Salvia, J., & Ysseldyke, J. E. (2004). *Assessment in special and inclusive education* (9th ed.). Boston: Houghton Mifflin.

Shavelson, R. J., & Baxter, G. P. (1991). Performance assessment in science. *Applied Measurement in Education, 4,* 347–362.

Shavelson, R. J., & Stern, P. (1981). Research on teacher's pedagogical thoughts, judgments, decisions, and behavior. *Review of Educational Research, 51*, 455–498.

Shepard, L. A. (1990). Inflated test score gains: Is the problem old norms or teaching the test? *Educational Measurement: Issues and Practice, 9*(3), 15–22.

Shepard, L. A. (1991). Interview on assessment issues with Lorrie Shepard. *Educational Researcher, 20*(3), 21–23.

Shepard, L. A. (1993). Evaluating test validity. *Review of Research in Education, 19,* 405–450.

Shepard, L., Hammerness, K., Darling-Hammond, L., & Rust, F. (2005). Assessment. In L. Darling-Hammond & J. Bransford (Eds.), *Preparing teachers for a changing world* (pp. 275–326). San Francisco: Jossey-Bass.

Shuell, T. J. (1990). Phrases of meaning learning. *Review of Educational Psychology, 60,*531–548.

Simon, H. A. (1973). The structure of ill-structured problems. *Artificial Intelligence, 4,* 181–201.

Sireci, S. G. (2005). Unlabeling the disabled: A perspective on flagging scores from accommodated test administrations. *Educational Researcher, 34*(1), 3–12.

Stiggins, R. J. (2005). *Student-involved assessment for learning* (4th ed.). Upper Saddle River, NJ: Merrill/Prentice Hall.

Stiggins, R. J., Conklin, N. F., & Associates. (1992). *In teachers' hands: Investigating the practice of classroom assessment.* Albany, NY: SUNY Press.

Stiggins, R. J., Frisbie, D. A., & Griswold, P. A. (1989). Inside high school grading practices: Building a research agenda. *Educational Measurement: Issues and Practice, 8*(2), 5–14.

Swiderek, B. (1997). Parent conferences. *Journal of Adolescent and Adult Literacy, 40,* 580–581.

Tallmadge, G. K., & Wood, C. T. (1976). *User's guide* (ESEA Title I Evaluation and Reporting System). Mountain View, CA: RMC Research Corporation.

Terry, P. W. (1933). How students review for objective and essay tests. *Elementary School Journal, 33,* 592–603.

Test-Takers' Rights Working Group. (1999). *Statement of test-takers' rights.* Washington, DC: American Psychological Association, Joint Committee on Testing Practices.

Tunstall, P., & Gipps, C. (1996). Teacher feedback to young children in formative assessment: a typology. *British Educational Research Journal, 22,* 389–404.

Turner, J. C., Thorpe, P. K., & Meyer, D. K. (1998). Students' reports of motivation and negative affect: A theoretical and empirical analysis. *Journal of Educational Psychology, 90,* 758–771.

Tyler, R. W. (1966). The objectives and plans for a National Assessment of Educational Progress. *Journal of Educational Measurement, 3,* 1–4.

U.S. Department of Education. (May 10, 2005). *New flexibility for states raising achievement for students with disabilities.* Washington, DC: No Child Left Behind, Author. (Downloaded from http://www.ed.gov/policy/elsec/guid/raising/disab-factsheet.pdf.)

U.S. Department of Education. (September 13, 2006). 34 CFR Part 200, Title I – Improving the academic achievement of the disadvantaged. Amendment to Section 200.6. (Downloaded from http://www.ed.gov/legislation/FedRegister/finrule/2006-3/091306a.html)

Valencia, S. W., & Place, N. A. (1994). Literacy portfolios for teaching, learning, and accountability: The Bellevue Literacy Assessment Project. In S. W. Valencia, E. H. Hiebert, & P. P. Afferbach (Eds.), *Authentic reading assessment: Practices and possibilities.* Newark, DE: International Reading Association.

Vallance, T. R. (1947). Comparison of essay and objective examinations as learning experiences. *Journal of Educational Research, 41,* 279–288.

Viadero, D. (1995). New assessments have little effect on contract, study finds. *Education Week, 14*(40), 6.

Waltman, K. K., & Frisbie, D. A. (1994). Parents understanding of their children's report cards. *Applied Measurement in Education, 2,* 223–240.

Wang, X., Wainer, H., & Thissen, D. (1995). On the viability of some untestable assumptions in equating exams that allow examinee choice. *Applied Measurement in Education, 8,* 211–225.

Wenglinsky, H. (2004). Facts or critical thinking skills? What NAEP results say. *Educational Leadership, 62*(1), 32–35.

Wesman, A. G. (1971). Writing the test item. In R. L. Thorndike (Ed.), *Educational measurement* (2nd ed.). Washington, DC: American Council on Education.

Wiggins, G. (1990). *The case for authentic assessment.* (EDD-TM-9010). Washington, DC: ERIC Clearinghouse on Tests, Measurement, and Evaluation, American Institutes for Research.

Wiliam, D., & Leahy, S. (in press). A theoretical foundation for formative assessment. In J. H. McMillan (Ed.), *Formative classroom assessment: Research, theory, and practice.* Teachers College Press.

Wiliam, D., Lee, C., Harrison, C., & Black, P. (2004). Teachers developing assessment for learning: impact on student achievement. *Assessment in Education, 11,* 49–65.

Winger, T. (2005). Grading to communicate. *Educational Leadership, 63*(3), 61–65.

Wiser, B., & Lenke, J. M. (1987, April). *The stability of achievement test norms over time.* Paper presented at the Annual Meeting of the National Council on Measurement in Education, Washington, DC.

Wolf, D. P. (1989). Portfolio assessment: Sampling student work. *Educational Leadership, 46*(2), 4–10.

Wolf, D. P. (1993). Assessment as an episode of learning. In R. E. Bannet & W. C. Ward (Eds.), *Construction versus choice in cognitive measurement* (pp. 213–240). Hillsdale, NJ: Lawrence Erlbaum.

Wood, R. (1977). Multiple choice: A state of the art report. *Evaluation in Education: International Progress, 1,* 191–280.

Woolfolk, A. E. (1995). *Educational psychology* (6th ed.). Boston: Allyn & Bacon.

Young, M. J. & Zucker, S. (2004). *The Standards-Referenced Interpretive Framework: Using Assessments for Multiple Purposes.* (Harcourt Assessment Report). San Antonio: Harcourt Assessment.

Name Index

Subject Index